Behavior Management

Principles and Practices of Positive Behavioral Interventions and Supports

Behavior Management

Principles and Practices of Positive Behavioral Interventions and Supports

FOURTH EDITION

John J. Wheeler
East Tennessee State University

David Dean Richey
Tennessee Tech University, late of

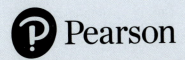 **Pearson**

New York, NY

Director and Publisher: Kevin M. Davis
Content Producer: Janelle Rogers
Media Producer: Lauren Carlson
Portfolio Management Assistant: Casey Coriell
Executive Field Marketing Manager: Krista Clark
Executive Product Marketing Manager: Christopher Barry
Procurement Specialist: Carol Melville
Full-Service Project Management: Thistle Hill Publishing Services
Cover Designer: Cenveo® Publisher Services
Cover Image: Qweek/Getty Images
Composition: Cenveo® Publisher Services
Printer/Binder: LSC Communications/Willard
Cover Printer: Phoenix Color Corp.
Text Font: 10/12pt ITC Garamond Std

Credits and acknowledgments borrowed from other sources and reproduced, with permission, in this textbook appear on the appropriate page within the text.

Every effort has been made to provide accurate and current Internet information in this book. However, the Internet and information posted on it are constantly changing, so it is inevitable that some of the Internet addresses listed in this textbook will change.

Library of Congress Cataloging-in-Publication Data
Names: Wheeler, John J., author. | Richey, David Dean, author.
Title: Behavior management : principles and practices of positive behavior
supports / John J. Wheeler, East Tennessee State University, David Dean
Richey, Tennessee Tech University, late of.
Description: Fourth edition. | New York, NY : Pearson, [2019] | Includes
bibliographical references and index.
Identifiers: LCCN 2017050760| ISBN 9780134773681 (pbk.) | ISBN 0134773683 (pbk.)
Subjects: LCSH: Classroom management. | Behavior modification.
Classification: LCC LB3013 .W465 2019 | DDC 371.102/4—dc23
LC record available at https://lccn.loc.gov/2017050760

1   18

ISBN 10:   0-13-479218-1
ISBN 13: 978-0-13-479218-7

This book is dedicated to the memory of my dear friend and colleague Dr. David Dean Richey, who sadly left this earth much too soon, but who in his time here made a lasting and significant impact on the lives of so many; to my wife Karen for her ongoing support; and to my children Ben, Alli, and John who inspire me.

JJW

About the Authors

John J. Wheeler, Ph.D., is currently Professor of Special Education at East Tennessee State University. Dr. Wheeler has served in many roles during his 35-year career including service as a special education teacher, professor, researcher, associate dean, and dean. His career has focused on the provision of technical assistance, program development, and research in the delivery of positive behavioral interventions and supports to children with autism spectrum disorder and other developmental disabilities in rural and underserved areas.

David Dean Richey, Ph.D. (1943–2014). Dr. Richey received his Ph.D. in 1974 from the University of North Carolina–Chapel Hill and had many professional roles while at Tennessee Tech University, including Professor, Associate Dean, and Interim Dean of the College of Education. He worked tirelessly for the care and well-being of young children with special needs and their families, specifically in his pivotal role in the establishment of Tennessee's Early Intervention System in the Upper Cumberland region of Tennessee. Dr. Richey was a devoted husband to his wife Linda; father to Patrick, Amy, Amanda, Hicham, Adam, and Gervan; and active grandfather to Noor, Lena, and Kaja. He was also a compassionate advocate for families and children, a mentor to countless students, a scholar, and a prolific gardener.

Preface

Welcome to the fourth edition of *Behavior Management: Principles and Practices of Positive Behavioral Interventions and Supports*. I am delighted that you have selected this text, as it represents a new and revised edition designed to assist in the preparation of undergraduate and graduate students in positive behavioral interventions and supports (PBIS). The content of this text is intended to provide an overview of both the principles that undergird PBIS as a philosophy of practice and the practical applications of PBIS as a proactive approach in promoting optimal behavior across schoolwide, classroom, and individual levels.

There has been significant progress in the development of PBIS since its inception in 1997. The reauthorization of IDEA in 2004 clearly mandated the use of PBIS as an evidence-based practice aimed at proactively addressing challenging behavior in students with disabilities. This progress can be measured in the growing number of professionals and schools using PBIS across primary, secondary, and tertiary levels. In fact, the National Technical Assistance Center on Positive Behavioral Interventions and Supports (2017) reports that 23,363 schools nationally are implementing PBIS. A central focus of this text is the application of this evidence-based practice with learners of all ages and abilities across learning environments. PBIS has been demonstrated to be a viable technology for improving the quality of educational experience for all persons within the school community. It is our hope that this text will help meet your professional development needs in the area of PBIS.

NEW TO THIS EDITION

A new edition implies new content, and we have made it our goal to better address the needs of readers through the addition of new material based in the research literature to reflect current practices in the field of PBIS. Teachers and school administrators continue to express that one of their greatest concerns is how to proactively address the behavior of students both in terms of prevention and also when students need extensive tertiary support for more severe behavioral challenges. This ongoing need, coupled with the increasing levels of performance evaluation required of teachers, speaks to the need for professionals to better understand how PBIS can be fully used to provide behavioral and educational supports to all learners.

In this edition, you will find:

- Student vignettes throughout the text that will provide applied illustrations of how PBIS can be employed across the continuum of age(s) and abilities and at primary, secondary, and tertiary levels
- Information about response to intervention (RtI) and how RtI and PBIS can complement one another in the delivery of behavioral and educational supports to learners

- Expanded focus on prevention of challenging behavior through effective instructional strategies
- Examination of the applications of PBIS within classrooms, including practical strategies for how to collect functional behavior assessment (FBA) data within classroom settings and how to teach replacement behaviors
- An increased emphasis on evaluating student performance, including student progress monitoring and the application of single-case designs in the classroom as a tool for monitoring student performance
- Practical applications for developing behavior support plans (BSPs)
- Explanation of the role of reinforcement across schoolwide, classroom, and tertiary levels of PBIS
- An expanded emphasis on schoolwide PBIS and how it can be applied towards preventing and minimizing challenging behavior
- Recognition of the importance of self-determination and how PBIS can be a tool for promoting self-determination and improving the quality of life for all students
- Updated information and references on PBIS and how this evolving evidence-based practice can be applied across multiple tiers with all learners as a proactive means of promoting meaningful educational and behavioral outcomes

These changes within the text are aimed at providing you with up-to-date and relevant material on PBIS and the application of these principles within educational settings.

ACKNOWLEDGMENTS

This edition represents a departure from our previous work in that I flew this mission solo, but I was inspired along the way by my creative memory of Dr. Richey's vast influence in my life as a friend and colleague. I would like to sincerely thank all of our colleagues at Pearson who have provided us with continued support and direction on this project. A special thank you to Kevin Davis, editor, who has provided me with guidance and leadership throughout this creative process; Janelle Rogers, program manager, for helping me shepherd the project to completion. I would also like to thank the reviewers who shared their expertise in providing us with guidance in the development of the text: Paulette Walter, Ph.D., University of North Texas at Dallas; Grace Francis, George Mason University; and Kelly Kathleen Metz, University of Southern Mississippi.

And, finally, my heartfelt thanks to my family, for their continued love and support and encouragement that made the completion of this text possible.

Brief Contents

Contents

Understanding Behavior in Children and Youth

CONCEPTS TO UNDERSTAND

After reading this chapter, you should be able to:

- List and describe the common theories used to understand human behavior, including the biomedical, developmental, psychodynamic/psychosocial, ecological, behavioral, and social learning models.
- Describe the foundations and applications of applied-behavior analysis.
- Describe the components of positive behavioral interventions and supports (PBIS) and the application of PBIS across the three tiers of prevention (primary, secondary, and tertiary).

KEY TERMS

Applied Behavior Analysis (ABA)

Behavioral Model

Biomedical Model

Developmental Model

Ecological Model

Positive Behavioral Interventions and Supports (PBIS)

Psychodynamic/Psychosocial Model

Social Learning Model

As a professional educator, your ability to understand teaching and learning is important in facilitating meaningful instructional outcomes for all students. One critical prerequisite skill for teachers is a fluent understanding of the diverse learning and behavioral support needs of all students, as these skills are critical to student success. Teaching and reinforcing the use of appropriate behaviors in the classroom are critical for student engagement and learning, and also for socialization with one's teachers and peers.

This chapter will provide you with a comparative overview of the common conceptual models used in understanding human behavior. Information is also provided on the historical development of positive behavioral interventions and supports (PBIS) as a school-based model of behavioral prevention and its applications across school-wide (primary), classroom (secondary), and individual (tertiary) levels. We will also explore how PBIS has been viewed by some as an outgrowth of applied behavior analysis (ABA). Finally, the chapter will explain the many virtues of ABA and PBIS across a range of learners and environments including classroom and school-wide implementation.

THEORETICAL MODELS FOR UNDERSTANDING BEHAVIOR

The focus of this text is on the use of PBIS to practically and positively address the behavior support needs of students across educational environments. This includes children and youth from pre-k settings through grade 12 including students considered typically developing, and those with disabilities.

In addition to PBIS, there are many that are frequently used to explain and understand human behavior and learning. It is important as a teacher to understand contrasting viewpoints as you formulate your own philosophy of practice and better equip yourself to appreciate the efficacy and limitations of each model.

Biomedical Model

The **biomedical model** examines the presence of atypical development and behavior from an organic viewpoint. For example, the medical profession addresses changes in physiological functioning (optimal health) within the context of presenting symptoms. These physical symptoms are often present as the result of pathogens in the body or other organic causes. Pathogens alter the body's equilibrium and are defined as any causative agent of disease resulting in changes in one's health and optimal levels of functioning. In other words, an illness can change the way a person typically feels, behaves, thinks, etc. Within the field of special education, we frequently encounter the biological or medical model when explaining the presence of specific disabilities that affect cognitive and behavioral functioning in children and youth. Many of these conditions stem from organic causes that alter typical development in children, thus producing disabilities. An example of this model is how autism was once believed to be a psychogenic disorder (a disorder with no known organic basis but was likely caused by emotional stress) and in fact many at the time believed that the condition was attributed to a lack of maternal nurturing (Kanner, 1943). Later in 1967 the infamous term "refrigerator mom" was coined by Bruno Bettleheim (1967) to describe this lack of maternal bonding that he perceived as the cause of autism in children. Many mothers of children diagnosed with autism were made to feel as if they were the cause. Sadly, the lives of many individuals were adversely affected as a result. It was later discovered in the late 1970s that autism was a neurobiological disorder caused by genetic and biological differences (Folstein and Rutter, 1977).

Further advances in medical science have contributed to our understanding of the causal factors associated with many disabilities, including autism, such as the origins of this disorder, not only the genetic factors associated with it but the impact of these on brain functioning (Gliga, Jones, Bedford, Charman, & Johnson, 2014). Biomedical research continues to explore the underlying genetic and environmental factors related to autism (Anderson, 2015). Some early examples of this type of research point to multiple causal factors as evidenced by varied biomarkers identified in individuals with autism across the body's four basic systems: gastrointestinal, immunologic, neurologic, and toxicological (Ratajczak, 2011). These findings are important because they assist us in accurately diagnosing these conditions and in designing appropriate treatment programs.

There are many other examples of how the biomedical model has contributed to the knowledge base for the diagnosis and treatment of other forms of intellectual, behavioral,

TABLE 1–1
Theoretical Models for Understanding Human Behavior

Theoretical Model	Key Concepts Relating to Behavior
Biomedical model	• Views behavior from an organic standpoint • Emphasis on pathogens as explanation for disease • Has medical/health implications
Developmental model	• Jean Piaget is a noted theorist in this area • Stresses a child's adaptation to environment is largely innate rather than learned • Application of model seen through widespread use of developmentally appropriate practice (DAP) by educators
Psychodynamic/Psychosocial model	• Pioneered by Sigmund Freud and expanded upon by Erik Erickson • Emphasis on unconscious processes (e.g., id, ego, & super-ego), underlying motives of behavior • Development of personality is key to understanding abnormalities
Ecological model	• This model is associated with the theorist Uri Bronfenbrenner • Focus on relationships between and within levels of ecosystems • Adaptations of this model have been applied to serving students with emotional/behavioral (E/BD) disorders
Behavioral model	• Ivan Pavlov, John Watson, and B. F. Skinner were significant theorists in the development of the behavioral model • Behavior is viewed from a functional perspective—measured and observed • Applied Behavior Analysis is how we refer to it today and it is widely used in the treatment of autism
Social learning	• Albert Bandura was significant in the development of this model, emphasis is placed on modelling—imitation of models as an important element in learning • Merges cognitive and behavioral models
Applied Behavior Analysis (ABA)	• Emphasis on the applied study of socially relevant behaviors • Focus on measurable and observable behaviors with precise measurement
Positive Behavioral Interventions and Supports (PBIS)	• Reliance on person-centered planning and supports • Stresses positive approaches to behavior change and seeks to enhance quality of life for the learner • PBIS is the method for addressing challenging behavior in public schools as recognized in the Reauthorization of the Individuals with Disabilities Act (IDEA) of 2004

and learning disabilities. These contributions include the organic factors associated with intellectual disabilities that encompass chromosomal abnormalities in conditions such as Down syndrome, multiple congenital disabilities, prenatal difficulties, gene defects, and postnatal brain damage. As special educators, we now have a fuller understanding of the etiology or causal factors associated with these disorders and their impact on fetal development.

The biomedical model has also assisted in the identification of the neurobiological origins of attention deficit/hyperactivity disorder (ADHD), a condition prevalent among many school-age children today. Through the use of magnetic resonance imaging (MRI), medical researchers have identified structural differences between the brains of persons affected with ADHD and persons not diagnosed with the condition, and they have observed diminished neuronal activity among persons found to have ADHD (Friedman & Rappaport, 2015). As with autism, earlier research had pointed to psychopathological origins rather than organic causal factors.

We also know that some children diagnosed with ADHD have co-occurring learning disabilities (DuPaul, Gormley, & Laracy, 2012). This means that for some children these conditions can result in learning and behavioral challenges if left untreated. The use of stimulant medications continues to be widely used in the treatment of children diagnosed with ADHD. These have been noted to be effective in improving attention and cognitive functioning in children and adolescents but concerns have been expressed about the evidence guiding the practice of using these medications to treat ADHD (Cortese et al., 2013). This criticism is due in part to the view held by many concerning the overreliance of this form of treatment for ADHD in children which is estimated to be as high as 3.5% of the school-age population by Zukevas and Vitiello (2012).

The limitations of medication as the primary form of treatment for children diagnosed with ADHD have also been questioned in the literature. These limitations include side effects, their lack of maintenance and generalization of behavior change when discontinued, issues of medication compliance meaning adhering to the prescribed dosage levels on a daily basis, and that some individuals do not respond favorably to the medication (Charach, Yeung, Volpe, & Goodale, 2014). There has also been concern expressed by many in the field that the use of medication seems to be the standard response when treating ADHD without fully understanding the potential for misuse of these medications (Greydanus, 2015). It has been advocated that the most effective method for successful treatment of children with ADHD is through the use of multimodal interventions that combine medication and positive behavioral interventions and supports (PBIS; DuPaul, Weyandt, & Janusis, 2011). This trend of using medication paired with PBIS continues to grow among professionals and families. Medical science has made progress in the diagnosis and treatment of conditions such as ADHD, and we continue to see that the outcomes from the merger of bio-medical and behavioral forms of intervention are more effective than medication alone in successfully treating these conditions on a long-term basis.

Consider This

- How could you envision the biomedical model better informing your practice as a teacher when addressing the learning and behavioral support needs of some students?
- What are your questions and concerns as a teacher regarding the use of medications in the treatment of ADHD?

In summary, the biomedical model contributes to our understanding of the underlying causes of disability and/or physical conditions that affect our health and well-being including our physical, emotional, and behavioral health and also assists us in the selection of treatment options designed to restore optimal health and functioning. Though informative in our practice, the biomedical model does not give us the complete picture and should be paired with PBIS and other evidence-based instructional practices to fully complement one another when addressing the educational and behavioral support needs of students.

Developmental Model

The developmental perspective has traditionally been associated with Swiss-born biologist Jean Piaget (1896–1980). Piaget's contributions are noteworthy in the field of human development and have served as a cornerstone among developmental theorists. His theory was built on the premise that children's adaptation to their environment was contingent on two processes: assimilation and accommodation. *Assimilation* is the process by which children fit new stimuli into their "comfort zone" or their current ability to understand this new information. *Accommodation* refers to how children modify their cognitive processing to fit these new or novel stimuli.

The **developmental model** has evolved over time; it essentially maintains that children develop in a predictable and predetermined manner that is internally organized (Cobb, 2001). Developmental theorists also contend that as children age, they proceed through several stages of development, each with its own unique set of characteristics. Similar to how a child first learns to crawl, then stand, and then walk; developmental theorists describe children's cognitive processes emerging in similar patterns as they interact with their environment.

The developmental model is most prominent in the education of young children. Contemporary early childhood educators and early childhood special educators rely on the principle of developmentally appropriate practice (DAP) as the philosophical foundation for the provision of education and related services to young children.

Copple & Bredecamp (2009) outline a synthesized list of research-based principles that undergird DAP. These principles include the following: (a) recognizing that physical,

Jean Piaget

Bettmann/Getty Images

cognitive, social, and emotional domains associated with child development are related, and that development in each of these areas is interdependent; (b) development is an orderly sequence whereby skills are developed in a stepwise fashion with new knowledge and skills building on existing strengths and previous learning; (c) development among individual children is unique, and variation for every child is important (i.e., no two children are alike); (d) learning experiences for children have a cumulative effect and long-term implications in terms of the child's growth and development in later years; (e) cognitive development advances from concrete to abstract in terms of the child's ability to acquire and transfer knowledge and skills; (f) child development is influenced by environmental factors; (g) children learn through their active engagement in environments and the events that surround them; (h) development and learning result from a combination of physical maturation and the environments that encompass the child; (i) play is an essential avenue for promoting development and learning in every child; and (j) optimal development is promoted when children are presented with new and enriching experiences that take into account present skill levels and those skills deemed to be emerging.

One limitation of the developmental model in understanding children with disabilities is that this model, when used exclusively, fails to inform us completely as to how to adapt the developmental model to children who display atypical development, as in the case of children with disabilities. It is important that all teachers of young children learn about typical and atypical development and that this method of instruction used in early childhood education settings can be modified and adapted to be inclusive of all children, including children with disabilities. The developmental model when paired with early intervention and/or early childhood special education is greatly enhanced and can be used to provide meaningful educational experiences for all young children. Young children should be provided a range of individualized activity-based interventions that are evidence-based and designed to support the optimal development of the child (Odom, 2016).

Psychodynamic Model

The **psychodynamic model** is a stage theory used to explain human development and behavior. The stage theory viewpoint is best characterized by a series of progressive developmental life stages that we experience as we move from childhood into adolescence and later periods throughout our lives. The psychodynamic model emphasizes the critical importance of unconscious processes (i.e., psychodynamic) as the determinants for atypical behavior. Although the psychodynamic model represents a cognitive perspective, it does acknowledge that environment contributes to development through internal processes and the battle between internal processes and these external events (Cobb, 2001). In short, the view held by psychodynamic theorists is that all people have internal states or thought processes operating as they attempt to process the environmental events that influence the development of these thought processes and, subsequently, their personalities. The challenges for educators when relying on psychodynamic approaches are that we cannot observe these internal states or processes in students and attempts to change these processes usually take lengthy periods of time.

The most noted psychodynamic theorist was Sigmund Freud (1859–1939), a well-known Austrian-born psychoanalyst. He is best known for his theory of personality development and the terms *id*, *ego*, and *superego*, which are associated with the formation of personality. Each of these components of Freud's structural model serves a unique function, yet they must ultimately balance one another to accommodate the development of the personality. The id is the area of the personality that demands immediate gratification of biological impulses, thus operating on the "pleasure principle" (Freud, 1961).

Sigmund Freud

The ego, on the other hand, attempts to satisfy these impulses in a more socially accept-able manner. The superego is the area of the personality that serves as the moral con-science as one attempts to internalize moral standards. Freud acknowledged the interaction between biological and environmental forces in the development of the id and superego in the development of personality (Cobb, 2001). In Freud's view, develop-ment occurs as a result of the conflicts between a child's internal drives and his or her social environment. As a result, a psychological balance must be obtained that channels, represses, and/or redirects these drives and thus lays the foundation for the development of the child's personality (Tharinger & Lambert, 1990).

Erik Erikson (1902–1994) expanded Freud's theory on personality through his own theory of psychosocial development. Erikson's theory maintained the importance of ego identity and the healthy personality. This perspective asserts the importance of the ego and emphasizes the process of adaptation and the resolution of opposing forces.

Erik Erikson

Erikson is best known for his eight stages of moral development, each of which is critical for subsequent development and involves a conflict involving maturational and social expectations on which the child progresses before moving to the next stage of development (Erikson, 1950). His stages extend from birth through the senior years, and each of these life stages brings with it a psychosocial crisis, referred to by Erikson (1950) as the epigenetic principle that serves as a developmental milestone. These stages include: (a) Basic Trust versus Basic Mistrust (birth to 18 months of age), when a child learns to develop trust; (b) Autonomy versus Shame and Doubt (18 months to 3 years of age), when a child learns to become independent by achieving some mastery of basic self-help skills; (c) Initiative versus Guilt (3 to 5 years of age), a stage characterized by a child role-playing and modeling adult life roles through creative play; (d) Industry versus Inferiority (6 to 12 years of age), when children learn and develop a sense of purpose or industry and when feelings of self-doubt or inferiority can also ensue, which may affect a child's self-esteem; (e) Identity versus Role Confusion (12 to 18 years of age), the point of development when the child begins to emerge in a more self-determined manner; (f) Intimacy versus Isolation (18 to 35 years of age), a stage of development marked by the forming of significant relationships (if we are not successful in forming these relationships, social isolation ensues); and (g) Generativity versus Stagnation (35 to 65 years of age), when the individual remains focused on making a contribution through work and family involvement—conversely, as children age and we grow older, we are faced with becoming more self-absorbed or stagnant. In Erikson's final stage, (h) Ego Integrity versus Despair (ages 65 years to death), adults pause for reflection on their lives and ideally draw on their contributions and accept the full circle of life, although some may experience regret and despair concerning paths not taken. Erikson contended that each of these stages of development is consistent for all people and that at critical periods within each stage, the developing personality is most sensitive to outside influences.

One prominent characteristic of the psychodynamic model that should be emphasized is its focus on the underlying motives that govern behavior. The psychodynamic model assumes that the developmental stages previously described are consistent across individuals and that they rely on internal processes to explain subsequent development and learning. This characteristic has become one of the major areas of criticism concerning the application of this model. Given the focus of the psychodynamic theory on the development of personality with regard to the internal processing of environmental influences, it is difficult to empirically validate the role these forces play in individual human development making it impossible to observe and measure the internal thoughts and feelings of individuals. Thus the application of this model in educational environments serving children has been limited in terms of its applied efficacy. There has been an increase in the use of cognitive/behavioral approaches that are a merger of meta-cognitive (psychodynamic) theory with a behavioral component.

Ecological Model

The ecological model perspective on behavior and learning is a very important viewpoint, especially given the focus of this text—that is, positive behavioral interventions and supports—and the importance of understanding behavior within the relevant environments (home, school, community) in which the learner lives and functions. These environments and the individuals found within them constitute one form of an ecological system. What occurs within this system affects not only one individual but also all who function within it. The **ecological model** is focused on the interactions that occur within these environments and how they influence behavior and learning in each of us.

Felicia Martinez/PhotoEdit, Inc.

Lev Vygotsky

An early theorist who achieved much notoriety in recent times from his work in the area of young children and learning was the Russian psychologist Lev Vygotsky (1896–1934). His theory stated that children learn by engaging and participating in activities that they enjoy and that learning is enhanced when children are in social contexts, working with other children who have the same aims (Vygotsky, 1978). Thus environment and social context are important aspects in Vygotsky's theory. Vygotsky emphasized the development of cognitive processes and behaviors in the child through interactions within the social context. His theory pointed out how children who approximate a certain skill level can learn from other children who are more skilled at a particular task. He termed this phenomenon the *zone of proximal development*, meaning the distance separating a person's current performance level from that of optimal performance levels. Although not exclusively an ecological theorist, Vygotsky reminds us of the importance of social interaction in meaningful environmental contexts and how such interactions foster cognitive development in children.

Urie Bronfenbrenner (1917–2005) is widely known for his application of the ecological model in reference to families. Bronfenbrenner (1994) asserted that a child's development is inseparable from the environments in which they function, which thus constitute his or her ecology. Bronfenbrenner's theory comprises a concentric circle that has the child at its center and five systems emerging from the core of the circle: the microsystem, the mesosystem, the exosystem, the macrosystem, and the chromosystem. The microsystem is basically the child's immediate environment, such as a home and family, or peer group association for an adolescent child. The mesosystem is composed of the interactions among contexts in the microsystem, such as school, home, and community. The exosystem refers to settings that influence the child with which he or she does not have a direct interface, such as school administrators or the employer of the child's parents. The macrosystem is illustrative of a set of philosophical or ideological patterns of a culture or subculture, such as the effect on a child's development of a school culture that practices corporal punishment. The chromosystem refers to changes that occur over time to a child within his or her environment. Examples of the chromosystem include the birth of a sibling, divorce, and effects of relocating to a new home and school system (Richey & Wheeler, 2000). Certainly it is easy to ascertain from Bronfenbrenner's theory how interactions across these systems can ripple and affect the child (our point of concern is at the center of this model). This theory supports what we have learned thus far—that is, the importance of the interactions between environment and individual and the cumulative effect that alterations within these ecologies can have on the optimal learning and development of children and youth. Vignette 1.1 provides more insight into the ecological model applied to children and families affected by poverty.

Vignette 1.1

The Ecological Model Applied to Children and Families in Poverty

An elementary school teacher working in an Appalachian community beset by high poverty and unemployment rates commented to a state representative that people do not really understand the complexities and impact of poverty and its effects on children and families as far as development and learning are concerned and the importance of education in these communities.

In this example, the community was once a thriving coal-mining region in which people were gainfully employed; however, when the demand for coal diminished, the mines closed, and subsequently the community's economy was destroyed. As a result, stores closed, people were left jobless, and some families left the region in search of new opportunities; whereas those families who remained behind worked at less fruitful jobs paying minimum wage and offering no insurance or benefits for themselves or their families. The impact began to be felt within all facets of the community, including the local schools. Evidence of this impact was seen as greater numbers of children began to receive free breakfasts and lunches through subsidy programs. Increasing numbers of children began coming to school without their basic needs met. Local teachers began to see the impact on individual children as well, including addressing the needs of children who were homeless. Other changes were noted within the community, such as increased alcohol and drug abuse, family problems, and criminal activity largely due to lack of opportunity and the hopelessness resultant from job displacement and unemployment.

Reflective Moment

Respond to the problems posed in the vignette by examining the following questions:

- How do the environmental challenges affecting families described in the vignette impact the work of teachers and educational systems within such a region?
- What strengths does the ecological model provide for educators in attempting to meet the educational needs of the students served in such a setting?
- What are the limitations of this model in assisting us as classroom teachers in facilitating optimal learning outcomes for children affected by such conditions?

Another example of an ecological-based approach to service delivery was a program known as Project Re-ED directed by Nicholas Hobbs (1915–1983). Dr. Hobbs was historically one of the most prominent leaders to provide educational and behavior support to children with emotional/behavioral disorders (EBD). Best known for his theory on the re-education of troubled children and youth, Hobbs had many formative experiences that led to the design of the Re-ED (Re-Education of Emotionally Disturbed Children) program. These experiences included studying how

Western European countries provided educational supports to children with disabilities. He was most impressed with the model that he had witnessed in France and the role of childcare workers known as *psychoeducateurs*, a title for which there was no equivalent in the United States (Hobbs, 1974). The psychoeducateur was essentially a child care specialist who had been cross-trained in the disciplines of child development, psychology, education, and child care and was responsible for working with children both during school hours and after school hours (Juul, 1977). Hobbs borrowed from this idea and framed the role of teacher–counselor, emphasizing teacher disposition as being the most important attribute for professionals who worked with troubled children.

The defining role of the teacher–counselor emerged, and these professionals were taught to develop trusting relationships with the children and youth in their care and to teach and model positive affirming behaviors that were offered within a context of support and inclusiveness, rather than one of failure and exclusion. Hobbs believed strongly in the development of interpersonal skills in the teacher–counselor and the importance of understanding feelings and expressions of anger and hurt in children and adolescents. He believed in promoting the idea that each child had a bright future and abilities from which to draw and to build from (Hobbs, 1974).

The Re-ED model came about largely from Hobbs's mounting frustration that psychotherapy, as a form of treatment, was ineffective in dealing with the life problems of troubled children and youth. Hobbs believed that Re-ED offered a positive and more holistic alternative to treatment models at that time and recognized the importance of working not only with the child but also with the child's family and other contacts in natural settings such as the home, community, school, and other relevant settings. An example of the ecological model used in the Re-ED program is illustrated in Figure 1–1.

The supporting theory behind the Re-ED model was that the child is inseparable from his or her social system or ecological unit. The child and the child's family, school, and neighborhood or community compose this ecological unit. The ultimate goal of

FIGURE 1–1

Ecological Model

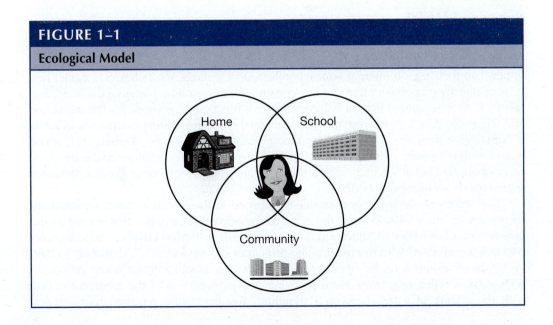

treatment was to be able to move each component of the child's life, including those significant others, above threshold (Hobbs, 1974). In the Re-ED model, the parents and family, teachers, and others who are significant in the life of the child were considered collaborators in promoting the desired outcomes. The Re-ED model attempted to maintain the child in his or her home and supported residential placement options for those children and youth who demonstrated a need for intensive re-education or whose family was incapable of providing in-home supports (Hobbs, 1974).

Re-ED was responsible for demonstrating model practices in the education of children and youth who were challenged by EBD. Many replication programs were developed from the original schools developed by Hobbs. In reflection, the Re-ED model represented a new and innovative philosophy and practice in educating children with some significant emotional and behavior challenges. It was a model of practice built on the delivery of child-centered and holistic educational services and supports and was inclusive of natural environments and significant others in the delivery of these behavior supports.

In contemporary practice, we see much of the early Re-ED model reflected in the delivery of wraparound services within special education and mental health settings that serve children with EBD and other high-risk youth (Fries, Carney, Blackman-Urteaga & Savas, 2012). These wraparound services mirror the ecological model in that they involve child, family, school, community, mental health professionals, and others in the design and delivery of supports to children and their families. The ecological model is important in promoting the implementation of educational and behavior supports across multiple environments with persons who are significant in the life of the learner. This approach views the persons within these settings as agents for change and, indeed, targets for change.

Consider This

- Identify how you, as a teacher, can have a meaningful influence in the life of a child?
- How can you as a teacher be sensitive to the needs of a child when they are experiencing challenges beyond school such as within their home or community?

Behavioral Model

One defining characteristic of the **behavioral model** is that it views behavior from a functional perspective in terms that are both measurable and observable. This means that rather than focusing on internal issues, conflicts, and feelings, the behavioral model first focuses directly on behavior that can be seen and documented by parents, educators, and others. It also recognizes that all behavior serves a function or purpose for the individual and has evolved as a direct result of the individual's learning history coupled with interactions within their environments over time (Sulzer-Azaroff, Mayer, Wallace, 2013). The historical development of the behavioral model provides the foundation for the development of applied behavior analysis and the subsequent development of Positive Behavior Interventions and Supports (PBIS).

The origins of the behavioral model are steeped in the research of many prominent theorists who empirically derived the scientific principles of behavior that served as the cornerstone of behavior modification. These include Ivan Pavlov (1849–1936), a Russian psychologist credited with discovering the principles of respondent conditioning. In Pavlov's famous experiment, he demonstrated that a dog would salivate when presented with meat (a reflex response). He then paired the presentation of the meat to the dog with the ringing of a bell (a neutral stimulus), and later, after repeated trials, Pavlov

Ivan Pavlov

would ring the bell alone, and the dog would salivate (Pavlov, 1927). This is referred to as *respondent conditioning*.

Later research began to explore the effects of consequences on behavior through the research of Edward Thorndike (1874–1949), who is credited with the discovery of the Law of Effect. The Law of Effect (Thorndike, 1911) states that if a behavior produces a favorable outcome on the environment, it is more likely to be repeated in the future. Thorndike established this principle through his research with animals (primarily cats). He trained cats to open their cage doors by pressing a lever to access their food; on learning of the positive outcome (obtaining their food), the cats not only repeated the process but also did it faster.

As the field of behavioral research continued to evolve, John Watson (1878–1958) coined the term *behaviorism*, which served to emphasize the relationship between environmental events and the responses they produced (Watson, 1924). The most prominent force in the development of behavior modification and the application of these principles to human conditions was, of course, B. F. Skinner (1904–1991), known for his work in the

B. F. Skinner

area of operant conditioning. Skinner furthered the earlier theories of Watson and Pavlov to more complex behaviors in humans, which he termed *operants* (Skinner, 1953). Operants are behaviors that are to a considerable degree controlled by their consequences (Sulzer-Azaroff & Mayer, & Wallace 2013). Operant conditioning occurs when a behavior is followed by a reinforcing consequence that results in the behavior being more likely to occur in a similar context in the future.

Skinner's work on operant conditioning began to be applied in settings outside the laboratory by other researchers and was most evident in the field of developmental disabilities, thus earning the clinical label of behavior modification (Scheerenberger, 1987). Researchers such as Sidney Bijou explored the application of Skinner's theories in working with children and adults with intellectual disabilities. Bijou (1963) advocated the use of applied behavior analysis procedures such as functional analysis in understanding the variables that influence learning and performance in persons with mental intellectual disabilities and the involvement of systematic instruction and support for parents. Until this time, many persons with intellectual disabilities were condemned to live their entire lives in state institutions with little or no active treatment aimed at learning new skills or fulfilling their learning and life potential. Many lay persons and professionals alike including many from the medical profession thought the condition of these individuals was beyond hope and that people with intellectual disabilities lacked any potential for learning; consequently, many persons were reduced to custodial care in these facilities. Behavior modification represented an avenue for hope in the design and delivery of interventions aimed at maximizing the human potential of these previously discarded persons.

It was during this time that numerous skill-acquisition studies using behavioral approaches began to emerge in the literature. Much of the early literature was directed toward understanding the value of reinforcement in teaching functional skills to persons with developmental disabilities (Reid, Phillips, & Green, 1991). As the research began to provide more evidence in support of behavior modification to enhance the learning potential of persons with intellectual disabilities, active programming became more prevalent within state institutions (Anderson & Freeman, 2000).

The application of behavioral research to the field of education was strongly encouraged by Skinner in his book entitled *The Technology of Teaching* (1968). Bijou (1970) also advocated that the principles of applied behavior analysis be used within the field of education. These include: (a) the importance of understanding the interaction between behavior and environmental events from a scientific perspective that placed emphasis on studying these relationships in terms that were observable, measurable, and reproducible; (b) the interactions between the behavior of individual and environmental events as lawful and as a function of an individual's instructional history and the context in which the behavior occurs; (c) the importance of understanding the variables that influence complex behavior, such as setting conditions, stimulus control, and reinforcement schedules; and (d) that emerging theories should adhere to stringent criteria such as being tied to observable events, having functional utility, and not overlapping existing principles previously identified from research. Bijou (1970) supported the perspective held by Skinner that the teacher was a facilitator of learning by arranging the contingencies within the environment to promote the desired outcome in the child and the use of systematic instruction procedures to promote acquisition of desired skills.

In summary, the behavioral model evolved from basic scientific research aimed at understanding reflexive behaviors in animals to examining complex human behavior, learning, and human development. The behavioral model is committed to the understanding of human behavior from a scientific perspective in terms that are observable and measurable. It places emphasis on the relationship between environmental events and behavior, it deemphasizes past events as being directly related to the occurrence of problematic behavior, and it attempts to identify cause-and-effect relationships, or what is termed a functional relationship, to explain behavior. The field of applied behavior analysis has had noted advancements over the years in the application of evidence-based practices in educational environments and other settings. Perhaps the greatest limitation of this model was the lack of widespread acceptance of it within educational settings. This trend was prevalent for some time, as many perceived the model as far too clinical, non-humanistic, and lacking in functional utility for widespread use in school settings. This resistance was attributable in part to a lack of uniform understanding within the field of education, as applied behavior analysis' origins are in the field of psychology. Fortunately this trend has faded and applied behavior analysis is widely recognized for its many contributions, most notably as an evidence-based practice in the education and treatment of persons with autism.

Social Learning Model

The **social learning model** (Bandura, 1977) advanced the understanding of learning and behavior to become more inclusive of multiple influences on human development (Kazdin, 2012). Albert Bandura advocated that people learn within a social context and that the environment and models within the environment influence learning in children. For example, children who grow up in an environment where they see other children being kind may more readily learn to be kind themselves. Whereas in contrast, children growing up in an environment where they see other children being cruel may more readily learn to be cruel themselves. One of Bandura's major contributions was studying the relationship of social learning to aggression in children (Bandura, 1973). His famous "Bobo Doll" experiment demonstrated the influence of modeled aggression on the behavior of young children (Bandura, Ross, & Ross, 1961). In this study, 36 boys and 36 girls between the ages of 37 and 69 months who were enrolled in Stanford University's nursery school participated in the famous experiment, which illustrated that children exposed to aggressive and violent modeling were more apt to imitate it, whereas those children not exposed to such behavior were less inclined to demonstrate such responses. Modeling is central to the social learning theory, which believes that the imitation of models is the most important element in learning for children in the areas of language,

Jon Brenneis/The LIFE Images Collection/Getty Images

Albert Bandura

social behavior, and gender-appropriate behaviors (Martonell, Papalia, & Feldman, 2013). The selection of models that children choose to identify is influenced by the characteristics and accessibility of the model, the child's preferences, and the environment to which the child is exposed. The social learning model's perspective on understanding behavior acknowledges the cognitive influences on behavior and the role of models within the child's environment as being very important to subsequent learning in the child (Martonell, et al., 2013). The social learning model attempts to merge the cognitive and behavior models and expands the view of each toward a more comprehensive understanding of behavior.

Applied Behavior Analysis

Applied behavior analysis (ABA) is the study of socially relevant human behavior in applied settings. ABA emphasizes the applied study of socially relevant behaviors within naturally occurring contexts. The focus is on overt behaviors that are measurable and observable, the influence of environmental variables on the occurrence/nonoccurrence of the behaviors in question, and precise measurement of these responses. In other words, ABA examines how factors in the environment influence behaviors. ABA studies behavior over time in relevant environments and employs research-validated teaching procedures that are replicable and specific to the individual needs of the learner. These procedures are socially acceptable, are implemented by people such as teachers and caregivers in everyday life, and are designed to promote increased lifestyle outcomes for the learner. Anderson and Freeman (2000) stated that no other subdiscipline within the field of psychology has had such a profound impact on the quality of services provided to persons with developmental disabilities than the field of applied behavior analysis. Persons with developmental disabilities were most often perceived as having a lack of potential for learning, yet with the advent of applied behavior analysis people began to see otherwise through the use of behavioral learning principles, as research to the contrary began to rapidly emerge (Anderson & Freeman, 2000).

Applications of ABA

Applications of ABA are evident across many areas, such as special education, in which applied behavior analysis research has resulted in the development of instructional inroads for children and youth with disabilities. These interventions have been refined over time from the early research conducted in the 1960s and 1970s within residential facilities serving individuals with severe disabilities. The research and applications of ABA were at first most evident in the area of systematic instruction or teaching approaches designed to facilitate the acquisition of new skills in learners.

An early leader in the use of systematic instruction to teach meaningful vocational skills to young adults with intellectual disabilities was Marc Gold (1939–1982), an applied researcher from the University of Illinois. Gold tirelessly advocated that persons with intellectual disabilities should be provided with meaningful opportunities for learning and gainful skills that would promote employability. Gold (1980) was a proponent of the effectiveness of behavioral teaching principles and adhered to the philosophy that "a lack of learning in any particular situation should first be interpreted as a result of the inappropriate or insufficient use of teaching strategy rather than an inability on the part of the learner" (p. 15). Gold's work demonstrated that persons with severe intellectual disabilities could be taught complex vocational skills where many had perceived these individuals as having a limited capacity for performing functional skills. To illustrate his point about people with severe intellectual disabilities having the ability to learn, Gold taught these individuals how to perform complex assembly skills by applying the use of task analyses and instructional prompts.

The use of behavioral teaching principles has been acclaimed in the area of autism, largely through the research of Ivar Lovaas. Lovaas demonstrated through his research (1993; McEachin, Smith, & Lovaas, 1993) that the use of discrete trial teaching with children younger than 2 1/2 years of age resulted in dramatic performance increases in these children that were maintained over time. No other form of treatment resulted in such significant treatment outcomes in the education of young children with autism (Martin & Pear, 2014). ABA treatment has been endorsed by the former Surgeon General of the United States, David Satcher (1999) and discrete trial training has become a staple within treatment programs for young children with ASD, as it has been widely recognized as an evidence-based practice that is effective in the education and treatment of autism.

ABA is recognized as an evidence-based practice in developing educational and behavioral intervntions for children with a range of challenging behavior and learning needs, including the areas of attention deficit disorder (ADD) and ADHD (Fabiano, Pelham, Coles, Gnagy, Chronis-Tuscano, & O'Connor, 2009), anger management in adolescents with emotional/behavioral disorders (Barnes, Smith & Miller 2014), the use of cognitive behavioral interventions such as self-management to teach academic and social skills in adolescents and young adults with behavior disorders and intellectual disabilities (Miller, Miller, Wheeler, & Selinger, 1989; Wheeler, Bates, Marshall, & Miller, 1988), and more recently the re-emergence of self-management to teach social conversation skills to children with autism spectrum disorder (2014). These are a just a few of the numerous research studies supporting the use of ABA procedures in educational environments serving children and adolescents with learning and behavioral challenges.

ABA has also been applied in a variety of other areas including the area of behavioral medicine. Behavioral medicine is interdisciplinary in nature and is aimed at understanding the connections among illness, wellness, and behavior (Martin & Pear, 2014; Poppen, 1988). Martin and Pear (2014) point to the application of behavioral medicine, particularly in health psychology, that has resulted in enhancements in the treatment of health conditions, the area of treatment compliance, wellness, management of caregivers, and stress reduction. ABA has also been active in working with geriatric populations for conditions such as chronic pain (Wisocki & Powers, 1997) and dementia (Engelman, Altus, & Mathews, 1999; Heard & Watson, 1999) associated with Alzheimer's disease (Dwyer-Moore & Dixon, 2007).

Consider This

- What do you consider to be the strengths and limitations of each of the theories described?
- Which theory do you think you identify most with and why?

POSITIVE BEHAVIORAL INTERVENTIONS AND SUPPORTS

The evolution of ABA as a method of promoting behavior change has resulted in the widespread application of behavioral procedures as has been described. This trend continues with the refinement and application of these procedures within new and challenging circumstances. Most noteworthy in this development was the emergence of **positive behavioral interventions and supports (PBIS).** Some have viewed PBIS as an outgrowth of applied behavior analysis relying on the use of person-centered interventions that depend on the use of positive approaches to engineer environments, teach alternative behaviors, and employ meaningful consequences to enhance the quality of life for the individual.

PBIS is linked to the initial work of Horner and colleagues (1990) who advocated for the use of nonaversive behavioral supports for persons with severe disabilities largely within integrated community-based residential and employment settings. But as Dunlap, Kincaid, Horner, Knoster, and Bradshaw (2013) indicate, PBIS was influenced by a convergence of the social and civil rights initiatives aimed at deinstitutionalization of persons with severe disabilities, the foundations of applied behavior analysis, and research in the functional analysis of behavior. Changes in the philosophy of service delivery for persons with severe disabilities resulted from the increased community integration initiatives and, as a result, behavioral interventions became more functional and nonaversive (Anderson & Freeman, 2000).

Many within the field of ABA have argued that PBIS is no different from ABA, yet others view it as an enhancement of ABA (Koegel, Koegel, & Dunlap, 1996). Anderson and Kinkaid (2005) point out that PBIS adheres to the main components of ABA such as it is applied and behavioral, analytic and conceptual, technological, effective and generality. There are those that also believe elements associated with the implementation of PBIS has not been sufficiently validated through sufficient research. Despite these viewpoints, PBIS was introduced in legislation as part of the IDEA Reauthorization in 1997 and in 2004 whereby it called for the use of functional behavior assessment (FBA) as a method for understanding challenging behavior and toward capacity building in schools as a formative measure for addressing schoolwide disciplinary practices. PBIS operates from a values base that highly regards the quality of life of the individual and the input from their family. PBIS is composed of intervention methods that are behaviorally based, empirically validated, and congruent with the value of nonaversive intervention embedded within this values-based philosophy. PBIS is characterized by three prominent characteristics: (a) PBIS operates from a person-centered values base and is designed and delivered specific to the needs and preferences of the individual, thus representing socially valid goals; (b) PBIS recognizes the individuality of each person in the delivery of services and supports and therefore takes into consideration the need for flexibility to accommodate the individual's needs as necessary, given life demands in the delivery of behavior supports; and (c) PBS works toward meaningful outcomes that enhance the overall quality of life for the individual, including participation in inclusive educational and community environments (Anderson & Freeman, 2000; Dunlap et al., 2013).

Components of PBIS

As Horner and Sugai (2015) point out, PBIS consists of three tiers of support that encompass schoolwide, classroom, and individual levels of behavioral support. Tier 1 is directed towards primary prevention of challenging behavior and is embedded within and across the school culture. This level of PBIS is referred to as schoolwide behavioral supports and engages all school personnel and students in the recognition of proactive behaviors within the school. Generally speaking, this level of prevention addresses approximately 80% of the student population. Tier 2 is referred to as secondary prevention and provides additional behavioral and instructional support for approximately 15% of the student population who may display signs of at-risk behavior. These strategies can be readily employed across classroom settings. The final tier, Tier III or tertiary supports are specialized individualized interventions directed towards students with high-risk behavioral support needs. This generally constitutes 5% or less of the student population.

Important to the delivery of PBIS especially at the secondary and tertiary levels is the use of assessment and intervention practices designed to identify and understand the variables that correspond with the occurrence of challenging behavior and the delivery of interventions designed to teach positive replacement behaviors. The use of functional behavior assessment (FBA) is an essential component of PBIS and is intended to assist in the identification of variables that precipitate and/or maintain challenging behavior, including the setting events and antecedent variables that trigger these behaviors in an individual and the consequences that maintain these responses. It is important that the data gathered from the functional assessment process lead to the development of meaningful instructional interventions (Dunlap & Fox, 2011).

Specific methods associated with functional behavior assessment include the structured interview with key stakeholders such as teachers, family members, and often the learner as a means of identifying the target behavior and those variables of concern that influence this behavior. Other components include the collection of observational data on the learner within relevant environments and, on occasion, actual manipulations of instructional and/or environmental variables. Hypothesis statements are generated concerning the behavior, such as: "What setting events or antecedents appear to trigger the problem behavior?" and "What function(s) does the problem behavior serve for the individual?"

Sugai, Horner, and Sprague (1999) identified five outcomes associated with the functional assessment process: (a) operational definitions of target behaviors, (b) identification of conditions that predict when challenging behavior will and will not occur, (c) identification of consequences that maintain challenging behavior, (d) hypothesis statements that state when and where the target behavior will occur and the associated antecedents and consequences, and (e) direct observational data that confirm the accuracy of the hypothesis statements.

Functional analysis, a term you will learn more about later in the text, represents a form of functional assessment. Functional analysis involves the experimental manipulation of antecedents and consequences to demonstrate a cause-and-effect relationship between specific antecedent and/or consequence variables and the occurrence or nonoccurrence of the behavior in question. Functional assessment has been widely used within learning environments such as classroom settings, given its practicality, whereas functional analysis has been historically confined more to experimental research settings.

Functional assessment offers the classroom teacher a more user-friendly method for understanding challenging behavior. An applied illustration of how functional assessment can be utilized in the classroom is contained in Vignette 1.2.

Vignette 1.2

Functional Behavior Assessment Within a Classroom Setting

The behavior specialist, Ms. Thomas, a young and energetic teacher with a master's degree in special education and applied experience in the delivery of positive behavior supports, was recently asked to lend her assistance within her school district. She received a request to serve as a consultant in reference to a 12-year-old boy named Stefan, who was receiving services in a self-contained classroom for children with moderate and severe disabilities. He was displaying some chronic episodes of

continued

challenging behavior, and his team needed assistance in the application of functional assessment procedures as a means of understanding his behavior and providing intervention.

Given Ms. Thomas's expertise and strengths in the areas of positive behavior supports and consultation, she was deemed an appropriate liaison for the team to consult. She began the process by meeting with the child's team and discussing the details prior to initiating the formal assessment process.

During this phase, Ms. Thomas assembled relevant information that included the child's age, information on the child's family and his disability, current Individualized Education Program (IEP), learning strengths, and greatest areas of challenge. She then proceeded to ask each member of the child's immediate team, including Stefan's mother, to complete a functional assessment interview (i.e., structured interview questionnaire) related to the behaviors of concern. The functional assessment interview consisted of a series of questions that probed the specifics of the behavior in question, elements of the environment that consistently coincided with high and low occurrences of the behavior, and what Stefan may be getting by engaging in the challenging behavior. Other relevant questions pertaining to changes in medical and physical health, family and living circumstances, changes in the routine at school and home, and other information deemed important by the team were then posed.

Upon obtaining the completed interviews, Ms. Thomas compiled, sorted, and collated the information contained in each of the completed interviews. In all, four total questionnaires were completed. These included one from Stefan's teacher, one from the classroom assistant, one from the speech and language therapist, and one from Stefan's mother. After reviewing the results, Ms. Thomas ascertained that the target behavior of concern was task avoidance. Stefan was identified with severe mental retardation and had limited communication abilities. It appeared from reading the interview responses that the behavior would frequently escalate if Stefan were not redirected early in the cycle.

Ms. Thomas collaborated with Stefan's team in sharing these immediate hypotheses and then began the next phase of the functional assessment. With the team's assistance, she operationally defined each of the target behaviors in question. The definitions were in terms that were observable and measurable. Once the behaviors were defined, she asked Stefan's teacher and his mother to record occurrences of these behaviors across 15-minute time blocks using a scatter-plot data sheet. After 5 days of collecting the scatter-plot information, she could see patterns of behavior emerging. Stefan had virtually no occurrences of the target behaviors at home, high frequencies of the behaviors during specific points of the day while at school, and periods of time in school when the behaviors were minimal, if present at all.

In conducting subsequent observations during both the peak times of the behaviors and times when the behaviors were not present, the hypotheses became clearer. Stefan was not given opportunities for choice, and when in need of help in performing a task, he would seek to escape rather than seek assistance. A functional communication method was developed for Stefan that included a laminated index card. One side of the card displayed a red circle with the word *help* written beneath it. Stefan was instructed to turn his card over to seek help when he needed the teacher's assistance. This small intervention was responsive to his needs and the need of his teacher in preventing problematic behavior from occurring.

Reflective Moment

1. After reading the vignette, do you feel that you have a better understanding of the importance of systematic data collection as part of the functional behavior assessment (FBA) process?
2. What skills are important to facilitate the completion of such a process while serving as a consulting teacher?
3. What strategies would you use to initiate collaboration among your fellow team members in such a role?

REAUTHORIZATION OF IDEA

The use of functional behavior assessment was introduced into legislation in the 1997 Reauthorization of IDEA (the Individuals with Disabilities Education Act). This legislation mandated the use of functional behavior assessment and the design of behavior intervention plans (BIP) to address the needs of learners with problem behaviors. The BIP component of IDEA stated that the BIP must be developed based on a functional assessment and developed with the intent of ameliorating the problem behavior (IDEA Amendments of 1997, Public Law 105-17). The mandate served as a catalyst for examining these issues and for building the case for the use of positive behavioral interventions and supports.

The most recent Reauthorization of IDEA occurred in 2004. Some changes in the Reauthorization related to PBIS worth noting included the increased emphasis on the use of PBIS in addressing challenging behavior. Whereas the 1997 Reauthorization says one should "consider" using positive behavioral interventions and strategies to address a behavior that is impeding the student or other student's learning, the 2004 Reauthorization stated that one "must consider" the use of positive behavioral interventions and strategies to address a behavior that is impeding the student's or another student's learning. Other changes stress that the IEP must give priority to PBS strategies for addressing challenging behavior (20 U.S.C. § 1414(d)(3)(B)(i), 34 C.F.R. § 300.324(a)(2)(i)). In summary, the 2004 Reauthorization of IDEA served to strengthen the role of PBS and embed PBIS as the recommended practice for addressing challenging behaviors in the schools.

THE APPLICATION OF PBIS ACROSS LEARNERS AND LEARNING ENVIRONMENTS

PBIS has evolved into a recognized evidence-based practice for addressing the prevention and remediation of challenging behaviors. Early research validated the use of these practices largely at the tertiary level for students with more significant needs including students with intellectual disabilities (Horner & Carr, 1997), emotional and behavior disorders, and learning disabilities (Dunlap et al., 1993; Dunlap, Kern-Dunlap, Clarke, & Robbins, 1991; Dunlap, White, Vera, Wilson, & Panacek, 1996; Kern, Childs, Dunlap, Clarke, & Falk, 1994; Umbreit, 1995).

The application of PBIS across the three-tiers of support illustrates a behaviorally-based systems approach to enhance the capacity of schools, families, and communities in designing effective environments. In focusing attention on creating and sustaining school environments that improve lifestyle results for all children and youth by making problem behavior less effective, efficient, and relevant and making desired behavior more functional, PBIS is the integration of (a) behavior science, (b) practical interventions, (c) social values, and (d) a systems perspective (Sugai, Horner, Dunlap, et al., 1999; Dunlap et al., 2013).

SCHOOL-WIDE APPLICATIONS OF PBIS

School-wide PBIS has become increasingly more widespread as experts have recognized the utility of these principles of instruction and support as a prevention tool for promoting safe learning environments for all students. Horner and Sugai (2000) identified the common features of schools that were actively using school-wide behavior supports and they included the following:

- The use of school-based support teams in the design and delivery of PBIS
- Administrative buy-in and support for schoolwide behavioral supports
- School culture defined by a limited number of behavioral expectations
- Behavioral expectations taught to all students
- Students given recognition for positive behaviors
- Students who engaged in disruptive and dangerous behavior being corrected, not ignored or rewarded
- Evaluation of student performance collected in an ongoing manner by school-based teams and used for decision making

School-wide PBIS has been successful in minimizing problem behavior and school violence and reducing discipline referrals through prevention (Sadler, 2000; Taylor-Greene & Kartub, 2000). Since its inception, school-wide PBIS has been used successfully in over 21,000 schools nationwide (Horner & Sugai, 2015). Historically, many school systems relied on rapid-suppression procedures for managing problematic behavior. Students who engaged in problematic behavior were usually administered punitive consequences such as expulsion, in-school suspension, and even corporal punishment. These procedures were after-the-fact interventions that were directed at suppressing or controlling the problem behavior. The merits and disadvantages of such approaches have been the source of constant debate over time among professionals, parents, and child advocates. In short, the use of rapid-suppression approaches does nothing to promote positive behavior, nor does it promote prevention through the active teaching and reinforcement of prosocial behaviors. These approaches do not enrich the culture or climate within the learning environment, and, finally, they are not sensitive to the environmental factors that influence challenging behavior.

FACTORS INFLUENCING THE DEVELOPMENT OF PBIS

One of the most important elements promoting the use of PBIS is the training of educational professionals at the in-service and preservice levels. Such training includes preservice teachers who are in the initial stages of professional preparation and professionals who are already on the job working as teachers. At present, most teacher training programs allot one course within the curriculum devoted to behavior management or classroom management issues. For preservice teacher training in the field of special education, students typically receive training in one or more courses devoted to ABA or behavior management. Given the outgrowth of PBIS, teacher training programs have expanded to become more inclusive of competencies in PBIS. Effective training practices of preservice and in-service educational professionals will hopefully lead to improved practices in the provision of behavioral supports within learning environments and result in greater quality assurance.

Another issue that is important to the success of PBIS with children and youth is the partnership between professionals and families. Families are key players in the process of functional assessment and in the development and success of behavioral intervention plans. Parents and families contribute a perspective on the child that is unique and exclusive to them and their role as the child's parents. Also important to the success of school-wide behavioral supports is the use of a school-based team comprised of administrators and teachers all with the goal of achieving a durable and lasting system-wide impact. This impact can be evaluated through such indicators as a reduction in office referrals, suspensions, and expulsions as one example. Vignette 1.3 provides an illustration of the use of school-based teams in the provision of behavior supports.

Vignette 1.3

School-Based Behavior Support Teams and the Provision of PBIS

Adams Elementary School and the regional state university have entered into a unique partnership involving the development of school-based teams in the delivery of behavior supports within their school. The partnership is part of a pilot grant project that facilitates the development of systemwide behavior support teams within schools. Adams Elementary School was selected to participate in the project based on several factors. The student body at Adams Elementary is composed of children primarily from lower socioeconomic conditions, and the patterns of problematic behavior that have emerged within the district as the children transition to middle school and junior high school have pointed to the need for early intervention and prevention at the preschool and elementary levels. Thus school officials and university project personnel have developed an innovative project aimed at the development of school-based teams in the area of behavior supports.

To initiate the newly formed partnership, the university project personnel and school-based team from Adams Elementary formulated an agreement to establish goals and objectives for the program and benchmarks for team progress. This agreement also detailed the roles and responsibilities of each team member and the appointed role of the university technical assistance team. A special education teacher trained in behavior supports, a school psychologist, a school counselor, an assistant principal, and a general education teacher participated as team members. The university-based technical assistance project consisted of one doctoral-level behavior analyst and two graduate students who worked as partners with the local school-based team.

The next phase of the project implementation was to provide extensive in-service training in the use of PBIS for members from the school-based team. The goal of the in-service preparation phase was to ensure that all members of the team from Adams Elementary and team members from the university-based behavior support project were well versed in a common knowledge base. This knowledge base included the

continued

principles of PBIS, functional behavior assessment, behavior support plan development, collaboration and consultation, and working in unison with families. The purpose was to build a sense of community within Adams Elementary among all relevant parties, including administrators, teachers, teaching assistants, cafeteria workers, bus drivers, and administrative personnel.

Once the team at Adams Elementary and other school personnel had received training and were aware the purpose of the project, the university-based technical assistance team served as on-site consultants at the school. They began working with the local school-based team in the delivery of PBIS practices with children referred to the project. They worked in tandem with classroom teachers and related education personnel with identified children who were experiencing problematic behavior. Applications of PBIS practices such as functional behavior assessment and development of behavior support plans were implemented for children identified with such conditions as autism, intellectual disabilities, emotional/behavior disorders, attention deficit disorder, and learning disabilities. The purpose of this phase was to model the implementation of these practices for the school-based team and assist in problem solving as they began to implement evidence-based practices for children within classroom settings. As the team began to sharpen their skills and positive outcomes began to be realized, teachers and administrators became more enthusiastic and supportive. As the first year of the program concluded, school officials were pleasantly surprised with the evaluation outcomes from the project, which included a reduction in office referrals and incident reports and measures of teacher and family satisfaction. During the second year of the program, the team began to generalize these practices throughout the general school population through the formation of school-wide PBIS and began involving students in the process by establishing school policies that promoted a sense of community for the students with the intent of improving school climate, such as school-wide incentives for appropriate conduct and behavior.

The project has resulted in improvements at all levels (individual student, classroom, and school) and continues with intermittent involvement of the university-based technical assistance team. Adams Elementary has become a model school in the district with its innovative approach to promoting positive student behavior through the use of PBIS. The district now uses the team from Adams Elementary as district wide consultants to provide professional development throughout the district as other schools are beginning to undertake the implementation of PBIS within their respective schools.

Reflective Moment

1. What are some indicators of positive school climate based on your observations within schools?
2. Identify some methods you could use to develop effective behavior support teams within your school.

Consider This

- How does PBIS fit or not fit with your theoretical orientation?
- What, in your view, are the strengths and limitations of PBIS?

SUMMARY

In this chapter, the common theories used to understand behavior and development in children and youth were described; these include the biological, psychodynamic/psychosocial, developmental, ecological, behavioral, and social learning theories. The origins and distinguishing features for each of the theories were described, and examples of each theory applied to practice were presented. The major theorists were introduced, as were their contributions to their respective fields, and the strengths and limitations of each of the theoretical frameworks were also discussed.

Given the focus of this text, much attention was given to the development of the behavioral model and more specifically applied behavior anlaysis and its relationship and contributions to the evolution and development of PBIS as it is today. Related to the behavioral model were the ecological and social learning perspectives, given their close association with the behavior theory. The work of theorists such as Urie Bronfenbrenner and Nicholas Hobbs (ecological theory) and Albert Bandura (social learning theory) were highlighted. The early history of the behavioral model applied to animal learning and the later applications to complex human behaviors, pioneered by the work of B. F. Skinner and advanced by such leaders as Sidney Bijou and others, were elaborated upon, including the development of applied behavior analysis, the outgrowth of positive behavioral interventions and supports, and the application of these methodologies to learners and learning environments.

Applied vignettes provided throughout the chapter described how to generalize the various theoretical frameworks discussed toward solving applied problems involving children, families, and educational systems relative to the delivery of PBIS. Finally, the chapter closed with a section devoted to understanding the application of PBIS across learners and learning environments. The utility of these procedures was discussed relative to individual and school-wide applications of PBIS. The barriers to full-scale acceptance and implementation of PBIS, including enhanced preservice and in-service training of teachers and related professionals, systemwide implementation at the local and statewide educational agency levels, and future trends in the development of the field, were examined.

ACTIVITIES TO EXTEND YOUR LEARNING

1. Develop a matrix for comparing and contrasting the various theoretical viewpoints described in Chapter 1. Identify and list major components of each theory and their applicability to understanding the behavior of children and youth.
2. Identify and list the merits associated with PBIS from Vignette 1.2. Would you have followed the same procedures as Ms. Thomas, and do you agree with her conclusions following the functional assessment? What would you have done differently?
3. Which of the theoretical viewpoints presented in Chapter 1 in your opinion has the most practical application with children and youth in learning environments? Explain why.
4. Compare and discuss the three-tiered model of PBIS and evaluate each of the levels, Tiers I, II, and III, and how they fit within your current philosophy of behavior management.

FURTHER READING AND EXPLORATION

1. Visit the OSEP (Office of Special Education Programs) Technical Assistance Center on Positive Behavioral Interventions and Supports at www.pbis.org.

Family/Professional Partnerships

CONCEPTS TO UNDERSTAND

After reading this chapter, you should be able to:

- Describe how education reform has affected the partnerships between families and professionals, and how education reforms are relevant to positive behavioral intervention and supports (PBIS).
- List and describe the six types of involvement from Epstein's model of family–professional partnerships.
- Discuss the historical and current roles of families served through special education.
- Delineate the legislative mandate for partnerships and parent involvement.
- Define and differentiate among the terms *partnership, empowerment, collaboration, parent involvement*, and *family-centered supports and services.*
- Describe and provide examples of the desired roles of families in the development, implementation, and evaluation of PBIS.
- Summarize research literature that supports the roles of parents and families related to PBIS.

KEY TERMS

Alliance

Behavioral interventions and supports

Collaboration

Empowerment

Family-centered support

Intervention

No Child Left Behind Act of 2001 (NCLB)

Parent involvement and participation

Partnership

Reform

Response to Intervention (RtI)

Special education principles

THE NATURE OF FAMILIES AND PARTNERSHIPS IN EDUCATION

What is a partner? As you think about this question, you might respond by providing any number of examples from your experience. There are many forms of partnership, and they may be either formal or informal. A **partnership** in general between two or more persons is characterized by a sense of sharing and common purpose, a close, cooperative working relationship, and a reasonable balance of rights and responsibilities between the two parties. Some partnerships are successful, some are successful for a period of time but not lasting, others are tenuous and on shaky ground, and still others are failures. What are the factors that contribute to the building and maintaining of a successful partnership?

Of particular interest in this chapter is how this question relates to the partnership between educators and family members. We focus in particular on how professionals should seek to understand, establish, and take advantage of this partnership to improve and enrich the lives and self-determination of children and youth with challenging behavior through application of positive behavioral intervention and supports (PBIS). However, we take a broader view of this partnership because in large measure the basic tenets and practices of partnership around PBIS are the same as those detailed more generally in education.

A common assumption in education is that parent and family involvement is critically important and is the best predictor of academic success for children and youth in school. A body of research evidence and expert opinion has historically supported the powerful influence of parent involvement in schooling (Henderson, 1987; Henderson & Berla, 1995; McWayne, C. M., Melzi, G., Schick, A. R., Kennedy, J. L., & Mundt, K., 2013). Take a moment to reflect on what the statement "parents should be involved" might mean to different people. For some people, "parent involvement" might mean that parents passively support and back up the teachers and the school and that they refrain from interfering with teacher and school decisions. For others it translates into the idea that parents will do what is asked of them by teachers and schools. For example, they will ensure that their children do their homework, they will respond to notes sent home by the teacher, they will provide refreshments for a special classroom event, or they will serve the school as part of a fund-raising campaign. Still others might think of parent involvement as parents serving as tutors, extra hands, volunteers, and classroom teaching assistants. And those who have an understanding of special education may associate parent involvement with participation in Individual Education Programs (IEPs), Individualized Family Service Plans (IFSPs), or the provision of training experiences for parents. Finally, some might see parent involvement as including some or all of the preceding descriptions.

Although we will be considering in some detail these different forms of parent involvement, it serves us now to first pose some questions. How do we account for cultural differences and diversity when determining how parents might be involved? What are the relationships between parents' and families' developmental status (ages, maturity levels, education, parenting abilities, economic well-being) and their involvement as individuals? How do we as professionals relate to parents who have beliefs, values, and goals that differ from ours? Can we genuinely make a place in our professional philosophy and practices for parents to be in an alliance with us—to become our partners and collaborators? And do we have, or are we willing to attain, the knowledge and skills necessary to prepare us to be successful in working with the parents and families of the children whom we teach or to whom we provide other services?

For us to be successful as educators in developing and maintaining strong partnerships with families, we must have some knowledge of how the characteristics and functions of families have changed over time. It is important to understand what families look like today as compared to what they were like in the past and what they will be like in the future. Professionals will be better prepared as partners and collaborators if they understand and are accepting of the increasing diversity represented in families and the children who are members of those families.

Families have become increasingly diverse in their structure and in the way they function. The 2016 census data for the United States reported that the majority of American children under the age of 18 (50.7 million children) live with two parents, 17.2 million children live with their mother only, 2.8 million live with no parent present, and 3 million live with their father only (U.S. Census Bureau, 2016). Our nation is also becoming increasingly more diverse with regard to race, ethnicity, and religion. One may view these changes as evidence of a decline of the family—for example, children being raised in families without a father or as the changing demographic of families. One of these changes that represent an interesting and unique challenge for partnering is the increasing role of grandparents in raising grandchildren. In the U.S., approximately 2.7 million grandparents are raising their grandchildren with about one-fifth of these grandparents having incomes below the poverty line (Cancino, 2016). The reality is that the families with whom educator's work may at times look and behave increasingly different from their own families.

Many years ago, Bengtson (2001) acknowledged that families in the future would become increasingly more diverse in structure and function and stated that "multi-generational bonds" would become more important. As a result of several factors, including the increasing importance of grandparents and other extended family members in fulfilling family functions and our increasing longevity (life span), ultimately with families having become more connected across generations. Think about how this might affect you as a professional. As an example, you might be serving as an early interventionist, and your work is primarily to provide home-based support in a family-centered manner. Suppose the nuclear family is the grandmother of an infant with disabilities, the great-grandmother, and the infant's great-aunt. They are generally there when you arrive at the home, and they are your partners. Suppose that you are their child's fifth-grade teacher and that, as a part of your parent involvement plan for the year, you have sent a letter inviting family members to be a part of your classroom mentoring and volunteer program. Most of your thinking and planning has been done with the assumption that the responses you get to this invitation will be from the mothers of your students. One of your "takers" may be a grandfather. Or suppose that you are a special education teacher at the high-school level responsible for developing and helping others implement positive behavior support plans for adolescents with challenging behavior. At the IEP or PBIS planning meeting, you might have the student, her stepmother, and her paternal grandfather and grandmother, all of whom are members of the student's nuclear family and very important in her life. Or you might have an adult sibling.

The relationships between parents and other family members and various educational environments and professionals have evolved over the years. A cursory discussion is undertaken here to set the stage for consideration of current issues and practices. Many factors, related both to general education and to special education, have influenced the changes that have occurred. Certainly economic changes in the United States, population trends, increased levels of education of the citizenry, scientific and technological advances, increased cultural diversity, societal shifts related to the roles of families and parents, educational reform movements and research findings, and other factors have all influenced this relationship. You might think of your own family and extended family and how these factors may have affected great-grandparents, grandparents, parents, and others regarding their connections with schools and educational professionals. The shifts that have occurred over time have sometimes been challenging for families, given that they have naturally tended to apply personal models and experiences to guide their ways of understanding and interacting with the education of their children. An example is the parent(s) in a family who are reluctant to participate in determining educational goals, curricula, or learning experiences because they have been acculturated to believe that education is best left exclusively to the professionals.

EDUCATION REFORM AND FAMILIES

Turnbull, Turnbull, Erwin, Soodak, and Shogren (2015) provide a description of how reforms in both general education and special education have affected the partnerships between families and professionals in education over four decades. And we have begun to see over the past 25 or so years a merger of these reform movements or a "unified systems reform" (McLaughlin, 1998). The term **reform** suggests that actions are taken to improve the form or condition of something but also to put an end to something that may be viewed as outdated or ineffective. To reform means to change for the better. Although it is not always so, one would hope that efforts to reform (for purposes here primarily with regard to the matter of educational institutions and their views and treatment of parents and families) are driven by empirical evidence and systematic and thoughtful deliberation, as well as by the wishes and needs of consumers, so that the reform will produce a more desirable result.

GENERAL EDUCATION REFORM

Historically, reform in general education has included a number of national as well as state- and regional-level studies, reports, and related initiatives. You may be familiar with some of these initiatives through the study of the foundations, history, and philosophy of education. If so, think about the extent to which the reforms include content related to the partnership between families and educational settings. The research and demonstration models of Joyce Epstein (2010) have been the most frequently applied with regard to conceptualizing, planning, and implementing family professional partnerships in general education. In the Epstein model, family, school, and community are seen as "overlapping spheres of influence," and balanced roles of these influences represent the opportunity for partnership.

Epstein and Sanders (2002) suggested from their overview of theory, research, and practice that "in educational practice, more educators are moving away from isolation behind classroom doors and toward new models of family-school-community partnerships" (p. 431). They earlier described six types of involvement in which families and professionals both have roles and responsibilities in order to effectively make use of these partnership strategies. These strategies remain critical in today's schooling efforts when fostering family, school, and community partnerships. Each of these types of involvement may be applied to a variety of educational environments, children, and families, whether the children are infants, toddlers, preschoolers, school-age children, or youth and whether they have a disability. Obviously the presence of a disability, ethnicity and language diversity, cultural and religious beliefs, as well as factors such as poverty, single-parent family, education level, and personalities of family members influence the types and intensity of involvement chosen and the ways in which schools and families experience involvement. It is also possible to understand the types of involvement as being to some extent sequential, moving from basic to more complex, with one building on the other. Here are a few examples:

- Type 1 focuses on the basic obligations of families for parenting. Suppose that you are the lead teacher in a school-based, inclusive preschool classroom for children ages 3 to 5. You find that some of your preschool teacher colleagues, your teaching assistants, and some of the parents of the children in your room have expressed an interest in learning how to do CPR with very young children, including children who are medically fragile and who have other health and orthopedic impairments. You arrange for a CPR trainer from the local health department to provide a training workshop over a couple of evening sessions.

- Type 2 addresses the obligation of schools for effective communication. As a fourth-grade teacher in your second year of employment, you are beginning to see the unique challenges associated with effective partnering, given that you have more than 100 different sets of families with whom to communicate. In assessing your first year's experience and your own professional development needs, you determine that you need some new ideas regarding strategies for written, verbal, and electronic communication. You take a step forward with regard to your Type 2 obligation by signing up for a graduate summer class on "Practical Communication Skills for Elementary Teachers."

- Type 3 highlights the importance of families volunteering at school and sharing their time and talents. As a high school special education resource room teacher, you find that your responsibilities for consulting with the general education teachers on behalf of included students are leaving you with insufficient time for some of the direct instruction that you need to provide to your students in the resource room. You address this issue by establishing a cadre of peer tutors and community mentors who volunteer time in your classroom.

- Type 4 focuses on home activities and primarily on applying school learning and homework. Your second graders are learning about trees, and it's time to do the project on collection and classification of leaves. You develop a guide and a few helpful hints for families as they participate with their children in this homework activity, and you and your first-grade colleagues take turns making yourselves available through the "homework hotline" program to answer questions after school.

- Type 5 involvement encourages parents and families to take leadership and decision-making roles related to schooling. As the father of an adolescent daughter who is a student at the local alternative school for children with behavior challenges, you initiate (and get support and assistance from the teaching faculty) a parent–teacher organization.

- Type 6 involvement describes the opportunities both teachers and parents might have to foster collaboration and connections in the community in support of education. In your role as a service coordinator, you are responsible for partnering with 30 families in which there is an infant or toddler with a disability that qualifies the child for early intervention services. A number of these families express interest in having access to respite care services. Along with these family members, you and some of your prior, experienced family members develop and distribute a respite care resource guide.

SPECIAL EDUCATION REFORM

Up to this point, we have examined general education reform. We'll now turn our attention to special education. An examination of the history of parent and family roles in special education and other services for children with disabilities proves quite interesting. What comes to mind when one thinks about the parents and other family members of a person with a disability? One's views are significantly affected by his or her closeness to the family and to the person with the disability. This is especially true if the individual is a member of his or her immediate family. It is reasonable to assume that the closer the personal relationship, the *less* likely one is to hold any of the following widely held historical assumptions:

- Parents are given a child with a disability because they are especially equipped to handle such a challenge.
- Families are given a member with a disability as a form of punishment.
- Families in which there is a member with a disability are stronger and more prepared to cope with adversity.
- Families in which there is a member with a disability tend to be dysfunctional in terms of marital and other intrafamily relationships.
- Parents of children with disabilities have a tendency to be at one extreme or the other—either overprotective of their child or disconnected and distant.
- Parents of children with disabilities go through a highly predictable process in which they experience shock, denial, blame, resistance, and finally acceptance.
- Parents of children with disabilities are adversarial and demanding of school systems and other service programs and are quick to take legal action.
- Parents of children and youth with disabilities want to be the primary teachers and interventionists for their children.

It is likely that some of these statements sound familiar. It is also reasonable to think that elements of truth exist in some of the statements. However, taken as a whole, they represent the inaccurate stereotypes and myths that have hindered our ability to establish and maintain partnerships with families.

With the initial passage of IDEA in 1990 as Public Law 101-476, legislation emphasizing the importance of "person-first" language came to exist, meaning that an individual's status as a person comes before his or her special needs. One would refer, for example, to a "child with Down syndrome" rather than a "Down syndrome child." Although it may sound like splitting hairs or political correctness to some, it is not to those persons with disabilities and their families. They do not want to be primarily defined by their disability status. In Richey and Wheeler (2000), we suggest adding the dimension of "family-first" language to the concept of "person-first" language:

> We are better served as professionals if our starting point in thinking about and serving families is to view them first as families (like our own families), and then as having uniqueness based on their individual circumstances, including the accommodations needed for a family member with a disability. (p. 12)

What is the relationship between the changes that have occurred over the past 50 years in the delivery of special education services and the views and roles of parents and families with children and youth who are the recipients of these services? The reforms in special education over the period noted are intertwined with the actions of parents; professionals' changing views of parents and families; economic, social, and political changes affecting family life in the United States; and the expanding knowledge base regarding causes, prevention, treatment, and **intervention** for persons with disabilities.

This point is validated if you think about your own personal experiences and those of your parents, grandparents, great-grandparents, extended family, and the people with disabilities with whom they have been acquainted. Turnbull, Turnbull, Soodak, and Shogren (2015) provide a helpful framework for understanding the evolution of parents' and families' place historically—in special education specifically and related to disability generally (Table 2–1). They report that by understanding this history, we might better understand the present situation and the challenges that families face.

Considering how the field of special education has changed over the years, it is reasonable to attribute those reforms to several primary sources, including social, political, and economic factors influencing our attitudes toward and treatment of people with disabilities. Also influencing change has been research regarding causation and best and effective teaching and intervention practices and the advocacy efforts of many (but especially parents), leading to federal and state legislation and its associated rules and regulations, policies, and financial resources.

TABLE 2–1
Historical and Current Roles of Families

Role/Time Frame	Event(s)
Parents as the source: 1880–1960	Parents viewed as unfit. Eugenics movement advocated the need for selective breeding (Barr, 1913).
Parents as organization members: 1930s–Present	Parents take lead in local and national organizing—for example, United Cerebral Palsy, 1949; Autism Society of America, 1961; National Association for Down Syndrome, 1961; Association for Children with Learning Disabilities, 1964; Federation of Families for Children's Mental Health, 1988.
Parents as service developers: 1950s–1960s	Largely as a result of the organizations that they developed, parents established service programs.
Parents as recipients of professional decisions: 1960s–1970s	Parents expected to be passive recipients and appreciative and supportive of the teacher.
Parents as teachers: 1960s–1980s	Prompted by the research related to environment and children's intellectual development (Hunt, 1972) and the work of psychologist Urie Bronfenbrenner, Head Start and school-age programs for children with disabilities emphasized parents as extensions of the educator.
Parents as political advocates: 1970–Present	Parents' central role was through advocacy for success of two landmark litigations for rights to treatment and education, leading to passage in 1975 of P.L. 94-142, the Education for All Handicapped Children Act.
Parents as educational decision makers: 1975–Present	Legislation—found in P.L. 94-142 and in subsequent reauthorizations in 1986, 1990, 1997, and 2004—establishes the importance of parents as decision makers.
Families as Partners and Educational Decision Makers: 1990s–Present	Advanced by Part C of IDEA Infants and Toddlers Program changes focus for parents to families and a family-centered approach and the Individuals with Disabilities Improvement Act (2004).

Source: Based on information from Turnbull, A. A., Turnbull, H. R., Erwin, E. J., Soodak, L. C., & Shogren, K. A. (2015). *Families, professionals, and exceptionality: Positive outcomes through partnerships and trust.* Columbus, OH: Pearson.

Yell (2015) stated that the landmark case *Brown v. Board of Education* (1954), which resulted in a victory for the civil rights movement and determined that separate, segregated schools were inherently damaging and not equal and were inconsistent with the Fourteenth Amendment of the U.S. Constitution as applied to students with disabilities. The basic position upheld by the Supreme Court that racial segregation was stigmatizing and had negative consequences was interpreted to also include persons who were denied opportunity as a result of their disability. The *Brown* decision was important in establishing the rights of persons with disabilities. However, the role of parent advocacy can be associated with a major event that occurred some 44 years prior to the civil rights case (Yell, 2015). The first White House Conference on Children took place in 1910. One of the goals of the conference was to define and establish remedial programs for children with disabilities or special needs. This and related events of the time served as an impetus in the United States to be more responsive to children and youth with disabilities in school settings and to establish separate special education. The assumption was that this arrangement would provide smaller classes and would facilitate individualized instruction, less competition, and more self-esteem for students with disabilities.

Although the concept of equal opportunity (articulated as a result of *Brown v. Board of Education*) did extend to children with disabilities, it was a number of years before that decision was specifically applied in the federal courts to those children. Two landmark class action lawsuits—the *Pennsylvania Association for Retarded Citizens,* or *PARC* (1972) and *Mills v. Board of Education of the District of Columbia* (1972), along with other cases—were foundational in establishing the right to education for children with disabilities. Prior to *PARC* being argued in court, it was resolved by a consent agreement stating that children ages 6 to 21 with intellectual disabilities had the right to a free public education and that it was desirable to provide that education in educational settings such as those provided for same-age peers who did not have disabilities. In a summary of *PARC*, Yell (2015) emphasized four points: (1) children classified as intellectually disabled can and do benefit from education and training, (2) education is more than strictly academic experiences, (3) the state of Pennsylvania cannot deny access to public education, and (4) early preschool experiences are important for children with intellectual disabilities and should be provided just as they are for children who are typically developing. Although these statements may seem obvious to us given where we are today with legislative mandates for special education, they were quite remarkable in 1972.

Like the *PARC* litigation, *Mills v. Board of Education* was a class action lawsuit. However, it was filed in the District of Columbia by parents and guardians representing a variety of disabilities and children who were denied public education without due process. *Mills* resulted in the federal court mandating that all children with disabilities in the district be provided with public education. It also outlined procedural safeguards and due process procedures. Due process has become an established cornerstone of IDEA. Families have a right to due process related to the decisions made about their children in special education programs. Earlier in this chapter, the role of parents as political advocates was introduced. The central role of parents and families and guardians in advocating for the right to public education for children with disabilities, not discounting the importance of parent organizations as advocates, may be connected to these two lawsuits. *PARC* and *Mills* clearly pointed to the necessity for both federal and state legislation specific to the provision of special education services.

That legislation was forthcoming beginning in the mid-1970s, as states and the federal government hastened to pass laws establishing the right to public education for children with disabilities. The legislation education was prompted in part by parent and professional advocacy groups, such as the Council for Exceptional Children. Also, a growing understanding from research and model programs about children and youth with disabilities, which showed they were valuable and capable no matter what their disability or its severity, supported legislation. But it was also clear to politicians and other decision makers from the litigation, especially *PARC* and *Mills,* that legislation was necessary to avoid further lawsuits.

In 1975, P.L. 94-142, the Education for All Handicapped Children Act (EAHCA) was passed, becoming essentially a bill of educational rights for all children with disabilities between the ages of 3 and 18 by September 1978 and up to age 21 by September 1980. This landmark legislation became the foundation for special education services in all 50 states. Its amendments and reauthorizations continue to provide the direction and a significant portion of the resources available today for the provision of special education services, as well as for the preparation of qualified personnel, funding of demonstrations of model service delivery, and the conducting of research in special education. Since it was initially passed as EAHCA in 1975, the legislation has been amended in 1986 as P.L. 99-372, the Handicapped Children's Protection Act, allowing parents to recover attorney's fees and their costs when they prevail in lawsuits. P.L. 94-142 was amended and reauthorized as P.L. 99-457, the Education of the Handicapped Amendments of 1986. In recognition of the established and growing body of research evidence regarding the efficacy of early intervention for very young children with disabilities and resulting from the advocacy efforts of parents, professionals, and others (Safer & Hamilton, 1993), P.L. 99-457 included funds for states to participate, if they chose to, in the development of programs for infants and toddlers (ages birth to 3 years) and their families. This initiative was Part H (now Part C) of the law and provided funding for 5 years of phasing in, developing, and planning for states to make ready their own models of early intervention.

By September 1991, all states had put in place mandates for early intervention services in compliance with Part H and following the components required in the law. Silverstein (1989) had indicated that a growing recognition of and respect for the importance of family resulted in the inclusion of family-centered and family-focused language and emphasis that we now find in Part H. Safer and Hamilton (1993) summarized the importance of families in early intervention by noting that:

> Part H reflects not only a respect for families and what they know, but also an assumption that the family plays the key role in the development of the young child, and that the responsibility of the service system is to support that role. (p. 5)

There is a very significant distinction to be made here between the concepts of supporting families as contrasted with providing services (educational and otherwise) to children. These views might be different based on the age of the child and the nature of the environment, and clearly the family–professional partnership is substantially affected by these factors.

In 1990, the special education federal law was once again amended and reauthorized, this time as P.L. 101-476, the Individuals with Disabilities Education Act (IDEA). As noted previously, IDEA changed the title of the law to reflect person-first language. P.L. 105-17, the Individuals with Disabilities Education Act Amendments of 1997, reauthorized IDEA and included some changes and refinements, including a greater emphasis on the inclusion of children and youth with special needs in general education (referred to as natural environments for infants and toddlers) and the role of general educators in the planning and implementing of special education. Turnbull, Turnbull, Erwin, Soodak, and Shogren (2015) noted that reform in special education has progressed through two phases: (1) reshaping how free and appropriate public education (FAPE) is provided and (2) reshaping the educational placements of children and youth with disabilities to be more inclusive and to have greater access to the general curriculum. Certainly the basis for this reform in special education over the past many years is attributable to the legislative mandates summarized earlier and the changes and refinements associated with their amendments and reauthorization.

Consider This

- What do you consider significant about the relationship between the federal legislation in special education as a source of reform and the partnership between parents and families of children and youth with disabilities and professionals?
- How might future legislation affect this partnership?

It is important first to remember that the relationship between the reform and partnerships has been reciprocal. That is, parents and families—through advocacy, litigation, and in other ways—have affected not only the initial passage of the law (EAHCA) now IDEA but also the changes that have been made and the ways in which IDEA has been implemented from its regulations at the level of state and local education agencies. Legislation has been the foundation for the establishment and refinement of the family–professional partnership in special education. From the initial passage of the law in 1975 through the most recent reauthorization in 2004, parent involvement has been emphasized as not only positive and desirable but also necessary. Six **special education principles** that underlie IDEA and that must be met if states are to participate; the relationships between them; and both the family-centered focus of Part C early intervention for infants, toddlers, and their families; and the parent involvement focus of Part B (special education for children and youth ages 3 years through 21 years) are all emphasized in the 2004 IDEA reauthorization. We are assuming that you have been exposed to these principles in previous special education classes, or maybe you have learned and applied them in educational settings. Although all six are relevant to our consideration of the roles of parents/families, we will focus here on Principle 6: Parent Participation.

THE PARENT PARTICIPATION PRINCIPLE UNDERLYING SPECIAL EDUCATION PROGRAMS

The sixth and last principle underlying IDEA is parent participation. This principle specifically addresses parents' rights to have access to the records of their children as well as control of others' access to those records. More generally, this principle may be understood as closely related to the six types of parent participation introduced earlier as a part of the model of home–school partnership developed and researched by Epstein (2010). The parent participation principle, interpreted somewhat loosely, supports the involvement of parents and families at all levels of special education service development and delivery, including leadership and decision-making roles at the school and system-wide level. With regard to how we may quantify and measure the satisfaction of families and the quality of the family–professional partnership, increased attention is noted in the professional literature. Summers and colleagues (2005) described the development of the Family–Professional Partnership Scale—an instrument that includes six domains of partnering and is divided into both child- and family-focused relationships. Last, a perspective that has not been sufficiently addressed in research and practice is the understanding of parents and families as being in a developmental process of growth and change, just as their children with disabilities are, with regard to their interest in and willingness to be participatory and to be our partners.

UNIFIED SYSTEMS REFORM

The ongoing movement to restructure schooling and education in a way that merges special education and general education and that further erases the line between the two is difficult for some professionals to comprehend and accept. Early work by McLaughlin (1998) focused on unified systems reform as a means of accommodating and supporting diverse learners and, including those with disabilities, without categorizing students or program resources. She emphasized accountability by schools for the learning of all students. It is reasonable to associate united systems reform with the trends in special education as reflected in the 1997 amendments to and 2004 reauthorization of IDEA and their emphasis on participation of general education, inclusion for children ages 3 through 21, and natural environments for infants and toddlers and their families. Subsequent research followed—Stichter and Caldicott (1999) discussed some of the issues involved in collaboration between families and schools in the context of the 1997 IDEA Reauthorization and amendments and PBS. They emphasized that whereas IDEA advances the need for personnel preparation that supports partnerships between general and regular educators and partnerships between educators and families, the tendency of preservice programs in special education and general education to maintain distinct boundaries is problematic and continues today within teacher training programs in colleges and universities. This separation creates great difficulty in realizing the achievement of a shared vision and the sense of being in a partnership and collaboration, especially as it relates to dealing with challenging behavior and the development and implementation of positive behavioral interventions and supports for all learners.

United systems reform has focused attention on the educational needs of all children and has blurred the lines between children who have disabilities and their age peers and classmates who do not have disabilities. The theory and practice of inclusion has become an accepted practice of schooling as the majority of students served in special education are being educated in general education settings. However, there are researchers and leaders in the field of special education who caution that unified systems reform (sometimes referred to as standards-based reform, high-stakes accountability, or minimum standards) has not necessarily been a benefit to children with disabilities, particularly as it relates to assessment and accountability. It has been reported that approximately 80% of students with disabilities take their states' standardized assessments either with or without special accommodations and another 20% take alternative forms of assessments. The outcomes in terms of their performance on these have been quite low leading one to question the efficacy of these practices.

Although it is difficult to pinpoint when reforms in special education and general education converged to become a unified effort, the beginnings can certainly be traced back to the 1980s and early 1990s. It was suggested (Kleinhammer-Tramill & Gallagher, 2002) that the National Goals 2000 legislation was the point at which the two converged. In 1989, President George H. W. Bush and the nation's governors established six national goals. In 1994, they were amended to include two additional goals. These eight goals were intended to provide the framework for reform and improvement in all of our nation's schools and for all of its diverse students. Goals 2000 specifically addressed the importance of including children with disabilities and the necessity for unifying special education and general education reform. The eight goals were: (1) children entering school ready to learn; (2) improving the high school graduation rate to 90%; (3) children achieving competence in core subjects; (4) excellence in math and science; (5) adult literacy and competing in the workforce; (6) safe, drug-free schools; (7) professional development for educators; and (8) increased parental involvement in learning. Of particular interest to us is the eighth goal: parent involvement. The full statement of the National Goal was as follows: "Every school will promote partnerships that will increase parental involvement and participation in promoting the social, emotional and academic growth of children." The inclusion of this goal specific to parent involvement and partnership came about largely as a result of advocacy efforts by the National PTA (2016).

Finally, with regard to national education reform movements and initiatives, and in particular how they are connected to parent and family involvement, we briefly address the connections among the **No Child Left Behind Act of 2001 (NCLB),** the Every Student Succeeds Act (ESSA) of 2015, the Response to Intervention (RtI) initiative, PBIS, and the place of parents and families in general and special education. NCLB, The Elementary and Secondary Education Act of 2001 (NCLB, 2001), which was the focus of education reform for the administration of President George W. Bush, was enacted January 8, 2002, and took effect in 2003. NCLB was controversial, especially in regard to costs to states, concerns about possible over-emphasis on testing, and potential negative impacts on students with disabilities. NCLB required, as a part of its quality of education focus, that schools implement scientific-based classroom practices and include parent involvement programs. It is also understood to require states and school districts to report their performance related to annual achievement to parents and to inform parents about whether their child is being taught by a "highly qualified" teacher. And according to the U.S. Department of Education website ED.gov (U.S. Department of Education, n.d.), NCLB "allowed parents to choose public schools, or take advantage of free tuition if their child attends a school that needs improvement. Also parents can choose another school if the school their child attends is unsafe." This law was amended in 2015 when President Barack Obama signed into law the Every Student Succeeds Act (ESSA). This new law afforded greater control back to the individual states and local authorities for addressing accountability and the educational needs of students in poverty, but it did maintain the required testing for all students in grades three through eight in math and in reading (Act E.S.S.A. 2015). The commonality between these two laws is that both teachers and parents alike were outraged with the increased and continued reliance on testing.

Response to Intervention (RtI) is an initiative that has gained in popularity and use primarily as an outgrowth of the 2004 IDEA Reauthorization. RtI is a process intended to assist educators with identifying students who are struggling early on and provide instruction that is based on research evidence and scientific studies. RtI is not without controversy with regard to its nature and purpose and how it is applied to support students who have special needs, particularly those with severe learning and behavioral needs. Although it is beyond our scope here, you should be aware that substantial differences of opinion exist. Fuchs, Fuchs, and Stecker (2010) detailed much of the controversy. They suggested that there are two "camps," an IDEA group focused more on a traditional special education perspective and an NCLB group that emphasizes the addressing of special needs more in the context of general education. This list is a summation and represents an oversimplification of the issues and concerns, but the point is that although all of the reforms and associated initiatives (NCLB, RtI, IDEA, and PBIS) are intended to improve education for children who are most at risk (including those with challenging behavior) and to involve parents and families in the process, the continuing confusion and disagreement about how and why to implement reforms may serve as a hindrance to meaningful parent involvement and parent partnerships.

RtI, like PBIS, is a three-tiered process that is intended to serve as a schoolwide model. Two notable, essential components of RtI are: (1) the requirement for research-based instruction, and (2) parental involvement in the process. These are consistent with the tenets of PBIS. The similarities between the two models are also notable. RtI focuses primarily on academic problems and PBIS on the prevention and intervention of challenging behavior, but they have in common emphasis on applying a problem-solving approach using a range of evidence-based practices, differentiated instruction, and parent involvement.

SUMMARY OF EDUCATIONAL REFORMS

Up to this point in the chapter, the intent has been to provide you with some perspective on the current status of P–12 education, especially with regard to the relationships of schools and teachers with parents and families. Reforms that have occurred in both special education and general education, especially over the past four decades or so, were reviewed. How these reform efforts have begun to merge into a unified systems reform was also summarized. The unified systems reform movement, including NCLB, ESSA, and RtI, carries with it very significant implications for all stakeholders, including the citizens who fund education, policy makers, researchers and leaders in education and related disciplines, children and youth with disabilities and those who do not have disabilities, and the families of those children and youth. It certainly has ramifications not only for how education is delivered in the United States but also for how professionals are prepared in teacher preparation and related programs from infancy through high school.

Consider This

Think about the preservice programs with which you are familiar or the one in which you are currently enrolled. How is the relationship between special education and general education presented in your coursework and by your professors? Are they treated as merged, as having some overlap, or as totally separate disciplines with unique and different goals, methods, and desired outcomes? Where might you place the program(s) on this continuum? How is the subject of understanding families and partnering with parents and families treated in those preservice programs? Is there any coursework at all related to families? Perhaps some family content is infused in a course or courses across the curriculum. Maybe the preservice program addresses parents and families in the programs aimed at preparing professionals to teach or intervene with very young children but minimally or not at all in programs at the upper elementary, middle school, or secondary level. Do the courses and field experiences in an undergraduate or graduate degree and/ or licensure program focused on parents and families treat the families with children who have disabilities as distinct and separate entities from families with children who do not have disabilities?

These are all important questions and considerations. Education professionals in training need a level of confidence that their preservice experiences are reasonably consistent with the expectations that others will have for them in the classroom. Legitimate questions remain about how unified systems reform, despite its potential, will affect all children and their families. From the special educator's perspective, there may be concern not only that students with disabilities might be excluded from the assessment and accountability process introduced earlier but also that the specialized needs of children with disabilities—especially those with more comprehensive and significant delays—will be unmet or inadequately met in the context of inclusive or natural environments. And a general educator might have this response: "I am overworked, underpaid, and undervalued, and now you expect me to include students with disabilities (with all the associated paperwork) and to partner with their parents and families! Not only do I now have these children with very specialized, intensive special needs, but some of them have behaviors that are very foreign to me, unacceptable in my classroom, and disruptive to the other students!" It is important to acknowledge the challenges and concerns associated with unified systems reform, but it is also important to understand that families are families first, and their status as having a member with a disability is secondary. The authors' experiences in partnering with parents and families suggest that at the heart of the matter, families often want two things: they want their child's specialized needs to be met, but they want a recognition and appreciation for their child as a child first, rather than a disability. Finally, it is important to recognize that you, as a professional educator, have provided an opportunity to benefit and grow professionally from the process of developing and nurturing a partnership with the parents and families of the children and youth with whom you work.

BUILDING RELIABLE ALLIANCES: A FRAMEWORK FOR THE FAMILY–PROFESSIONAL PARTNERSHIP

You will encounter a sometimes confusing and seemingly overlapping maze of terminology associated with the relationship of education to parents and families. Some of these terms are *family centered, parent involvement and participation, partnership, collaboration, empowerment,* and *reliable alliances.* In this section, these terms are defined and clarified, and the relationships among them are explained. A framework for the partnership between professionals and families is provided. Finally, an examination of the specific connections between PBIS and family–professional partnerships is addressed.

In the broadest sense, one of the goals of an educational professional in service to children and youth should be to have an **alliance** with their parents and families. An alliance means a positive connection and bond between two parties. Building reliable alliances suggests that achieving an alliance requires some work, effort, and maintenance (building) and that an alliance is reliable when there is trust and dependability between the two parties. As stated at the beginning of the chapter, a successful partnership is one in which a sense of sharing and common purpose, a reasonable balance of rights and responsibilities between the two parties, and a close, cooperative relationship exist. **Empowerment** means to have the ability to get what one wants and needs.

A fundamental question might be, "Are we willing and, if so, do we know how to support parents and families in becoming empowered related to their children's development and education?" The term **collaboration** has historically been used to describe what professionals do with each other, rather than to describe the relationship between professionals and families. Collaboration (joint decision making) is more apt to be viewed as a strategy that is appropriate in special education (and especially early childhood special education) than it is in general education. The beliefs and practices associated with **parent involvement and participation** emphasize, especially in general education and in Part B of IDEA, the importance of parents' roles in education in a variety of ways, at different levels, and as associated with their children's achievement and success in educational environments. **Family-centered supports** and services are associated primarily with Part C of IDEA and an approach to planning the IFSP process as well as providing service coordination and delivering early intervention that has developed since the initial passage of the law in 1986. One way to summarize the meaning of "family centered" is as follows:

> services to infants and toddlers with disabilities must not be delivered in a way that fails to consider the child as a part of the family unit, and that the family's participation—in ways that take advantage of their strengths, needs, and wishes—is essential. (Richey & Wheeler, 2000, p. 8)

How does one make sense of these terms and convert them into an overall statement of recommended practice in relationships with families? As a professional, one believes that an important part of his or her mission is to establish and maintain a partnership (an arrangement) with parents and families and to carry out that partnership through ongoing collaboration (activities and actions). As a result of this partnership and collaboration, a professional intends to build a reliable alliance with parents and families (a positive connection and bond—i.e., we trust each other and we are in this together). From collaboration and alliance comes increased empowerment (ability to get needs met) for both the professionals and the parents and families with whom they partner. The approach that is employed will tend to be either that of parent involvement and participation (child focused and emphasizing parents rather than the family as a whole) or family centered (family focused and emphasizing the family unit and its needs, strengths, routines, and goals).

Turnbull and colleagues (2015) provide a framework that emphasizes the importance of taking into account the resources (knowledge, skills, and motivation) that both families and professionals bring to the partnership or collaboration. They further describe the opportunities that might arise during the process for collaboration, and they list eight obligations that professionals have to build and maintain a reliable alliance (see Figure 2–1).

These eight obligations provide a useful guide, without regard for the ages of the children, whether they have disabilities, and the level and type of participation of parents and families. Some of these obligations are more focused on personal attributes of the professional and his or her beliefs, attitudes, and behavior style. Others are more specific to skills and abilities as a professional. That is, if one wishes to be successful in family–professional partnerships and to be able to meet these eight obligations, he or she must be engaged not only in the development and refinement of his or her own professional competencies but also in personal growth in relationships with others. Some would argue that the distinction between the two is artificial and unnecessary. Think about the traditional view of professionals (specifically teachers, for our purposes) as needing to maintain a "professional distance" and "objectivity," to not get "too close" in their dealings with the parents of their students. Some might argue that this view is wise and necessary, but think about how it might affect your ability to carry out the eight obligations for a reliable alliance.

FIGURE 2–1

Obligations for a Reliable Alliance

1. *Know yourself:* having accurate self-knowledge—knowing and appreciating your own perspectives, opinions, strengths, and needs
2. *Knowing families:* being able to identify the unique aspects of each family's characteristics, interactions, functions, and life cycle and to respond in ways that are personalized and individually tailored to respect families' uniqueness
3. *Honoring cultural diversity:* relating to others in personalized, respectful, and responsive ways in light of values associated with factors such as ethnicity, race, religion, income status, gender, sexual orientation, disability status, occupation, and geographical location
4. *Affirming and building on family strength:* identifying, appreciating, and capitalizing on families' strengths
5. *Promoting family choices:* selecting the family members to be involved in collaborative decision making, deciding which educational issues should take priority over others, choosing the extent to which family members are involved in decision making for each educational issue, and selecting appropriate goals and services for the student
6. *Envisioning great expectations:* recognizing that one can have an exceptionality and also have an enviable life
7. *Practicing positive communication skills:* using nonverbal skills (such as physical attending and listening), verbal communication skills (such as furthering responses, paraphrasing, and summarizing), and influencing skills (such as providing information, providing support, and offering assistance) in ways that most sensitively and respectfully connect with families
8. *Warranting trust and respect:* having confidence that everyone is pulling in the same direction in a supportive, nonjudgmental, and caring way

Source: Based on information from Turnbull, A. A., Turnbull, H. R., Erwin, E. J., Soodak, L. C., & Shogren, K. A. (2015). *Families, professionals, and exceptionality: Positive outcomes through partnerships and trust.* Columbus, OH: Pearson. Reprinted by permission of Pearson Education Inc., Columbus, OH.

PARENTS AND SPECIAL EDUCATION— THE PARADIGM SHIFT

A *paradigm* is a philosophical and theoretical framework of a scientific school or discipline within which theories, laws, and generalizations and the experiments performed in support of them are formulated. In the discipline of education—and, more specifically, special education—the paradigm over the past four decades related to parents and families has been well established. It accepts that the contribution of parents is helpful in the process of evaluation and assessment of their children (even though the inclination may be to give their input less weight, to qualify it with a "parent reports" statement, or to disallow it in formally determining performance scores). Special educators have come to accept and value the important role that parents play in the education of their children as is evidenced by, for example, the legal mandate for their participation in the planning processes of the IEP and the IFSP. The importance of parents as teachers (even saying that they are the "first and most important teachers") has been emphasized.

The need for consistency between the content and the methods that we employ in educational settings and the experiences that children have at home and elsewhere with their families has been emphasized. Special educators have stressed that new learning and behavior or the replacement of an unacceptable behavior with a more acceptable one (e.g., learning to not be aggressive toward other children—to refrain from hitting them and to substitute an alternative behavior) requires a commitment to generalization. Generalization, or the generality of behavior change, is described by Martin and Pear (2015) as transferring new behaviors to new settings (including natural environments such as home), making those new behaviors last, and sometimes having behaviors that have been learned lead to the development of new behaviors that have not been learned. Educators and special educators have had the expectation that parents would learn from them what generalization is and why it is important for them at home to be extensions of our behavior change objectives and associated intervention approaches.

This description is by no means a complete picture of the paradigm that has been employed related to parents of children with disabilities, but it does summarize some of the main points. Special educators have considered the active participation of parents as critically important, but they have also tended to view that participation as being subject to the direction of professionals. One could conclude that desirable parent participation was to some extent dichotomized into those parents who were appropriately involved (following the lead of and doing what professionals directed) and those who were not involved (not being responsive to professional direction) or were inappropriately involved (being pushy, demanding, and overstepping their bounds). Education generally and special education specifically are in the midst of a paradigm shift with regard to our disciplines' fundamental position on the relationship between parents and families and professionals. The theoretical and philosophical frameworks that have been employed no longer seem sufficient. However, it is important to note that the suggestion is not being made that there will be no continuing need for parents and families to be educated by professionals. There are numerous examples in the professional literature in special education of how training and education have been and can be successfully applied to assist parents of children with special needs—in particular, those children and youth with challenging behavior. One example, Meadan, Halle, and Ebata (2010), in a study focused on stress and support needs in families with a child with an autism spectrum disorder, found that all family members may experience stress and may need support. They suggest that needs may exist for respite care, formal and informal supports, and educational program and professionals to help them understand and respond to challenging behaviors. It may be useful to think of this issue in terms of a balance rather than unidirectional (i.e., professionals training parents). Appropriate times exist for parents and family members to be the providers of training and education for professionals and others concerning their children's disabilities, abilities, needs, preferences, and routines.

Another consideration related to how educators are prepared to implement partnerships with families is the increasing focus on cultural and linguistic diversity (CLD). Harry (2008) reported that given the representation of children from CLD families is disproportionately high in special education classes, it is especially important that we have a commitment to and skills for collaboration with CLD families. She noted that barriers to this relationship include deficit views of these children, cross-cultural misunderstandings related to disability, and differing values in goal setting. As one example specific to PBIS and cultural issues, Wang, McCart, and Turnbull (2007) examined the need for enhancing competence of professionals who collaborate with Chinese American families in planning and implementing PBIS. They found that merely knowing PBIS concepts and practices was insufficient. Professionals (educators and others) need a working understanding of the cultural values of PBIS, culturally specific knowledge of families, and motivation to learn and grow continually as professionals.

Described in this chapter thus far have been some of the factors and events that led to the paradigm shift toward a partnership between professionals and families.

Now attention shifts to the application of a new paradigm, the family–professional partnership, related specifically to the provision of positive behavior supports for children and youth who experience challenging behavior in various educational and developmental environments.

POSITIVE BEHAVIORAL INTERVENTIONS AND SUPPORTS AND THE FAMILY–PROFESSIONAL PARTNERSHIP

Chapter 1 introduced positive **behavioral interventions and supports** (PBIS) as an approach to serving individuals with challenging behavior in various educational settings. As explained in Chapter 1, PBIS may be understood as one fundamental means of applying and expanding on the tenets of applied behavior analysis. Like the paradigm shift related to the relationship between the special education discipline and its connection to families, PBIS may be viewed as a shift in the paradigm with regard to how behavioral theory, principles, and practices are applied to help individuals with challenging behavior. In a significant position paper describing the historical and current relationship between applied behavior analysis and positive behavior support, Anderson and Freeman (2000) concluded that "the approach [Positive Behavior Supports] emphasizes using behavior-analytic assessment and treatment strategies to address both challenging behavior and global quality-of-life issues such as helping a person to develop meaningful friendships and participate in the community" (p. 92). This perspective is especially important in understanding the connections between behavior supports and the family–professional partnership. Considering quality of life, the community, and meaningful relationships, one should recognize that families are frequently at the center of the educator's work.

Turnbull and colleagues (2015) described the contribution of PBIS to achieving a "rich lifestyle" for persons with disabilities. They pointed out that although PBIS has made significant contributions to enriching the lives of persons with disabilities, the need remains for a great deal of research and related improvement and expansion of practice. Vaughn, White, Johnston, and Dunlap (2005) were one of the first to highlight the importance of a family-centered approach in the planning and delivering of positive behavior support to children. They indicated that this approach not only can increase the durability and sustainability of child interventions but also has lifestyle and quality of life benefits for all family members. The goal should be to better use PBIS to support persons with disabilities in experiencing a rich lifestyle, as evidenced by the enhanced quality of their lives as individuals and within their families and by their improved abilities and opportunities for self-determination. Self-determination is defined as "acting as the primary causal agent in one's life and making choices and decisions regarding one's quality of life free from undue external influence or interference" (Wehmeyer, Martin, & Sands, 1998, p. 192).

As noted earlier, the 1997 IDEA Reauthorization has had a central role; it relates to reforms in general education and special education and to its focus on establishing and using the partnerships between parents and families and professionals. Specifically, in the regulations established to guide implementation of the 1997 IDEA amendments, the law is interpreted to:

> provide an opportunity for strengthening the role of parents, and emphasize that one of the purposes of the amendments is to expand opportunities for parents and key public agency staff (e.g., special education, related services, regular education, and early intervention service providers, and other personnel) to work in new partnerships. (*Assistance to States,* 1999, pp. 124–72)

The federal special education law stressed the need for a closer relationship between general education and special education as well as a partnership between parents and professionals, but it also required that positive behavior interventions and supports be provided when the IEP process determines that challenging behaviors are a concern (i.e., "behavior problems that interfere with his or her learning or that of others" [*Assistance to States*, 1999, pp. 124–41]). In summary, the law mandated that positive behavior interventions and supports be provided when appropriate, and it stressed the importance of a team approach in which parents are partners with educators and other professionals.

The specific relationship between PBIS and the family–professional partnership has rapidly expanded since the reauthorization. Numerous studies have been conducted demonstrating the efficacy of parent and professional partnerships in the design and delivery of PBIS with children and youth.

Lucyshyn, Blumberg, and Kayser (2000) offered three suggestions designed to create and further these relationships. These included: (1) provide family-centered, home-based positive behavior support services; (2) expand the unit of analysis and intervention to focus on family routines; and (3) teach professionals to build collaborative partnerships. In the first suggestion, professionals view and treat family members as equals and address challenging behaviors in all relevant contexts, including home. In the second, interventionists must understand problem behavior in the context of the family's daily activities and routines.

In one early study, Buschbacher, Fox, and Clarke (2004) demonstrated that a parent–professional collaboration focused specifically on family activities and routines and with a comprehensive, family-centered approach was highly effective in improving the behavior of a 7-year-old with autistic-like characteristics and Landau-Kleffner syndrome and also enhanced family overall quality of life. Lucyshyn and colleagues (2007) report on the effects of a longitudinal PBIS intervention conducted over a 10-year period with a girl who had autism and her family. They found that this intervention was socially valid, durable, and lasting and was a contextual fit with the life and routines of the family. Problem behavior was reduced, and generally improvements were noted. This study was especially important because the positive effects of PBIS intervention were demonstrated to be maintained over a substantial period of time, the family members were consistently active partners, and the family quality of life was improved. A subsequent study by Brookman-Frazee and Koegel (2004) compared a parent–professional partnership approach to a more traditional clinical-directed model in a program-serving children with autism. Their results and conclusions suggested that the collaborative approach was preferable and resulted in reduced stress, increased confidence, more positive affect, and more appropriate engagement with and responding to parents by children. Other researchers (Blair, Lee, Cho, & Dunlap, 2010; Steiner, 2011) have more recently provided evidence of the positive impacts on children with autism of using positive behavior support in collaboration with families and by using a strengths-based approach with parents.

Finally, it is essential that university preservice teacher training programs should prepare professionals to be partners and collaborators with families. In a relevant article contributed by the mother of a young adult with autism (Fisher, 2000), six recommendations were provided from the perspective of a parent and family member regarding PBIS and the relationships among professionals, schools, families, and communities. One of the recommendations made by this parent is that universities that prepare educators should ensure that those students understand the science of positive behavioral interventions and supports. We trust that you will understand PBIS, but also want to make sure that you are committed to delivering it in a family-friendly and collaborative fashion.

THE BEHAVIOR SUPPORT TEAM

Later chapters in this text address the composition and functioning of the behavior support team specific to planning, implementing, and evaluating PBIS. Membership on the team varies widely in both number of members and their roles. The central substantive participation of family members on the team is how a reliable alliance, partnership, and collaboration are manifest. Of course, the manner and extent to which family members served on the team is highly individualized. Cultural differences may also play an important part in how family members view the behavior support team so cultural competence becomes an important skill set for team members to possess.

APPLICATIONS OF PBIS AND FAMILY–PROFESSIONAL PARTNERSHIPS

Vignettes 2.1, 2.2, and 2.3 provide a sense of the various ways in which families and professionals might experience PBIS. These vignettes come from a combination of the author's experiences in working with children, educators, and other professionals and in partnering with families over the span of his career. Also, some ideas have been included from recent literature on applications of PBIS. As you read each, you may wish to consider the ways in which they demonstrate both the levels of family involvement and the obligations for a reliable alliance (see Figure 2–1). The intent here is not to address the specifics of functional behavior assessment and positive behavioral interventions and supports but rather to present the broad strokes relating family experiences to intervention planning and implementation. As you progress further into this text, you will see that we expand in other chapters the focus on applying PBIS in partnership with parents/families. The Vignettes, Reflective Moments, and Consider This sections are provided purposefully to illustrate and hopefully make more "real" the principles and practices as they are experienced by children and youth and families at home as well as in school and other contexts.

Vignette 2.1

Aaron and His Mom, Dad, and Big Sister

Aaron Thompson is 2 years old and is the youngest child of Donna and Horace Thompson. He has a 10-year-old sister, Anna. Aaron was recently diagnosed with autism, and the family has been referred to their state's early intervention system. Aaron has been determined to be eligible for early intervention, and the family's service coordinator, Mrs. O'Connor, feels that they are off to a good start in their partnership. She has made several home visits to get acquainted with the Thompsons before any intervention planning got underway. An IFSP has been developed for Aaron and his family. The IFSP team includes Mr. and Mrs. Thompson; Mrs. Thompson's mother, who frequently takes care of Aaron; Mrs. O'Connor, a developmental psychologist; Aaron's pediatrician; Aaron's caregiver at nursery school; and an early interventionist representing the local program. In accordance with early intervention public policy and effective practice, it is family centered and emphasizes natural environments and inclusive experiences for Aaron. Present levels of functioning for Aaron and the

continued

family's resources, priorities, and concerns were determined through a functional assessment and through talking with the family to understand their family routines.

The family-centered intervention planning routines-based approach developed by McWilliam (2009) was used to better understand the family and their daily activities and to facilitate the embedding of intervention in an activity-based approach (Bricker, Pretti-Frontczak, & McComas, 1998). The IFSP team established major outcomes and associated action steps. One of the outcomes is specific to implementing a PBIS plan to address Aaron's pinpointed challenging behaviors. The plan is practical, supported, and understood by everyone and can be implemented across various settings, including home, grandmother's house, Aaron's three-mornings-a-week preschool, church, and other places in the community. Another IFSP goal is that Mr. and Mrs. Thompson want to learn more about autism and especially want to do some reading and perhaps be a part of a parent-to-parent connection. Mrs. O'Connor provides them with a handbook on parent-to-parent programs information about autism, and a contact for a local support and advocacy group. Because the grandmother watches Aaron during the times that he isn't at nursery school while Mr. and Mrs. Thompson are at work, she wants to volunteer at the nursery school to help out and to observe and get some ideas on how to be more effective with her grandson and to share her knowledge and experience. The early interventionist will consult and help the grandmother and the caregiver to facilitate this outcome and help them develop and use a communication plan. Aaron's sister, Anna, has an understanding of her brother's special needs beyond what might be expected from her developmentally, and she wants to be a part of helping him. Mrs. O'Connor and the early intervention professional agree with Anna and her parents that this is a workable idea, find some examples in the literature of how sibling interaction and social play have been facilitated, and help them develop activities.

Reflective Moment

What, if any, special considerations might be made to include the grandmother as a volunteer at the preschool and how might her wish to be a resource to others and to share her experiences be accommodated?

When it is time for Aaron's transition to a preschool setting, what will be necessary to maintain the family-centered partnership and inclusive nature of her services and supports?

Vignette 2.2

Mr. Rodriguez's Kindergarten Classroom

Emilio Rodriguez is in his third year of a job that he loves—teaching in a kindergarten classroom. He teaches in an inner-city school, and the children in his class represent a very heterogeneous group with regard to their families' income levels as well as cultural, ethnic, and religious diversity. He has 18 children in the room and a full-time teaching assistant. Partly as a result of his first 2 years of teaching experience and partly prompted by some graduate coursework in early childhood education in which he is currently enrolled, Mr. Rodriguez wants to address two professional development issues. He wants to merge his understanding of the developmentally appropriate practices of positive child guidance as described by the National Association for the Education of Young Children (NAEYC) with what he has learned about PBIS. He also wants to further develop and refine the parent involvement program that he has been using for the past 2 years. Mr. Rodriguez sees these two needs as closely related.

His parent involvement program has consisted of a parent group that meets monthly (usually with low attendance) for the purpose of responding to needs identified by the teacher, such as bringing refreshments for a birthday or chaperoning a field trip. Also, monthly individual parent conferences to review progress, conferences as requested by parents, a weekly newsletter done by the children and taken home, parent attendance at schoolwide functions such as the parent–teacher organization, special occasions (performances, holiday celebrations), and open houses are part of his plan. Mr. Rodriguez wants to improve his parent program to be more comprehensive and collaborative and to have more of a family systems perspective. He has in mind to use the variety and continuum of strategies suggested by Turnbull and colleagues (2015), including accommodating cultural and linguistic diversity, respecting family preferences, and written strategies of communication. Written strategies will include handouts, newsletters, letters, notes and dialog journals, progress notes and report cards, and occasional messages. Some of these he had in his old plan. Mr. Rodriguez will also use some nonwritten strategies, including phone contacts, email, possibly a class website, and face-to-face interactions. He is planning a series of monthly family meetings to be held at times most convenient for the families and at varied sites, including school, perhaps one of the family homes, and elsewhere in the community. The first meeting will be preceded by a letter of explanation of his plan and views on partnership, along with an invitation to the first meeting. It will focus on assessing the interests and needs of families. Two of the families of Mr. Rodriguez's kindergarteners speak Spanish, and fortunately he also speaks Spanish. He will develop with each family (of course there will be a good deal of overlap) an individual plan of collaboration and alliance.

With regard to Mr. Rodriguez's positive behavior support plan, he wants to develop a more systematic approach to fostering and maintaining positive behavior and social skills in his classroom, and he wants to be more effective in helping several students who are at risk for problem behavior. At present he does not have in his classroom a child with chronic and intense problem behavior. The behavior support planning that Mr. Rodriguez wants to implement is at two levels: the primary level, which is intended to reduce (prevent) the number of new instances of problem behavior; and the secondary level, which is focused on students who are at risk for problem behavior (Sugai et al., 2000). These are also referred to in the literature (Turnbull et al., 2015) as Level 1 (clear expectations and positive feedback) and Level 2 (individualized support in school settings). Mr. Rodriguez intends to merge his new and improved family partnership plan and his PBIS plan in several ways. He will present at the first family meeting his preliminary plan for Level 1 (Primary) PBIS strategies, including ideas related to redesigning the layout of the classroom, organizing materials, centers and tables to facilitate cooperative learning, developing transitions between activities and routines of the classroom, and more consciously providing positive, descriptive praise for desired behaviors. Mr. Rodriguez will incorporate the suggestions provided by families and thereby make the plan more responsive to the uniqueness of the individual children and also foster a shared ownership of the plan with the families. Another thing that he has in mind is showing the families an example of a home-school journal and inviting the families to begin keeping one. This activity allows families who wish to do so to make daily or periodic written journal entries. In addition to being helpful

continued

to families, this activity can contribute to communication between the teacher and families in general, specifically as related to classroom behavior and socialization. For Level 2 (Secondary) PBIS strategies, one of the connections between the classroom and the families that Mr. Rodriguez wants to explore the development of a cadre of classroom volunteers and mentors to provide extra hands, some of whom might learn to do observations to assist in completing functional assessments.

Reflective Moment

What are some ways in which Mr. Rodriguez might use the work he has done for primary and secondary behavioral support planning when he needs Level 3 (Tertiary) planning for a child with intensive challenging behavior in his class?

To what extent and in what ways do you feel his kindergarten teacher colleagues in the school might use Mr. Rodriguez's parent involvement plan?

Vignette 2.3

Making Middle School Work for Brianna, Her Mom, and Teachers

Brianna lives with her mother and her grandmother. She is 12 years of age and is just beginning seventh grade at Mt. Jackson Middle School. Brianna has spina bifida, and her means of mobility is a wheelchair. Brianna does have an IEP, as has been the case since she started preschool, but at this point the only issues are related to catheterization and Brianna's participation in physical education class. She has done quite well in her academic subjects and routinely makes the honor roll. But this is a new year and a new school for her. Also, there is some concern on the part of her family as well as her homeroom teacher that she is having some difficulty making and keeping friends because she seems to be "bossy" and demanding of them. To address this concern, a behavior support team was established. The membership of the team consists of Brianna's mom and grandmother, five of her teachers, the school counselor, the consulting special education teacher, and Brianna. Although this is a large team, the need for Brianna to learn social skills will allow her to make friendships and better integrate into her school and community.

Brianna needs Level 2 or Secondary behavioral supports: intervention is required, but her needs are not comprehensive enough to warrant Level 3 or Tertiary supports. A functional behavior assessment was conducted. Brianna, her mother, and her grandmother determined her goals for establishing and maintaining friendships. Family members and professionals have agreed to use a daily journal summarizing Brianna's daily progress. Entries made by everyone (including Brianna, who is quite verbal) have resulted in improved communication between school and home. The team agrees on the following strategies: more opportunities will be provided for Brianna to cooperate with peers on classroom assignments. Practical aspects of friendship and respect will be addressed in the classroom as curricular content. Brianna will be instructed on replacement behaviors for being demanding. Also, Brianna will engage in self-monitoring to track her progress in these areas. All members of the team will verbally reinforce Brianna in the form of genuine praise when she is engaged in behavior that addresses her goals. Directed efforts will be made to help Brianna continue the friendships she has made at school through visits at home and outings in the community, such as going to the movies and having sleepovers.

Reflective Moment

The team will genuinely praise Brianna when she is engaged in behavior that addresses her goals. What, in your view, might be the difference for Breela between genuine and disingenuous praise?

How might the daily journal of progress be used effectively? Should some structure be used to facilitate entries, and, if so, what should it be?

SUMMARY

The purpose of this chapter was to introduce the philosophical and theoretical bases for and overview of the history, current status, and future directions and practices associated with family–professional partnerships in a variety of educational environments for children and youth from infancy through high school. Specifically, the goal has been to set the stage for how a partnership with families is integral to successful use of positive behavioral interventions and supports for children who have challenging behaviors. Partnering with families is a theme that will be carried out in the remainder of the chapters in this text. Views of how parents and families can and should be participants and partners have been influenced in part by the reforms that have occurred in general education and in special education, resulting in what is referred to as unified systems reform. Epstein's (2010) model of six levels of parent involvement has been very influential in the development of general education policies and practices related to parent and professional partnerships. A resource worth consulting is the PTA's National Standards for Family-School Partnerships (www.pta .org/nationalstandards). This document recommends six standards which include:

- Standard 1   Welcoming all families into the school community
- Standard 2   Communicating effectively with families
- Standard 3   Supporting student success through family-school collaboration
- Standard 4   Speaking up for every child
- Standard 5   Sharing power
- Standard 6   Collaborating with the community

Reforms in special education specific to parents and families have followed the course described in Table 2–1 and have been promoted by federal legislation beginning in 1975. In particular, the 1986 passage of Part H of Public Law 99-457 (now Part C of IDEA), Early Intervention for Infants, Toddlers, and Their Families, and its subsequent reauthorizations, has brought into focus family empowerment and family-centered supports and services. Indeed, one of the challenges that professionals and families continue to face is the nature of the parents' and families' roles as children with special needs transition from early intervention into preschool environments.

This chapter has defined the various terms associated with the relationships we desire as professionals related to parents and families, including *alliance, partnership, empowerment, collaboration, parent involvement and participation*, and *family centered*. As a professional, whether one is a general educator, special educator, early interventionist, therapist, caregiver, counselor, psychologist, or otherwise, it is important to believe that a part of one's mission is to establish and maintain a partnership arrangement with parents and families and to carry out that partnership through ongoing collaboration (activities and actions). As a result of this partnership and collaboration, the professional educator will build a reliable alliance with parents and families. From collaboration and alliance will come increased empowerment (ability to get needs met) for both professionals and the parents and families with whom they partner. The approach that is employed will tend to be either that of parent involvement and participation (child focused and possibly emphasizing parents more than the family as a whole) or family centered (family focused and emphasizing the family unit and its needs, strengths, routines, and goals). Professionals have eight obligations (Turnbull et al., 2015) for achieving a reliable alliance: knowing yourself, knowing families, honoring diversity, affirming and building of family strengths, promoting family choices, envisioning great expectations, practicing positive communication, and warranting trust and respect.

Special education as a discipline and profession—specifically, the area of applied behavior analysis and intervention for children with challenging behavior—has experienced a paradigm shift over the past 10 or so years. Where special educators historically might have thought in terms of the parents (and possibly the mother in particular), now they are more likely to view the family as a unit. Where special educators historically might have seen parents as the recipients of training in content determined by the professionals and intended to foster generalization of behaviors into the home setting, now they are more likely to see themselves as in a partnership in which they learn, teach, and share. Where special educators historically might have viewed parent involvement in a more formalized, legalistic way, they are now less likely to be adversarial and more inclined to view families as collaborators, allies, and partners. It is hoped that professionals will be more focused on interventions that meet the criteria of supporting children with disabilities and their families to be self-determining, to function in the community as a whole, and to have a richer lifestyle.

ACTIVITIES TO EXTEND YOUR LEARNING

1. Interview a respected teacher in your community's school system. Ask about the teacher's plan for parent involvement, what the teacher has found useful, and how the teacher's ideas have been developed and refined over time. This could be a general education teacher, a special education teacher, an early interventionist, or a professional from a related discipline.

2. Make arrangements to attend a local meeting of a parent and family organization, such as the school PTO or an advocacy group for children with special needs. Listen to the content of the meeting and attempt to relate what happens in the meeting to the types of involvement and the issues introduced in this chapter.

3. In pairs or small groups in class, study the vignettes provided in this chapter. Identify the ways in which obligations for an alliance and levels of participation are addressed as they are described. Then brainstorm additional potential levels of participation and connections with the obligation for a reliable alliance.

4. Visit the site: Foundation for Grandparenting at www.grandparenting.org. Look for specific information and ideas about grandparents and their response to challenging behavior of grandchildren.

5. In pairs or small groups, each assigned or selecting one site, go to one of the websites listed in this paragraph and review and make notes for a class presentation over what the site offers with regard to partnerships with families in general education and special education. In particular, look for partnerships focused on challenging behavior/positive behavior support. Websites: (1) Harvard Family Research Project (www.hfrp.org), (2) OSEP Technical Assistance Center on Positive Behavior Interventions and Supports (www.pbis.org), (3) Family Friendly Schools (www.familyfriendlyschools.com).

FURTHER READING AND EXPLORATION

1. This chapter emphasized the work of Ann and Rud Turnbull and their colleagues related to partnerships and collaboration (building a reliable alliance) with families of children with special needs. Do a literature search to see what you can find out about how the Turnbulls' personal and professional experiences influenced their ideas on partnerships and their contributions to the literature. You might want to visit the website of the Beach Center on Families and Disability at www.beachcenter.org.

2. The magazine *Exceptional Parent* is an excellent resource. Take a look at some copies of the magazine. In particular, look at the Editorial Mission and how the magazine has historically presented and currently presents the topic of the relationships between professionals and families. How has terminology and emphases changed over time? Do you see any connections between articles found in the magazine and topics introduced in this chapter? Visit the magazine's website at www.eparent.com.

3. For a focus on early childhood development, very young at-risk children and families, family-centered approaches, and descriptions of models of support and parent training, see the *Bulletin of Zero to Three: National Center for Infants, Toddlers, and Families* at www.zerotothree.org. In particular, look for examples of how family-centered approaches have been successfully used with young children at risk and with culturally diverse families.

4. Visit the website of the National PTA (www.pta.org), review their resources, and get a copy of the National Standards for Parent/Family Involvement Programs.

Ensuring Ethical Practices in the Delivery of PBIS

CONCEPTS TO UNDERSTAND

After reading this chapter, you should be able to:

- Define *ethics* and *ethical conduct*.
- List and describe the nine organizing themes for understanding ethical practices.
- Understand accepted standards of ethical conduct.
- Understand the unique position of positive behavioral interventions and supports (PBIS) within an ethical framework.
- Evaluate the extent to which behavioral interventions are consistent with ethical standards of conduct.
- Compare and contrast different professional organizations' standards for ethical conduct.

KEY TERMS

Ethical conduct	Principles
Ethics	Quality of life
Organizing themes	Standards

What are ethics, and what does it mean to engage in ethical behavior? And what guidance do we as professionals have and use to hold us accountable to ethical practices in our service to children and their families as we plan, implement, and evaluate positive behavior supports? These are the fundamental questions that are addressed in this chapter. For our purposes, **ethics** are defined as the **principles** of conduct governing us as individual professionals as well as our particular group or discipline. Whether it is general education, special education, counseling, psychology, the various therapy disciplines, or related areas, there are established principles of conduct that govern ethics. To be ethical as a professional means to conform to accepted professional standards of conduct. You might ask yourself to what extent—given your current status with regard to professional development and preparation to be licensed in your discipline and specialty area(s)—you are familiar with the ethical standards of your discipline. Have you taken courses in which ethics were addressed in a substantive manner? If not, are you aware of a point in your preparation where you will get such a focus? To what extent do your professors and the textbooks used in your classes include ethical standards, guidelines, and practices? Is it assumed that textbooks would not include—nor would professors advocate—theories, beliefs, or practices that are unethical?

When you participate in field experiences and other professional development activities, are the standards governing ethical conduct obvious in some manner (e.g., posted somewhere or included in a procedural or policy handbook)? Children with special needs are typically served by at least two and frequently three or more professionals whose disciplines have produced standards or codes of ethical conduct. Do you have an understanding of what those standards might be and the extent to which they are complementary or possibly incongruent? Of course, much of our focus in this text is on children and youth who have challenging behavior and who would benefit from PBIS to enhance their skills, achievement, self-determination, and inclusion. One might argue that it is especially important to know and adhere to ethical standards of conduct when serving children and youth with challenging behavior and when partnering with their families and other professionals. Factors such as cultural and societal values, religious beliefs, personal beliefs, upbringing and parenting models, theoretical perspectives, and other factors all affect our views of challenging behavior.

In this chapter, we examine the ethical standards governing our professional conduct as they relate specifically to applying PBIS across a variety of educational environments. To do this, you must first understand what professional organizations and learned societies believe and advocate with regard to influencing behavior, so we study content provided by the National Education Association (NEA), the Learning First Alliance (LFA), the Council for Exceptional Children (CEC), the Council for Children with Behavioral Disorders (CCBD), the National Association for the Education of Young Children (NAEYC), and the Division for Early Childhood (DEC) of the CEC. Finally, the Standards of Practice from the Association for Positive Behavior Support (APBS) and the Behavior Analysis Certification Board (BACB) are addressed.

Turnbull, Turnbull, Erwin, Soodak, and Shogren (2015) describe how educational systems reform is likely to be unified rather than enacted with special education and general education on isolated and separate tracks. We see increasing numbers of students with disabilities now being educated in general education settings prompting is to re-think how our preparation of preservice teachers is currently structured (Lewis, Wheeler, & Carter, 2017). We might assume that codes and standards of **ethical conduct** will also begin to be somewhat unified. Beyond understanding accepted **standards**, you will be provided with a framework for understanding the elements required in meeting standards and evaluating the extent to which PBIS are consistent with ethical standards of conduct. This framework of nine **organizing themes** will be used to examine relatedness among various sources.

In Chapter 1, you were introduced to the primary theoretical models as applied to explain human behavior. One useful way to think of ethics and ethical standards in education is to view them as a connector between theory and practice. That is, standards of conduct are outgrowths of one's theoretical point of view, but they also provide, at least in a general sense, guidance for our practices—what we should and should not do as professionals (e.g., teaching, intervening, playing, and providing therapy). In this chapter, we are especially interested in ethical considerations as they apply to behavioral theory and the practices of positive behavioral interventions and supports with which they are associated (e.g., antecedent-based intervention, functional assessment, behavior support plans, and positive, consequence-based interventions and evaluation of behavior support plans).

NINE ORGANIZING THEMES FOR UNDERSTANDING ETHICAL PRACTICES

Nine major themes occur in the ethical standards of professional behavior provided by the various professional organizations introduced later. Historically, the preparation of special educators, general educators, and other school personnel (e.g., school psychologists and counselors) in preservice programs has been rather isolated and distinctly separate. That isolation was, of course, reflected in the way we delivered services to children with special needs (with emotional and behavior difficulties or otherwise) in various school environments. Programs preparing teachers and other school personnel have begun to reflect more collaborative approaches and shared content. Standards of ethical behavior have been developed in some respects to reflect the lack of shared philosophy and practice. As we consider ethical standards provided by the organizations included herein, we need to take into account the congruence, or lack of congruence, among them that is specifically related to what they have to say regarding how to influence the behavior of children and youth. Beyond the degree of congruence, we can relate the various standards to the following themes in terms of emphasis and specificity. Nine organizing themes are presented in Figure 3–1.

FIGURE 3–1

Nine Organizing Themes for Understanding Ethical Practices

- Each student as an *individual human being has worth and dignity*, despite the nature or severity of his troubling behavior.
- The *behavior* of children and youth (challenging and otherwise) always *reflects a need*. People respond out of need, and all behavior serves a function. Often skill limitations paired with unresponsive environments result in the display of challenging forms of behavior in an attempt to communicate these needs.
- Systematic and thoughtful management of learning environments and understanding of individual differences and uniqueness will serve to *prevent* some challenging behaviors. And *early intervention* will serve to prevent or lessen the severity of many challenging behaviors.
- Families, children, and youth should be central to all aspects of PBIS, including *active participation* in planning, implementing, and evaluating interventions.
- The uniqueness of children and youth, as reflected by their *family's diversity* (race, ethnicity, religion, and culture) should be taken into account in understanding behavior and responding to challenging behavior.
- Natural environments and *inclusive settings are desirable* for children and youth with troubling and challenging behavior, but school personnel must assume ownership in those settings, and a full continuum of services and settings should be available.
- *Natural and logically occurring consequences* are preferable to extraneous and contrived reward systems to foster self-discipline, independence, and self-determination.
- Behavior interventions should be *positive* and should not include corporal punishment or other punitive measures.
- Actions taken by professionals to either suppress undesirable behavior or foster desired behavior of children and youth should be associated with meaningful and *functional* attitudes and skills and should be positively related to *quality of life*.

Much has been written over the past four decades about the rights of children and youth and ethical conduct in the provision of services to them. It is not our purpose here to undertake an historical review of that literature. It is important that you know that this body of research and writing exists, and it may be seen on a continuum from very broad descriptions of the rights of all children and youth as reflected in social policy to the rights of children and youth with comprehensive disabilities to specific types of behavior treatment. For example, Garfinkel, Hochschild, and McLanahan (2001), suggested that children have rights that social policy should reflect in seven arenas: child care, schooling, transition to work, health care, income security, physical security, and child abuse. Ethics and ethical conduct in the delivery of PBIS could certainly have a beneficial impact on most of these areas.

At the other end of the continuum, we might consider the position advocated by several of the prominent leaders in applied behavior analysis (Houten et al., 1988) at the point in history when applied behavior analysis was being refined and pointing in the direction of PBIS. They suggested that individuals in need of behavioral interventions have six rights: a therapeutic environment, services whose overriding goal is personal welfare, treatment by a competent behavior analyst, programs that teach functional skills, behavior assessment and on-going evaluation, and the most effective treatment procedures available. It may seem challenging to find a fit between two such seemingly disparate viewpoints, but they both provide important guidance about how we as professionals should understand our ethical responsibilities related to children and youth.

CODES, STANDARDS, AND PRINCIPLES OF PROFESSIONAL GROUPS

Professional organizations and associations in education provide information, support, guidance, and leadership to their members and opportunities for participation through various means of communication, including journals, newsletters, websites, and conferences. One central function of these groups is to develop, disseminate, and revise ethical codes of professional conduct that reflect their mission and the standards, beliefs, values, and principles of their organization. These standards provide guidance to teachers and other practitioners as they carry out their professional responsibilities. The NEA, the LFA, the CEC, the CCBD, the NAEYC, the DEC, APBS, and the BACB are all introduced in the following pages, and their positions of ethical standards, beliefs, values, and principles are considered. There are a number of associations and organizations that could have been included here but are not, given constraints of space and scope.

National Education Association

The National Education Association (NEA) has a membership of more than 3 million members who work at various levels of education. NEA was founded in 1857 and has been the principle advocate and professional organization for public education in the United States. NEA has considerable influence at the local, state, national, and international levels in all aspects of public education. Many of you may become NEA members as you enter the profession as educators from preschool through university environments or may already hold student membership. In 1975, the NEA adopted the *Code of Ethics of the Education Profession*. The Code was intended to be the standard by which to judge the professional conduct of its members. Although the Preamble of the Code does not provide any specific guidance related to ethical conduct of educators and the behavior of children and youth (students), it does include wording that is important as a foundation for the standards that we consider later in this chapter. Specifically, the phrases "believing in the worth and dignity of each human being" (i.e., presumably including those with disabilities and/or challenging behavior), "guarantee of equal educational opportunity for all," and "desire for the respect and confidence of students" (National Education Association [NEA], 2017) all seem relevant as we think about our responsibilities related to problematic and challenging behavior.

Two overriding principles (I: Commitment to Students and II: Commitment to the Profession) with associated standards are the essence of the NEA Code of Ethics. Principle I states, "the educator strives to help each student realize her potential as a worthy and effective member of society" (NEA, 2017). Again, these standards do not specifically address student behavior; however, they may be taken as a start point or foundation for educators.

Learning First Alliance

The Learning First Alliance (LFA) was founded in 1997. It is a permanent partnership of 13 leading educational associations representing 10 million members. The LFA is committed to partnering innovative and successful solutions to the challenges facing our educational system. To that aim, LFA believes that based on the evidence that safe and supportive schools contain four distinct elements. These include: (1) a supportive learning community; (2) systematic approaches to supporting safety and positive behavior; (3) involvement of families, students, school staff, and the surrounding community; and (4) standards and measures to support continuous improvement based on data (LFA, 2017).

It is reasonable, although these are not stated as codes of ethical behavior and conduct, to treat and use the core elements published by the LFA as such. Of course, of particular interest here is the information provided in the second core element—systematic approaches to supporting safety and positive behavior. Each of the four elements is seen as connected to desired outcomes focused on preventing and/or reducing aggressiveness, violence, delinquency, and drug and alcohol use; increasing social competence and positive behavior; increasing concern for others; improving connection to school and educational aspirations; and improving academic motivation and achievement. It is interesting and encouraging to many professionals to note that these desired outcomes are broad based with regard to the role of schooling and not narrowly limited to academic performance. Major points addressed in core element 2—systematic approaches to supporting safety and positive behavior, in particular those most relevant to the provision of positive behavior supports to children and youth who exhibit challenging behavior—include emphasis on the following: (1) establishing a school atmosphere of civility and not accepting bullying, intimidation, and taunting; (2) having fairly and consistently enforced rules that are clear and modelled and reinforced by school staff; (3) student and family participation in determining rules; (4) opportunities for students to learn and practice positive approaches to getting along with others; (5) attention to arrangement of classroom/physical environments; (6) celebrating success; (7) nurturing self-management for students; and (8) clear and consistent consequences for violation of rules. In addition to these approaches, core element 2 includes avoiding harsh and punitive discipline styles and excessive punishment, celebrating and rewarding appropriate behavior, a continuum of supports, a range of services for improving behavior and enlisting parents and students in the process, and effective alternative programs when needed with positive behavior support and community involvement. Several things are particularly noteworthy as we think about these beliefs and approaches. They reflect agreement among partnering organizations, which represent the majority of the professional constituency of public education in the United States. There is substantial attention given to the school's role in addressing behavior issues of all students and doing so in a positive way with a focus on prevention, early intervention, student participation, and family involvement. And positive behavior support is specifically identified as a desirable and effective approach.

The Council for Exceptional Children

The Council for Exceptional Children (CEC) is the primary professional organization for special educators. There are 12 core values in the CEC Ethical Principles and Professional Practice Standards for Special Educators and they are as follows: (1) Maintaining challenging expectations for individuals with exceptionalities to develop the highest possible learning outcomes and quality of life potential in ways that respect their dignity, culture, language, and background. (2) Maintaining a high level of professional competence and integrity and exercising professional judgment to benefit individuals with exceptionalities and their families. (3) Promoting meaningful and inclusive participation of individuals with exceptionalities in their schools and communities. (4) Practicing collegially with others who are providing services to individuals with exceptionalities. (5) Developing relationships with families based on mutual respect and actively involving families and individuals with exceptionalities in educational decision-making. (6) Using evidence, instructional data, research, and professional knowledge to inform practice. (7) Protecting and supporting the physical and psychological safety of individuals with exceptionalities. (8) Neither engaging in nor tolerating any practice that harms individuals with exceptionalities. (9) Practicing within the professional ethics, standards, and policies of CEC; upholding laws, regulations, and policies that influence professional practice; and advocating improvements in the laws, regulations, and policies. (10) Advocating for professional conditions and resources that will improve learning outcomes of individuals with exceptionalities. (11) Engaging in the improvement of the profession through active participation in professional organizations. (12) Participating in the growth and dissemination of professional knowledge and skills. (CEC, 2017).

The CEC, an international organization formed in 1922, has grown in 2017 to a membership of more than 27,000 members, all who share an interest in the education of individuals with exceptionalities. Although membership is international, the majority of the members are in the United States or on the Canadian Council for Exceptional Children. CEC currently has 18 divisions that provide a structure for members to address particular exceptionalities or phases of special education. All of the advocacy efforts, publications, and other supports provided through the CEC may be assumed to be largely consistent with and reflective of its ethical code. The *CEC Standards of Professional Practice Professionals in Relation to Persons With Exceptionalities and Their Families* provides specific standards, three of which include instructional responsibilities, management of behavior, and support procedures (i.e., the nature of expectations placed on special educators in such matters as the administration of medication, parent relationships, and advocacy). The standards of particular interest to us are the ones associated with behavior management. The five behavior management standards, summarized and abbreviated, focus on: (1) use approved methods that do not undermine dignity, and that avoid corporal punishment; (2) have specified goals and objectives in the IEP; (3) conform to policies, statutes, and rules; (4) take appropriate measures when a colleague's behavior is perceived to be detrimental to a student; and (5) refrain from aversive techniques, unless repeated trials of other methods have failed and only after parent and agency consultation. What are some of the main points that we might take from these five standards related to behavior management and special education? One is that in the management of challenging behavior, professional special educators should see themselves as part of an interdisciplinary team, one that includes parents as valued members and equal partners on the team. Another point is that without regard for the type or severity of the disability or the nature of the challenging behavior, the child is worthwhile, and his or her dignity is maintained in the selection and application of behavior management approaches. Behavior management is individualized as reflected by the IEP. Punitive and aversive techniques are ill advised and should be undertaken only in rare instances and with strict oversight. It might be useful for you to compare these five standards to the information provided so far in the chapter from other organizations that are not focused on children with special needs.

PREVENTION AND EARLY INTERVENTION

What existing ethical codes and standards of professional behavior establish the necessity for prevention, early identification, and early intervention for young children who have or may develop challenging behaviors? Much of the literature related to programs, services, and interventions for children with behavior and emotional disabilities emphasizes the importance of prevention and early response to troublesome behavior. We recognize that most of you do not have a specific career focus on young children from birth through grade 3. However, it is very important for teachers and other professionals who serve school-age children and youth and their families to understand the importance of the early years specific to social–emotional development and the acquisition of behaviors that may minimize or contribute to challenging behavior in later years. To assist in understanding the guidance that is provided in this regard and to understand the related issues, two leading professional organizations are considered: the NAEYC and the DEC of the CEC.

National Association for the Education of Young Children

The National Association for the Education of Young Children (NAEYC) exists for the purpose of leading and consolidating the efforts of individuals and groups working in the education of all young children. It was founded in 1926 and is the nation's largest and most influential organization focused on the educational, developmental, service, and program needs of children from birth through age 8. NAEYC has a *Code of Ethical Conduct and Statement of Commitment*. Since its adoption, the Code has been through three revisions, one in 1992, the second in 1997, and in April 2005 (NAEYC, 2017). Every 5 years, the Code is reviewed for possible revision, and in May 2011 the Governing Board reaffirmed the 2005 Code. NAEYC takes the position that a code of ethical conduct and its standards are based on core values, and they provide six such value statements. These are important because they are to a large extent aligned with statements found from other sources and organizations, and they can be readily connected to more specific ethical guidance policies that might be used for dealing with young children and used for responses in preventing or intervening young children's challenging behavior. The NAEYC's (2011) core values state that the organization's members have committed to the following:

- Appreciate childhood as a unique and valuable stage of the human life cycle.
- Base our work on knowledge of how children develop and learn.

- Appreciate and support the bond between the child and family.
- Recognize that children are best understood and supported in the context of family, culture, community, and society.
- Respect the dignity, worth, and uniqueness of each individual (child, family member, and colleague).
- Respect diversity in children, families, and colleagues.
- Recognize that children and adults achieve their full potential in the context of relationships that are based on trust and respect (NAEYC, 2017).

In 2010, the NAEYC Governing Board approved a revision of the *NAEYC Standards for Early Childhood Professional Preparation: Baccalaureate or Initial Licensure Level* (NAEYC, 2017). These standards, which are intended to provide guidance in the development and implementation of preservice preparation of early childhood professionals, were developed in collaboration with several other professional organizations, including the DEC. In fact, a significant reason for the revision of the standards was the recognition that the context of early childhood education is rapidly changing—that early childhood educators will have the opportunity to serve an increasingly diverse group of children and families including children with a variety of special needs and disabilities.

The revised standards are intended to represent a shared vision and to be empowering for children and professionals alike (NAEYC, 2017). These ethical standards, intended to form the baseline of what an early childhood educator should know and be able to do at an entry level of the profession, have several sections and specific statements describing the standards that are helpful related to influencing the behavior of young children.

The Division for Early Childhood of the Council for Exceptional Children

The Division for Early Childhood (DEC) of the CEC promotes policies and advances evidence-based practices that support families and enhance the optimal development of young children who are at risk for developmental delays and disabilities. Like NAEYC, the DEC has a focus on children from ages birth through 8 years. DEC, however, describes the population as children from birth through age 8 *and their families*. Note the similarities between the two statements of purpose. Although the DEC has contributed significantly through to the understanding of and response to challenging behavior of young children, of particular interest here are the ethical guidance and related standards and principles that they have provided.

In 2014, the DEC issued *DEC Recommended Practices* (DEC, 2017). This document was important because it gave guidance that was consistent with the DEC beliefs and standards to professionals who worked on behalf of young children with disabilities and their families. One section of the *DEC Recommended Practices* addresses instruction. There are 13 recommendations governing practice and addressed within these is a practice relevant to challenging behavior. That recommended practice is as follows:

> INS9. Practitioners use functional assessment and related prevention, promotion, and intervention strategies across environments to prevent and address challenging behavior.

In August 2007, the DEC adopted a concept paper on the identification of and intervention with challenging behavior (DEC, 2007). The concept paper, was also endorsed by the NAEYC and the Association for Childhood Education International (ACEI).

DEC believes strongly that many types of services and intervention strategies are available to address challenging behavior. For some young children, the use of adult vigilance and developmentally appropriate positive guidance techniques is insufficient to successfully respond to their challenging behaviors. For these children, positive behavioral interventions and supports are warranted to effectively address their needs. Without systematic intervention, it is likely that chronic challenging behavior will escalate and become more problematic for the child and others.

The DEC suggests that services and strategies might include four areas: designing environments and activities to prevent challenging behavior, using positive behavior interventions that address both the form and function of behavior, adopting curriculum modification and accommodation strategies, and providing external consultation and technical assistance. Further, the DEC believes that effective intervention includes comprehensiveness, individualization, and positive programming and is multidisciplinary and data based. *Comprehensive* interventions are those that include more than one strategy. Young children may engage in the same challenging behavior for different reasons. Therefore, it is necessary to *individualize* and understand both how to assess and quantify what (form) the behavior is and why (function) the child is engaging in the behavior. Because many challenging behaviors of young children result from a deficit in social and communication skills, *positive programming* is needed to foster development and learning of those skills. Typically the collaborative efforts of a *multidisciplinary* team (e.g., early interventionist, early childhood educator, behavior analyst, and speech therapist) will result in more effective interventions. Interventions that are *data based* and apply systematic methods of collecting data specific to challenging behaviors will serve best in that they will assist with accountability, facilitate communication, and increase the ability of adults to be consistent in responding to behavior across varied settings.

DEC believes that families play a critical role in designing and carrying out effective interventions for challenging behaviors. Recommended practices suggest that early childhood education and early childhood special education should have a strong family focus. A coordinated team effort between professionals and families is critical for success in behavior interventions. In fact, in early intervention programs and state-wide systems for children with disabilities from ages birth to 3 years, a family-centered approach is mandated. The family is the smallest unit of intervention. Historically, families have been blamed, especially with regard to children who exhibit challenging behaviors. This is frequently incorrect or at least grossly oversimplified, given the numerous complex factors that typically contribute to the establishment and maintenance of challenging behaviors. Families are best viewed as partners in the process of planning, implementing, and evaluating behavior interventions.

Behavior Analysis Certification Board (BACB)

The ethical practice of applied behavior analysis is overseen by the Behavior Analyst Certification Board (BACB). They have developed a Professional Ethical Compliance Code for Behavior Analysts that contains 10 sections relevant to the ethical and professional conduct of behavior analysts. These sections are as follows: (1) Responsible Conduct of Behavior Analysts, (2) Responsibility to Clients, (3) Assessing Behavior, (4) Behavior Analysts and the Behavior-Change Program, (5) Behavior Analysts as Supervisors, (6) Behavior Analysts' Ethical Responsibility to the Profession of Behavior Analysts, (7) Behavior Analysts' Responsibility to Colleagues, (8) Public Statements, (9) Behavior Analysts and Research, and (10) Behavior Analysts' Ethical Responsibility to the BACB. As you can see, the list is comprehensive and encompasses all aspects of ethical practice and professional conduct, including the roles and responsibilities to clients and the practice and delivery of behavior analysis (BACB, 2017).

SUMMARY OF ETHICAL CODES, STANDARDS, AND PRINCIPLES FROM ASSOCIATIONS/ORGANIZATIONS

In this chapter, we have reviewed the ethics, standards, principles, and underlying beliefs of a variety of professional associations and organizations. Although this exercise may have seemed somewhat disconnected from the question of what the ethics are that specifically guide professionals in the area of positive behavioral interventions and supports (PBIS), it is important for you to understand the broader context of ethics in education and the place of prevention and intervention for challenging behaviors in that context. Further, one may assume that in the future, as special education and general education systems continue to unify with regard to reform, the revisions and further development of ethical codes will be more inclusive of varied constituencies.

The inclusion of particular associations and organizations has been purposeful and intended to guide you from the broadest perspective on education and ethical codes and conduct to a focus on ethics and conduct specific to PBIS. A number of other associations and organizations could have been included—for example, the National Middle School Association and their mission and position statements; the National Association of Secondary School Principals, particularly the information that they provide about special education; and the Council of Administrators of Special Education. (See websites in Figure 3–2.) Also, TASH, an organization actively involved in a variety

---

FIGURE 3–2

Selected Websites

Association for Persons with Severe Handicaps (TASH)
http://www.tash.org

Council for Children with Behavioral Disorders
http://www.ccbd.net

Council for Exceptional Children (CEC)
http://www.cec.sped.org

Council of Administrators of Special Education (CASE)
http://www.casecec.org

Division of Early Childhood of the Council for Exceptional Children (DEC)
http://www.dec-sped.org

ERIC Clearinghouse on Disabilities (ERIC)
http://eric.ed.gov

National Association for the Education of Young Children (NAEYC)
http://www.naeyc.org

National Association of Secondary School Principals
http://www.principals.org

National Education Association (NEA)
http://www.nea.org

National Middle School Association (NMSA)
http://www.nmsa.org

The OSEP Center on Positive Behavioral Interventions and Supports (PBIS)
http://www.pbis.org

of professional and advocacy activities aimed at improving the lives of persons with comprehensive and severe disabilities, could have been included. NAEYC and DEC are included and are especially important because of their focus on early identification, prevention, early intervention, and participation of and partnerships with families. Also, these organizations have demonstrated willingness over time to and success in collaboration, including joint efforts aimed at supporting young children with challenging behaviors and their families. It is understood that you are preparing to work with children and youth at various levels from infancy through preschool, middle school, and secondary school as well as in various settings, including general and special education settings. It is important to have a foundation in the development and learning of young children and the ethical standards that guide practice. Obviously, young children become older, and challenging behaviors of young children, in the absence of successful and lasting interventions, frequently become chronic and more severe. Finally, the professional and ethical code for behavior analysts developed by the BACB was presented. This document encompasses the professional and ethical practice of behavior analysis including services to clients.

PBIS AND ETHICAL STANDARDS AND PRACTICES

As introduced in Chapter 1, the field of PBIS is built largely as an outgrowth from the foundations of applied behavior analysis. Historically, research focused on behavior change over the past five decades have included ethical considerations related to assessment, planning, delivering, and evaluating interventions. Sulzer-Azaroff and Mayer (1991) pointed out that in the use of applied behavior analysis and behavior procedures, ethical responsibility requires that behavior interventions "are based on the laws of behavior, use scientific methods of evaluation, and improve the quality of peoples lives and society by helping those persons to enhance their repertoires of constructive and reinforcing behavior options" (p. 103). Sulzer-Azaroff and Mayer further stated that the primary sources for professional ethical standards have been the Division of Experimental Analysis of Behavior of the American Psychological Association (APA) and the Association for the Advancement of Behavior Therapy (AABT).

The use of PBIS in schools has its basis in federal legislation. The 2004 amendments to IDEA provide for both positive behavioral intervention and support and functional behavior assessment (FBA) for children with disabilities and for whom behavior issues impede success in educational settings. However, PBIS is viewed much more broadly as having relevance for all children and youth in a variety of educational contexts as evidenced by the three-tiered model that symbolizes the PBIS model. Schoolwide PBIS represents an example of universal supports intended for all students to provide a positive learning environment. We now know that in order for schoolwide PBIS to be successful, schools must clearly define behavioral expectations for all students and actively engage in teaching these behavioral expectations to all students, openly acknowledge and reinforce students for engaging in appropriate behaviors, engage in on-going program monitoring and evaluation and modifications as needed through a team-based model and identify and develop the necessary behavioral supports for those students needing more intensive and long-term supports (Sugai et al., 2000). PBIS may be developed and maintained at three systems levels, including primary, or reducing new instances of problem behavior; secondary, or reducing current instances; and tertiary, or reducing the intensity and complexity of current instances. To apply this universal and systems perspective to the uses of PBIS in educational contexts, you must understand the tenets of PBIS in relation to other education profession codes, standards, principles, and beliefs specific to facilitating desired behavior, preventing undesirable behavior, and intervening with challenging behavior. Vignette 3.1 describes how PBIS was used in one school.

Vignette 3.1

Riverdale School

Riverdale is a public elementary school located in a rural, Midwestern community. There are 300 students in preschool through fourth grade. The student body is quite diverse and includes children with various ethnic, cultural, socioeconomic, racial, and religious backgrounds. Riverdale has a significant focus on their English as a Second Language (ESL) program, largely to serve a growing Hispanic population. Inclusion of children with special needs is also a priority at Riverdale, and approximately 10% of the children have a variety of types and severities of disability and are included in general education classrooms from preschool through fourth grade. Special education teachers serve as team teachers with general education teachers, whereas others are in a consulting role, and on occasion they provide pull-out services. For the last 5 years, Riverdale has been recognized annually by the state department of education for excellence as a result of readiness and academic achievement scores, for its model practices in inclusion of children with special needs, for its commitment to children for whom English is not the primary language (ELL learners), and for its program of partnering with parents.

During the most recent cycle of Riverdale's school improvement planning process, which was implemented during the past school year, the consensus of teachers, administrators, other school personnel, and family representatives in their self-assessment was that an area of needed growth and improvement was specific to fostering desired behavior in school, preventing behavior problems, and intervening more effectively in response to individual challenging behavior. It was agreed that for the upcoming school year, the school improvement focus would be on development of a schoolwide PBIS plan, and the target date for implementation would be the beginning of school in the fall. During the previous year, a series of meetings and workshops open to all stakeholders (Riverdale's parents, teachers, the principal and assistant principal, school psychologist, counselor, bus drivers, dietary staff, office staff, custodians, and even a few of the older students) were held for the purposes of achieving a shared vision, commonly held beliefs regarding behavior, and some broad goals for the schoolwide PBIS plan including the establishment of a representative team of 8 to 12 members and develop the specific plan for implementation.

One thing that became clear during the process of the broader participation of all interested stakeholders was that it was important to take into account the ethical standards, codes, and principles related to behavior and provided by the various professional organizations represented by the faculty and other professional staff at Riverdale. It was agreed that a subgroup of these individuals would work on merging content of ethical positions from their organizations and would develop an ethics statement for consideration by the larger group. Having this formalized ethical position

continued

statement would be an important element of the school's belief system and would help guide the work of the schoolwide PBIS team. Borrowing from content on ethics provided by the NEA, the LFA, the CEC, the CEC Division for Children with Behavioral Disorders (CCBD), the NAEYC, and the DEC of the CEC, the subgroup came up with the following general ethical position statement for Riverdale School:

> We believe in the worth and dignity of all of our students, their access to equal educational opportunity, and we will help each student realize his or her potential. We will avoid the use of disciplinary procedures as a means of excluding students from school settings until all other alternatives have been exhausted. We will not use corporal punishment as a means of discipline. We will give priority to prevention, early intervention, student participation, and family involvement in matters of student behavior. We will take into account the uniqueness of individual children, their family diversity, and their developmental status in any decisions about behavior in school. We will use a variety of positive, proactive methods of influencing behavior, and these methods will be relevant to helping our students develop self-determination, independence, and an improved quality of life. When intervention is required, we will use an evidence-based, systematic, team approach and will always select the least intrusive and most typical response to challenging behaviors. This is our ethical position related to the behavior of students at Riverdale School.

Reflective Moment

The statements made in Riverdale School's ethics position are related to the various codes and standards of NAEYC, DEC, and other associations or organizations. What are some examples?

How might some of the unique features of Riverdale School affect further development and implementation of its schoolwide plan?

How might the large and growing population of ELL learners at Riverdale influence the ethical position statement?

One of the central features of PBIS is its emphasis on social values. Sugai and colleagues (2000) asserted that to be judged as socially significant, behavior change through PBIS must be *comprehensive*—that is, it must have relevance across a child's day in school and in other important social contexts. It must be *durable*, that is, lasting. It must be *relevant* and foster skills that are functional and useful in daily living. The necessity for PBIS to result the enhancement of the **quality of life** and the ability of individuals to self-determine has also been emphasized as PBIS principles have been articulated. There are numerous sources of information for educators about the ethics, principles, and beliefs associated with PBIS and its application in a broader sense with all children and youth in educational settings as well as with those who have substantial and comprehensive challenging behaviors. Two key sources of information and guidance in this regard are the Technical Assistance Center on Positive Behavioral Interventions and Supports (PBIS) and the *Journal of Positive Behavior Interventions*. The mission of the Technical Assistance Center, which was established by the U.S. Office of Special Education Programs largely in response to the emphasis in the 1997 and 2004 amendments to IDEA, is to support schools in planning and implementing schoolwide discipline. The *Journal of Positive Behavior Interventions* is a quarterly publication whose purpose is to provide a publication outlet for research in the area of positive behavioral interventions and supports.

Consider This

As a member of the community-based behavior support team for a 30-year-old man with severe physical disabilities and mental illness, you become aware that his direct support staff are ignoring his choices and providing only maintenance care for him. You recognize the position of the agency in a time of high turnover, but you want to ensure quality of life and self-determination for this man.

- How do you approach this challenge from an ethical standpoint?
- Whose help do you enlist?

Vignette 3.2

Eastwood High School

Eastwood is a large, comprehensive high school located in a suburban community in the Southwest. There are about 1,500 students, and the vast majority of them will continue their education following high school at a community college or 4-year institution of higher education. The school is very well funded; it has a faculty of highly qualified teachers, counselors, and school administrators, and it has been consistently evaluated as one of the most successful high schools in the state with regard to academic achievement and on a number of other outcome measures. The school climate can be described in general as very positive, healthy, and safe. Eastwood emphasizes a partnership approach with the community and with the parents of the students with regard to school activities and governance.

Raynel, a 17-year-old senior at Eastwood, takes some of his classes through the gifted/accelerated program and has consistently achieved high grades in school. Ray is a starter on the football team and he is being recruited by several major universities for a football scholarship. Over the period of the summer and during the beginning of the fall school term, Ray's family, friends, coaches, and some of his teachers have noticed that Ray seems to have "gone into a shell." He seems sullen and distant and doesn't want to talk about what is bothering him, and his work in class as well as his commitment to the football team has diminished significantly. Ray is at risk of failing his classes, which will affect his ability to earn a scholarship, and he might also be dropped from the team for failing to attend some practices and for speaking disrespectfully to the coaches.

All of the seniors at Eastwood have appointments with one of the several school counselors during the first 6 weeks of the fall term for the purpose of providing them with some initial guidance about what they will do following high school—especially what steps to take in order to make good decisions about college choices. Ms. Hamilton is the school counselor who has Ray on her list. In addition to being licensed in school counseling, Ms. Hamilton is a certified behavior analyst. In her appointment with Ray, Ms. Hamilton takes note of his seeming lack of interest and unwillingness to engage with her. Ray only says that he doesn't care and that it doesn't matter. Ms. Hamilton wants to be a support and resource for Ray to help him resolve what is troubling him. She asks Ray to come back to see her in a week just to talk, and he agrees. Over a period of a couple of appointments, Ray begins to open up about what is troubling him and resulting in his failure to complete class assignments, miss football

continued

practices, and cut off communication with people close to him. Ms. Hamilton is familiar with and adheres to the standards from the APBS for practitioners. As a result, she knows that positive behavior support planning and intervention are not limited in their usefulness to children and youth with disabilities. And she knows that PBIS has relevance not just for reduction of problem behavior but also for the improvement of quality of life. Ray could really use some quality-of-life improvement about now, and he hasn't been able to pull out of his troubles on his own. Ms. Hamilton has gained Ray's trust, so he agrees to a meeting with her, his parents, the head coach, and his homeroom teacher. Ray knows that the purpose of the meeting will be to begin formulating a plan (of which he approves) that will help him pinpoint what is troubling him and come up with steps to make things better.

PBIS, ETHICAL STANDARDS, AND PRACTICE: NINE ORGANIZING THEMES

At the beginning of this chapter, we stated that nine organizing themes (see Figure 3–1) would be used as a summary and one representation of how to understand the major domains of ethical standards, beliefs, principles, and related practices in the provision of PBIS in educational contexts for children and youth with challenging behaviors. These themes also serve as the basis for examination of the common elements and differences across the professional associations and organizations related to their positions on behavior.

Individual Worth and Dignity

Each student (child or youth) is an individual human being with worth and dignity, regardless of the nature or severity of his or her challenging behavior. This position is found, sometimes using different terms such as *quality of life* or *human rights*, in essentially all the organization and association references that we have examined. The phrase "regardless of the nature or severity of his or her challenging behavior" is, however, not always articulated, but rather implied. In the Preamble to the National Education Association's *Code of Ethics of the Education Profession*, emphasis is given to the educator's belief in human worth and dignity. One of the five core values of the NAEYC is respecting worth, dignity, and individual uniqueness, and this is reinforced as an ideal in the NAEYC *Code of Ethical Conduct and Commitment*—specifically, section I-1.3—to recognize and respect the uniqueness and the potential of each child (NAEYC, 2011).

In special education, advocating for the worth and dignity of children and youth, without respect for the severity or type of their disability, has long been central to the mission. In the CEC standards specific to behavior management, the first standard requires that special educators use methods and procedures that do not undermine dignity or human rights. In discussing the public policy foundations for positive behavior interventions, strategies, and supports, Turnbull and colleagues (2015) included a constitutional precedent: the Fifth Amendment, which prohibits the federal government from denying any person life, liberty, or property. Also included are the right to education and the right to treatment legislation and other moral and democratic precedents. These are certainly public policy foundations associated with PBIS, but they also more generally serve as a basis for advocating the worth and dignity of persons with disabilities.

Behavior Reflects a Need

The behavior of children and youth (challenging and otherwise) always reflects a need on the part of the individual. People respond out of need, and all behavior has a form and serves a function. The important point here is that the challenging behavior of children and youth is all too often misread, leading to responses that do not facilitate positive behavior. Although this specific theme is not found stated as such in the positions of the associations and organizations reviewed previously, the emphasis on viewing children and youth as individuals supports the theme of behavior reflecting a need. In a sense, all the ethical standards and principles reviewed that focus on behavior suggest that professionals must seek to understand the function (purpose or need) addressed by a discrete behavior in order to intervene effectively.

Prevention and Early Intervention

Systematic and thoughtful management of learning environments and understanding of individual differences will serve to prevent some challenging behaviors, and early intervention can serve to eliminate or lessen the severity of such behaviors. The theme of prevention is found in numerous places in the various codes, standards, and statements of principles and beliefs. The second core element of the document provided by the LFA targets systematic approaches to supporting safety and positive behavior. Many of these approaches are focused on prevention of challenging behavior in school settings through communication, clear rules, modeling, nurturing student's self-management, celebrating success, arrangement of the environment, and avoidance of harsh and punitive styles.

The NAEYC (2011), in its *Code of Ethical Conduct and Commitment*, provides Ideal I-l.5: to create and maintain safe and healthy settings that foster children's social, emotional, intellectual, and physical development and that respect their dignity and contributions. In fact, the NAEYC focus on developmentally appropriate practices with young children and the emphasis on positive child guidance may all be understood as intended to foster desired behavior and to prevent the need for an intervention. In the 2001 revision of the *NAEYC Standards for Early Childhood Professionals*, the section on addressing children's challenging behaviors includes a statement that early childhood educators understand the importance of a supportive, interesting classroom environment and relationships as ways to prevent many challenging behaviors.

It is interesting to note that the practices advocated by the DEC appear to be similar to the guidance provided by NAEYC. Prevention is associated with environmental arrangement, child initiations, play and socialization, engagement, and communication. The DEC emphasizes routines, structure, prompting, consequences, and consistency. A common belief is that an "ounce of prevention is worth a pound of cure." That maxim is clearly underscored in the professional guidance provided to educators in responding to the behavior of children and youth. We are reminded of the continuum of positive behavior support introduced earlier (Sugai et al., 2000) in which universal interventions (schoolwide) serve to reduce the number of new instances of problem behavior and as preventive measures.

Family Partnerships

Families, children, and youth should be central to all aspects of PBS, including active participation in planning, implementing, and evaluating interventions. Chapter 2 emphasizes the rationale for and recommended practices associated with treating families as team members, collaborators, and partners in all aspects of PBS. Ethical codes and standards have recently begun to reflect this emphasis. One of the three overriding goals stated by the LFA is to involve parents and other community members in helping students achieve meaningful outcomes and in-turn for developing safe and supportive schools (LFA, 2017). Specifically, one of the LFA core elements states the family role in determining school rules related to behavior and how rules are communicated and enforced. Also included in the LFA core elements are beliefs that parents should (to the degree possible) be active participants in behavior change, and effective alternative programs should include active family involvement (LFA, 2017).

The ethical code of the CEC has only one reference to families, and its focus is on activities delivered to families rather than partnerships with families. However, the CEC professional practice standards specific to behavior management are introduced by a statement suggesting that parents (rather than families) are a part of an interdisciplinary team, along with other professionals in an effort to "manage" behavior. In its mission statement, the CCBD includes a part of the mission being to foster collaborative relationships among families and professionals.

Focusing now on early childhood as represented by both the NAEYC and DEC, a number of standards, values, beliefs, and principles associated with the place of families are to be found. As one of its six core values, the NAEYC commits professionals to value the relationships children and their families have. As addressed earlier in the chapter, NAEYC complemented its core values with the addition of related professional responsibilities in four areas, including families. Respecting family child-rearing values and decision-making, helping families learn and grow in parenting skills, and involving families in significant decisions affecting their children are all stated as professional responsibilities. The DEC, as noted earlier, has worked closely with NAEYC over the last 10 to 15 years. In the NAEYC mission statement is recognition of the role of families in the successful development of children. They state that their policies and practices should support families and ultimately the optimal development of children. The concept paper produced by DEC, and endorsed by NAEYC, on identification of and intervention with challenging behavior supports the critical role of families related to interventions for challenging behavior. Although some might argue this point, it seems clear that one of the most significant changes that may be seen in the evolution of behavior theory and applied behavior analysis to PBIS is the role of the family. PBIS stresses the movement away from parents as targets for intervention, as extensions of the professional, as trainees, and toward families as partners in all aspects of PBIS, including functional assessment, planning processes, designing and implementing positive behavior interventions, and evaluation.

Family Diversity

The uniqueness of children and youth, as reflected by the diversity of their families (race, ethnicity, religion, and culture) should be taken into account in understanding and responding to challenging behavior. The National Education Association Code of Ethics continues to be the guiding philosophy of ethical practice for the organization and its members. The Code of Ethics in summary upholds the belief in the worth and dignity of all and that the freedom to teach, the freedom to learn, and access to equal educational opportunity should be a guarantee for all citizens. The Code of Ethics defines the ethical roles and responsibilities for educators to students and to the profession.

Consider This

In partnering with the family of a school-age child, you are confronted with their stringent belief in corporal punishment as a means to discipline the child. These beliefs are strongly held cultural assumptions for this family.

- How do you, as a teacher and part of the behavior support team, deal with this challenge?
- How do you maintain ethical standards for the child and in your partnership with the family?

The NAEYC (2017) includes as one of its six core values that children should be understood and supported in the context of family and culture. Also, one of the ideals provided in the NAEYC ethical code directs early childhood professionals to be respectful of family child-rearing values. The DEC includes as one of its recommended practices in child-focused intervention that practices not stigmatize the child or family and that they should be culturally and linguistically sensitive.

Natural Environments and Inclusive Settings

Natural environments and inclusive settings are desirable for children and youth with troubling and challenging behavior, but school personnel must assume ownership in those settings, and a full continuum of services and settings should be available. The literature in education, special education, and related disciplines is rich, in both empirically based and position statements, with information about natural environments, inclusion, and least restrictive environments. The consideration here is limited to examining the extent to which these issues are addressed in codes, standards, and statements of principles and beliefs. Although the review of organizations and associations provided in this chapter is certainly not exhaustive, neither in terms of numbers nor the extent to which information provided by the organizations and associations is complete, it is surprising to find that natural environments and inclusion apparently receive little attention in ethical codes and standards. The NEA does provide in its resolution on discipline wording that indicates that "discipline" should not be misused as a reason to exclude children from school settings. However, the resolution does provide that children could be excluded after other means of intervention have been exhausted.

The LFA, in their core elements related to supporting safety and positive behavior, stress the necessity of a continuum of services for children who engage in challenging behavior. When the NAEYC revised its standards for early childhood personnel preparation in 2001 from the prior 1996 version, they emphasized the importance of professionals being prepared to teach children with and without developmental delays or disabilities. This statement reflects the growing movement, especially for young children, of inclusive processes and environments. In 1999, the DEC adopted a concept paper, endorsed by the NEA, in which they pointed out that many young children experience challenging behavior as a part of development and that most of them respond to developmentally appropriate management techniques (positive guidance and PBIS). Further, the DEC takes the position that even when specific intervention strategies are necessary to address challenging behavior, sometimes changing adult behavior or the environment (inclusive and natural) serves to minimize or prevent challenging behavior.

Natural and Logically Occurring Consequences

Natural and logically occurring consequences are preferable to extraneous and contrived reward systems to foster self-discipline, independence, and self-determination. The fundamental question here is, of course, what educators should do in response to the behavior (desirable and undesirable) of children and youth. What are the consequences of behavior? There is a common assumption in education and special education that logical and natural consequences are desired. What guidance do educators find for this point of view in the ethical codes and standards that have been introduced in this chapter?

One of the core elements of the LFA is a systematic approach to supporting safety and positive behavior. This core element emphasizes the importance of rules for behavior that are clear, consistent, logical, inclusive of student input in development, and fairly and consistently enforced. This emphasis provides the opportunity for use of natural and logical consequences for both desired and undesired behavior. The LFA core element also emphasizes the importance of celebrating the success of students who meet behavior expectations. PBIS brings to professionals the focus on prevention as well as emphasis on positive consequences that are meaningful to children and families (natural and logical).

Being Positive Rather Than Punitive

Central to the philosophy and practice of PBIS is an emphasis on being positive. Behavior interventions should be positive and should not include corporal punishment or other punitive measures. Represented in the various codes and standards is a clear movement toward using positive and avoiding negative consequences, which may be where the largest gap continues to exist between general education and special education. In the NEA *Code of Ethics of the Education Profession*, educators are obligated, among other things, to not intentionally expose students to embarrassment or disparagement and to protect students from conditions harmful to learning or to health. Although some will disagree, one reasonable assumption is that the use of corporal punishment and other punitive methods could be inconsistent with these ethical standards.

In its core elements for safe and supportive learning communities, the LFA states that harsh and punitive discipline styles tend to result in resentment and resistance and that excessive punishment puts the student in the position of trying to find ways to escape and takes attention away from the problematic behavior. This organization highlights the importance of teachers rewarding appropriate behavior and alternative programs including PBIS. The CEC standards for professional practice related to behavior management give guidance on this theme. Corporal punishment is given as an example of a violation of basic human rights, and aversive techniques are to be avoided unless other methods have failed repeatedly and after consultation with parents and appropriate agency officials. The CCBD, in a position paper on behavior reduction strategies, notes that progress has been made in developing less aversive ways of responding to behavior disorders in children and youth and that the CCBD does not sanction the use of corporal punishment.

Arguably the most important principle in the NAEYC (2017) *Code of Ethical Conduct and Commitment* is P-l.1: "Above all, we shall not harm children. We shall not participate in practices that are disrespectful, degrading, dangerous, exploitative, intimidating, emotionally damaging, or physically harmful to children." In their concept paper on identification of and intervention with challenging behavior, the DEC states that children who require specialized interventions may need positive behavior interventions that address both the form and function of behavior.

Functionality and Quality of Life

The PBIS movement, both as specific practice for children and youth or adults with challenging behavior and as a universal school model, has focused attention on a topic that many researchers and leaders in special education have begun to address in some detail: the relevance of behavior interventions for how a person functions in the "real world" and how the intervention affects their quality of life. One prominent writer on the subject of quality of life for persons with intellectual disabilities reviewed the evolution of the concept in the 1980s and 1990s and how it might be pursued for persons with disabilities in the immediate future (Schalock, 2000). He provided a definition as follows: "Quality of life is a concept that reflects a person's desired conditions of living related to eight core dimensions of one's life: emotional well-being, interpersonal relationships, material well-being, personal development, physical well-being, self-determination, social inclusion, and rights" (p. 121). This definition serves our purpose as we consider the ethical support for positive behavior support and quality of life.

Finally, supporting persons with disabilities in achieving a quality of life that is functional for them and assisting them in achieving a "rich" lifestyle (Turnbull et al., 2015) is certainly a guiding principle in the ethical conduct of PBIS.

PBIS STANDARDS OF PRACTICE

As we noted at the beginning of this chapter, in order to be ethical a professional must know and follow the standards of practice of his or her professional organization(s). In March 2007, at the annual conference of the APBS, the board approved a document intended to provide guidance to practitioners as they plan and deliver positive behavior support. This document, entitled *APBS Standards of Practice*, and specifically SP-I (Association for Positive Behavior Support [APBS], 2008), is the result of a developmental process that started in 2006 and is expected to continue and lead to revision and expansion as the standards are further studied and applied. Visit the APBS website (www.apbs.org/standards_of_practice.html) and look at the complete listing. Thinking about the use of these standards to guide PBIS to children and youth in school environments, it is reasonable to assume the following: the term *practitioners* applies primarily to professionals, such as behavior specialists, behavior analysts, and others who have primary responsibility to address the needs of students with challenging behavior. However, teachers, counselors, school psychologists, coaches, school administrators, family members, and others who are outside the field of PBIS and who may have different philosophical orientations will benefit from having knowledge of these standards, especially as they are likely to be involved in PBIS planning and intervention processes for students with challenging behavior.

There were six standards provided under SP-I: (I) Foundations of PBS; (II) Collaboration and Team Building; (III) Basic Principles of Behavior; (IV) Data-Based Decision-Making; (V) Comprehensive Person Centered and Functional Behavior Assessments; and (VI) Development and Implementation of Comprehensive, Multi-Element Behavior Support Plans. Each of these six standards has been extensively outlined and described. For our purposes, we will address only highlights and selected points. Note that there is substantial overlap between the emphases of the standards and the nine organizational themes presented previously. Again, you are encouraged to study the standards of practice in total; they have a great deal of relevance for essentially all of the content of your text and are not exclusive to Chapter 3.

Standard I (Foundations of PBIS) states that practitioners should have a historical perspective on the evolution of PBIS from applied behavior analysis and the disability movement, should follow basic assumptions of behavior (e.g., understanding the environmental context and keeping in mind that behavior always serves a function), and should apply 11 key elements in PBIS development (e.g., collaboration, person-centeredness, and enhancing self-determination). Additionally, practitioners are engaged in continuous professional development and know and follow legal requirements associated with assessment, planning, and implementation of services for individuals with challenging behavior. Standard II (Collaboration and Team Building) emphasizes the importance of professionals working collaboratively with other professionals, persons with disabilities, and families. Skills such as clear communication, flexibility, learning from others, and managing conflict are important. Practitioners should also understand the importance of the team and the strategies associated with successful team functioning.

Standard III (Basic Principles of Behavior) states that practitioners should use methods that are based on operant learning (e.g., the assumption that behavior is based on the antecedent–behavior–consequence model), should understand and use the manipulation of antecedents to influence behavior (e.g., changing routines, curriculum, or instruction) and should understand and use consequence manipulations (e.g., using various reinforcement strategies) to increase desired behaviors. Practitioners also understand the use of consequence manipulations to decrease undesirable behaviors. Finally, practitioners use basic principles to facilitate generalization and maintenance of skills. Standard IV (Data-Based Decision-Making) includes a focus on operational definitions of behavior, using established methods form measuring target (defined) behaviors, using graphic displays of data to support decision making, and using data-based strategies to monitor behavior (e.g., sharing data with team members).

Standard V (Comprehensive Person Centered and Functional Behavior Assessments) reflects the necessity of multi-element assessments (elements such as quality of life, environment, setting events, and antecedents and consequences) and comprehensive assessments of the individual that include lifestyle, preferences/interests, communication/social abilities, ecology, health and safety, problem routines, and the variables that promote and reinforce problem behavior. Standard V also includes the necessity of assessing quality of life, the conduct of functional behavior assessments, the use of both indirect and direct assessment strategies, collaborating with the team in hypothesis development, and finally, the understanding and use of functional analysis when appropriate as differentiated from functional assessment. Standard VI (Development and Implementation of Comprehensive, Multi-Element Behavior Support Plans) focuses on the needs for plans to be comprehensive. Under this standard, importance is given to collaboration, person-centeredness, contextual fit, planning to improve quality of life and self-determination, social interactions, and interventions that promote prevention of problem behaviors. Standard VI also includes evidence-based instructional strategies, sound consequence intervention strategies (e.g., function-based reinforcement using natural consequences as much as possible), and finally, the use of data to evaluate interventions and make modifications. As you think about these PBIS standards of practice, keep in mind that what is provided in this chapter represents only highlights from the document and that these standards are in a continuous development process. Also remember the connection between standards and ethical behavior of professionals. To engage in ethical practices as a professional educator, one must know and follow the standards of their discipline.

SUMMARY

Ethics are defined as the principles of conduct governing us as individual professionals as well as in our particular discipline. To be ethical as a professional means conforming to accepted professional standards of conduct. The intent of Chapter 3 is to introduce you to the basic ethical codes, standards, principles, and beliefs of key and representative organizations and associations. More specifically, the chapter examines the standards targeting behavior in educational environments and draws some comparisons about the overall guidance provided to professional educators regarding fostering desired behavior, preventing problematic behavior, and intervening with challenging behavior. The logic of introducing associations and organizations outside the discipline and subdisciplines of special education is the growing trend toward unified systems reform in public education and the perspective that PBIS represents principles and practices that have universal relevance for schools and other educational environments. Nine organizational themes for understanding ethical practices are suggested, and the standards, principles, and beliefs from the selected associations and organizations are related to the themes. Finally, the standards of practice from the ABPB were briefly introduced.

ACTIVITIES TO EXTEND YOUR LEARNING

1. Interview a faculty member who teaches course(s) in history and philosophy of education and social foundations at your institution. Ask him or her to assist you in finding additional references and resource material dealing with ethics and ethical behavior in education and in special education and/or challenging behavior in particular.
2. In small in-class groups of three to five participants, develop together your own code of ethics for the use of PBIS, first for a schoolwide, universal perspective and then from the standpoint of children and youth with challenging behavior.
3. With fellow class participants, discuss the extent to which ethics and ethical behavior is addressed in your preparation. At what point in your programs of study and in what courses and to what degree are these issues covered?
4. If you are in field experiences in schools or agencies or have access to various educational settings, look for evidence of ethical standards being displayed or shared in those settings. Ask teachers and other personnel how they keep abreast of codes of ethical conduct.
5. Look at some textbooks in education, special education, and psychology that were published prior to 1960 and note how they presented ethics and ethical standards. Use this information to compare to current information as introduced in Chapter 3.
6. In small groups of three to five participants, search online for a discipline plan from an area school system. Study the plan with regard to whether it addresses ethical conduct and standards and the extent to which the plan's mission and practices are consistent among mission, ethics, and practices and also consistent with the standards in Chapter 3 and the themes.

FURTHER READING AND EXPLORATION

1. Visit the websites of the organizations and associations introduced in Chapter 3 and review the content that they provide related to ethical codes, standards, principles, and beliefs. These websites are listed in Figure 3–2.
2. The *Journal of Positive Behavior Interventions* (JPBI) is a quarterly journal that premiered in 1999. Review parts of JPBI and develop an annotated bibliography categorized by the nine themes presented in Chapter 3.

Prevention Through Effective Instruction

CONCEPTS TO UNDERSTAND

After reading this chapter, you should be able to:

- Understand the relationship between setting events and antecedents and the importance of preventing challenging behavior through effective instruction.
- Describe how to identify probable antecedents or "triggers," related to challenging behavior.
- Identify and describe how to prevent challenging behavior through effective instructional approaches.
- List and describe effective instructional strategies such as engineering supportive learning environments, managing instructional antecedents and RtI (Response-to-Intervention).

KEY TERMS

A-B-C recording

Antecedents (triggers)

Engineering learning environments

Functional behavior assessment (FBA)

Indirect assessment

Interval recording

Scatter-plot analysis

Setting events

Universal design

During the past 20 years in the field of special education, we have witnessed a greater emphasis being placed on the importance of effective instruction as a means of preventing challenging behavior in learners. This focus has largely been aimed at better understanding of those causal relationships that influence these behaviors. Since the inception of PBIS as part of the 1997 Reauthorization of IDEA, research in the field of PBIS has fostered a greater awareness among professionals toward furthering their understanding of the relationship between distant **setting events** (i.e., physical, social, and environmental variables that serve to establish operations, or "set the stage") and **antecedents (triggers)** (i.e., events that trigger behavior) and challenging behavior. This relationship was initially viewed by many as a new way of thinking, though the concept has been around for much longer. The noted psychologist and researcher Sidney Bijou (1908–2009) addressed the importance of understanding these relationships, especially within classroom and instructional settings (1970). The use of antecedent management strategies provides a mechanism for minimizing and in many cases preventing the occurrence of challenging behaviors. Understanding and managing antecedents is a departure from traditional behavior management practices whereby in the past, professionals would frequently place greater emphasis on consequence events following the occurrence of an inappropriate behavior, often in the form of punishments. With the advent of PBIS, professionals have begun to address challenging behavior from a more proactive framework that includes the use of antecedent management strategies as a mechanism for the prevention of problematic behaviors.

The purpose of this chapter will be to explain the role that antecedents can play in triggering challenging behaviors in learners and how we can better utilize effective instructional practices including antecedent management strategies in the prevention of challenging behaviors. Such intervention options can include how tasks are presented to the learner by the teacher, the type of instructional cues used by the teacher during the presentation of tasks, the presence or absence of choice-making opportunities, and the level of behavior supports provided to individual learners as necessary to maximize their performance and make better use of their individual learning strengths. We hope that you have a better understanding of these concepts after completing this chapter.

PREVENTION OF CHALLENGING BEHAVIOR THROUGH THE MODIFICATION OF ANTECEDENTS

The assessment of antecedents or the triggers that are associated with challenging behavior can be most helpful to us in understanding these relationships and in our attempts to prevent challenging behaviors. Once we determine what these relationships are we can then design interventions aimed at lessening or even preventing their impact on behavior. These interventions can range from differentiating our instructional practices such as how tasks are designed and presented or in modifying the learning environments. These adjustments can have a positive impact on lessening and in preventing challenging behaviors leading to more enjoyable life experiences for students. A key point to bear in mind is how modifying certain environmental variables—such as seating, noise level, and room temperature, for example—when paired with differentiating how instruction and learning tasks are designed and delivered can play a significant role in how learners respond. The way instructional materials are presented, scheduled, and arranged within the physical environment can all have an impact on a learner's behavior and his or her subsequent performance (Conroy & Stichter, 2003; Wheeler, Carter, Mayton, & Thomas, 2002).

It is important in our effort to provide effective and meaningful educational outcomes for every child that we first understand how to provide effective behavior supports to children and youth including and most importantly strategies aimed at prevention. The assessment of antecedents provides us with the critical information needed to aid in the development of student-centered interventions. The need for understanding the role of instruction to student behavior and academic performance is even more important, given the legislative mandate for RtI (Response-to-Intervention). Response to Intervention was created in response to the need for improving student outcomes as a result of legislative mandates—IDEA (2004) and the No Child Left Behind Act (2001)—and requires differentiated instruction for students deemed to be at risk for academic failure (Lewis, Wheeler, & Carter, 2017; Cummings, Atkins, Allison, & Cole, 2008), thus requiring greater attention to understanding the role of instructional antecedents to learner behavior. More specifically RtI states that the use of evidence-based intervention strategies be applied across students based on student need (Lewis, Wheeler, & Carter, 2017; Crosland & Dunlap, 2012).

In considering how a teacher can identify and manage antecedents within the classroom, we should always remember that a teacher is first and foremost a facilitator of learning. As a facilitator of learning, the teacher assumes the responsibility of organizing the learning environment and instructional structure needed by every child to learn and being sensitive to the individual characteristics, performance strengths, and limitations of every student. The outcomes derived from assessing potential antecedents can offer the teacher practical options in the organization and delivery of instruction, the design of the learning environment, and the level of individual supports needed by each student. The various antecedent management strategies to be explored in depth within this chapter include engineering learning environments, environmental modifications, instructional modifications, and quality-of-life enrichment strategies.

ENGINEERING LEARNING ENVIRONMENTS

The concept of **engineering learning environments** has been synonymous with PBIS since the inception of this methodology. Some illustrations of this philosophy include an emphasis on enriching the lifestyles or quality of life of individuals (as addressed later in the chapter), promoting opportunities for choice, and social inclusion within educational and community settings. PBIS has reinforced the focus on the learner and in designing educational, behavioral and lifestyle supports to enhance positive and pro-active behavior in learners.

Systems change within schools and classroom settings continues to be an evolving process with regard to the implementation of PBIS. To date, it has been reported (Childs, Kinkaid, George, & Gage, 2016) that 21,000 schools nationally have enlisted schoolwide positive behavior interventions and supports (SWPBIS). The increasing number of schools adopting SWPBIS is encouraging when faced with how to respond effectively to challenging behavior. This initiative has encouraged school systems to practice self-examination and focus their energies on understanding how learning and educational environments can positively affect student behavior and learning from both an individual and group perspective. Most people would agree that all learning environments should be designed to be safe, inviting, and supportive for the learners who use them. A concept that has become more widely accepted by professionals has been that of **universal design**. Universal design was a concept that originated in the field of architecture and was initiated to foster inclusion within environments by way of innovative design intended to create such access for persons with disabilities. Universal design has grown to incorporate more elements, including how instruction is designed and delivered allowing for equity and building on a concept of learning communities for all (Lewis, Wheeler, & Carter, 2017). Universal design is an example of how we as educators can "engineer" learning environments to promote a variety of pro-social responses in learners.

PBIS has advanced the concept of how to make learning environments more conducive to promoting positive behavior and learning outcomes through the process of engineering and redesign of these learning environments. The concept of engineering learning environments to promote successful performance outcomes can take on a broad (schoolwide) perspective or a more focused (individual classroom) perspective, depending on the goal of the intervention and whether it is aimed at schoolwide levels or focused on a specific individual.

SWPBIS has broadened our understanding of how to address problem behavior before it begins, in many cases through activities that promote awareness and prevention for all students. Within PBIS are three major strata in terms of schoolwide behavior supports. Sugai and colleagues (2000) referred to these strata as: (a) primary prevention (designed for the largest percentage of students, 80% to 90%, who do not experience serious problem behavior), (b) secondary prevention (directed toward those students, approximately 5% to 15%, who are at risk for problem behaviors), and (c) tertiary prevention (targeted for those students, approximately 1% to 7%, with chronic and intense levels of problem behavior).

The most noticeable areas of school environments that embrace a philosophy of positive behavior interventions and supports are school culture and climate. Schools with effective cultures and climates have the best interests of every child as their primary goal, an emphasis is placed on prevention of problem behavior, and school-based teams are in place to promote positive and proactive interventions that are designed to promote enhanced learning and quality-of-life outcomes for *all* children. These environments also emphasize team-based approaches to problem solving, have active and committed administrations, and direct their efforts on multisystems perspectives that include the district, schoolwide, nonclassroom, classroom, learner, family, and community environments (Sugai et al., 2000).

As Sugai and colleagues (2000) have indicated, effective learning environments are characterized by the following qualities:

- The behavioral expectations are defined and shared among administrators, teachers, families, and students.
- Expectations are published and visually apparent within all areas of the school. Students are aware and informed of the expectations. Subsequently, these expectations are taught to students and reinforced throughout the child's day. The skills are modeled and reinforced repeatedly by teachers and school personnel on a daily basis.
- Appropriate behaviors exhibited by students are frequently acknowledged and celebrated within these environments by teachers within classrooms and at schoolwide assemblies and functions.

Sugai and colleagues (2000) also noted that schools successful in promoting this type of learning environment typically reflect a pattern of interactions between adults and students that uses four times more positive feedback than negative. This pattern of interaction within schools among teachers and students characterizes the adage that a child will rise or fall to the level of expectation before them and the amount of support provided in meeting that expectation. This type of environment serves as a model for school improvement.

Some examples that can be tried when designing optimal learning environments include a change in seating, lighting, modulating noise in the classroom, and changes in classrooms or teachers to facilitate a better fit between the student and instructor. More specific modifications within the environment should be considered when attempting to promote acquisition and maintenance of replacement behaviors among learners.

Jolivette, Scott, and Nelson (2000) among others recommended two major strategies to employ relative to environmental design to promote the successful acquisition of replacement behaviors: manipulating the environment to increase the probability of success and minimizing the likelihood of failure. These strategies are best accomplished by designing the learning environment to reinforce the replacement behavior, which can be accomplished through the careful design of settings, individuals, and tasks. Minimizing the probability of failure is most important and is best facilitated by removing barriers that prevent the replacement behavior from occurring within the appropriate context. Jolivette, Scott, and Nelson (2000) termed this change "removing the predictors of failure." Other types of barriers sometimes exist and could include the level of distractibility within the classroom, the density (number of children within the class), and social interactions with specific students or staff. Any number of these factors could serve as potential barriers to the performance of replacement behaviors, ultimately resulting in a missed opportunity for reinforcement of the replacement skill (Jolivette et al., 2000). One consideration to remember is that when we are attempting to teach new behaviors and or ways of responding we as teachers must be mindful that we enhance the efficiency of these new behaviors for the learner to perform initially and that we certainly provide praise and encouragement as reinforcement for their attempts at responding.

One specific strategy directed at engineering supportive learning environments includes the use of individualized activity schedules. Activity schedules provide students with enhanced structure and also a means by which the daily routine of activities can be clearly and consistently communicated to the student. Activity schedules serve to reinforce the acquisition of new behaviors.

Activity schedules have been widely used with children and youth with autism as a means of communicating instructional demands, showing the sequence of activities, promoting increased task clarity, and communicating performance expectations. They have also been used as a tool to aid in the prevention and reduction of challenging behavior in children with autism (Massey & Wheeler, 2000).

Massey and Wheeler's (2000) study used a photo activity schedule with a young child (age 4 years) with autism in an inclusive preschool classroom as a method for increasing task engagement and minimizing the occurrence of challenging behavior. The primary behavior of concern was the child's difficulty with unplanned transitions between activities, which resulted in periods of crying and noncompliance. Following a period of instruction in the use of a photo activity schedule that consisted of photographs of activities arranged in sequential order on a schedule, the child demonstrated acquisition and fluency in his use of the activity schedule. This achievement was apparent when examining the decrease in teacher-delivered prompts across work, leisure, and lunch settings. During the work condition, the child needed a total of 265 prompts, which included 170 verbal prompts, 25 gestural prompts, and 70 physical (hand-over-hand) prompts. These figures were noticeably less during the leisure condition, where a total of only 190 prompts were needed. This number included 118 verbal prompts, 69 gestural prompts, and 3 physical prompts. The number of prompts used in the lunch condition consisted of 0 verbal prompts, 9 gestural prompts, and 23 physical prompts. This study demonstrates the child's ability to generalize the use of the schedule across settings as reflected by the systematic reduction in teacher prompts. The child also demonstrated increased levels of task engagement across three distinct conditions: work (performing developmentally appropriate class work and activities), leisure (unstructured play), and lunch.

Activity schedules are now recognized as an evidence-based practice (EBP) in the education and treatment of learners with autism (Mesibov & Shea, 2010) and have been successful in preventing the occurrences of challenging behavior, facilitating successful transitions between activities, and fostering increased levels of independence in learners (Mesibov, Browder, & Kirkland, 2002). The use of individualized activity schedules were first advocated by Division TEACCH, a comprehensive diagnostic and treatment program for individuals with autism as a component of their structured teaching model. Mesibov and colleagues (2002) pointed out that activity schedules served multiple needs such as assisting students with autism during transitions, fostering independent performance of tasks and activities by learners, teaching students to follow a prescribed schedule within school and home environments, and structuring leisure time. Activity schedules also promote independence when designed around the learning strengths of an individual.

Activity schedules should also be matched to the literacy level of individual learners (Mesibov et al., 2002). The model recommended by Division TEACCH includes the following hierarchy of forms: (a) objects—actual objects that are used within activities, such as a toothbrush, a bar of soap, or toilet paper; (b) symbolic miniature objects that represent the activity, such as magnets; (c) photographs of the activity; (d) line drawings of an activity or an object used in an activity; (e) sight words, such as *Restroom*, *Exit*, and *Entrance*; and (f) short phrases pertinent to an activity (Mesibov et al., 2002).

Learners need to receive individualized instruction in the use of an activity schedule in terms of understanding the symbolic representations of the various objects, pictures, or symbols and written phrases included on the schedule. Other considerations include determining the complexity of a student's schedule, given age, and developmental levels.

In summary, it is important to be sensitive to the idea of structure within the learning environment specific to the behavior support needs of individual learners. The need for engineered learning environments and environmental supports, such as the presence of a routine within a classroom and an individualized activity schedule, cannot be overstated. These serve as mechanisms for ensuring meaningful learning outcomes, preventing challenging behaviors, and promoting a stimulating and supportive environment in which every student can learn and grow.

ENVIRONMENTAL INTERVENTION STRATEGIES

The occurrence of challenging behavior can often be linked to environmental triggers such as overcrowding, noise, room temperature (too hot or too cold), a lack of visual clarity within tasks or within a classroom for some learners, and in general a lack of structure and organization within the classroom. For some students, these very events can pose significant challenges and result in the onset of challenging behaviors that interfere with their learning and or impede the learning of other students. One important pre-consideration is that these behaviors are frequently caused by a combination of skill limitations on the part of the learner coupled with an insensitivity found within the environments in which they learn and function (Durand, 1990). An important first step in addressing such responses in the classroom is attempting to understand the contributing factors found within the environment. Unfortunately, we often find ourselves arriving at a judgment without considering these important contextual factors. A simple reminder: "see the BIG picture, before arriving at a judgement."

One good example to consider of why it is important to structure the environment for learner success is in the education of learner's autism. For learners with autism, structuring the learning environment can compensate for skill deficits they may experience such as organizational skills, the need for visual clarity in assigned tasks to serve as cues, and the need for supports through transitions between activities (Lord & Schopler, 1994). Environmental accommodations are therefore made to ensure positive learner outcomes and minimize the occurrence of challenging behavior, thus serving as an example of how environmental supports can be used to promote positive behavior and learning outcomes.

Given the importance of environment on learning and behavior, teachers should ask the following questions when trying to understand how the classroom environment might be influencing the behavior and learning of their students.

Is the Environment Pleasant?

This question may seem obvious to some. Certainly what is pleasant to some is not to others—how can one operationally define and ascertain this? One observable and measurable indicator is the degree to which the environment is stimulating to learners. Are the learners engaged in their work or creative activity? Do they appear to enjoy the surroundings? For example, is the classroom colorful and inviting? Are classroom materials age-appropriate and pleasing to the eye? Are the social interactions between the learners and the teacher offered in a kind and caring manner? Is the noise level within the classroom tolerable? Other important pre-instructional considerations include the temperature of the classroom: Is it comfortable and seasonably appropriate? Is the classroom well-organized and uncluttered? Is the classroom overcrowded, and what is the condition of the learners' desks and chairs? Vignette 4.1 discusses how the environment can influence learning.

Are Environmental Cues Clear and Consistent?

Within most classrooms and learning environments, visual cues are found that assist learners with regulating their behavior. These include aisles for walking and negotiating the classroom space, assigned seats and work areas for learners, and often a classroom

Vignette 4.1

Environmental Influences on Classroom Behavior

Consider Michael, a fifth-grader who has just begun middle school. He had attended a small neighborhood elementary school prior to his transition to the fifth grade in the middle school. His school is large and very old with many structural problems in the building; for instance, the classrooms are too hot both in winter and summer, and the restrooms have antiquated plumbing that results in bathroom overflows on a regular basis. Aside from these building issues, his year has been one of adjustments with both a homeroom and changing classes as a member of his team, new teachers, and a considerably larger school. He has begun to complain to his parents about his dislike for school on a weekly basis. Given these challenges, Michael is an exceptionally gifted and talented student who is very skilled and capable, yet the distress he finds in his school environment has begun to diminish his desire to excel academically, and he appears to be withdrawing socially.

Reflective Moment

- Given the apparent environmental challenges that Michael encounters in his classroom, how can his teachers minimize their effects by creating a more inviting learning community for him within their respective classrooms and in assisting him and other students through the transition to a new school?

schedule displayed for all to see. Some teachers use individual schedules for all learners as a method of promoting self-determination skills. Attention to these types of environmental supports is an excellent way to design environments conducive to learning and the support of children and youth.

INSTRUCTIONAL INTERVENTION STRATEGIES

Often the behaviors that learners engage in within educational environments can be directly linked to curriculum and instruction. Research has demonstrated the relationship between instructional variables and their influence on the behavior of learners within educational settings (Dunlap & Kern, 1996; Kern-Dunlap, Clarke, & Robbins, 1991). Challenging behaviors experienced during the school day are often precipitated by instructional demands, teacher–student interactions, and school climate issues. Challenging behavior can also be attributed to instructional variables. These behaviors can result from an interaction between instructional demands (how instructions are provided, the difficulty of the work, the amount of work) and a lack of congruence with the learning style and abilities of the student.

In response to some of these challenges, Response to Intervention (RtI) was identified in the 2004 Reauthorization of IDEA and No Child Left Behind as a method for assisting in identifying learners with specific learning disabilities (Berkeley, Bender, Peaster, & Sanders, 2009). What RtI represents is also a three-tiered intervention model similar to PBIS; it does seem to interface well, as it is designed around prevention of academic and behavioral challenges. Basically, RtI allows for Tier I, Core Instructional Interventions, a tier that is designed for all students as a proactive method of prevention, Tier II represents targeted group interventions aimed at students deemed at risk; Tier III interventions are designated for intensive and individual interventions specific to individual students (Lewis, Wheeler, & Carter, 2017).

Generally speaking, there are two major classes of learning problems that students may confront: (1) skill deficits, or the insufficient level of skill needed to perform a desired task; and (2) motivation problems or a lack of desire to attempt performance. "Skill deficit" refers to a lack of ability on the part of the learner to perform a desired skill or behavior because he or she has not been taught the skill, lacks certain prerequisites that are critical for performance of the skill, or lacks fluency to perform the skill independently. A lack of motivation displayed on the part of the learner can be linked to many factors, including the individual's learning history, the absence of reinforcing consequences present in his or her classroom, and a general fear associated with performance (Mager & Pipe, 1997). Teachers and educational personnel can promote learner engagement and minimize the occurrence of challenging behavior through careful attention to instructional antecedents and management of those variables that impede learning and behavior outcomes. Many of these fall under the category of preinstructional considerations and result in a learner profile for each student and include the following:

1. *Learning strengths: what learning strengths does the learner have that can be emphasized in the development of successful instructional formats?*

   Too often, the learning and behavior challenges experienced by children and youth are addressed from the perspective that remediation is needed to "fix" the academic and social challenges experienced by these individuals without any attention being given to their individual strengths. Each learner has a set of skills or attributes that— once identified—can be used in the development of instructional programs directed toward setting the learner up for success. Subsequently, by capitalizing on individual strengths and using a compensatory approach aimed at minimizing skill deficits through the design of PBIS within environments, as one example, we can promote enhanced learning outcomes.

2. *Are there successful teaching and response formats that have been used successfully in the past?*

It is important to confer with the child's former teachers, parents, and family members to assist in the identification of teaching and response formats that have been demonstrated to be successful with the child in the past. Understanding what works for a child is important when teaching new skills. How tasks are presented, the types of cues used in their presentation, and error correction procedures that have met with success in the past are all very important preinstructional considerations for setting a child up for success.

Language and communication skill levels are also central to this area and identify the communication abilities of the learner; their ability to process cues such as gesture, visual, and auditory cues; and their preferred response modes, such as verbal or gesture.

3. *Consider the age of the learner and any identified learning difficulties or disabilities that may be present.*

It is important to consider the age of the learner, the presence of any pre-existing learning difficulties or disabilities before initiating instruction. These considerations will allow you to differentiate instruction around the individual needs of the learner.

4. *What are the preferred activities of the learner?*

This preinstructional consideration attempts to identify the likes and dislikes of the learner. It is important to identify what subjects the learner enjoys and the types of academic skill instruction (e.g., drill and practice, computer-assisted instruction, creative endeavors, kinesthetic activities, and experiential learning) that are most and least preferred by the learner. It is also important to be aware of the activities that the learner enjoys for fun and leisure beyond classroom work, such as games and activities.

We have examined the major areas of preinstructional considerations when attempting to address instructional antecedents. Next, we'll explore the use of instructional interventions aimed at antecedent management that also have functional utility across various types of learners and learning environments.

As we have eluded to the role of curriculum and instruction can play a significant role in the performance of learners and in the promotion of task engagement. They can also serve as triggers for problematic behavior in some students. A review conducted by Kern and Dunlap (1998) broadly defined the term *curricular variables* to include: (a) content and objectives, (b) materials used in their performance, (c) behaviors associated with performance, (d) scheduling and sequencing, and (e) the ecological and social conditions in which they are presented. Their review identified that curricular modification has been inclusive of three major areas of study: (1) task modification, (2) instructional modification, and (3) modification of setting events. Basically, these areas equate to how tasks are designed for the learner, taking into account the individual's learning strengths, interests, and the selection of socially valid instructional goals. This concept also includes how tasks are delivered to the learner in terms of instruction. Tasks need to be presented in a systematic manner, prompts used in the initial stages of acquisition to assist the learner, and reinforcement used throughout as a means to promote engagement on the part of the learner.

The modification of instructional antecedents by teachers and caregivers represents an effective and systematic method for minimizing the effects of problem behavior across learning environments (schools, day care settings, home, community). The difficulty has been making the methods identified within the research portable and practical for educators within these environments to use (Stichter, Sasso, & Jolivette, 2004). Some of these research-based practices are expanded upon in the next section.

MODIFYING INSTRUCTIONAL ANTECEDENTS

This section provides a sample of suggested strategies aimed at the modification of instructional antecedents as a method for minimizing the frequency of challenging behavior. These are presented within two major categories: task design and presentation of tasks. These strategies are also applicable across ages and learning environments.

Task Design

When designing instructional tasks for learners, several intervention strategies can be used to prevent the occurrence of challenging behavior:

- *Make tasks relevant to the learner*—Tasks should be directed toward the learner. They should be age and developmentally appropriate, socially valid, and functionally relevant. Teachers should be mindful to be inclusive of these elements in the selection and design of tasks. Often task demands are not geared for a learner's age or developmental level and are not socially or functionally relevant to the learner's needs or interests.
- *Matching tasks to the learner's abilities*—Tasks should be modified to the level of the learner. The learner can become frustrated, and subsequent behavioral challenges may ensue if tasks appear too difficult and beyond the learner's current skill level.
- *Build in opportunities for choice*—All of us respond better when we are given the opportunity for input and the ability to have choices. Allow time and ample opportunity for learners to select tasks at different intervals throughout their day. One useful option is to identify the teaching objective, select three to five tasks, and provide the learner with choice-making opportunities from this list of options. For example, the goal might be a language arts activity; the list of task options could include: (a) a skills worksheet, (b) a kinesthetic activity requiring the learner to move about the learning area collecting materials, (c) a peer buddy activity in which more than one child works together, and (d) a computer-based exercise. The teacher can allow the students to select two of the four options for completing their activity in language arts during the period. By creating opportunities for choice potential, problem behaviors can be avoided.
- *Determine the appropriate length of activities*—The length of activities is very important across all age groups and levels of ability. Activities should have time limitations that coincide with the age and developmental levels of the learner. Preschool-age children should engage in activities that do not exceed 15 minutes in length, such as group story time. Primary-grade-level learners should not exceed 30 to 40 minutes per activity, middle school youngsters no more than 45 minutes per activity, and high school students no more than 60 minutes per activity.
- *Vary activities within the classroom*—Structure and predictability within the classroom are no doubt important; however, activities should be varied and alternated to

control for boredom and fatigue. Alter the types of activities used to teach specific content, and provide novelty and alternative activities on an intermittent basis to achieve this goal. Teachers should also be aware of how frequently learners engage in the same task over and over as they fulfill the objectives stated on the learner's IEP. Often, problematic behavior results from children and youth being assigned the same tasks or worksheets every day with no new instruction or activity being offered.

● *Use of classroom and individual schedules*—Classroom schedules are important components of an organized learning environment. The efficacy of this intervention tool as a means of promoting positive behavior in learners within inclusive settings has been documented (Massey & Wheeler, 2000). The schedules can be centrally located in the classroom or learning setting and can include times and written and pictorial listings of the scheduled activities for a given day. It serves as a reference point for both the learner and teacher. Individualized schedules can also be helpful for promoting self-management skills in learners and for reinforcing organization and task engagement. They have been widely used with children and youth with autism as a learning support mechanism. Individualized schedules are developed for each learner and tailored to his or her needs in terms of level. They can be developed using objects for learners with intense support needs, such as children who are nonverbal and with severe disabilities, or for younger children who are at prelanguage stages of development. Schedules can also be developed using photographs, picture symbols, and written words paired with these or alone. The level of visual cue represented on the schedule is an individual decision based on the abilities of the learner. As children age and develop language and sight-word reading schedules, they can graduate to become more abstract and ultimately lead to the use of a smartphone to assist with a calendar or list of events.

The importance of task design as a mechanism for the prevention of challenging behavior has been described in detail. However, this concept is explored in Vignette 4.2 in terms of its application with a learner having severe disabilities.

Vignette 4.2

Structuring Tasks for Learner Success

Josh was a 16-year-old learner with severe intellectual disabilities who spent his entire school day within a self-contained classroom for adolescents with comprehensive disabilities. He used functional signs to communicate his needs and was suspected of having auditory processing difficulties. Josh displayed out-of-seat behavior, general agitation, and ultimately aggression toward himself and others. His behaviors would usually escalate in that order if left unattended.

A functional behavior assessment (FBA) was conducted that consisted of: (a) a structured interview with his teachers and family, (b) a scatter-plot analysis, (c) an A-B-C analysis, and (d) a 10-second partial interval recording using videotape analysis. From the data gathered, it appeared that there were inconsistent teacher cues used during instruction, the majority of the time verbal instructions were used and there was an absence of environmental cues present in the classroom, such as a visual schedule for Josh to refer to. There was also an absence of reinforcing consequences associated with his attempts at performance and the functions of his behavior appeared to be escape and sensory related.

Further observations revealed an absence of an appropriate curriculum for Josh. An example of this was the teacher reading a children's book to Josh and his peers during a group instruction period, at which point Josh left several times. The FBA also revealed that the prevalence of these behaviors corresponded with periods of group instruction. During these periods, his rate of challenging behavior averaged approximately 70%. In contrast, his challenging behavior during individual instruction time averaged less than 25%.

The behavior support team collaborated on the possibilities and concurred that during group instructional periods more auditory cues were used with an absence of visual cues such as gestures. The opposite was true during the individual instructional periods, with more visual cues embedded within tasks, thus making the ability to discern performance expectations clearer for Josh. Upon modifying the instructional presentation and developing instructional supports such as a picture schedule, Josh's behavior improved quickly and significantly.

Reflective Moment

Why were the visual cues so important in helping Josh understand the performance expectations required of the task?

Task Presentation

The ways in which tasks are presented to learners can serve as antecedents that trigger problematic behavior. Often, little thought is given to understanding how to modify the presentation of academic task demands to facilitate appropriate learner responses. There are several key points to consider when presenting instructional demands:

- *Use of clear and consistent cues*—The selection of instructional cues is important when initiating instruction with learners. The cues that a teacher selects should be geared to the specific learner's needs, and they should also be clear and consistent. Often, a failure to clarify cues leads to learner confusion and subsequent frustration, resulting in disengagement and the potential for problematic behavior that interferes with instruction and task completion.

   Instructional cues should be direct, brief, and clear. In teaching new tasks, these recommendations are most important because the goal of instruction during the skill-acquisition stages of learning is to teach the components of a new skill with minimal or no errors. Also important is the type of cue used. Verbal, gestural, or physical cues may be used or paired with one another. For example, the use of a verbal cue paired with a gesture or physical cue is not uncommon when teaching a new task to a learner. The form of cue used is important and should be determined based on the assessment of the learner's needs and strengths. Some children with disabilities such as ADD need short and direct verbal cues paired perhaps with gesture cues to lend clarity in their presentation.

- *Use embedded cues within the task*—The use of embedded cues within the task is also important. For example, learners can be taught to identify cues embedded within the performance of a task that will serve as a visual stimulus for correct learner performance. For example, when teaching a match-to-sample problem, a lined outline of the sample can be provided so that the learner will use to make the correct match. Another illustration is the use of highlighted instruction within written text and color-coded cues within tasks.

- *Interspersed requesting*—One method that has been very successful in promoting momentum related to task approach and completion has been interspersed requesting, also referred to as high probability requests. It is an approach that uses high-probability requests throughout the delivery of a task as a means of fostering learner compliance and task completion (Wehby & Hollahan, 2000). An example of this method applied to an academic task such as math problem completion would be to intermittently present math problems that are within the learner's performance range (skills currently in his or her repertoire or skill set) within a group of problems, some of which are more difficult, as a method for promoting task engagement and reducing escape-motivated behavior in learners.

- *Systematic instruction*—Systematic instruction represents an instructional methodology designed to teach skills in a structured and stepwise manner. It employs the use of prompts and error-correction procedures sometimes referred to as *prompt hierarchies*. Prompt hierarchies vary depending on the type of task to be taught and the needs of the learner. Most often, a system of least-to-most prompts is used in the delivery of instruction. Such a prompt hierarchy would look like this:

  I = Independent performance—Teacher allows for the learner to independently perform the task.

  V = Verbal prompt—The teacher initiates the task with a verbal prompt such as "begin working."

  G = Gestural prompt—If, after 3 to 5 seconds, the learner does not initiate the task, the teacher may point or use another gesture to help the learner initiate the step in the task that he or she is working on.

  P = Physical prompt—Again, the teacher allows 3 to 5 seconds to elapse; if at this point the learner fails to respond to the component step in the task, the teacher then uses a hand-over-hand procedure to assist the learner.

  In using such a system, the teacher would initiate a task with the learner and allow for a 3- to 5-second time delay to occur before initiating the next level of prompt to assist the learner. The prompt hierarchy should be structured in such a way that the teacher would then proceed through the remainder of prompts on the hierarchy as needed, based on the learner's performance and need for assistance.

- *Use of naturally occurring reinforcers*—Often, learners approach the performance of a task with greater interest if functional and naturally occurring reinforcers are a consequence for task completion. We are not recommending the extensive use of edibles and stickers and things that are contrived but instead consequences that are functional and naturally occurring within the learning environment. Consequences such as free time paired with choice serves as a good example. Upon completion of an activity, the learner is given free time if he or she completes the task in the allotted time frame. During this free time period, the learner may select from a list of choices such as computer time, library time, reading time, or assisting the teacher in running errands or with classroom organization. This is not to say that the use of stickers and treats occasionally, when paired with verbal praise, is not warranted or meaningful for some children and youngsters. Tangible reinforcers such as stickers and snacks are usually very effective and looked upon with favor by children, but an overreliance on them is not recommended.

The use of a preferred activity as a reinforcing consequence is featured in Vignette 4.3.

Vignette 4.3

Enhancing Learner Performance

Richard is an 18-year-old young man with Down syndrome and a severe intellectual disability. He is currently being served for half the school day in a transition program. As part of this program, he is working on a paid job contract for 4 hours each day. His job is to assemble drapery pulleys for a company that manufactures and sells blinds. His job-training specialist has noticed that Richard engages in some stereotypical behavior that she has termed "self-cleansing behavior." This behavior is characterized by excessive rocking, licking the palms of his hands, and running his palms through his hair. Following the completion of a functional assessment, the function of this behavior is thought to be sensory related. After direct observations of Richard in his work setting, the behavior support specialist, Ms. Holmgren, determined that the job-training specialist on average provided two verbal cues per 50-minute session to prompt Richard to work. Furthermore, a preassessment of Richard's skills on performance of the job task was not conducted.

Ms. Holmgren developed a systematic intervention that included the use of a system of least-to-most prompts, a task analysis of the job task, and a method for recording data on performance that included a 15-second partial-interval scoring procedure. The intervention also used a preferred reinforcer at the completion of the task and a graduated system of increased work units over time. Ms. Holmgren also initiated a teaching method that included a workbasket that contained the drapery pulleys, a second workbasket containing component parts, an empty basket for completed pulleys, and a small plastic basket containing Richard's preferred reinforcement (his iPhone and ear buds).

Systematic instruction procedures were implemented following a baseline to determine the percentage of intervals that Richard engaged in the challenging behavior across the conditions. Upon completion of his assigned work found within his workbasket, Richard could select a song from his iPhone and listen to one song of his choice while on his break. During this time, as he listened to his music, he would rock to and fro to the music as he enjoyed his favorite activity. The results of this successful intervention are displayed in Figure 4–1. It is also interesting to point out that during the initial stages of instruction, Richard was able to complete only 10 pulleys on average with assistance. Ultimately, as a result of sustained instructional efforts, he was able to assemble 50 pulleys consecutively.

Reflective Moment

How would you modify the intervention developed by Ms. Holmgren? What could you do to increase the maintenance and generalization of Richard's newly acquired skills?

As you can see in Figure 4–1, the percent of intervals that Richard engaged in self-cleansing behavior averaged 75% of intervals observed during baseline. During the first phase of intervention (systematic instruction), Richard's behavior decreased to 55%. The final phase of the intervention (workbasket and self-reinforcement) resulted in a further decrease of Richard's self-cleansing behavior to below 20%. The results of this intervention demonstrate the efficacy of systematic instruction as a means of enhancing the delivery of instruction and as a viable method for reducing challenging behaviors that interfere with learning.

continued

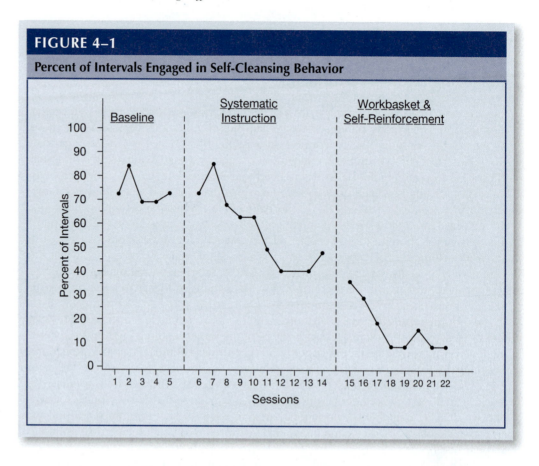

FIGURE 4–1

Percent of Intervals Engaged in Self-Cleansing Behavior

QUALITY-OF-LIFE ENRICHMENT

Much research has emerged over the past three decades on the significance of quality-of-life factors in the lives of persons with disabilities. Schalock (2000) was one of the first to initiate the study of quality of life and the important role it serves for all of us, not simply the students we serve. This concept is congruent with the philosophy that underlies positive behavioral interventions and supports. Quality-of-life factors are often sorely overlooked when designing interventions to address challenging behavior in learners. Although this area may be the most difficult area in which to have an impact as a teacher, attentiveness to the quality of life of learners is nevertheless very important. Schalock (2000) offers eight quality-of-life indicators as identified by extensive studies in the area that remain relevant today:

1. Emotional well-being
2. Interpersonal relations
3. Material well-being
4. Personal development
5. Physical well-being
6. Self-determination
7. Social inclusion
8. Rights

Schalock (2000) further addressed how these elements can be better attained through the delivery of services and supports to individuals with disabilities. One of these areas is matching persons with their environments as a method for diminishing the discrepancies between a person and his or her environment (Schalock, 2000). Promoting a good fit between an individual and his or her environment is a basic and important step to ensuring an individual's quality of life, but it can also serve as a means to prevent the occurrence of challenging behaviors. This is an example of how environments can be engineered to promote success for individual learners.

How does this approach translate to the notion of prevention through effective instruction within learning environments? As discussed in the preceding chapters, PBIS supports the engineering of environments as a critical factor in the success of individual learners and the prevention of challenging and or undesired behaviors. Teachers should be mindful to promote this relationship between learners and their learning environments. Second, teachers can seek to implement educational services and supports within their classrooms that are learner centered and inclusive of quality-of-life features. Enrichment of learning environments and programmatic efforts can result through attention being given to this very important aspect of intervention, promoting the overall well-being of the learner. Third, the resulting outcomes from such approaches can be meaningful learning outcomes for all learners, including a sense of happiness, self-determination, satisfaction, safety, and general well-being. Last, such practices can be very helpful in reducing challenging behavior in students by promoting a greater sense of belonging.

Through the material discussed in this chapter, we have discussed several key factors that directly or indirectly address the quality of life of children and youth within learning environments. As previously mentioned, a sensitivity to the learner and those antecedent variables that influence the behavior of a child or adolescent and the use of proactive assessment and intervention practices will lead to better outcomes for all concerned.

SETTING EVENTS, ANTECEDENTS, AND BEHAVIOR

All behaviors, whether desirable or challenging, are influenced by antecedents. Antecedents are also referred to as discriminative stimuli (SD), which are prompts that trigger specific behaviors. Setting events (Bijou, 1970) are broad contexts that alter antecedent–behavior relationships (Horner & Carr, 1997) and are distant to antecedents yet can be volatile when paired with the right trigger (or antecedent). Setting events often "set" the stage for problem behaviors to occur.

Carr (1994) identified three major categories of setting events: biological, environmental, and social or interpersonal. Biological setting events include such things as thirst, hunger, sleep, medication effects, and level of energy. Environmental setting events refer to the quality of the home setting, classroom, school setting, temperature, climate, dense or overcrowded work area, and level of noise in the classroom. Finally, social and interpersonal setting events include social interactions with peers or significant others in both home and school environments, friendships, and personal space. Figure 4–2 provides an example of each of these.

It is easy to understand how one or many of these setting events, when combined with a specific trigger or antecedent event, can spark the occurrence of challenging behavior. Vignette 4.4 provides a context for understanding these relationships.

FIGURE 4–2

Examples of Setting Events

Biological
- Thirsty
- Hungry
- Poor sleep, not enough sleep, too much sleep
- Drowsy, irritable from medication
- No energy or hyperactivity

Environmental
- Clutter in the home
- Not enough play materials in classroom
- Cannot see the blackboard in classroom
- Too hot or too cold
- Crowded environment
- Too loud

Social/Interpersonal
- Misunderstanding with store clerk
- Argument with peer or family member
- Personal space infringed upon

Vignette 4.4

Setting Events and Antecedents

Annie is a 12-year-old child with chronic allergies and asthma who often must rely on a variety of medications to control her condition. A sudden change in weather conditions can spark an attack that can lead to an infection such as bronchitis or, even worse, bronchial pneumonia. She has experienced recurring periods of illness in which she will arrive at school not having slept well the previous night because of her respiratory condition. To make matters even more difficult, her school building is in a declining state of disrepair and has very poor ventilation, thus resulting in building temperatures that are often varied extremes, such as too hot or too cold. On the days when she is not at her physical best and she is presented with a difficult task demand by her teacher, she will become agitated and will often get frustrated and place her head on the desk and not complete the assigned work. These behaviors do not occur on days when she has had sufficient rest and is feeling well. Thus, the setting event in this example is that her physical illness has made her sleep deprived, the antecedent is the task demand made by her teacher, and the behavior is Annie's inability to complete the task due to frustration and exhaustion. If Annie's teacher can better understand these relationships, she can utilize a behavior support strategy and alter how the task demands are given on those days when Annie is challenged by her medical condition.

Reflective Moment

- What would you do if you were the teacher in this situation?
- What are some strategies that you could try to minimize Annie's frustration?

It is important as a teacher to be sensitive toward identifying the relationships between setting events, antecedents, behaviors, and the consequences that result, often referred to as the four-term contingency. These relationships are reflected in the following diagram:

SE_____A_____B_____C
(setting event[s]—antecedent[s]—behavior[s]—consequence[s])

An illustration of this diagram, in practice, is as follows:

Jason does not go to bed early on school nights; he thus arrives at school very tired each morning (setting event); Jason's first class is rather demanding; and when his teacher places a work demand (antecedent), he refuses and often gets verbally abusive with his teacher (behavior). His teacher later takes him to the office, where he receives a suspension (consequence). Jason is negatively reinforced for his behavior as he has successfully escaped performing the work required of him by his teacher by being removed from class.

In the previous examples, we have focused on how setting events can set the stage for antecedents or triggers that can result in challenging forms of behavior. Understanding these relationships can also result in the promotion of positive forms of behavior in the learning environment as well. As an example, if the teacher can better identify the learner's strengths and the level of structure needed by the individual learner for optimal performance, then the teacher can better design effective instructional antecedents to correspond with these distinct learner characteristics. An illustration of this approach is provided in Vignette 4.5.

Vignette 4.5

Promoting Positive Learning Experiences Through the Arrangement of Instructional Antecedents

Aaron is an 8-year-old child with ADHD who is easily distracted in his classroom environment and therefore needs enhanced structure during periods of instruction. In an effort to accommodate his learning style and behavior support needs, his teacher utilizes a visual schedule at his desk containing the list of tasks to be completed in their respective order and a filing system of colored folders containing tasks listed on his schedule. Prior to the presentation of new tasks, the teacher reviews the use of Aaron's individualized schedule and color-coded filing system with him. By attending to these instructional antecedents (designing the instructional system around Aaron's learning strengths and the provision of behavior supports to minimize his distractibility), Aaron is afforded a greater likelihood of success and enhanced learning and behavior outcomes.

Reflective Moment

- What strategies would you as a teacher use in the design of instructional antecedents that would promote a learner's engagement?
- What were some of the strategies used by Aaron's teacher?

continued

It may be difficult for a teacher to identify the distant setting events associated with some behaviors displayed by their students. The teacher may often not be made aware of the events that may have occurred prior to school or before the learner has entered the classroom. However, good instructional strategies that are designed to reinforce student engagement through structuring the learning task, the classroom environment and designing relevant learning tasks can help minimize the influence of these on student behavior and learning.

METHODS USED IN THE ASSESSMENT OF ANTECEDENTS

Functional behavior assessment (FBA) has many components that assist us in the assessment of antecedents and in furthering our understanding of how they influence behavior in learners. There are several methods that a classroom teacher can use to help in the identification of antecedents and their relationship to behavior responses in learners (both positive and negative). These include the collection of descriptive data such as structured interviews, behavior rating scales, and observational data. Each method of antecedent assessment will lead to the development of hypotheses related to the design of interventions. The processes are described in the following sections.

Structured Interview

The process of collecting descriptive assessment data is initiated with the structured interview. Typically, the structured interview is completed by the classroom teacher, other instructional personnel, family members, and any significant contacts in the learner's life. The content of the structured interview seeks to identify the various elements associated with the behavior(s) of concern. These elements include a description of the behavior, patterns of occurrence or nonoccurrence of the behavior, antecedents and consequences associated with the behavior, life events that may have had a relationship to the behavior, and physical events such as medication changes or health factors that could serve as precursors to the behavior.

There are numerous examples of structured interviews that exist and several that have been adapted by school personnel to accommodate the specific needs of learners within their respective learning environments. Figure 4–3 provides an example of a structured interview form for use in a school setting.

Upon completing the structured interview with key informants, the teacher should then collate and synthesize the information. The data obtained from the interview should be analyzed to determine the patterns associated with the behavior, such as:

- A description of the target behavior
- Antecedents, or "triggers," that commonly precede the behavior
- Consequences that consistently occur following the behavior
- Life events that could account for the behavior (a sudden change, such as death of a parent or loved one, parental separation, divorce)
- Hypotheses statements related to the function or (purpose) of the behavior, causal factors, and things to consider in terms of remediation

FIGURE 4–3

Functional Assessment Interview Form

Student: _____ Date: _____

Completed by: _____

Description of the Target Behavior(s)
1. What are the specific target behaviors in observable and measurable terms?

Predictability of the Target Behavior(s)
2. Are there events (antecedents) that consistently happen prior to the behavior?
3. What typically happens after the behavior occurs (consequences)?
4. Do the target behaviors occur at predictable times during the day?
5. If you answered yes to question 4, please indicate the time periods and the activities that coincide with the occurrence of the behaviors.

Function(s) of the Target Behavior(s)
6. What are the function(s) of the target behavior(s), or what does the behavior accomplish?
7. What is the communicative intent of the target behavior(s)?

History
8. Are there any significant life events that could account for the behavior(s) exhibited?
9. Which behavior intervention methods used in the past have been demonstrated to be effective in reducing the target behavior(s)?

Setting Events
10. Are there medical/physical issues that could account for the target behavior(s)?
11. Does the occurrence of the target behavior(s) coincide with demands placed on the student in instructional settings, transition periods, or while the student is alone?
12. Is there a predictable schedule for the student during the school day?
13. What form does the schedule take (e.g., written, symbol, picture, object)?
14. Are there times and activities in which the behavior(s) does not occur?
15. Please indicate preferred reinforcers that the student enjoys (i.e., activities, tangibles).

Behavior Rating Scales

Behavior rating scales represent another tool that can be used to gather preliminary information about the specifics surrounding challenging behavior. There are numerous behavior rating scales designed to identify problem behaviors through the use of questionnaires. One instrument in particular, the Motivation Assessment Scale (MAS), is very helpful in understanding the functions associated with challenging behavior.

The MAS (Durand & Crimmins, 1988) is a relatively easy instrument to use. When combined with other sources of data, such as a structured interview and behavior observation, it can be very helpful in the identification of probable antecedents and consequences that are associated with problematic behavior. The MAS is also very helpful in the identification of the function associated with the behavior(s).

The MAS comprises 16 items presented on a Likert scale and is designed to assess the functions of challenging behavior: attention, tangible, social, and self-stimulation. The

MAS examines both antecedents and consequences. The 16 items are equally distributed across the four major functions of challenging behavior: sensory, escape, attention, and tangible. The items are then tallied, resulting in total and mean scores with the relative ranking of perceived function being the final product. Once the perceived function of the target behavior has been identified, intervention plans can result with an emphasis on the arrangement of antecedents, the teaching of positive alternative behaviors, and/or the modification of consequence events.

Emphasis is given to the development of behaviors that serve the same function as those of the challenging behavior yet are directed at allowing the individual's needs to be met through the development of appropriate behavior responses. Thus the function of the behavior is never altered; however, the form (or what the behavior looks like) is the focus of the intervention effort.

There are limitations associated with indirect forms of assessment such as behavior rating scales. These methods rely totally on informants to provide information based on memory that could be potentially limiting in terms of a respondent's accuracy. They may also encourage exaggerated responses on the part of respondents, especially when challenging behaviors are concerned.

One method that can lend greater reliability to the use of **indirect assessment** tools such as structured interviews and the MAS is the sampling of multiple respondents. This method allows synthesis of the comments or ratings across respondents, thus providing feedback in terms of the degree of similarities and consistency across raters.

The best method is use of indirect assessment methods such as rating scales as part of an assessment package along with behavior observation and other components (Miltenberger, 2015). The benefits of behavior observation as the best method for understanding the relationship of antecedents to behaviors cannot be overstated in terms of reliability. This method provides the observer with a hands-on view of the learner within the relevant setting of his or her natural environment, thus providing an understanding of the interaction that is occurring between the learner and the pertinent environmental variables. This method can, of course, be more time consuming than others, yet it lends itself to ensuring the reliability and accuracy needed to understand the issues surrounding challenging behavior.

Observational Methods

As previously described, direct observation offers many advantages when attempting to understand the events surrounding behavior, including antecedents and consequences. There are three different methods of behavior observation that are useful to consider in the assessment of antecedents associated with problematic behavior: (1) scatter-plot analysis, (2) A-B-C (antecedent–behavior–consequence) recording, and (3) interval-based recording of behavior. An additional method that has been quite useful in the assessment of antecedents is structural analysis (Stichter, Lewis, Johnson, & Trussell, 2004; Wacker, Cooper, Peck, Derby, & Berg, 1999). Structural analysis is a form of functional analysis that seeks to better understand the relationship of specific antecedent events to challenging behavior through the manipulation (i.e., the adding or removal) of these antecedents and noting the effects on the rate of behavior.

Scatter-Plot Analysis

Scatter-plot analysis (Touchette, MacDonald, & Langer, 1985) is a simple and portable method that provides information concerning the frequency, time, and setting in which the target behavior occurs. It enables us to understand the pattern of behavior over time, such as time of day in which the behavior occurs or does not occur, activities or demands associated with high frequencies of the behavior, and also activities and demands associated with an absence of the behavior. Scatter-plot analysis allows us to correlate high rates of behavior with one or more of these corresponding variables and better identify the important antecedents associated with challenging behavior. It is a relatively easy procedure to implement within educational environments and is preferred by many teachers because of its ease and utility within busy learning environments. A scatter-plot data sheet consists of a series of grids that are associated with time increments and days of the week. The time increments may vary based on the specific needs of the classroom teacher, but they generally range from 15- to 30-minute intervals. When the target behavior occurs during the designated time interval, a slash is placed in the corresponding box. If the behavior occurs multiple times during the designated time period, the box is blackened completely through, and if the behavior does not occur at all during the designated time period, the box is left blank.

Typically, scatter-plot data must be collected over a period of time such as 1 week before trends can be determined visually. Most often these trends reveal high rates of problematic behavior corresponding consistently with certain times of days and activities occurring within these time frames. An example of a scatter-plot data sheet is contained in Figure 4–4.

A scatter-plot data sheet allows the teacher to link the high rates of behaviors to specific times of day and to the activities associated with these time periods. In this example, the learner has peak periods of behavior that are associated with math and reading. The remaining portions of the day are relatively free from disruption. Given this information, the teacher can now examine the nature of those activities with the learning style and challenges associated with the learner.

In this example, the child, Peter, has a diagnosed learning disability, and math and reading are two areas that pose significant learning challenges for him. He becomes frustrated during these activities. The teacher can now use this information to examine more critically the types of learning tasks and how these tasks are presented to Peter. This type of microanalysis allows Peter's teacher to better understand the instructional antecedents that prompt Peter's work refusal behavior. She can now attempt to modify her instruction and at the same time teach Peter new behaviors that will better accommodate and redirect his frustration.

Consider This

The use of a scatter-plot assessment can assist teachers in documenting not only the frequency of a behavior but also the contextual variables that surround the occurrence of a behavior, such as the time of day the behavior occurred and the class or activity the student was engaged in.

In the example provided, Peter's outbursts are directly related to his apparent skill deficits in reading and math. Given that his behavior coincides with each of these classes, it would enable a teacher to strategize about instructional methods and curriculum changes needed to facilitate Peter's engagement in each of these areas.

A-B-C (Antecedent–Behavior–Consequence) Recording

A-B-C recording represents another more commonly used behavior observation technique. This method is most helpful and relatively practical for use by classroom teachers and instructional staff. It is also referred to as anecdotal or narrative recording.

FIGURE 4–4

Scatter-Plot Data Sheet

Name: _____   Behavior: _____

	Monday	Tuesday	Wednesday	Thursday	Friday
8:00–8:15					
8:15–8:30	✓✓✓✓	✓✓✓✓	✓✓✓	✓✓✓✓	✓✓✓
8:30–8:45		✓✓		✓✓✓	
8:45–9:00	✓✓✓	✓✓	✓✓✓✓	✓✓✓✓✓	✓✓✓✓
9:00–9:15	✓✓	✓✓✓✓	✓✓✓	✓✓	✓✓✓✓✓
9:15–9:30					
9:30–9:45					
9:45–10:00					
10:00–10:15	✓✓	✓✓✓	✓✓	✓✓	✓✓✓
10:15–10:30	✓✓✓	✓	✓✓✓	✓✓✓	✓✓✓
10:30–10:45	✓✓	✓✓✓	✓	✓✓	✓
10:45–11:00	✓			✓✓	
11:00–11:15	✓✓				✓
11:15–11:30					
11:30–11:45					
11:45–12:00					
12:00–12:15					
12:15–12:30					
12:30–12:45					
12:45–1:00					
1:00–1:15					
1:15–1:30					
1:30–1:45					
1:45–2:00					
2:00–2:15					
2:15–2:30					
2:30–2:45					
2:45–3:00					
3:00–3:15					
3:15–3:30					

A-B-C recording is conducted by selecting an observational period—for example, 20 minutes of an hour, or perhaps one short class period per day. Often, the selection of the observation period can be guided by the data from the scatter plot. Upon examining the trends found within the scatter-plot, the observer can plan to observe using A-B-C recording both during the peak times when behavior occurs at the highest frequency and also during periods in which the behavior does not occur at all. The contrasting observation periods will shed light on the antecedents and consequences that coincide with periods of high-frequency occurrences versus those of the periods in which little or no occurrences of the behavior occur.

When conducting anecdotal or A-B-C recording, the observer is interested in observing a specific learner within the context of his or her natural environment, such as the classroom or home setting. The observer attempts to be noninvasive and records the antecedents, behaviors, and consequences as they naturally occur. This tracking is done on a data sheet specifically designed for this type of recording (see Figure 4–5). It is important when conducting A-B-C recording for the observer to maintain focus and records the events as they happen in a manner that is descriptive.

Another variation of the A-B-C recording method has been suggested as well (Miltenberger, 2015; O'Neill et al., 1997). It is referred to as the *checklist method* and it involves a data sheet that lists specific antecedent, behaviors, and consequences associated with an individual. This method permits the observer to check the corresponding box when noting the occurrence of a specific antecedent, behavior, and consequence.

Interval Recording

The third method used in the A-B-C assessment is interval-based recording. Typically, a 5- to 10-second interval scoring procedure is used to note the occurrence or nonoccurrence of specific antecedents, behaviors, and consequences as they occur. There are two types of interval scoring procedures to select from: partial interval scoring or whole

FIGURE 4–5

A-B-C Recording Data Sheet

Observer: _____

Date: _____

Time: _____

Antecedent	Behavior	Consequence

interval scoring. Partial interval scoring is most commonly preferred and is most frequently cited within the literature.

When using partial **interval scoring**, the target behavior must occur during a portion of the interval to be scored as an occurrence. Whole interval recording specifies that the target behavior must occur throughout the entire interval (e.g., 5 or 10 seconds) before an occurrence is scored. There are some obvious limitations to the use of whole interval scoring within busy classrooms and learning environments. In reality, teachers have little time to conduct this level of analysis. One method that could serve to provide teachers with the information they need and allow for more detailed analysis is the use of videotape and subsequent analysis at a later time. Recording a video of the interactions within the classroom or learning environment provides a permanent product that can be later scored. See Miltenberger, Rapp, and Long (1999) for an excellent description of how to use video analysis for scoring behaviors in applied settings such as the classroom, home, or community. They describe how the use of video recordings allows behaviors to be scored using the automated counters commonly found on video cameras and playback software, thus making the analysis much easier, as the intervals on the screen correspond with those on the data sheet. Figure 4–6 serves as an example of an interval scoring data sheet.

FIGURE 4–6

Interval Recording Data Sheet

Name: _____   + = on task

Behavior: _____   − = off task

Date: _____

Time						Interval							Percentage
1:00	+	+	+	−	+	−	−	−	+	+	−	+	−
	−	+	−	−	+	+	+						55%

FIGURE 4–7

Interval Data Sheet with Codes

Observer: _____

Date: _____

Conditions   **Behaviors**

P = play   + = hair pulling

I = instruction   ✓ = screaming

A = alone   − = nonoccurrence

Time	Condition											Interval
10:05	I	+	+	−	−	−	✓	✓	+	+	−	−

While using an interval recording procedure, the teacher can develop a checklist of probable antecedents, behaviors, and consequences specific to a particular learner and use the checklist while conducting an analysis of videotaped sessions (Miltenberger, 2015). Another variation is the use of a code sheet that reflects the specific antecedents, behaviors, and consequences relevant to a specific setting. An illustration of this type of data sheet is contained in Figure 4–7. The data sheet reflects specific antecedent, behavior, and consequence variables related to the instruction of a young child with autism.

Structural Analysis

Structural analysis (Wacker et al., 1999) has been used to evaluate the effects of various antecedent conditions on the behavior of children within clinical settings (Wheeler, Carter, Mayton, & Thomas, 2002). It represents a form of functional analysis (the experimental manipulation of antecedent and consequence events to note their effects on behavior). In structural analysis, various antecedents are presented and removed so that the effects of these manipulations on behavior can be noted (Wacker et al., 1999). Antecedent variables include how tasks are presented, the number of tasks presented, the type of instructions used, and in general the instructional delivery. In using structural analysis, we hope to identify the specific antecedent conditions that trigger the target behavior. Conversely, we also hope to identify antecedent conditions that promote positive behavior in the learner. Structural analysis serves as a mechanism to experimentally validate functional relationships (i.e., cause and effect) between antecedents and behavior.

The obvious limitation associated with this type of assessment is that it requires a level of control (i.e., ability to manage all the variables to the degree of experimental control that is needed to validate results) that is typically not possible within educational settings. In spite of its portability within traditional learning environments, it has been demonstrated to be effective within home settings and shows promise in the assessment of antecedents that frequent problematic behavior.

Points to Remember

- Antecedent assessment is important for understanding those factors that trigger challenging behaviors in learners.
- The most commonly used methods used in the assessment of antecedents include:

    1. Structured interview
    2. Scatter-plot analysis
    3. A-B-C recording
    4. Interval recording
    5. Structural analysis

- Antecedent assessment assists in the identification of variables that influence challenging behavior, thus providing essential information used in the development of proactive intervention strategies.
- An antecedent that serves to trigger problematic behavior in learners may include physical, social/emotional, environmental, and instructional components.

SUMMARY

This chapter examined the relationship between setting events and antecedents and challenging behavior in learners. You learned that there are three major categories of setting events: biological, environmental, and social/interpersonal. Biological setting events include thirst, hunger, sleep, the effects of medication, and fatigue factors. Environmental setting events involve factors such as the quality of environments (temperature, density, noise, climate, and design). And social/interpersonal setting events address the quality and scope of social relationships, friendships, social interactions, and personal space factors.

The first section of the chapter addressed the importance of preventing challenging behavior through the modification of instructional antecedents. Research conducted by Dunlap and colleagues (1995) and subsequent research conducted by Kern and Dunlap (1998) was highlighted. The rationale for understanding the relationship between instructional antecedents and problematic behavior was described, and methods for prevention were explored. Other important areas that were introduced include the use of environmental intervention strategies aimed at the enhancement of learning environments and the use of instructional intervention procedures as a means of preventing problematic behavior.

Instructional interventions include preinstructional considerations. These considerations occur prior to the implementation of specific strategies and are designed to provide a better understanding of individual learning strengths, challenges, and general characteristics of the learner. Also mentioned were task design (how tasks are selected and designed), task delivery (how instruction is given to the learner), and quality-of-life enhancements such as the development of self-determination skills and the design of environments that interface with the needs and choices of the individual.

The assessment of antecedents was also presented with a number of methods for assessing antecedents being described. These methods include the use of a structured interview as used in a functional assessment of behavior. The purpose of the interview is the identification of target behaviors and the development of hypothesis statements related to the causal factors associated with problematic behavior. The use of other indirect forms of assessment such as behavior rating scales was also described. As pointed out in the chapter, the use of indirect forms of assessment used in isolation is considered a limitation, given their reliance on secondary sources for information concerning a learner's behavior and not within the context that the behaviors occur. The MAS was recommended as a method for generating interview data relating to the functions of challenging behavior, especially concerning learners with more severe disabilities.

The section on antecedent assessment also described observational methods such as scatter-plot analysis, A-B-C recording, and interval-based recording and the merits of each for use within classroom settings. Scatter-plot analysis represents a relatively easy-to-use method for determining both the frequency of occurrence of target behaviors as well as the time of day in which they occur and more contextual features that are related to their occurrence, such as the teacher and content area with which they correspond. A-B-C or anecdotal recording was reviewed as a method for identifying antecedents, behavior, and consequences using a narrative recording format. The use of interval-based recording was also described as a means by which to gather observational data related to antecedents and consequences related to behavior. In addition, the use of video analysis as a practical method for the analysis of behavior was discussed. Finally, structural analysis was described as an experimental method for determining functional relationships between antecedents and problematic behavior with discussion on its potential applications. The value of structural analysis in the experimental analysis of antecedents that precipitate behavior is noteworthy; however, the obvious question mark has been the utility of this procedure within classrooms and applied learning environments.

ACTIVITIES TO EXTEND YOUR LEARNING

1. Conduct an assessment of antecedents within an applied setting and use the following methods: (a) structured interview or (b) the MAS, and at least one of the following: (c) scatter-plot analysis, (d) A-B-C recording, or (e) interval-based recording. Compare and contrast each method in terms of its utility within the learning environment you selected and the data derived from each approach.
2. Describe one antecedent management strategy that you would consider using within your classroom to address a specific challenging behavior, and present your approach to your classmates. Provide the rationale behind your selection.
3. Discuss numerous methods of preventing challenging behavior in learning environments, and develop a list of strategies that you could employ as a teacher.
4. Conduct an assessment of a selected learning environment and identify methods for enhancing the learning environment with an emphasis on identifying and controlling for potential antecedents.

5. Conduct a literature search on one of the antecedent management strategies described in the chapter, and develop a resource file of those references for future reference when teaching.

6. Brainstorm how antecedent management strategies could be developed and used schoolwide to prevent discipline problems.

FURTHER READING AND EXPLORATION

1. Consult the Positive Behavior Supports website at www.pbis.org and research any references to antecedent management strategies.

2. Consult the National Center on Response to Intervention's website at www.rti4success.org.

Understanding Functional Behavior Assessment

CONCEPTS TO UNDERSTAND

After reading this chapter, you should be able to:

- Describe the importance of functional behavior assessment (FBA) in understanding behavior.
- List and discuss assumptions concerning challenging behavior.
- Describe the components of FBA including: identifying and operationally defining target behaviors, conducting behavioral observations, interpreting the data and generating function-based hypotheses.
- Define functional analysis and its application when needed as part of the FBA process.
- List, describe, and recommend how data obtained from the FBA can be used in the development of a behavior support plan (BSP).

KEY TERMS

A-B-C analysis (anecdotal recording)   Frequency recording

Behavior Support Plan (BSP)   Functional behavior assessment (FBA)

Challenging behavior   Interval recording

Duration recording   Scatter-Plot Analysis

Event recording   Target behavior

Functional behavior assessment (FBA) is a method that continues to be widely used in the assessment of challenging behavior within schools and educational settings since the 1997 Reauthorization of IDEA. This piece of legislation mandated that educational teams use FBA and positive behavioral interventions and supports (PBIS) in the assessment and development of interventions for students whose behaviors impede their learning and or the learning of others (IDEA, 1997). This mandate has been strengthened under the last authorization of IDEA in 2004, which stated that the IEP team must consider the use of positive behavioral intervention and support as the intervention of choice. One can assume that the FBA therefore is the starting point for the design of PBIS in that a reliable behavioral assessment is required to ascertain the reason for the behavior and contributing factors that both trigger and maintain the behavior and finally for determining how to effectively design a **behavior support plan (BSP)** to address the concerns in question.

The FBA is a multistep process that is designed to identify causal factors associated with challenging behavior and to generate a "best guess" or hypotheses about the functions (purpose) of challenging behaviors and to develop possible interventions aimed at replacing such behaviors. We have learned that challenging behaviors do serve a function for the individuals who engage in them from research as early as Skinner (1974), who stated that all behavior had a purpose and promoted the analysis of this throughout his research in the area of operant conditioning. Subsequent research by Carr (1977) examined hypotheses on the motivation of self-injurious behavior and also on escape-related behaviors (Carr & Newsom, 1985) in persons with developmental disabilities.

This line of research extended further as Iwata, Dorsey, Slifer, Bauman, and Richman (1982) examined the function of behavior related to self-injurious behavior (SIB) in an original study that established the basic model for conducting what is referred to as functional analysis. Their study presented a new and innovative model for determining functional relationships between self-injurious behavior and specific environmental events. This study and subsequent investigations over time have examined these methods and provided insight into the factors that contribute to challenging behaviors and the functions that these behaviors serve. As a result, we understand that challenging behavior is not maladaptive; rather, it does serve a purpose or function for the individual, such as attempting to gain attention or to meet other needs, whereas maladaptive behavior fails to do so (Carr, Langdon, & Yarbrough, 1999; Dunlap & Fox, 2011).

Functions associated with problem behavior can include one or more of the following, the need for (a) tangible reinforcement, (b) attention, (c) sensory reinforcement, and (d) escape (Carr & Durand, 1985; Horner, Sprague, O'Brien, & Heathfield, 1990; O'Reilly, 1997). Challenging forms of behavior can often coincide with communication difficulties and can represent a form of communicative intent generally around obtaining a basic need such as gaining access to food or a desired toy and/or seeking attention from others. Often something as simple as "I need help" might be communicated with a more challenging form of behavior such as a form of aggression like hitting that has occurred largely out of frustration. Another example is an individual's need for escape from an activity that he or she finds unpleasant yet is unable to communicate in a more functional manner, such as "I need for a break," or "could you please help me?" Given these basic human needs paired with skill limitations on the part of the learner, such as in the area of communication, challenging behavior results.

The purpose of this chapter is to describe the components and process of FBA. The chapter also explores the applications of this methodology across learners and learning environments and how teachers can better use functional behavior assessment to understand the behavior of children and youth and how the information derived from this process can be used in the development of meaningful interventions.

THE IMPORTANCE OF FUNCTIONAL BEHAVIOR ASSESSMENT

Functional behavior assessment (FBA) has been identified as an effective practice in the assessment of **challenging behavior** as recognized by the 2004 Reauthorization of IDEA. The reauthorization of this legislation first mandated the use of FBA and PBIS to address chronic and excessive problem behavior (Dunlap & Kinkaid, 2001; Bruni, Drevon, Hixon, Wyse, Corcoran, & Fursa, 2017). As indicated by Yell, Shriner, and Katsiyannis (2006) a manifestitation determination is required under the IDEA Reauthorization of 2004 when considering the exclusion of a student with a disability that results in a change of placement. As Yell and colleagues (2006) pointed out, the law states that:

> a child with a disability who is removed from his or her current placement because of weapons, drugs, or infliction of injury or because of violation of school code— irrespective of whether the behavior is determined to be a manifestation of the child's disability—must continue to receive educational services that enable the child to continue to participate in the general education curriculum and receive the services required in the IEP. The student should also receive a functional behavior assessment, behavioral intervention services and modifications to address the behavior violation so it does not recur. (p. 18)

In the case of a manifestation determination that a child has violated a code of student conduct or if a violation has involved weapons, illicit drugs, or infliction of serious bodily injury, the student's IEP team must convene within 10 school days and determine whether the conduct was directly related to the child's disability or was the conduct due to the LEA's (Local Education Agency) failure to implement the IEP. If the conduct is deemed to be a manifestation of the child's disability, then the IEP team should conduct an FBA and develop a BIP, or behavioral intervention plan, for the student (Yell et al., 2006).

What does functional behavior assessment refer to? Functional behavior assessment was defined by Sugai and colleagues (2000) as a "systematic process of identifying problem behaviors and the events that (a) reliably predict occurrences and nonoccurrences of those behaviors, and (b) maintain the behaviors over time" (p. 137). One important point to understand about the terms *functional assessment* and *functional behavior assessment* is that they are synonymous.

The FBA combines both direct and indirect forms of assessment and is conducted within natural environments such as the classroom or home and relies on multiple data collection methods using indirect methods such as file review and interview and direct methods such as behavioral observation. An FBA is completed through a systematic process of data collection consisting of interviews and observations within the learner's relevant environments, including classroom settings, home, and community. The data collection process usually includes a structured interview paired with observational data collected within natural environments to gain a contextual understanding of the behavior in relevant environments, which is important in that the FBA will assist us in understanding how environmental variables influence problem behavior.

The goal of an FBA is to understand the factors that occasion or reinforce problematic behavior and the subsequent function(s) that this behavior serves for the individual. This information allows educational personnel to generate hypotheses concerning the relationship between these events and behavior. In turn, the outcomes of FBA should translate into effective learner-centered interventions that are also function based and designed to ameliorate the problem behavior. In contrast, traditional forms of behavioral assessment have often relied exclusively on secondary reporting through the use of indirect methods such as interviews, checklists, and rating scales to identify the frequency and severity of problem behavior. Behavior rating scales have been frequently used in school settings, because of the high volume of children and youth served within these environments and the ease and efficiency of completing these types of instruments. The main limitation of these methods is that without behavioral observation measures, they are incomplete and do not provide an accurate portrayal of the behavior within relevant environmental contexts such as the classroom or home settings. In short, there still appears to be a great degree of variability in how FBAs are carried out across state and local education agencies, perhaps in large part as a result of teacher workload and or a lack of consistent and agreed-upon policy within school districts.

This point was reinforced in an earlier study conducted by Weber, Killu, Derby, and Barretto (2005) of state education agencies (SEAs) throughout all 50 United States to determine whether they had developed resources and guidelines for completing FBAs. Weber and colleagues used 14 items identified as standard practice for completing FBAs that were derived from the extant research and from resources obtained through the U.S. Department of Education's OSEP Center on Positive Behavioral Interventions and Supports (1999). The 14 components were: operational definition of the target behavior, review of student records, checklist data, student interviews, other interviews, team meetings, direct observation with no manipulation, scatter-plot analysis (Touchette, MacDonald, & Langer, 1985), A-B-C analysis, the Functional Analysis Observation Form (O'Neill et al., 2015), reinforcer assessment, ecological context, development of hypotheses, and analog analysis. The results from this study indicated that 41 states supplied information, 7 states did not have resources identified, and 2 states elected to not participate. Of the states that responded, a majority indicated that they required teachers to operationally define target behaviors and conduct behavioral observations as part of the FBA, and only 18 states provided the researchers with reference or training materials that were used by their respective SEAs. Weber and colleagues (2005) surmised from their data that for the most part, SEAs were not using scientific-based practices in conducting FBAs based on the quality of responses received from study participants. One can somewhat understand these findings given this study was conducted shortly after the mandate to incorporate FBA's in the schools. However, more recently Strickland-Cohen and colleagues (2016) confirmed the need of many school districts to receive technical assistance and support in developing the capacity to perform FBA's in the schools. This finding is quite disconcerting in that there remains less than a consensus in terms of understanding these requisite skills when one considers how vital the functional assessment process is in the identification and design of meaningful interventions aimed at addressing challenging behaviors. As the field of special education has evolved more into the use of evidence-based practices it is paramount that we continue to promote quality assurance in conducting FBAs across teachers, school psychologists, and related services personnel. The development of policies and procedures within state and local educational agencies for conducting FBAs and in developing BIPs is therefore needed to carry out this mandate with any degree of credibility.

The adoption of FBA procedures continues to be a challenge for many school systems, even though the initial mandate is now many years old. These problems have stemmed largely from limited training and experience early on in the development of these procedures and partly from philosophical differences in how challenging behavior has been traditionally viewed within these settings. Most educational systems have maintained discipline policies that are punitive in their response to challenging behavior and view such behavior as intolerable, as evidenced by the "zero-tolerance" policies commonly found within schools. There are notable exceptions, especially given the growth of schoolwide PBIS, with approximately 21,000 school systems participating nationwide (Horner & Sugai, 2015). Though many of these participating schools have done outstanding jobs with implementation of schoolwide PBIS gaps still remain in the implementation of these services within schools, most notably the issues of fidelity—that is, ensuring that policies and practices are implemented as intended and ensuring the sustainability of these practices within programs (Horner & Sugai, 2015). It is important that evidence-based practices in the area of SWPBIS are implemented with the same degree of consistency across schools before inferences from the data can be used to make any accurate determination about the efficacy of this model at scale (Kincaid, Childs, Blasé, & Wallace, 2007). As Kincaid and colleagues (2007) have indicated, this is not an easy task given the multiple variables involved. An important factor in the adoption and implementation of PBIS within school settings across the three-tiered model (individual, classroom, and schoolwide) is the degree to which teachers, administrators, and related services personnel understand the philosophy and methodology associated with PBIS. Yet models for evaluating the implementation of schoolwide PBIS have been developed and refined (Algozzine et al., 2010), so it is hoped that there will be more data available on these implementations in the future for consumption by researchers and practitioners.

Along these lines, Horner and Sugai (2015) in a retrospective analysis of PBIS over the past 20-years have identified the following components as being essential for maximizing PBIS. These are (a) the emphasis on core features and the use of evidence-based strategies, (b) developing systems of support within school settings to support the use of EBP's, (c) the use of data for informed decision making, and (d) evaluating the process of implementation and refining these practices. More empirical study of these elements is needed to fully ascertain their impact on educational and social outcomes.

With respect to the use of functional behavior assessment to better understand challenging behavior, the merits of the FBA process are many. FBA is aimed at understanding the variables that contribute to challenging behavior and gathering information that lends itself to the development of effective interventions through the BIP. The FBA provides a constructive framework for understanding challenging behavior and addressing these problems from a solutions standpoint. Such a viewpoint is necessary to promote meaningful change. Counter to this philosophy is the reactive model (responding to problem behavior after the fact) is too frequently used within classrooms and schools, resulting in children who fail to exhibit desired behavior being viewed as the problem, without any concern as to why these behaviors occur or to contextual variables that influence these responses in children. The burden most often falls entirely on the learner within such a mindset. On the contrary, FBA offers teachers and families research-based practices that are user friendly and effective in understanding behavior and the factors that influence it and in promoting solutions-based responses designed to address these challenges from a win-win perspective.

ASSUMPTIONS CONCERNING CHALLENGING BEHAVIOR

Frequently, when professionals encounter learners who display challenging behavior, they conjecture about the causes of these behaviors; this conjecture often translates into false assumptions and/or generalizations about the learner. This approach is obviously less than professional approach; many times, it can result in blame for why a particular child has such difficult behavior to manage. Often, the child or family is made the scapegoat. This type of practice is wrong and counterproductive, as it offers nothing in terms of a solution to address the challenging behavior. Again, one of the merits of PBIS and the use of the FBA as a starting point is that it is solution based.

Chandler and Dahlquist (2002) addressed this problem and categorized the negative assumptions that are often made about children with challenging behavior into five major areas: (1) the bad child (the child misbehaves because he is bad), (2) the child's disability (problem behavior occurs as a direct result of the child's disability), (3) the bad family (problem behaviors are the result of ineffective parenting and poor family dynamics), (4) the bad home (problem behaviors occur because of problems in the home), and (5) trauma suffered earlier in the child's life (the child's behavior can be attributed to some form of trauma, such as abuse, neglect, or sexual abuse). Many factors influence challenging behavior, such as previous learning, stress within the home or family, academic or social skill challenges, and physical factors, to name just a few. It is important to view challenging behavior from a comprehensive perspective and to take into account the many variables that can trigger and maintain such responses. Care must be taken to consider all these factors if we are to be effective in the delivery of PBIS.

As with PBIS, the FBA process reinforces the belief that all behavior is purposeful, including challenging behavior. This statement is especially true for young children and individuals with disabilities who are often challenged by developmental limitations that may prevent them from effectively communicating their needs to caregivers. If caregivers and family members are insensitive to these attempts on the part of the individual, frustration ensues, and challenging behavior often follows. It is extremely important for parents and professionals to recognize these communicative attempts as a means of preventing challenging behavior. For example, when a child cries or has tantrums, these behaviors may result from increased levels of frustration that have not been addressed or anticipated by caregivers, fatigue on the part of the child, or frustration at not being able to obtain his or her basic needs. Sensitivity to understanding causal factors and being mindful of communicative intent are core values found within PBIS.

Consider This

- Does challenging behavior have communicative intent for many children with disabilities and represent an attempt on the part of the learner to communicate a need? Think of some examples from your own experience.

Behavior is not only purposeful but may also represent a lack of congruence between the demand being placed on the learner and the skill limitations they experience. For learners with disabilities, challenging behaviors should not be viewed as abnormal responses; rather, these behaviors reflect the skill limitations frequently experienced by the learner and a lack of sensitivity on the part of the environment (Durand, 1990). This point was emphasized by Demchak and Bossert (1996), who, in a synthesis of the research on FBA, offered the following principles concerning challenging behavior: (a) challenging behaviors serve a specific purpose or function for the individual, (b) challenging behaviors have communicative intent, (c) challenging behaviors are directly related to events in the environment that influence or reinforce such behaviors, and (d) a single challenging behavior can serve multiple functions for an individual.

FBA is a process that seeks to understand these behaviors and the factors that underlie them so that effective interventions can be designed. The goal of PBIS is to promote supportive environments that place emphasis on engineering learning environments for student success, the teaching of replacement behaviors that increase the learner's options, and intervention practices that address the overall quality of life of the individual.

COMPONENTS OF FUNCTIONAL BEHAVIOR ASSESSMENT

As previously stated, the FBA is a multistep process. The basic components of an FBA consist of: (a) gathering descriptive information or data concerning the target behavior through a structured interview and or use of behavior rating scales, (b) conducting behavioral observations to determine the antecedents and consequences associated with the target behavior and any patterns that might exist, (c) formulating hypotheses related to the function(s) of the behavior and variables that are contributing to the behavior, and, if necessary, (d) conducting a functional analysis consisting of systematic manipulations of antecedent and consequence variables to validate their relationship to the behavior and also to confirm the function of the behavior (Demchak & Bossert, 1996; O'Neill et al., 2015).

It is important when working within classrooms and schools to consider the portability of these interventions so as to enable classroom and school personnel to use them to the fullest extent. A common criticism of researchers is that they do not consider the demands of the "real world." In some cases, this statement may be true. However, one of the most important things to do as a teacher is to fully use the array of available instructional and behavioral support tools. PBIS provides an array of approaches for teachers and other professionals to consider; there are times when adapting some of these tools will be necessary given the specifics of one's assignment as a teacher. Important points to remember when conducting a functional behavior assessment are: (a) attempt to follow a protocol that is consistent with what we know to be evidence-based practice recognizing that if you abridge these procedures, you may not be able to get a complete and/or accurate understanding of what is occurring; (b) creatively explore and consider all options for support and assistance from paraprofessionals and or other colleagues such as school psychologists when conducting data collection during the FBA process; (c) decide on a plan and data gathering procedures that are—above all—manageable within your current classroom setting; and (d) recognize that data is required to make informed decisions that will result in the best instructional and or behavioral supports needed to promote learner success.

Identifying and Defining Target Behaviors

The initial step of a functional behavior assessment is identifying and defining the **target behavior** of concern. The best method to do so is a structured interview. The structured interview should be conducted with relevant individuals in the learner's life, such as the child's teacher, teaching assistants, principal, parents, and family. There are various models of the structured interview available within the literature; in short, it should include the following questions:

- What time of day does the behavior typically occur?
- How often does the behavior occur?
- Does the behavior coincide with specific events such as particular classes or academic or social activities?

- Are there antecedent events that consistently coincide with occurrences of the behavior?
- What typically happens after the behavior has occurred?
- What does the behavior accomplish for the individual?
- What is the communicative intent of the behavior?
- Are there significant life events that could account for a change in behavior?
- Are there any medical or physical problems that could be contributing to the behavior?
- Is there a predictable schedule for the learner each day?
- Is the learning environment pleasant and safe?
- Are classroom expectations clear and consistent?

Once the structured interview has been conducted, the results should be compared and contrasted across raters resulting in the identification of the target behavior, characteristics of the behavior, probable antecedents and consequences associated with the behavior, and other relevant points. Behavior rating scales might also be used in conjunction with the structured interview, as previously described in Chapter 4. Another option is a student-assisted interview. The student-assisted functional assessment interview developed by Kern, Dunlap, Clarke, and Childs (1994) is an assessment aimed at identifying student preferences in terms of school content areas such as reading, math, and spelling and also how students perceive various types of tasks and whether they feel they receive adequate attention or reinforcement for performance. This form of assessment is most conducive to understanding triggers within the environment and general perceptions about academic content, perceived strengths and challenges respective to such content, and how reinforcing consequences (or lack thereof) are viewed from the learner's perspective.

Upon completing the structured interview, probable target behaviors are then identified. Target behaviors should be defined in terms that are measurable and observable so that data collection can occur and there is reliable agreement among professionals on what the target behavior looks like. When identifying the target behavior, it is important to be specific in your description, as in the following example.

Effective Behavioral Definitions

- When presented with a written task, Laura pushes the materials aside and place her head on her desk.
- Emily manipulates assigned task materials consistent with their use.
- Brenda wipes with a sponge both the front and back of each cafeteria tray and then rinses each side before sending it through the dishwasher.
- Jacob's competing behaviors are defined as verbal or physical aggression, including name calling and slapping, noncompliance with teacher requests (as evidenced by refusal to comply with teacher directives), and tantrums when presented with a task demand.

These definitions are characterized by a description of specific behaviors that can be identified and measured by observers. The final example shows how a class of related behaviors can be grouped for purposes of data collection. Several behaviors are referred to as competing behaviors or behaviors that compete negatively with instruction. Often, teachers within busy classrooms will employ this strategy if there is more than one target behavior of concern, provided that these behaviors are related. If there are multiple target behaviors that cannot be grouped, prioritize them by their level of severity. If certain behaviors pose an eminent risk or threat to the safety of the individual or others, then that behavior should take priority over others. Contrast the previously stated examples with the following example.

Ineffective Behavioral Definitions

- Bob will behave in class.
- Julie will be kind to others during recess.
- Josh will be compliant during classroom instruction.
- Sandra will wait her turn during instruction.

These examples are vague and ambiguous. The reader is left with questions about what the desired behaviors really consist of. These examples also fail to provide the needed detail for an observer to reliably and accurately measure and observe the behaviors.

Conducting Behavior Observations

As discussed in Chapter 4, behavioral observations are necessary for understanding the relationship between behavior and environmental events. They provide us with a context, in that we personally witness the behavior in the setting of the natural environment. Observations provide us with baseline data so that we can document the severity of the problem behavior (Dunlap et al., 1993). Behavioral observations are initiated after the structured interview is conducted and consist of the following methods for collecting data on the target behavior.

Anecdotal Recording or A-B-C Recording

A-B-C analysis, a type of **anecdotal recording**, is a form of data collection effective for identifying: (a) the antecedent variables that serve as triggers for the behavior, (b) the actual behaviors exhibited by the learner in response to these triggers, and (c) the consequences that are maintaining these behaviors.

Frequency or Event Recording

Frequency or **event recording** is used to determine how frequently a learner engages in a behavior. It is often used by teachers within classroom settings because of its relative ease for use within these busy environments. Frequency or event recording is most effective when the behavior has a clear beginning and end that can be distinguished. This method of data collection can also be paired with permanent product recording. Permanent product recording is useful in classroom settings as it involves collecting work samples (or a permanent product) from learners. These work samples can include homework assignments, writing samples, and in-class work assignments. Frequency or event recording can be coupled with this method to monitor how frequently a student completes homework or in-class assignments and hands them in to the teacher.

Frequency data is typically converted to rate, which is calculated by taking the frequency or number of times that a behavior occurs and dividing it by the amount of time the behavior was observed (see Figure 5–1).

An example of calculating the rate of behavior follows. The frequency of Richard's out-of-seat behavior during a 6-hour school day totalled eight times. Here is how the teacher would calculate the rate of his behavior:

Frequency of out-of-seat behavior = 8 times

Total observation time = 6 hours

Frequency ÷ time = rate, 1.3 per hour

FIGURE 5–1

Frequency/Event Recording Data Sheet

Student _____   Observer _____

Target Behavior _____

Date	Start Time	End Time	Frequency of Occurrence	Total

When using frequency/event recording, the following points should be remembered:

- Select an observation time that is consistent in time length so that data can be easily computed.
- Select behaviors that have a clear beginning and end.

Scatter-Plot Recording

This type of analysis (Touchette et al., 1985) is an effective method for measuring not only the frequency of the behavior but also the pattern of these behaviors, such as setting, time of day, presence or absence of certain people, an activity, or a contingency of reinforcement. Use scatter-plot data in 15-minute intervals or less throughout the course of the day and record the frequency of the behavior. The data is then transferred to a scatter chart (see Chapter 4), and the code is used to designate the frequency of the behavior. The code indicates whether the behavior occurred at a high, low, or zero frequency. Another option commonly used by teachers to simplify the process is to record slash marks within the 15-minute interval and count the frequency of occurrence of the target behavior.

Duration Recording

Duration recording is used to determine the length of time that a student engaged in a behavior. Duration recording involves making a notation of when the behavior begins and ends and computing the amount of time that has elapsed from beginning to end (see Figure 5–2).

Interval Recording

The **interval recording** method involves breaking down an observation period into smaller and equal intervals. These include whole interval and partial interval. Whole interval recording involves noting the occurrence of a behavior with a plus (+) if the behavior occurs throughout the entire interval and a minus (−) if it does not. Partial interval recording, on the other hand, would score an occurrence of the behavior (+) if it occurred at any point during the interval and a nonoccurrence (−) if it did not occur at all during the interval (see Figure 5–3).

FIGURE 5–2

Duration Recording Data Sheet

Student _____ Observer _____

Target Behavior _____

Date	Start Time	End Time	Total Duration

Momentary Time Sampling

The **momentary time sampling** method of data collection is similar to interval record-ing in that it breaks a large period of time into smaller time units; however, unlike the interval recording methods previously described, less time is required of the teacher in carrying out the procedure. Momentary time sampling requires that a teacher observe a student at the end of an interval and record an occurrence (+) or nonoccurrence (−). Vignette 5.1 provides an example of this method of data collection.

FIGURE 5–3

Interval Recording Data Sheet

Student _____ Observer _____

Target Behavior _____

Interval Length _____

INTERVALS

1	2	3	4	5	6	7	8	9	10

Vignette 5.1

Momentary Time Sampling

Mr. Harrison, a secondary transition teacher, spends much of his day in the community monitoring the performance of his students in various community job settings. His most recent supported employment placement involves Peter, a young man age 17 with developmental disabilities, who is employed at a local pizza restaurant. Peter's job is to load the commercial dishwasher each shift; to complete the task, he must work at a steady rate without stopping. Mr. Harrison wants to assess his progress in staying engaged in his work task and will use momentary time sampling to collect task engagement data. Mr. Harrison begins by observing Peter at the end of each 1-minute interval and continues for a 20-minute period. At the end of the 20 minutes, he examines the data. He notes that Peter was engaged in performing his task for 14 of the 20 observations. Mr. Harrison converts this to a percentage by taking the 14 occurrences and dividing it by 20, the total number occurrences, and then multiplying it by 100, thus equaling 70% ($14/20 = 0.7 \times 100 = 70\%$). Mr. Harrison can now graph Peter's percent of task engagement for that day (see the following figure).

Student Peter Smith _____   Observer Mr. Harrison _____

Target Behavior Task engagement _____

Interval Length 1 minute _____

INTERVALS

1	2	3	4	5	6	7	8	9	10
+	+	+	−	+	+	+	−	+	+

11	12	13	14	15	16	17	18	19	20
−	−	−	+	+	+	+	+	+	−

Reflective Moment

Why is it important for the teacher to collect performance data on Peter's level of task engagement? How would you use such data to improve Peter's performance?

It is important that teachers select an observational method that fits comfortably within their schedule so that they will be amenable to it. A simple rule of thumb for teachers to consider when in the data process is to be consistent when conducting behavior observations so that comparisons can be made across observations. Data should be taken for a minimum of 1 week, because at this point trends in the data will be most likely to appear. O'Neill et al. (2015) recommended gathering data for 2 to 5 days or until a minimum of 10 to 15 occurrences of behavior have been documented.

Consider This

Many teachers often remark that they feel constrained when it comes to having the necessary amount of time to collect data on challenging behavior. It is important to remember that indeed there is an initial investment of time on the front end, but with persistence and the selection of appropriate data collection methods, the investment will be worth it over time for both you and the learner.

UNDERSTANDING THE DATA AND FORMULATING HYPOTHESES

At the conclusion of the FBA, the data are summarized and hypotheses statements are generated regarding the environmental events associated with the behavior and the function(s) of these behaviors. Interventions are then developed that address the hypotheses and whether there are consistent triggers that elicit the target behavior. Finally, the consequences following the behavior should be examined to ascertain whether they maintain the response. Figure 5–4 shows examples of hypotheses culminating from FBAs.

FIGURE 5–4

FBA Hypotheses Statements

Student:	Jacob	*Grade Level:* 3
Target Behavior:	Refusal to Complete Assigned Work	
FBA Components:	Structured Interview	
	A-B-C Analysis	
	Scatter-Plot Analysis	

Hypothesis: When Jacob is presented with worksheets and prompted to complete them, he fails to make any attempts at completing his assignments, and upon receiving a second prompt from his teacher, he turns away and ignore the teacher. The teacher then attends to Jacob, thus providing him with negative attention.

Function:	Attention
	Escape/Avoidance

Intervention Strategies: These include conducting a criterion-referenced assessment to determine whether Jacob can indeed perform the work he is being asked to do or if he has a skill deficit in this area. Second, modify the task by presenting fewer problems and worksheets at one time, use a red light/green light card on each student's desk, and instruct the students to display red on their card if they need teacher assistance and green if they are not in need of teacher assistance as a method of antecedent management. Teach Jacob the necessary skill requisites for task completion and also how to appropriately seek teacher assistance. Finally, use redirection techniques if Jacob engages in work-refusal behavior and provide him with differential reinforcement for attempts at task engagement and immediate verbal praise for task attempts and completion.

Student:	Sharon	*Grade Level:* 7
Target Behavior:	Cursing in Class	
FBA Components:	Structured Interview	
	A-B-C Analysis	
	Scatter-Plot Analysis	

continued

Hypothesis: Sharon frequently curses in class. This behavior coincides with teacher-delivered instruction or when assignments are given. The behavior consists of an impulsive outburst that results in laughter from other students and a reprimand from the teacher, including a verbal warning that if Sharon persists she will be sent to the principal's office.

Function: Attention

Intervention Strategies: Teach Sharon how to appropriately communicate her frustrations when in class. Use a self-recording form for Sharon's talk-outs and establish goals for changing the behavior over time. Pair this approach with a point structure for appropriate behavior and a plan for redeeming the points. Consequence-based strategies include the use of differential reinforcement in the form of teacher attention for appropriate communication and consistent consequences for engaging in the behavior, such as point loss. Develop a point system for the entire class for appropriate classroom communication and conduct as a means of promoting a positive peer culture.

Student:	Ray	*Grade Level:* HS/CDC
Target Behavior:	Rocking and Hand Flapping	
FBA Components:	Structured Interview	
	Motivation Assessment Scale	
	A-B-C Analysis	

Hypothesis: During functional skills training while in the classroom, Ray will frequently engage in rocking and hand flapping if he is not actively engaged in an activity.

Function: Sensory Stimulation

Intervention Strategies: Provide Ray a picture schedule of his daily activities so that he can anticipate his daily routine. Provide instruction on new tasks, and develop a systematic method of structuring tasks so that Ray can work independently on maintaining the skills he has already learned. Enrich his environment with new opportunities for learning (novel skills or routines), and allow him opportunities for choice within his daily routine. Redirect him prior to the onset of the stereotypical behavior, and provide intermittent verbal reinforcement in the form of praise for task engagement.

The hypotheses provided in this figure offer a description of the antecedents and consequences associated with each target behavior. These examples were derived from FBAs conducted within school settings by the authors. The information contained in the hypothesis statements provides us with insights that are most helpful in the development of interventions.

Consider Vignette 5.2 for an example of a completed functional assessment.

Vignette 5.2

A Functional Behavior Assessment

Student:	David	*Age:* 13
Diagnosis:		Emotional/Behavior Disorders
Educational Placement:		Self-Contained Class and Inclusive Art, Physical Education, and Lunch

Description: David's classroom teacher referred him for an FBA because of his chronic behavior problems within the self-contained and inclusive classroom settings. These disruptive behaviors have been ongoing and persistent and have disrupted David's ability to learn and also that of his classmates.

FBA Components: Structured Interview
                        Scatter-Plot
                        A-B-C Analysis

Target Behavior: David will speak out in class without raising his hand and will not engage in assigned tasks for extended periods of time. During these frequent periods of task disengagement, David will interrupt the work of other students with ongoing chatter until they tell him to stop, which results in a hostile verbal exchange between David and other students. Summarized results from the structured interview conducted with his teachers revealed the following comments:

Structured Interview

1. *What are the specific target behaviors of concern?* Excessive talking out in class, negative attention-seeking behaviors such as his "cartoon voices," which consists of David imitating the voices of his favorite cartoon characters for attention and general off-task behavior.
2. *Are there antecedent events that consistently happen prior to occurrences of the behavior?* His behavior escalates when given a written assignment unless he receives teacher assistance on the front end. If he does not prefer a task or has any difficulty, he will lose his patience and go off task, and then it becomes increasingly difficult to redirect him.
3. *What typically happens after the behavior occurs?* David will continue to talk and chatter, which causes a great deal of frustration on the part of his class-mates, until one of them will boldly tell him to "shut up," which makes him very angry, at which point he yells at them. He has been dismissed and sent to time-out on repeated occasions and has also been sent to the principal's office.
4. *Do the target behaviors occur at predictable times of day?* His worst periods are during the midmorning and early afternoons. These occur during math and physical education during the morning and during English in the afternoon.
5. *What are the functions of these behaviors?* Attention seeking.
6. *Are there significant life events that could account for the behavior?* Nothing new or different has occurred in David's life. These behaviors have been chronic for a long period of time, and past reports indicate that many of these same issues were unsuccessfully treated in his past educational placements.
7. *What behavior interventions have been used in the past to address the behavior?* Time-out, loss of privileges, and in-school suspension.
8. *Are there medical or physical issues that could account for the behavior?* No, he currently takes no medications.
9. *Are there times in which the behavior does not occur?* It does not occur during art, which is his favorite subject, nor does it occur during social studies as long as the class is on a topic of interest to him.
10. *Please indicate activities that the student enjoys.* He enjoys art, creative activities, music, and his vocational education class, and he loves computers and technology.

Results from the A-B-C analysis reveal that David has some consistent antecedents and consequences that occasion his off-task and disruptive behaviors. A sample of these comments is illustrated in the following figure.

continued

Observer: *Mrs. O'Brien*

Time: *1:15–1:45 P.M.*

Date: *11/14/12*

ANTECEDENT	BEHAVIOR	CONSEQUENCE
Teacher prompts class to take out work materials	David continues to talk and interact with others	Teacher again prompts David
Teacher delivers instructions for the activity	David places head down and taps on his desk with a pencil	Teacher attempts to redirect him with a verbal cue
Confronted by the teacher to begin working	David mutters under his breath and attempts task	Teacher turns and walks about the room
"Time up" is announced by teacher	Students turn in work, David hands in an empty sheet	Teacher reprimands him for not completing his assignment

Hypothesis: When presented with task demands in specific courses—math, English, and physical education—David will frequently engage in off-task behaviors, including excessive talking and general noncompliance (an ability to redirect back on task given an instructional cue by the teacher). During these periods, he will engage in many negative attention-seeking behaviors, including whispering to his classmates and the use of "cartoon voices," which cause some laughter (negative attention) and serve to create more disruption in the classroom.

Function: Attention

Intervention Strategies: The following intervention strategies were generated from David's team after reviewing the data from the functional behavior assessment. (a) *Prevention strategies:* Modify the presentation and delivery of tasks in math and English. This includes providing David with preinstructions on each assigned task, the use of guided instruction, and high-probability requests embedded within the math problems and written assignments. (b) *Behavior change strategies:* Use self-monitoring and self-recording to enhance David's task engagement in math and English, and use direct instruction in how to appropriately request teacher attention. (c) *Consequence strategies:* Use differential reinforcement for appropriate classroom behavior, a point system for task engagement paired with the self-monitoring and self-recording program that would enable him to earn privileges such as computer access, increased art lab, and a free pizza upon the accrual of the necessary points depending on his choice.

Evident in this example is how data can reveal an obvious trend that assists us in the formation of hypotheses statements and intervention strategies.

However, if the trends in the data are not clear, and you have collected additional data (e.g., 7–10 days), and you still cannot identify the causal factors associated with the target behavior or the function, consider conducting a functional analysis (O'Neill et al., 2015).

Reflective Moment

What intervention strategies might you recommend other than those suggested? What is the rationale for using a comprehensive plan that identifies antecedent management, replacement behavior, and consequence strategies simultaneously?

CONDUCTING A FUNCTIONAL ANALYSIS

A functional analysis is a component of the FBA and is a method used to assess behavior under very controlled conditions. The efficacy of functional analysis procedures for identifying the function of challenging behaviors across settings has been well documented in the literature (Carr et al., 1999; Iwata, 1994; Iwata et al., 1982; O'Neill et al., 2015). In a recent review conducted by Beavers, Iwata, and Lerman, (2013) it was reported that over 981 FAs have been published in the research since 1961, with approximately 74% of these having been conducted with children and only 36% of these conducted in school settings. Many of these studies employed the analogue assessment model. An analogue assessment (Iwata et al., 1982) is when a functional analysis is conducted within a controlled setting (such as an unused classroom or clinic room) with experimental conditions being similar to those found within natural settings such as school (Asmus, Vollmer, & Borrero, 2002) and home environments (Peck Peterson, Derby, Berg, & Horner, 2002). Some have argued that analogue assessment is not as socially valid, given that the target behavior is not exposed to the same level of contingencies operating in the natural environment when in such a contrived setting (Conroy, Fox, Crain, Jenkins, & Belcher, 1996). Despite these limitations, research in the area of functional analysis has helped advance our understanding of how to experimentally validate hypotheses concerning the functions of challenging behavior.

A functional analysis is conducted by changing various environmental events or situations to determine their effect on behavior (O'Neill et al., 2015). These manipulations are designed to test the hypotheses that were arrived at through the functional assessment process. Demchak and Bossert (1996) suggest that when conducting a functional analysis within a school setting, the manipulations should be selected for their potential to invoke the target behavior of concern. An example of this approach is selecting manipulations based on the hypotheses and perceived function of the target behavior, which would require setting up brief conditions, approximately 10 minutes in length, to assess the behavior that would coincide with the perceived function, such as Attention, Access to Tangibles, Escape, and Sensory Stimulation, as described by Iwata and colleagues (1982). Functional analysis, therefore, serves to validate and confirm what function the problem serves for a learner. When conducting a functional analysis, the following conditions are typically assessed using a multi-element design, and the effects of these manipulations on the target behavior are noted (Asmus et al., 2002; Wacker, Cooper, Peck, Derby, & Berg, 1999).

Conditions Associated with a Functional Analysis

1. *Attention:* If you suspect that a learner is engaging in a problem behavior for the purpose of gaining attention, use the 10-minute time period and set up a series of activities for the learner to engage in while you sit in the room totally preoccupied on some other activity. Each time the learner engages in the target behavior, provide him or her with attention. If the behavior occurs at a high rate of occurrence, one could assume that a probable relationship exists, with attention serving as the function for the problem behavior.

2. *Escape:* If you believe that the learner's behavior is related to escape, then you could provide the learner with a nonpreferred task. Instruct the learner to work on the task for the duration of the 10-minute period. If the learner should engage in the target behavior, allow him or her to stop working, have a brief break, and then resume

the task. If the problem behavior should reoccur, repeat the procedure, allowing the child to take a brief break before returning to the task. Note the occurrences of the behavior to determine the relationship between task presentation and the learner's behavior. High frequencies of escape behavior from the task indicate that the function of the target behavior is escape.

3. *Sensory stimulation:* This condition allows the learner to be alone without any reinforcing materials, toys, or other forms of stimulation. If the child's behavior is aimed at providing sensory stimulation, the behavior should occur within this condition.

4. *Access to tangibles:* Assess whether the learner's behavior is directed at obtaining tangibles such as a preferred toy, food, drink, or other items. Select a preferred toy and place it in view of the learner. When the learner engages in the target behavior, allow the child to interact with the preferred object for a brief period, and then have him or her resume the task. Repeat the procedure again until the brief 10-minute period has elapsed and note the occurrences of the behavior. If the target behavior occurred numerous times, the behavior is aimed at obtaining tangible reinforcement.

5. *Play:* This condition is characterized by the learner being given noncontingent access to high-interest materials and attention, with the expectation being that the problem behavior will not occur. The play condition also serves as a control condition (Carr et al., 1999; Demchak & Bossert, 1996).

Most functional analyses are conducted using either a multi-element or reversal design. These research designs as well as others are described in greater depth in Chapter 6. The multi-element design (Iwata et al., 1982; Sidman, 1960; Ulman & Sulzer-Azaroff, 1975) has also been referred to as the alternating treatment design (Bailey & Burch, 2002).

O'Neill and colleagues (2015) recommend guidelines for conducting experimental manipulations as part of a functional analysis. These include: (a) conducting manipulations only when you can control relevant situations, (b) determining the level of potential risk involved for learners and staff, (c) obtaining permission and approval to conduct systematic manipulations, (d) using protective procedures and equipment as necessary for learner and staff safety, (e) considering assessment of "precursor" behavior as alternative strategies, and (f) using manipulations to evaluate specific ideas or hypotheses about the situations that are related to challenging behaviors and the functions they serve.

DEVELOPMENT OF AN INTERVENTION PLAN

Following the completion of the functional analysis, it is time to develop a comprehensive intervention using the data derived from the assessment. When developing an intervention, it is important to consider the data that have been gathered (O'Neill et al., 2015). These data include some of the following elements:

1. An operational definition of the target behavior.
2. Factors that could be influencing the behavior, including a change in major life events, medication, physical illness, or other such factors.
3. Setting events and antecedents that consistently serve as triggers for the problem behavior: are they settings, tasks, individuals, time of day, instructional cues, and/or others?
4. Events that follow the behavior that serve to maintain the behavior such as negative reinforcement.
5. The function of the behavior and how it serves the individual.
6. Potential replacement behaviors that would serve the same function as that of the problem behavior.

7. A list of attempted interventions that have been used in the past to address the target behavior.
8. Quality-of-life variables that may need to be addressed as part of a comprehensive intervention package. These could include enriching environments, providing increased opportunities for choice, scheduling changes, and other environmental supports designed to increase the individual's quality of life.
9. Socially valid data from the learner or learner's parents and family concerning their perspectives on the problem behavior and input on the development of a behavior support plan. The development of a behavior support plan requires that we consider the type of intervention that will best address the problem behavior; therefore, the hypotheses are important in helping us determine how to intervene.

When addressing challenging behavior, perhaps the best place to begin is at the antecedent and setting event stage. To address these behaviors on the front end, so to speak, is a proactive approach that will hopefully result in the prevention of these problem behaviors or at least their significant reduction in the future.

Bambara and Knoster (1998) recommended strategies for antecedent and setting event modifications that include: (a) Avoid giving assignments that are repetitive or overly difficult in an area that the learner has problems with. (b) Modify a problem event such as adapting lessons or instructional cues. (c) Intersperse difficult and easier tasks. (d) Add tasks and learner preferences that promote desired behavior. (e) Block or neutralize the impact of events that trigger challenging behavior.

Other strategies to consider when modifying antecedents and setting events as part of a behavior support plan include the following:

Modifying Setting Events and Antecedents

- How can changes in the environment help to prevent occurrences of the problem behavior?
- What can be done to alter specific antecedents that trigger the problem behavior?
- How can daily schedules and routines be enriched to increase the likelihood of appropriate alternative behaviors?

Teaching alternative replacement behaviors that serve the same function is also a critical element of an effective behavior support plan (BSP). This goal is accomplished through the identification of some essential skills that could assist the learner in obtaining his or her needs as well as eliminating the need for the problem behavior. It is important to note that when teaching, Bambara and Knoster (1998) identified three areas when contemplating replacement behaviors, these are (1) teaching replacement behaviors (behaviors that are designed to serve the same function as the target behavior); (2) general skills (skills that build on current competencies and expand and generalize the skills that enable the individual to have greater options and thus reduce the need for problem behavior to occur); and (3) coping skills (strategies for the individual to use when challenging and difficult situations are encountered).

Other questions to consider when selecting replacement behaviors could include some of the following.

Teaching Positive Replacement Behaviors

- What positive alternative behaviors can serve as acceptable replacement behaviors?
- Does the learner have strengths that could assist them in acquiring these replacement behaviors?

- What are some specific self-management skills that would enable the learner to cope with difficult situations?
- What are the specific areas of intervention needed to teach replacement behaviors (social or communication skills, self-management skills such as self-instruction and self-monitoring, or others)?

Traditionally, behavior change programs within schools have placed a great deal of emphasis on consequence-based approaches with the administration of reinforcers or punishers. Although important to the behavior change process, they are part of a larger, more comprehensive approach toward the development of a behavior support plan. Some important considerations in the use of consequence-based intervention practices are described in the following section.

Consequence-Based Interventions

- How can consequences be altered to reduce the frequency of the problem behavior?
- What type of strategy will be used (differential reinforcement, redirection, planned ignoring)?
- How will replacement behaviors be reinforced so that they will become more efficient than the problem behavior?
- Have crisis intervention procedures been identified to protect the child or others in the event that they are needed?

Finally, an area of great importance in the design of a BSP is the individual's overall quality of life. This point cannot be overstated, as the major goal of positive behavior supports is the enhancement of an individual's quality of life (Horner, 1999). Concern for the quality of life of the persons we serve through the design and delivery of PBIS is consistent with the promotion of self-determination skills, which are essential for promoting happiness and self-fulfillment among all people.

Many times, these rights have been denied to persons with disabilities because of challenging behavior and often because of an identified disability that has served to label these individuals as being incapable of performing such skills. The tools that enable us to assist individuals in obtaining such outcomes include PBIS. The FBA and functional analysis (FA) are tools by which we can assess these enhanced lifestyle avenues. Functional behavior assessment offers us an applied technology to facilitate positive life changes through the design and implementation of behavior support plans—with enhanced quality of life serving as the ultimate outcome.

SUMMARY

This chapter described the process of functional behavior assessment (FBA). The importance of FBA was identified in the 1997 and 2004 Reauthorization of IDEA and the more recent Reauthorization of the Individuals with Disabilities. One major point as noted from the 2004 Reauthorization is that it reinforces the use of FBA and PBS to address challenging behaviors. These assessment and intervention tools were mandated to address the behavior support needs of children whose behavior negatively affects their learning and/or the learning of others and represent evidence-based practices in the assessment and intervention of challenging behavior. Also addressed within the chapter were the assumptions that are often made by professionals and others concerning challenging behavior. Such false assumptions are simply conjecture and are not based on fact, nor are they supported by data, and thus they serve no purpose in addressing the problem. However, it is important to remember that challenging behavior serves a function or purpose. The process of FBA provides us with a systematic method for obtaining information that will lead us to a better understanding of challenging behaviors, the factors that influence its occurrence, the variables that reinforce it, and the function of these behaviors. The components of functional behavior assessment were also described and applications of these methods provided. The final portion of the chapter discussed how to conduct a functional analysis. Questions of the utility of functional analyses within school settings were addressed, as was the experimental manipulation of variables and how it can serve to validate the function of problem behavior. Finally, the chapter described how information compiled from an FBA could translate into the development of behavior support plans (BSP) and the various types of intervention alternatives available.

ACTIVITIES TO EXTEND YOUR LEARNING

1. Select a series of target behaviors and operationally define these behaviors in measurable and observable terms.
2. Conduct a series of behavior observations within your practical setting while focusing on the target behaviors you selected; practice each of the observational methods described within the chapter, such as interval recording and time sampling.
3. While in your practical setting, observe your cooperating teacher and other educational professionals as they conduct an FBA.
4. Interview a teacher, behavior support specialist, and school psychologist concerning their perspectives on conducting an FBA. Compare and contrast their viewpoints and approaches.

FURTHER READING AND EXPLORATION

1. Consult the website for the Office of Special Education Programs on Positive Behavioral Interventions and Supports for more information on functional behavior assessment: www.pbis.org
2. Develop an electronic resource file on materials related to FBA that includes data collection forms, interview forms, and information that you can use to inform both yourself and families of these approaches.

Single-Case Design

CONCEPTS TO UNDERSTAND

After reading this chapter, you should be able to:

- Describe the importance of measuring behavior change through the use of single-case designs.
- Understand the rationale for evidence-based practice in special education and how single-case research design assists us in determining efficacious practices in the area of PBIS.
- List and describe the applications of single-case designs within experimental research and in classroom settings.
- Identify and describe the most commonly used single-case designs found within experimental research and the designs most applicable for use by classroom teachers in attempting to measure and evaluate behavior change among students.

KEY TERMS

A-B design

A-B-A design

Alternating-treatments design

Baseline

Changing-criterion design

Dependent variable

Evidence-based practice (EBP)

Independent variable

Intervention

Multiple-baseline design

Reversal design

Single-case design

One of the basic tenets of applied behavior analysis is that it uses the scientific method in the study of human behavior. The scientific method is a process by which a research question is arrived at and then operationally defined in observable and measureable terms, data are collected relevant to the question and concerning any methods used to test the question, with the subsequent results being analyzed and conclusions drawn. As best described in a classic paper by Baer, Wolf, and Risely (1968), "analytic behavioral application is the process of applying sometimes tentative principles of behavior to the improvement of specific behaviors, and simultaneously evaluating whether or not any changes are noted" (p. 91). A key point worth noting in the quote from this landmark article is the word *evaluating*. Evaluation of behavior change is essential for us to determine the efficacy of our intervention packages and thus the rationale for **single-case design** also known as **single-case design**. The role of single-case design as a viable research tool is underscored by Horner and colleagues (2005), who reinforce that "single subject design is a rigorous, scientific methodology used to define basic principles of behavior and establish evidence-based practices" (p. 165). Teachers and other professionals can also use single-case design as a tool for evaluating student progress monitoring on instructional and behavioral goals and objectives relative to the student's IEP or BSP. Student progress monitoring is most important, given the mandate to evaluate student progress from evidence-based practices as part of RtI (Bolt, Ysseldyke, & Patterson, 2010; Lewis, Wheeler, & Carter, 2017). We will examine the fundamentals of single-case design in this chapter, including the rationale for this methodology and how it relates to evidence-based practices in the field of special education and, more specifically, the application of PBIS within classroom and school settings and the various types of designs used within research and applied settings. The goal of this chapter is to enhance your knowledge and skills about the benefits of this methodology applied to your work as teachers, consumers of research, and as future researchers.

EVIDENCE-BASED PRACTICES AND SINGLE-CASE DESIGN

The term **evidence-based practice (EBP)** in special education circles that was introduced by Carnine (1999). The term *evidence-based*, however, originated in the field of medicine (Odom et al., 2005) and referred to a method of instruction largely used in the preparation of physicians within medical schools (Grad, Macaulay, & Warner, 2001) and in the identification and delivery of medical practices deemed scientifically sound. The EBP movement within medical education was aimed at developing the ability of family practitioners to define the presenting problem being experienced by the patient, to then conduct a search of evidence-based literature from the research, and finally to critically evaluate the evidence gained from the literature and assess its implications relative to the needs of the individual patient (Guyatt, O'Meade, Jaeschke, Cook, & Haynes, 2000).

This method of training medical students has grown in popularity within medical education; it has focused on finding evidence-based solutions to the presenting clinical problems experienced by patients (Grad, Macaulay, & Warner, 2001; Green, 2001). Ironically, a recent study by Kortekaas and colleagues (2017) revealed that integrated training in evidence-based medicine does not change the clinical practice behavior of general practitioners. Though this is a recent finding from the field of medicine, more research is needed to fully ascertain the conclusions of this practice applied to teaching.

The impetus for evidence-based practice in the field of education is resultant from the research-to-practice gap fostered largely out of a genuine concern that effective educational practices that were research based were not being widely used in the schools (Odom et al., 2005). Researchers and practitioners have maintained separate viewpoints on where the problem lies with respect to what and/or who is responsible for this gap between research and practice. Over the years, researchers have stated that teachers and administrators don't understand the importance of research in terms of practice, and practitioners have held to the view that most research does not address matters of practical importance and/or is unrealistic given the demands placed on teachers and related professionals working in the schools especially given the competing mandates that teachers must juggle. With regard to the use of EBP in the area of PBIS in schools, more empirical study is needed to address the factors that preclude teachers from using EBP in the delivery of PBIS and other evidence-based practices in the classroom.

EBP has been supported through the 2004 Reauthorization of IDEA, which mandates that measureable progress toward annual goals be demonstrated, that progress monitoring ensue, and that services and supports that are provided are based on empirical research. This law requires professionals to be accountable for what we do and how we do it and to provide measures of performance. The relationship between EBP and the use of single-case design serve as a means by which to evaluate student's behavioral and learning outcomes could not be more evident, as it provides documented evidence on students' performance relative to their individual goals and objectives as stated in their IEP.

REFLECTIVE MOMENT

How can teachers verify the effectiveness of their instructional interventions without a formal means of evaluating progress? How can single-case design promote greater accountability and foster improved learning outcomes for students?

Public scrutiny and criticism of public education paired with federal mandates have served to foster a need for enhanced accountability within the field of special education. The field has since witnessed a move toward a standards-based model in the preparation of teachers and students alike, thus prompting researchers, teacher trainers, and practitioners to more fully realize the use of efficacious practices as determined by research within school settings (Gersten & Smith-Jones, 2001; Odom et al., 2005). The rationale for evidence-based practice was more fully established as a result. Not only is it important for practitioners such as teachers and related services personnel to utilize research to guide their practice in terms of teaching, but it is equally important for researchers to utilize the highest degree of professional ethics in the practice of research as a means of promoting valid and reliable findings in attempting to improve our practices. Given the expectations now placed on schools to support the academic and behavioral support needs of every student, some advocate that now—more than ever in the history of the field—special education teachers are becoming interventionists who identify evidence-based practices to provide these range of supports to all learners (Simonsen et al., 2010).

In response to the evidence-based movement, researchers advocated for the development of quality indicators for experimental research (Gersten et al., 2005) so that researchers would have standards by which to measure the quality of a research study, thus improving the likelihood that a degree of rigor had been attached. These quality indicators would assist not only researchers but also consumers such as teachers and practitioners in their evaluation of extant research, in the hope of leading to a more refined knowledge base of evidence-based practices that have been scientifically validated as being efficacious for promoting improved learning outcomes for children and youth with disabilities.

Single-case design evolved from the long and rich history of case study research in the field of psychology and has been refined, further developed, and used by researchers in disciplines such as psychology, special education, physical and occupational health, speech–language pathology, and others. The sophistication of these designs has also evolved and become more complex; still, the salient feature of single-case designs is the ability to evaluate the effect of an intervention on a single individual. Its applications can extend across larger numbers; however, like the case study method, emphasis on the single case is an enduring characteristic (Kazdin, 1982). Unlike case studies, single-case design provide researchers with a means by which to document experimental control, thus lending a greater degree of scientific validity to the outcomes from such studies (Horner et al., 2005).

Another benefit of single-subject research is that it promotes the study of socially valid behavior. Social validity reminds us as professionals that the behavior or skill in question must have social significance to the individual and or his or her family—in other words, that it has value in the life of the learner and his or her family (Carter, 2009). In turn, this element of social validity is enhanced by the collaborative nature of single-subject designs in promoting teaming among professionals and family members, thus improving the likelihood of more enduring socially important or valid outcomes for the learner in question.

Basic Elements of Single-Case Design

Before introducing the basic elements of single-case design as a methodology for studying and evaluating behavioral interventions, it is important to understand some basic terminology used in single-subject research. For example, the terms *research methodology* and *method* refer to the experimental procedures that were used in conducting a research study (Johnston & Pennypacker, 1993).

An important distinction to make when attempting to better understand research is to differentiate the terms *basic research* and *applied research*. *Basic research* is a term used to describe research studies aimed at the development or formulation of theory and/or the testing of an existing theory; applied research is aimed at addressing a more current problem (Carnine, 1999). The fields of applied behavior analysis and subsequently single-case design were developed in response to the need for applied research to address the behavioral, social, and learning challenges experienced by individuals with developmental, behavioral, or learning disabilities. The field of PBIS has incorporated the use of single-case design into the study of individual and classroom applications to students and continues to refine this form of research methodology within applied settings.

Two important terms to understand in research are *independent variable* and *dependent variable*. An **independent variable** refers to the intervention or treatment that is being used to promote behavioral change, whereas the **dependent variable** denotes the target behavior. For example, Ms. Thomas is using the PECS (Picture Exchange Communication System) with Jared, a young child with autism spectrum disorders, to promote his communication skills, and she is evaluating his progress using a single-subject research design—the independent variable (IV) is the PECS system (the intervention that we are using), and the dependent variable (DV) is "Jared's attempts at initiation using his PECS system" (the target behavior that we are seeking to promote).

As another example of these terms, Ms. Dotson is teaching a small group of her students subtraction with regrouping; to better teach this concept, and to more fully engage the students in their learning, she has developed a game format and is evaluating her students' abilities to identify the steps used in the regrouping process. The IV in this example is the subtraction regrouping game, and the DV is the percentage correct. For teachers and related services personnel, the goal of evaluating student performance is to demonstrate a marked increase or improvement in terms of skill development, whereas in research the goal is directed toward demonstrating experimental control or, as defined by Bailey and Burch (2002), to "demonstrate the functional relationship between an event and target behavior" (p. 143). This goal is not always possible, or practical, when working in applied settings such as schools and classrooms, but single-subject designs do provide for both researchers and practitioners a means by which to better evaluate the performance of learners with respect to specific target behaviors. As you have learned, each student's IEP states that measureable progress on goals and objectives must be demonstrated. Often, this area is lacking in IEPs of students with special needs; however, the use of single-subject methodology can serve as a useful tool for providing such evaluative data.

Two more important terms to understand are *baseline* and *intervention*. These are sometimes referred to as "baseline-phase" or "baseline condition." The **baseline** is the initial stage, or "pretest," before any intervention has ensued. You'll see that on a graph depicting a target behavior, the baseline condition is labeled with the letter *A*. The **intervention** or treatment phase is the condition by which an intervention has been employed; it is labeled with the letter *B*.

Single-subject designs have distinguishable features from more traditional group designs. Horner and colleagues (2005) offered a table of quality indicators found within single-subject research. Some of these basic elements, as described by Horner and colleagues, include: (a) the focus on the individual as the unit of analysis; (b) participants, setting, and procedures are operationally defined in terms that are measureable and observable; (c) dependent and independent variables are also operationally defined to reinforce validity and reliability and to promote replication by other researchers; (d) single-subject designs consist of a pretreatment condition referred to as baseline and a treatment phase, and thus comparisons are made across these conditions; (e) the determination of a functional relationship or a cause-and-effect relationship between an intervention (independent variable) and changes in the target behavior (dependent variable) is another important feature of single-subject designs; (f) single-subject designs address socially valid concerns relative to the individual learner; another, unique feature of this form of research design is that (g) they rely on visual analysis of the data related to trend (ascending or descending) and level (average or mean performance within a condition).

It is most important that consumers of these studies—that is, the practitioners—understand good research if the field of special education is to move forward in better operationalizing evidence-based practice. Along those lines, in one of the seminal works in the field of research methods in applied behavior analysis, Sidman (1960) offered a framework to consider when evaluating research findings. This framework is very much applicable to the challenge that consumers of research face when attempting to assess the quality of a research investigation. Sidman stated that one should evaluate research on the following topics: (a) the scientific importance of the data (how socially and scientifically significant the data from a study or set of studies are), (b) to what degree the results are reported within the study reliable, and (c) how well the findings presented in the study have generality across time, settings, and participants. Carnine (1997) provided a more condensed framework for consumers of research in special education that basically asked a series of questions: (a) whether a study presented evidence that a method was effective, (b) whether the study was described in detail in terms of procedure and outcome, (c) whether measures of accountability were reported, and (d) what the implications were for teachers and school administrators. This initial framework offers practical questions for researchers to consider, and if the research-to-practice gap is to be lessened, researchers and practitioners need to find a common dialogue so that research can be helpful in answering applied questions of importance to the delivery of educational services and supports to learners with special needs.

Applications of Single-Case Design

As has been eluded to previously, single-case designs have been a mainstay of ABA since its inception. In the late 1960s, applied behavior analysis was being widely used throughout state mental health settings serving clients with developmental disabilities and psychiatric disorders. ABA was the intervention of choice in promoting active treatment for individuals within these settings. However, applications of ABA within school settings also began to appear, as did the use of single-subject designs in these investigations. During the 1960s and 1970s, we witnessed the application of single-subject designs with behavioral training studies across children and adult populations within institutional (Ayllon & Azrin, 1968) and community-based settings, including school environments (Bijou, 1970). Examples of these are too numerous and exhaustive to list; some of these studies included the training of three beginning teachers in the use of systematic reinforcement procedures for use within the classroom (Hall, Panyan, Rabon, & Broden, 1968) and teaching persons with mental retardation coin summation as a functional living skill (Lowe & Cuvo, 1976).

In the 1980s through the 1990s, these methodologies were refined, that is, used in more inclusive school and community settings, in teaching complex skills, and in addressing challenging forms of behavior. Some examples of these include the development of toothbrushing skills in preschool children (Poche, McCubbrey, & Munn, 1982), the use of functional communication training as a means of reducing challenging behavior for children with developmental disabilities (Carr & Durand, 1985), the use of direct instruction as a means of improving spelling performance in second-grade boys (Gettinger, 1993), and increasing interactive communication skills in young children with autism with a voice output communication aid (Schepis, Reid, Behrmann, & Sutton, 1998). The field began to witness the advent of PBIS in 1997 with the Reauthorization of IDEA, and single-subject designs have been effectively used within PBIS among individual learners and in classroom applications, including inclusive classroom settings. Some of these applications have included the use of activity schedules with young children with autism (Massey & Wheeler, 2000), the use of video priming as a way to minimize disruptive behaviors during transitions for children with autism (Schreibman, Whalen, & Stahmer, 2000), the use of functional assessment and self-management for promoting task engagement and task completion (Brooks, Todd, Tofflemeyer, & Horner, 2003), and the use of computer-presented social stories and video models to increase social communication skills of children with high-functioning autism spectrum disorders (Sansoti & Powell-Smith, 2008). As PBIS has become more widely used within school settings, the need for evaluation of behavior supports across individual and classroom tiers remains as we refine the application of PBIS within school settings. The RtI movement has also increased the awareness among professionals regarding progress monitoring. It is important that teachers understand the application of this methodology not only within applied research but also the more important issue of how this approach to measuring performance can be applied to learners within their classrooms (Lewis, Wheeler, & Carter, 2017).

The purpose of the remainder of this chapter is to familiarize you with the most commonly used variations of single-case designs found within the research literature and also the designs most applicable for use by teachers within classrooms and other learning environments. In many cases, the designs used for research purposes are not easily applied within classroom settings, given the busy nature of a teacher's role within the classroom; yet there are designs that can assist teachers with evaluating a student's progress, monitoring performance, and the effectiveness of an intervention. More often than not, due to time constraints and limited supports, it is difficult for a teacher to ensure experimental control when utilizing an intervention. Experimental control is the degree to which a researcher can reliably verify that the results demonstrated are due to the intervention employed—a cause-and-effect relationship. As you will learn, there are single-subject designs well suited for teachers, others for researchers, and those that can serve the needs of both groups.

SINGLE-CASE DESIGN VARIATIONS

The various types of single-subject designs fall into categories such as: teaching designs, research designs, and designs that can be used across both classroom and research settings (Alberto & Troutman, 2012). Research designs allow us to determine a functional relationship between an intervention and behavior change, whereas teaching designs do not because of their lack of experimental control. Yet there are types of designs that can be utilized in the classroom and provide teachers with credible feedback on learner progress and degree of behavior change (Alberto & Troutman, 2012).

A-B Design

The simplest and the most commonly used single-case design within classroom and other educational settings is the **A-B design**. This design has two conditions: baseline and intervention. The A-B design is an example of a teaching design; a learner's progress with respect to a specific intervention can be monitored from baseline to intervention phases, yet it does not provide us with conclusive data due to a lack of experimental control and thus does not allow for the determination of a functional relationship between the intervention and behavior change to be conclusively verified. With the A-B design, baseline data are collected in the first phase (A) and then compared to data collected during the intervention phase (B). An example of an A-B design is contained in Figure 6–1.

Figure 6–1 presents an A-B design used by a teacher to evaluate her student's performance in computational skills on homework sheets in the area of multiplication. Remember that condition (A), or the baseline, is the condition wherein data are collected on a target behavior before any form of intervention has occurred. Note from the example the differences in terms of student performance in condition (B), intervention, from the performance during baseline. In this example, we can tally up this student's performance during baseline by adding each of the data points and obtaining

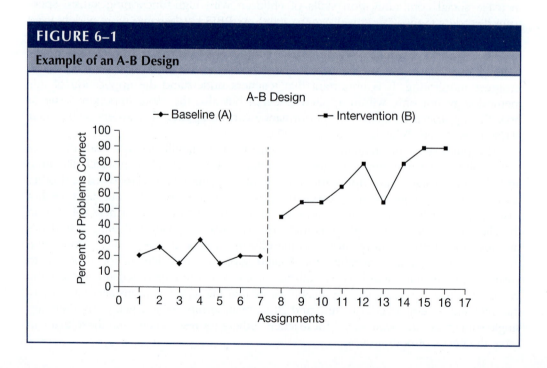

FIGURE 6–1

Example of an A-B Design

a mean, or average, for the baseline phase. The sum of the baseline data points is 145. Divide this figure by the total number of data points, or 7, which results in a mean or average across baseline data of 20.71% ($145 \div 7 = 20.71$). The mean is also referred to within single-subject design methodology as the *level*. Now compare the data from the intervention phase by summing all the data points from the intervention phase. These figures equal 68.33%—the mean for the intervention phase. In comparing the means in this example across baseline and intervention phases, we can see an increase in the level, or mean, during the intervention condition. We also see a change in the trend (the directionality of the data) when comparing the behavior from baseline to intervention. In looking at the student's performance during intervention, we see an ascending trend of increase in terms of performance. It is also important to note that when we speak of trends in the data, the trend is one of the following: ascending (increasing), descending (decreasing), or stable (basically flat, with little or no change).

The A-B design is an excellent design for teachers to use, as it will serve to evaluate and document learner performance and monitor individual educational or behavioral goals and objectives. This design is probably most useful in student progress monitoring relative to academic performance in the classroom.

The A-B design does not control for extraneous variables and their effects on behavior change, so in terms of its utility for research purposes, it is very limited because it does not allow for us to demonstrate a functional relationship between our chosen intervention and behavior change, as we have previously mentioned. Thus the findings cannot be reliably attributed to the intervention (internal validity), nor would the results of this intervention generalize to more than one student with similar needs (external validity). Yet for teachers, the A-B design serves as a simple and practical means by which to gather data and to monitor and evaluate student performance. (Bear in mind that teachers are held accountable for measuring student performance and monitoring progress on individualized goals and objectives as part of the IEP.)

A-B-A Design

A simple variation on the A-B design is the **A-B-A design**. Once again, you may see this design configuration used most often within school settings by classroom teachers. It is a design variation that is most conducive for teachers in obtaining feedback on learner performance. How is this variation different from the A-B design that we reviewed previously? The A-B-A design differs slightly in that in the second (A) phase, we return to baseline. You may hear teachers refer to this as a pretest/post-test method, because in the initial, or baseline, phase (pretest, A) we collect data on student performance in a given area and then administer an intervention (B) phase. Then we fade or withdraw the intervention and return to a second baseline condition (post-test, A).

In Figure 6–2, the A-B-A design has been used by a teacher, Ms. Dotson, to evaluate the use of mnemonics for teaching a student science facts. In the figure, we see the student's performance on quiz grades in science over vocabulary terms associated with accompanying units. Ms. Dotson then develops a method for teaching the student how to use mnemonic rhymes for remembering vocabulary terms. She provides the student with guided instruction and notes the improvement in the student's quiz grades. When the student reaches fluency in the skill, Ms. Dotson decides to eliminate the direct instruction on the skill and assess his performance, thus returning to baseline. Now let's evaluate the student's performance in this example. In the initial baseline phase, the student's mean performance on science vocabulary quizzes was 15 points. That number was obtained by adding the total points for each of the first five quizzes ($20 + 10 + 10 + 20 + 15 = 75$) and dividing by 5 (total quizzes). So, 15 is the mean, or average, for this phase.

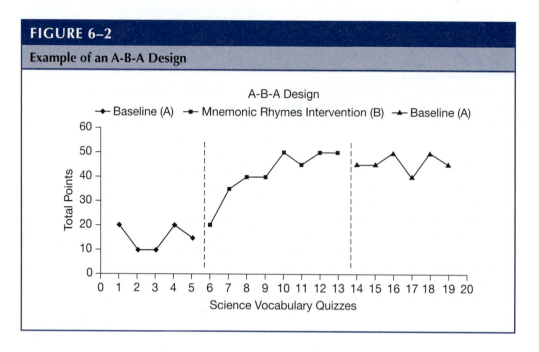

FIGURE 6–2

Example of an A-B-A Design

During the intervention phase, using the mnemonic rhymes, we see an increase in performance to a mean of 41. This figure was arrived at by adding scores from each of the individual quizzes during this phase (20 + 35 + 40 + 40 + 50 + 45 + 50 + 50 = 330) and divided by 8 (total quizzes). During the return to baseline, or second (A) phase, we see that the student has maintained performances well above the initial baseline and intervention phases with respect to quiz points earned. The mean for this phase is 45, which is derived from the sum of each quiz score (45 + 45 + 50 + 40 + 50 + 45 = 275) divided by 6 (total quizzes during this phase). From this example, we see that the student has increased in terms of his proficiency during intervention and even maintained these gains in the return to baseline phases. From this observation, we can assume that the student has reached acquisition and fluency of this skill, but we cannot accurately infer precisely what has contributed to his increased proficiency. Many times when using the A-B-A design, teachers will see a reduction in performance after a return to baseline, as you will see in the next section.

A-B-A-B or Reversal Design

The A-B-A-B, or **reversal design**, is an experimental design most often used in research investigations rather than in teaching and classroom settings. It provides a mechanism for experimental control, thus allowing the researcher to determine the presence of a functional relationship. How is this accomplished? In this design, we see baseline (A), intervention (B), return to baseline (A), and reintroduction of the intervention (B). By using this design, the researcher is most likely to determine the presence of a functional relationship by returning to baseline whereby learner performance most likely will return to near the level, or mean, from the first baseline phase. Upon reintroducing the intervention, the learner's performance will be likely to improve to the level attained in the first intervention phase if indeed there is a cause-and-effect relationship between the intervention and target behavior. Consider Figure 6–3.

In this example, the researcher is examining the use of self-instruction to assist the learner in performing word problems in math, hoping to improve the learner's proficiency

FIGURE 6–3

Example of an A-B-A-B or Reversal Design

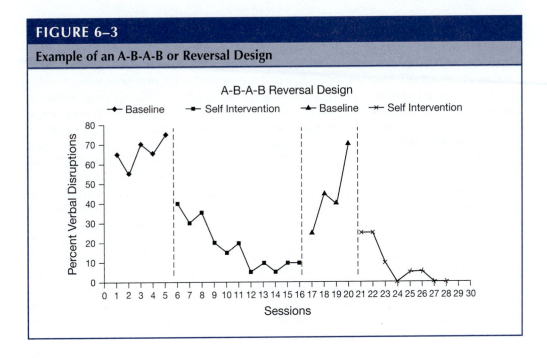

in math and increase task engagement. Also important to the researcher is reducing the level of verbal disruptions exhibited by this student, as such behavior has interfered with his learning and the learning of others. Figure 6–3 depicts the percentage of intervals at which the student engages in verbal disruptions. The example illustrates a mean level of behavior in the initial baseline at 66%. This figure is obtained by adding the data points (65 + 55 + 70 + 65 + 75) and dividing the sum of these numbers (330) by 5. The percentage of verbal disruption declined at a steady rate during the intervention phase, where the mean was 18%, which was arrived at by adding the data points for this phase (40 + 30 + 35 + 20 + 15 + 20 + 5 + 10 + 5 + 10 + 10) and dividing the sum (200) by 11. Upon returning to baseline, the researcher sees the learner's verbal disruptions rapidly increase to near the original baseline mean of 45%, at which point the intervention is reintroduced and the learner's behavior quickly reduces and maintains at a mean of 9%. This example highlights the presence of a functional relationship. The functional relationship is apparent given the lower rates of behavior during the self-instruction intervention, as this and the behavioral increase upon the return to baseline and the effects of reintroducing the intervention and the noted behavior reduction during this phase.

As discussed previously, one of the strengths of the A-B-A-B design is that it allows for experimental control, thus affording researchers the opportunity to determine whether a functional relationship exists between an intervention and behavior. A drawback of this design is that it is not necessarily the best design for teachers within classroom settings because the A-B-A-B design removes the intervention to return to baseline, and this is not consistent with how programs within schools operate.

If a teacher is working with a learner and witnesses an improvement in learner performance, the last thing and probably the least ethical choice to make is to pull the intervention that he or she thinks has had an effect in promoting improved performance. Yet for a researcher, this design provides robustness in terms of experimental control and the ability to ascertain the efficacy of an intervention through the determination of a functional relationship.

Changing-Criterion Design

One of the more effective designs that can be used in either the classroom or research domains is the **changing-criterion design**, which allows for teachers and researchers to evaluate the systematic increase or decrease of a target behavior over time using a series of preestablished stepwise criteria. This design is quite effective for shaping behavior; that is, reinforcing successive approximations of behavior. The changing-criterion design has a baseline and an intervention phase. As previously mentioned, this design is effective for evaluating behavior support programs aimed at systematically increasing a target skill or behavior, whether it is a social behavior or an academic skill. This design is also useful for systematically decreasing behaviors that are problematic for the learner.

This design is implemented by collecting baseline data on the target behavior. These data are assessed and the mean or average is derived for the target behavior. At this point, the initial performance criteria must be established as the intervention is implemented. Depending on the learner's performance in the baseline phase, the teacher will establish the initial criterion level and subsequent criterion steps that are large enough to illustrate changes but not so large as to frustrate the learner and impede performance. Also, criterion changes should be in small and equal units. For example, if a student averaged 6 responses on his math fact review quizzes that are held twice each week, and the ultimate criteria established by the teacher was 20, the teacher would implement the intervention by establishing the initial criteria at 8 × 2 quizzes, and then the next step would be 10 × 2 quizzes, 12 × 2 quizzes, 14 × 2 quizzes, 16 × 2 quizzes, and 18 × 2 quizzes until reaching the terminal criteria of 20. As the learner reaches the targeted criterion, his teacher provides access to his preferred reinforcer, such as a trip to the school library to select a book of his choice for the week. See Figure 6–4.

Now let's examine how a teacher used a changing-criterion design to monitor the use of a self-instruction aimed at reducing a student's inappropriate "talk-outs" during in-class assignments. This particular student was 11 years old and was labeled as E/BD. He also had challenges with ADHD and specified learning disabilities. A behavior of

FIGURE 6–4

Example of a Changing-Criterion Design

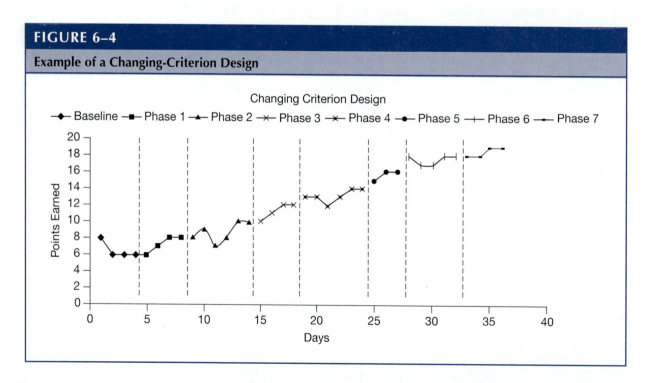

FIGURE 6–5

Changing-Criterion Design for Behavior Reduction

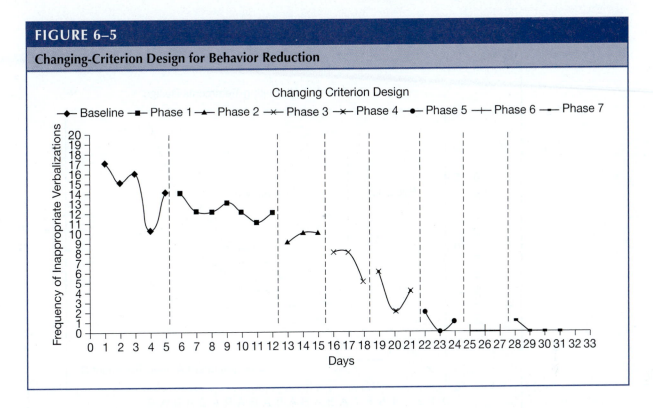

concern was the degree of impulsivity that he manifested during in-class assignments, which would result in inappropriate verbalizations that disrupted other class members. So his teacher developed a self-instruction intervention aimed at redirecting the learner when he felt the need to talk out. If you refer to Figure 6–5, you can see how systematically the behavior reduces over time. Each time the student meets his criterion, he earns 10 minutes of which he can participate in an activity of his choice. (In this case, he prefers instructional time on the computer.) If you average the data points from the baseline phase, you obtain a mean of 14. The teacher decides to make the criteria levels at 12 or fewer occurrences × 3 consecutive days, 10 or fewer occurrences × 3 consecutive days, 8 or fewer occurrences × 3 consecutive days, and so on, in the hopes of continuing until the student has zero occurrences of the behavior. As you can see from Figure 6–5, the behavior has reduced more rapidly than anticipated; however, the teacher has adhered to the criteria until convinced by examining the data relative to the student's performance that the student has reached the criterion target—in this case, zero occurrences.

Alternating-Treatments Design

The **alternating-treatments design** (Barlow & Hersen, 1984), also referred to as the multi-element design (Ulman & Sulzer-Azaroff, 1975) and simultaneous-treatment design (Kazdin, 1982), is used to evaluate two or more treatments or methods of instruction and involves the delivery of two distinctly different interventions within the same setting. It is important to note that when using multiple interventions, they should be evenly administered in terms of trials so as to be able to fully evaluate their efficacy. An example of how this works is illustrated in Figure 6–6.

When examining this figure, note that each of the two treatments (A and B) are administered an equal number of times (8) and in a sequential manner. It is also important

FIGURE 6–6

Example of an Alternating Treatments Design

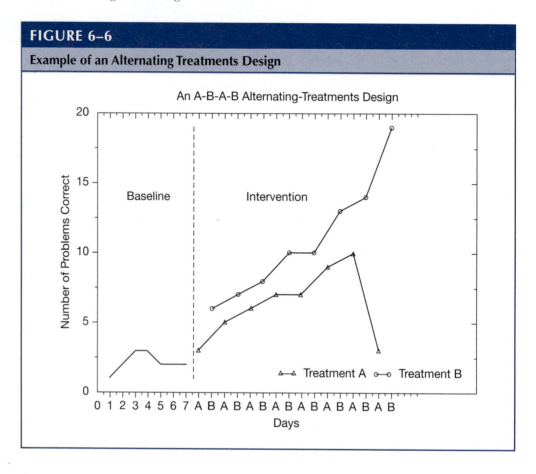

An A-B-A-B Alternating-Treatments Design

to note that each of the independent variables or treatments should vary enough so that a comparison of the two approaches can be fully evaluated. The sequence of interventions is at the discretion of the teacher or researcher; however, each treatment should be administered an equal number of times to allow for comparison.

Among the strengths of the alternating-treatments design is the ability to evaluate one or more forms of intervention (independent variables). After the initial baseline phase, as Sulzer-Azaroff and Mayer (1991) indicated, multiple treatments can be implemented in a somewhat timely manner, and one can decide to intersperse baseline conditions between treatments at any point in time. The alternating-treatments design is a very effective tool for teachers when comparing more than one type of teaching intervention and of equal value to researchers when seeking to study more complex behaviors across multiple instructional contexts (Sulzer-Azaroff & Mayer, 1991).

A disadvantage of this design is something called *sequence effects*, which occurs when one of the treatments inadvertently interferes with another. This effect has also been referred to as carryover effects or multiple-treatment interference (Sulzer-Azaroff & Mayer, 1991). This is where altering the sequence in a less-than-predictable fashion is advisable to control for this confound, as long as each treatment is delivered the same amount of times to allow for comparisons.

In summary, the alternating-treatments design is an effective design when the goal is to compare the effectiveness of more than one intervention and each of the treatments are different enough that participants can discriminate these differences (Richards, Taylor, Ramasamy, & Richards, 1999).

Multiple-Baseline Design

The **multiple-baseline design** is an effective design for use within classroom and research settings. It allows for the simultaneous comparison of multiple dependent variables. The multiple-baseline design is perhaps one of the most widely used research designs in applied behavioral research, yet it can be used by teachers in classroom settings and can be applied across behaviors, settings, and subjects (meaning students or individuals). For example, if a teacher wanted to address the efficacy of a self-management intervention across two or more students, multiple-baseline would be an appropriate design to consider; if the teacher wished to assess the efficacy of the self-management intervention with a single student across multiple settings, such as across classrooms, it would again be an appropriate design to consider. Finally, if the teacher desired to assess the efficacy of this same self-management intervention across more than one behavior with a single student, this would be the design of choice.

Among the many strengths of multiple-baseline designs are that they provide a simultaneous comparison of multiple dependent variables, they are relatively easy to implement (as they are an extension of the A-B design and are applied across multiple settings, behaviors, and or subjects with staggered intervals [Zirpoli, 2015]), and they provide for the replication and the determination of a functional relationship between the target behavior and intervention. Finally, another benefit of this design is that it does not require a reversal as with an A-B-A-B design and can be implemented within the context of a classroom.

Consider This

Many criticize the importance of maintaining data as a means of monitoring student behavior in the classroom. It has been documented in the professional literature and public media that teachers are often overworked and given little time to devote to classroom planning and data collection. The multiple-baseline design is an example of one method that can be used to assist in this capacity.

Massey and Wheeler (2000) used a multiple-baseline across activities (work and leisure) with a 4-year-old boy diagnosed with autism who was receiving his educational services within the context of an integrated preschool classroom. The dependent measure in this study was task engagement; the intervention was teaching the student how to use a photo activity schedule across classroom and leisure-time activities.

To implement the multiple-baseline design, whether across settings, behaviors, or subjects, follow these steps:

1. Collect baseline data across settings, behaviors, and/or subjects simultaneously.
2. Apply the intervention within either one setting, behavior, or subject.
3. Continue to take baseline across subsequent settings, behaviors, or subjects.
4. When criteria are obtained in the initial setting or behavior or with the initial subject, then administer the intervention in the second setting or with the second behavior or subject.
5. Continue baseline for any remaining settings, behaviors, or subjects until criterion is reached for treatment as indicated in Step 4.
6. Administer the intervention with the remaining settings, behavior, or subjects in the same manner until the intervention has been applied to all subsequent settings, behaviors, or subjects.

Examine Figure 6–7 for an example of the multiple-baseline-across-settings design. In this example, the resource special education teacher wants to evaluate the efficacy of a self-instruction/self-recording intervention to assist a student with ADD and learning disabilities to maintain his attention during in-class assignments and thus improve the student's level of task engagement. The teacher has decided to use a multiple-baseline-across-settings

FIGURE 6–7

Multiple-Baseline Across Settings Design

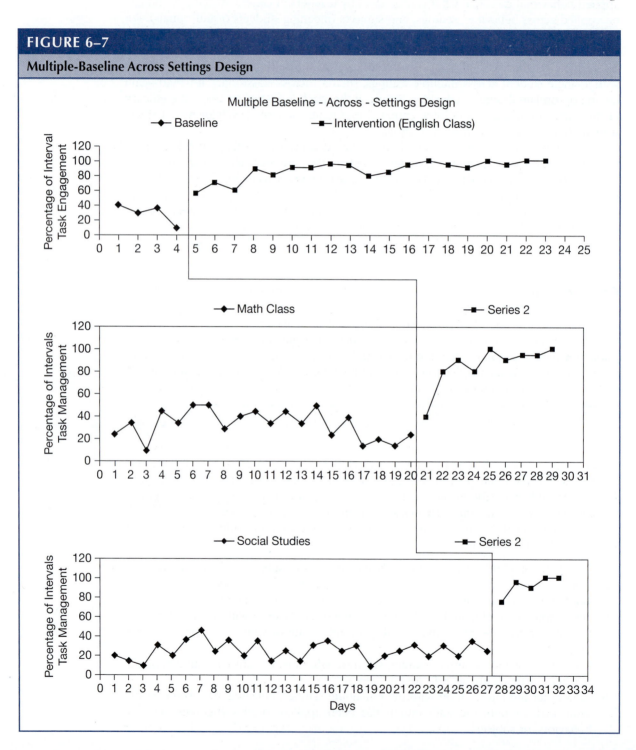

design because she feels that the intervention could have merit in assisting the student across these academic areas, where he is currently having difficulty. She records baseline data across the student's English, math, and social studies classes using a partial-interval recording procedure and initiates the self-instruction/self-recording intervention in the English class while continuing to take baseline data in the remaining two classes. Upon reaching the point of criteria (3 consecutive days at 90% or better on-task engagement) with the intervention in the English class, the teacher introduces the intervention in the student's math class while continuing to take baseline data on the student's percentage of task engagement in the social studies class. Once again, after the student has reached criteria (task engagement of 90% or better for 3 consecutive days), the intervention is initiated in the final setting: the social studies class.

By examining the data, you can see a similar pattern of performance across intervention phases in all three settings, thus replicating the results in multiple settings. The strength of the multiple-baseline design and, in this specific example, the multiple-baseline-across-settings design, is that the student was in need of assistance in more than one subject area and, as stated previously, the multiple-baseline design is a more appropriate choice given that reversal designs are not practical because in teaching and learning situations it is not in the best interest of a student to withdraw an educational intervention aimed at improving learner performance.

ANALYZING SINGLE-SUBJECT DESIGN DATA

The most commonly used method of data analysis when evaluating single-subject design data is visual analysis. In visual analysis, one attempts to examine the data within and across the respective phases, that is, baseline and intervention. Second, these trends in the data are then analyzed across phases. This is of course a dramatic difference from traditional group research, which uses statistical analysis to ascertain whether there is statistical significance in the findings. Statistical analysis may be used to study data from single-subject research designs and can include descriptive statistics such as mean and frequency. Additional analysis may be used, such as inferential statistics, but that will not be the focus of this section.

Single-subject research is largely concerned with social or educational significance of the data and the impact they have on the learning and behavioral outcomes for individual learners. Visual analysis allows for teachers and researchers to view subtleties in the data.

Earlier, the terms *trend* and *level* were introduced. These are two of the major indices used to evaluate data from single-subject designs. *Trend* refers to the directionality of the data. As indicated earlier, an ascending trend indicates an increase in the target behavior, whereas conversely, a descending trend is indicative of a decrease in the target behavior. A flat trend is indicative of stability and essentially no change in the target behavior. See Figure 6–8 for the various examples of trend lines.

Changes in level are mean level differences across phases. Determine level by calculating the mean in each phase and note the differences in trends across phases by drawing a horizontal line through the data at the mean from the *x*-axis through the respective phase.

When using visual analysis, one should be aware of the advantages to such a method. Cooper, Heron, and Heward (2007) stated that when visually inspecting data there are two questions that must be addressed: (1) Was there a socially significant change in the target behavior that occurred? and (2) Was this change due to the independent variable? Visual analysis allows for a careful inspection of all phases of a study and the ability to

FIGURE 6–8

Trend Lines

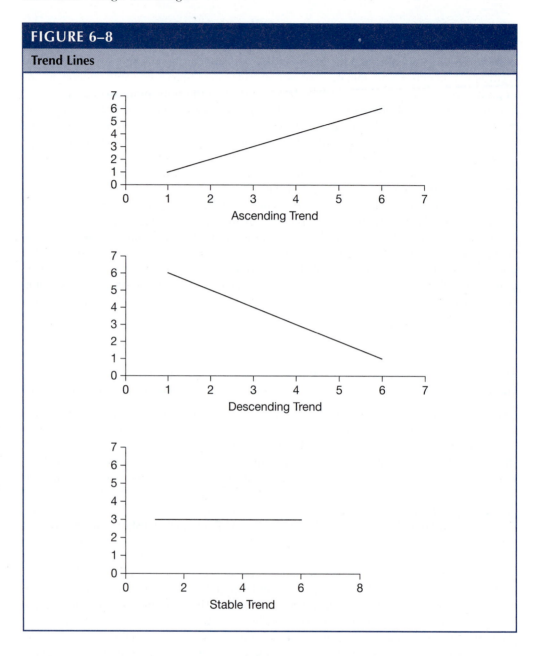

Ascending Trend

Descending Trend

Stable Trend

address issues of variability within the data. However, the disadvantage of this method of analysis is that it can be very subjective unless there are clearly defined rules applied for evaluating the data across multiple observers. This approach would lend itself to a greater degree of reliability among persons evaluating the data and thus promote a more objective analysis.

SUMMARY

In this chapter, we reviewed the fundamentals of single-case design, their utility across educational settings, and their value as tools used in research investigations aimed at furthering our understanding of evidence-based practices in the fields of positive behavior supports and special education. EBP (evidence-based practices) and the work by Horner and colleagues (2005) in this area were discussed relative to how the use of single-case design can assist in the development of evidenced-based practices in special education. After elaborating on the relationship between evidence-based practices and single-case designs, relevant terms pertaining to single-case research were introduced, including basic and applied research, independent variables, baseline, and treatment condition.

Single-case design variations were also introduced in this chapter. The utility of these designs was discussed as it pertains to their use within teaching and research domains and those that serve in both roles. The A-B design was identified as the most commonly used design in classroom and applied instructional settings. The A-B design is perhaps the simplest of all designs to implement. Yet, as we also discussed, the A-B design does not allow for the presence of a functional relationship to be reliably determined between an intervention and behavior change, and therefore it is not a research design.

The A-B-A design was also described, as it is also a design variation found within applied settings and often used by classroom teachers to evaluate a student's performance within academic areas. In some ways, this design can be considered a pretest/post-test measure, as we have discussed. The initial phase of this design is baseline with treatment followed by a return to baseline. We also discussed the ethical ramifications of withdrawal designs such as the reversal design or A-B-A-B design. As noted, teachers do not typically withdraw effective interventions that are serving to enhance the learning of their students. The A-B-A design will be used when an intervention is faded, and the return to baseline serves as more of a follow-up or post-test. Whereas the reversal or A-B-A-B design is a very widely used research design that addresses the validity of an intervention and the presence of a functional relationship. Given that following the intervention phase, the treatment is removed; this design is typically not used within educational settings. The ethical questions raised by removing a successful intervention within a school setting do not warrant the use of this design for answering a research question if it places the learner in peril.

The changing-criterion design was another design variation described in the chapter. The strengths of this design are in its application to learning settings, as teachers can utilize the changing-criterion design to systematically shape a student's behavior, whether it is aimed at increasing a particular learning response or decreasing a challenging form of behavior. This design allows for gradual, stepwise criterion shifts over time. Upon meeting each of these incremental criterion shifts, the criteria are incrementally raised or decreased, depending on the intended outcome of the intervention. As each criterion level is met, the student is provided with the appropriate reinforcement. The changing-criterion design is a very effective design for classroom settings and is also useful for researchers.

The alternating-treatments design was described as an effective design for comparing the efficacy of more than one treatment and for evaluating student performance within classroom settings and/or within the research domain. The problem of sequence effects and methods for controlling for multiple-treatment interference were discussed. Finally, multiple-baseline design was the last single-subject research design reviewed in this chapter. The multiple-baseline design is an effective design for teachers to monitor classroom-based interventions and also a widely used design within research investigations. The multiple-baseline design has three variations that can be used: the multiple-baseline-across-behaviors design, in which an intervention is implemented across more than one behavior; the multiple-baseline-across settings design, in which an intervention is implemented across two or more settings; and the multiple-baseline-across-subjects-or-participants design, in which the same intervention is implemented with two or more participants. Among the strengths of the multiple-baseline design is that reversals are not required; they promote experimental control or the presence of a functional relationship, given the replication effect across behaviors, settings, and/or subjects.

In conclusion, this chapter addressed how to evaluate single-case designs through the use of visual analysis. The terms *trend* and *level* were also discussed pertaining to visual inspection, and other methods of evaluating single-subject data were mentioned, including statistical analysis.

Finally, single-case design offers much in the way of functional utility to practitioners such as teachers, school psychologists, behavior analysts, and researchers, given the relationship of this research methodology to helping to define evidence-based practice in our field. It is important to consider a scientist–practitioner model in furthering your understanding of human behavior, as this is the basis for PBIS, and the use of single-case design is essential to supporting this understanding and in promoting meaningful learning and behavioral outcomes for our students and their families.

ACTIVITIES TO EXTEND YOUR LEARNING

1. Conduct a search of the literature in the areas of ABA and PBIS within your particular area of interest—for example, autism spectrum disorders, emotional/behavioral disorders, developmental disabilities—and examine some of the major journals and research studies that incorporate many of the various designs highlighted in the chapter. Be sure to examine the critical points concerning data collection and analysis.
2. Design a case study for teaching a specific skill to a student, and attempt to implement, under the supervision of your instructor, a simple A-B teaching design to allow yourself the opportunity to become more fluent on the collection and graphing of data.
3. Within your respective practicum settings, identify how plausible the use of more elaborate designs—such as the changing-criterion design or multiple-baseline design—might work as methods of evaluating student performance. Identify some of the barriers found within classrooms that teachers must contend with in attempting to collect performance data on learners.

FURTHER READING AND EXPLORATION

1. Compile a list of special education and/or behavioral journals that feature single-subject research, such as the *Journal of Positive Behavior Interventions*, the *Journal of Applied Behavior Analysis*, and *Education and Training in Autism and Developmental Disabilities*, to name just a few. Compare and contrast the types of articles and frequency of the designs used within studies contained in these journals.
2. Consult Horner and colleagues (2005) for a more thorough review on single-subject research design and its relationship to assisting in the identification of evidence-based practice in special education.
3. Identify a list of other resources from books, chapters, and articles on the use of single-case design, and complete additional reading on the topic to assist in your understanding of this important research methodology.
4. Visit the website http://www.rti4success.org/essential-components-rti/progress-monitoring for more information and resources pertaining to student progress monitoring.

Planning Positive Behavioral Interventions & Supports

CONCEPTS TO UNDERSTAND

After reading this chapter, you should be able to:

- List and describe the seven components of the planning process.
- List and describe the five factors that can influence the success or failure of a plan.
- Describe two planning processes typically used in programs for children, youth, and families.
- Compare and contrast individual education programs (IEPs), individualized family service plans (IFSPs), and person-centered planning (PCPs).
- Discuss the general role of planning in each of the three levels of positive behavior support (PBIS).
- Outline a Schoolwide Positive Behavioral Interventions and Supports (SWPBIS) plan for a preschool, a middle school, and a high school.
- Outline a Level 2 PBIS plan for a preschooler and a school-age child with challenging behavior.
- Outline a Level 3 PBIS plan for a preschooler and a school-age child with challenging behavior.

KEY TERMS

Behavior support plan: Level 1, Level 2, Level 3

Behavior support planning

Competing behaviors model

Constraints

Evaluation

Goals

Group action planning (GAP)

Impeding behavior

Implementation

Individual Education Program (IEP)

Individualized Family Service Plan (IFSP)

Objectives

Person-centered planning (PCP)	Resources
Primary, secondary, and tertiary prevention	Schoolwide positive behavior interventions and support (SWPBIS)
Rationale/mission	Strategies

Whether it is in our everyday lives or our roles as professionals in education and other disciplines, we are constantly in the process of assessing, planning, implementing, and evaluating. Often this process occurs rather informally and even unconsciously, but it certainly affects the quality of our lives and the lives of those we care for as well as the lives of the children and youth we serve as professionals. At one end of the continuum, some individuals appear to have an aversion to planning, preferring instead that events unfold as they will without any structure imposed by making a plan. Other individuals appear to enjoy spending an inordinate amount of time in the development of formal plans, sometimes to the detriment of carrying out the plan. Perhaps you know someone who fits one of these extremes. Maybe you know people who might state that they have no plan for the day—that they will just let it unfold, take whatever it brings, and make the best of it. On the other hand, maybe you know people who start every day with a list of things that they intend to do, the order in which they will be undertaken, and the criteria by which successful completion of each task will be measured. The point here is that everyone has a different perspective on planning and its place in our everyday lives. Given this fact, it is important to keep in mind that professionals, families, and persons targeted for a behavior support plan will also have differing views about the place of planning in their work and lives.

THE PLANNING PROCESS

Frequently, planning processes are described in seven components: a rationale or mission, goals, objectives, strategies, constraints and resources, implementation, and evaluation (Figure 7–1).

Although it is not our intent here to go into detail about these components of planning, it is useful to briefly introduce each. The relevance of each component will be clear as you progress further in the chapter and give consideration to the means by which behavior support planning is successfully done. The first component of a plan is the **rationale/mission**, sometimes thought of as a philosophy. Let us assume that you are a special education resource teacher in an elementary school. You have four class periods during the school day, and during each you have 10 to 12 students with a variety of mild to moderate special needs. Asked to state your mission/philosophy related to what you do in preparing lesson plans, you might include, among other things, the following: "I believe in the individual worth and dignity of each of my students; in their ability to learn; in hands-on, experiential learning; in positive methods of discipline and guidance; and in partnerships with the families of my students. My mission is to plan and carry out my professional responsibilities in a manner that reflects my philosophy/beliefs and is consistent with the standards of my profession and the expectations of my employer."

What about goals? **Goals** are broad statements of intent associated typically with what one believes. Continuing our scenario in which you are the special education teacher, as a part of your plan for the school year, you will have goals. Some will be given to you by the school and/or system, some might be focused on your classes as a whole or on your partnerships with families, and others will be related to the individual needs of your students (as stated in each student's IEP). You establish a goal of improving and strengthening your

FIGURE 7–1

Components of a Planning Process

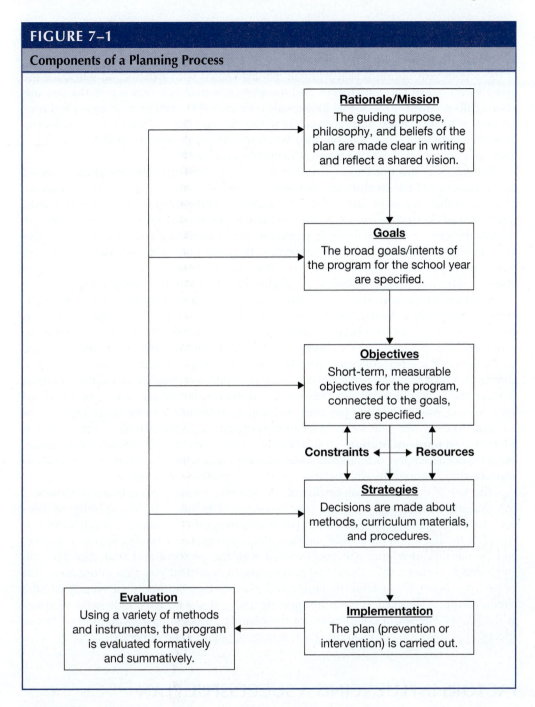

Rationale/Mission
The guiding purpose, philosophy, and beliefs of the plan are made clear in writing and reflect a shared vision.

Goals
The broad goals/intents of the program for the school year are specified.

Objectives
Short-term, measurable objectives for the program, connected to the goals, are specified.

Constraints ◄──────► Resources

Strategies
Decisions are made about methods, curriculum materials, and procedures.

Evaluation
Using a variety of methods and instruments, the program is evaluated formatively and summatively.

Implementation
The plan (prevention or intervention) is carried out.

partnership with the families of your students by implementing a variety of activities over the period of the school year. That is a goal—a broad statement of intent.

Objectives are more specific and measurable subsets of goals. How will you know that you have met the goals that you have in mind? One objective related to the goal example stated previously might be: "By January 15, I will have completed individual conferences with at least 50% of the parents (those who agree to an individual conference) of my students."

The **strategies** are the actions that you might choose to meet your goals and objectives. Some of the strategies available in our example might be related to the preparation that you do prior to individual conferences. Will you have a meeting at the beginning of the school year during which you will get acquainted with parents and introduce the intent to do individual conferences and the purposes that they will serve? Do you use phone calls or emails to schedule individual conferences? Do you arrange individual conferences at times that are most convenient to the parents? Do you adopt a format for the individual conference that will be used when meeting with parents? Will it be unstructured and open ended, semi structured, or highly structured?

The strategies that one chooses to address their goals and objectives are always affected by the presence of **constraints** and **resources**. Constraints and resources may be thought of as things that limit what one can do (constraints) and the things that support and assist what one can do (resources). Of course, constraints and resources are frequently different sides of the same coin. Two things in particular come to mind for you related to your plan for individual conferences: time and expertise. Time is a constraint because you are very busy with instructional responsibilities, but it is also a resource because you have some planning time and you are willing to do it after school and in the evenings. Expertise is a constraint for you because you have minimal experience with parent meetings; your preparation as a teacher is focused almost exclusively on teaching pedagogy. But expertise is also a resource because you have a willingness to learn, you have been reviewing information about effective methods for conducting individual parent conferences, and you have an experienced teacher colleague who has offered to share resources and mentor you. Obviously, you'll take into account your resources and constraints as you select strategies to meet goals and objectives. You have assessed the constraints and resources associated with meeting your goals and objectives, and you have considered various strategies. Now it is time to carry out your individual parent conferences. In the planning process, this is referred to as **implementation**—you schedule and implement your individual parent conferences, document the outcomes of your meetings, and apply the results of the visits to improve your partnerships with parents and your instruction with students.

The last of the seven components of the planning process is **evaluation**. How will you evaluate whether you have met your goals and objectives? Can you quantify or measure the outcomes of your individual parent conferences? (Of course you can!) Did you complete the minimum number of individual parent conferences stated in your objective, and by the time deadline? Are you satisfied with the protocol and strategies that you employed to conduct your individual parent conferences? Did you gain information that helped you better understand the family and plan for their further involvement? Did the families express satisfaction with the meeting and a desire to have individual meetings in the future? The seven components of the planning process have been applied in our special education teacher example. Each is important and interconnected.

FACTORS INFLUENCING A SUCCESSFUL PLAN

The seven components just introduced are useful in understanding the typical process, or cycle, of planning. What factors might be associated with a successful or unsuccessful plan? Think about some of the factors that have influenced the success or failure of a plan in your personal or professional life. Following are five such factors.

First of all, you might consider whether all the seven components are sufficiently taken into account. For example, you might have a plan that is heavy on constraints and limited on resources and therefore not probable for success. Maybe a plan is well conceived from a strong rationale, has meaningful goals and objectives, has strategies based on consideration of constraints and resources, and is implemented, but there are no means of evaluating how the plan worked. So one factor associated with a successful plan is the extent to which it includes all the components.

A second factor is the question of how much emphasis is given to collaboration and teamwork, the partnership, among the members responsible for designing and carrying out a plan. Plans are often doomed from the start if they do not provide for the meaningful involvement and participation of all who are stakeholders and who care about and will be affected directly by the result of the plan. Related to the functions of a planning team, it is obvious that if they do not have a shared vision, a comparable philosophy, and a similar mission in mind, they will have difficulty from the start of the process. Therefore, the second factor associated with successful planning is the use of a team approach in which members have a stake in the plan and the ability to influence decisions through meaningful contributions based on their knowledge and expertise.

A third factor is the extent to which the plan is a real, practical, and usable document that is applied, as opposed to one that is produced to satisfy an imposed requirement. This plan is likely to be filed away and forgotten, used only in the event of a need to provide documentation. Is the plan active or passive? Is it used as a roadmap over the period of time that it is intended to address? Is it updated, changed, and revised as circumstances dictate?

The fourth factor associated with the success or failure of a plan is the role played by the target of the plan: a person (or multiple persons). To the extent possible, have the individual who will be most affected by the plan directly involved in making decisions regarding all components of the process. After all, if an individual is the target of changes specified in a plan, then that person will hopefully feel ownership and investment in carrying out the plan. Further, the persons targeted in a plan should experience it as an effort to advocate, support, and facilitate for them, rather than an adversarial effort intended to require, force, and mandate changes that are imposed on them.

A fifth and final factor is the question of how doable and sustainable the plan is. It is possible, considering the establishment of goals and objectives based on constraints and resources, to make a plan that is too hard or impossible to achieve or one that is too easy and represents insignificant or irrelevant change. For example, it might be difficult for someone to sustain a plan in which his or her objective is to lose 25 pounds in 1 month. Conversely, the objective of losing 1 pound over the period of 1 month might also make the plan of limited use.

To summarize, one might understand the success of planning as dependent on five factors: (1) including all components of the planning process; (2) using a collaborative team approach; (3) having a meaningful, relevant, and useful document; (4) involving the person who is the target of the plan; and (5) making the plan challenging while doable and sustainable. Finally, when planning involves students and families we must ensure that the goals and objectives central to the plan are socially valid and meaningful to the individuals involved and incorporates their input.

PLANNING FOR CHILDREN AND YOUTH AND THEIR FAMILIES

As you are undoubtedly aware, there are numerous required or recommended planning formats and documents associated with the myriad services and programs for children and youth and their families. Although the focus here is specifically on planning as it relates to children and youth in educational environments (especially, of course, those manifesting or at risk for challenging behavior), it is useful to also consider briefly some of the planning approaches in related areas. It is important for professionals to keep in mind that these various plans are frequently mandated and required for individuals to gain access to needed services and resources. So in some respects, they are imposed, and that fact creates circumstances associated with the successful development and implementation of a plan. Following is a brief introduction to various planning formats, some of which you are most likely familiar with, possibly in a similar form.

PLANNING FOR CHILDREN AND YOUTH WITH DISABILITIES

The two prominent plan requirements in special education are the **Individualized Family Service Plan (IFSP)** and the **Individual Education Program (IEP)** plan. You might already be familiar with these two plans to some extent. The IFSP is required for infants and toddlers (ages birth to 3 years) with disabilities and their families who meet the various state definitions for early intervention services provided under Part C of the Individuals with Disabilities Education Act. The IFSP is different from the IEP in several significant ways, including its emphasis on services in natural environments, the expectation that a quality IFSP will be family centered and include outcomes and action steps focusing on the family unit, and the participation of professionals and disciplines outside education. The IFSP is completed on an annual basis, is reviewed at 6 months, and requires that a transition plan be done 1 year before the child moves to a preschool setting. Compared to the IEP, the development, refinement, and evolution of the IFSP is rather brief, having begun with its inclusion in the IDEA Reauthorization of the Education for All Handicapped Children Act Amendments of 1986 (PL 99-457).

The IFSP remains a work in progress, as does the IEP, but it is important to note that the differences between the two planning documents and their associated processes continue to be a source of contention between early interventionists and school personnel. Two reasons for this are the family-centered nature of the IFSP and the use of family-stated and often less measurable objectives (referred to as outcomes) in the IFSP and the inclusion of more broadly stated action steps in the IFSP, rather than curricula and specific strategies as often found in the IEP. It should be noted here that states might choose to use the IFSP for preschool-age children with special needs if they so choose.

In contrast to the IFSP, the IEP is child focused and intended to address exclusively the special educational needs of children who are eligible to receive special education services. Rather than the family-centered emphasis of the IFSP, the IEP has a focus on parent involvement and their participation as one of several stakeholders (note discussion of this term later in this chapter). The IEP is required to be done on an annual basis, including a reevaluation of the child or youth's eligibility and need for special education services. IEPs tend to include more measurable and educationally stated objectives than the IFSP. The IEP is applied for children receiving special education through age 21, and a transition plan, beginning at age 16, is required as a part of the process.

Consider This

When appropriate and desired, the student for whom the IEP is written should be a part of the team responsible for writing and implementing progress toward achieving the goals and objectives stated.

- In what ways might this involvement affect the planning process?

Although both the IEP and the IFSP require the plan to be the result of the efforts of a multidisciplinary team including professionals and family members, the IEP team is child focused and focused on educational matters only. The central mission and beliefs underlying these planning processes, the different roles of parents and families, and the different perspectives related to the approach of measurable outcomes are all important factors to be considered in using behavior support plans for children and youth of all ages in various educational environments.

Before getting into the specifics of behavior support plans, it is helpful to consider a few additional planning processes targeting children and youth with special needs. **Person-centered planning (PCP)** has been described as an effective method of involving parents, students, and family members (Turnbull, Turnbull, Erwin, Soodak, & Shogren, 2015). A primary example of PCP is the McGill Action Planning System (MAPS) (Forest & Lusthaus, 1990). The MAPS process provides the opportunity for a student with a disability and his or her friends, teachers, parents, and siblings to get together and to develop a vision and create an action plan for the student to achieve the vision.

Turnbull and Turnbull (1996) advocated another example of a planning process: **group action planning (GAP)**. The emphasis in the group action plan is on the family unit's need for positive behavior support, rather than exclusively on the child's, and more broadly on inclusive lifestyle change rather than behavior change. GAP is intended to provide comprehensive family support. Turnbull and Turnbull (1996) suggested that as compared to the IEP process, which tends all too often to be routinized, somber, tense, and distant, the key to group action planning is "to create a context in which people can enjoy themselves, feel a sense of renewal and rejuvenation, and obtain personal gratification and validation that they are making a difference in someone's life" (p. 107). GAP contains five elements: inviting support, creating connections, envisioning great expectations, solving problems, and celebrating success. In its emphasis on the family and natural and inclusive lifestyles, GAP may be seen as quite similar to the intent of the IFSP. However, there remains an emphasis frequently in the development of the IFSP on child-centered behavior outcomes to the exclusion or de-emphasis of family-centered and family-guided inclusive lifestyle actions and outcomes. Certainly, the GAP process is quite different from the intent and actualization of the IEP plan. Unlike GAP, the IEP tends to be formal (even quasi-legal), exclusively child centered and focused only on education, time limited, paper driven, and requiring highly measurable outcomes.

The purpose here is not to be critical of the IEP process. Since its beginnings and the inception of the IDEA in 1975, the IEP has certainly been a significant tool to ensure that children and youth with disabilities receive the individual services that they need. Rather, the purpose is to help you understand that there are various planning formats and processes and that they have different missions, emphases, and content. We have briefly considered the IFSP, the IEP, PCP and its related MAPS process, and GAP, and numerous other planning approaches could have been included.

Questions remain for the future: What should and will be the connections among these various planning approaches, especially as they relate to the needs of children and youth with challenging behavior? Will children and youth with special needs and their parents or families be subject to participation in planning processes (often because professionals have said they ought to be) that are quite different and even seen to be at cross purposes? Are there significant discrepancies in the various planning approaches—for example, with regard to child versus family focus, outcome measurability, education versus broader lifestyle—that create barriers, block progress, and create distance for children and youth with disabilities and their families? An example of the potential for incompatibility of plans may be seen when children in early intervention programs transition to preschool- or school-based classrooms. Because there is a great deal of difference between the two, educators, parents or families, and others sometimes experience difficulty in successful transition planning. Finally, what about the connection between the planning approaches introduced here and behavior support plans? Planning approaches and processes that we use as professionals, although they don't need to be uniform, should have sufficient consistency and unity of purpose that children and youth and their families are well served and can have a sense of partnership and ownership in the plan.

INTRODUCING BEHAVIOR SUPPORT PLANNING

As you have learned, the need for **behavior support planning** is a component of the PBIS model. In the 1997 Reauthorization of the IDEA (IDEA, 1997) is the following statement: "In the case of a child whose behavior impedes his or her learning or that of others, the child's IEP team must consider, when appropriate, strategies, including positive behavior intervention strategies and supports to address that behavior" (1414(d)(3)(B)(i)). Turnbull, Wilcox, Turnbull, Sailor, and Wickham (2001, p. 467) defined **impeding behavior** as any behavior that:

1. Impedes the learning of the student or of others and include those behaviors that are externalizing (such as verbal abuse, aggressions, self-injury, or property destruction); are internalizing (such as physical or social withdrawal, depression, passivity, resistance, social or physical isolation, or noncompliance); are manifestations of biological or neurological conditions (such as obsessions, compulsions, stereotypes, or irresistible impulses); or are disruptive (such as annoying, confrontational, defiant, or taunting behavior)
2. Could cause the student to be disciplined pursuant to any state or federal law or regulations or could cause any consideration of a change of the student's educational placement
3. Are consistently recurring and therefore require functional behavior assessment and the systematic and frequent application of positive behavior interventions and supports

Thinking back to the beginning of this chapter and the discussion of the components of program planning and evaluation, recall that prior to the establishment of a plan, the components include the mission/rationale/philosophy, the goals and objectives, the constraints and resources existing that affect the choices of goals and objectives, and the associated strategies needed to carry out the plan. Applying this perspective to PBIS and BSPs, we know that the philosophy of PBIS emphasizes schoolwide relevance, positive methods, teamwork and collaboration, parent or family partnerships, and quality-of-life and lifestyle improvements that are quantifiable. If those participating in the plan development do not share this point of view, success will be limited or non-existent. Goals and objectives to be included in a behavior support plan should be the result of a collaborative team effort and a partnership with parents or families and should be functional and meaningful and foster a sense of ownership by the children or youth targeted and their families. Further, the goals and objectives of the plan should be derived largely from the findings of a functional behavior assessment, especially for children and youth with more substantial and troublesome challenging behaviors.

It is very important to systematically take into account the constraints and resources available prior to the development of a behavior support plan. Certainly, these are not constant and will change over time. In fact, the successful beginnings of implementation of the plan will frequently increase the resources. For example, the plan might lead to more prosocial behavior, which gives a child access to more peer support and friends (resources). Consider that the behavior support plan for a student is being done in the context of the multidisciplinary team and the IEP meeting. Traditionally, IEP meetings have failed to give much attention to the constraints and resources associated with accomplishing the stated goals and objectives, except maybe to emphasize the placement option. In summary, one would desire that the behavior support plan be the result of a shared vision (mission/rationale/philosophy); include quantifiable objectives based on goals that are functional, meaningful, and related to improved quality of life; be the result of information provided by a functional assessment; and use a process of considering and delineating constraints and resources in determining goals, objectives, and intervention strategies.

PBIS has demonstrated its effectiveness and practical application for all children and youth in various educational environments, delivered across all three levels of support. These three levels will now be briefly introduced and then used as the basis for the vignettes and examples of behavior support planning provided later in this chapter. **Level 1** (schoolwide) support targets all students and emphasizes prevention of troublesome behavior by making expectations clear, including students in decision making and ownership of rules, teaching expectations, and providing positive feedback and regard for desired behavior. The percentage of students in a school for whom Level 1 support will be sufficient to establish and maintain desired behavior will vary substantially by the nature of the school and its population. But certainly, the failure to have a schoolwide behavior support plan will increase the number of students who will need more intensive behavior supports.

Level 2 (classroom) supports are individualized and more intense than Level 1 and are the result of functional assessments in school settings. A variety of individualized strategies might be used as a part of Level 2 supports. Turnbull and Turnbull (2001) suggested as examples environmental changes, predictability of schedule, increased choices, curricular adaptations, more attention to rewarding positive behavior, and teaching replacement skills. **Level 3** (tertiary) supports are intended for children and youth with the most comprehensive and pervasive challenging behaviors. Supports at this level would be for a relatively small percentage of students, applied across learning and living environments and resulting from a systematic functional behavior assessment.

Children who require Level 3 supports have impeding behavior that negatively affects their quality of life across multiple environments. Another way to understand the three levels of PBIS is by levels of prevention (National Center on Education, Disability and Juvenile Justice, n.d.) as they have been used to describe the prevention of juvenile delinquency as merely one example. **Primary prevention** corresponds to Level 1 PBIS and suggests universal strategies that may be applied to groups or populations, for example a schoolwide discipline plan. **Secondary prevention** corresponds to Level 2, or targeted PBIS, and the focus is on preventing repeated occurrences of problem behavior through targeted interventions. For example, students who have more than one disciplinary referral in a given month for fighting might be provided with special instruction in conflict resolution or social skills. **Tertiary prevention** equates with Level 3, or intensive PBIS. This level attempts to reduce the impact of a condition or problem on the individual's ability to function in the least restrictive setting. For example, the needs of students identified as having as emotion/behavioral disability are typically addressed through special education services and behavior intervention plans. Sugai and colleagues (1999) further connected these two perspectives. They indicate that primary prevention (schoolwide, Level 1) typically includes 80% to 90% of students without serious behavior problems, secondary prevention (Level 2) includes 5% to 15% of students at risk for problem behavior, and tertiary prevention (Level 3) is focused on the 1% to 7% of students with chronic and/or intense challenging behavior and in need of specialized and highly individualized interventions.

In addition to understanding PBIS planning by the levels introduced, it is helpful to consider planning by age ranges associated with typical educational environments. For purposes here, those environments include infant and preschool settings, early elementary and middle school settings, and high school/secondary environments. There are a number of factors that contribute to the uniqueness of PBIS and associated plans and that are dependent on the ages of the children and youth and the chronological ages associated with the settings. Some of those factors are the relative importance of peers, the role of parents or families, developmental ages and abilities of the child or children for whom planning is done, the nature and composition of the planning team, and the different standards, goals, and practices associated with each environment. For the remainder of this chapter, we will consider all three levels of plans, taking into account some of the special considerations associated with typical age-level educational environments.

PLANNING FOR LEVEL 1 SWPBIS

Although most of the literature related to PBIS planning describes efforts to prevent or intervene at Levels 2 or 3 for individual children or youth in a specific context, comprehensive **schoolwide positive behavioral interventions and supports (SWPBIS)** also requires systematic planning. The National Center for Positive Behavioral Interventions and Supports (www.pbis.org) is a primary source for current information about the design and implementation of schoolwide models of PBIS. In many respects, SWPBIS includes the basic elements that have long been considered desirable in education. Students know and understand what is expected and are provided opportunities to learn the expectations. Behavior expectations are stated positively, and students are acknowledged and rewarded for adhering to the expectations significantly more than they are sanctioned for not adhering to them. Additionally, the development, implementation, and evaluation of schoolwide behavioral support planning is the result of a team collaborative effort that (to the maximum extent possible) includes participation by the persons (students) who are the targets of the plan.

Consider the five factors introduced at the beginning of the chapter and associated with successful planning. The first factor is that all components of planning are included—that it is comprehensive. If, for example, a school develops what seems to be a good plan but does not specify the means by which it will be evaluated, then it will be difficult to determine when and whether it has succeeded.

The second factor is the extent to which teamwork is used. Suppose that a high school-wide plan includes the participation at all levels of high school students as members of the team; this obviously has the potential to improve the plan.

The third factor is the extent to which the plan is real, practical, and useable. Who are the primary persons directly affected by a schoolwide behavior support plan? Such a list would include the teachers and other school personnel, the students in the school, and families of the students. Of course, having a comprehensive plan (Factor 1) that includes representation from all of the stakeholders as members of the team (Factor 2) is going to contribute to the plan being real, practical, and useable (Factor 3). Suppose, for example, that a large, diverse, and urban high school administration, without the participation of the student body, determines that their schoolwide plan will include a strict dress code requiring a uniform. The students are the targets of this plan, so if they are represented in decisions about the dress code, then they are more likely to have a sense of ownership and commitment to successful implementation of the plan (Factor 4).

The fifth factor is the extent to which the plan is doable and sustainable. To summarize, all these factors are connected. A schoolwide behavior support plan that is comprehensive, is developed by a team, is relevant, involves meaningful participation by the persons targeted by the plan, and is doable and sustainable is most likely to be successful. Horner and Sugai (2000) provided seven key themes regarding the implementation of schoolwide behavior support. These themes provide the framework for the development of a SWPBIS plan.

Level 1 Behavior Support Planning for Young Children

In planning PBIS for very young children, it is especially important to keep in mind the guidance related to behavior provided by both the NAEYC and the DEC of the CEC. One of the primary principles and beliefs about the challenging behavior of young children is that "many young children engage in challenging behavior in the course of early development. This statement points to the importance of planning that is done by infant, preschool, and other early childhood educators related to establishing and maintaining learning and developmental environments (such as Head Start, preschool classrooms, home-based settings, and nursery schools) that facilitate desired behaviors. One example from the literature was provided by Fox and Little (2001) who described the successful development and implementation of a schoolwide behavior support plan in an inclusive, NAEYC-accredited community preschool. Seven themes provided by Fox and Little may be used as a guide for plan development. The seven themes, in summary, are: (1) local team development; (2) clear administrative direction and support; (3) identification of a small number of behavior expectations to define the school culture; (4) teaching students behavior expectations; (5) on-going system of recognition and reward for meeting behavior expectations; (6) neither ignore nor reward problem behaviors, with dangerous or disruptive behaviors corrected; and (7) continuous collections of information on student performance summarized for decision making by local teams. Recent success of this model in preschools is also evident from a study conducted by Steed, Pomerleau, Muscott, and Rohde (2013) who demonstrated program-wide PBIS in three rural preschool programs pointing to the utility of this practice across settings.

In general, we might conclude that an effective preschool-wide behavior support plan will include the characteristics to follow. It is the result of a collaborative team process that includes meaningful input from all the stakeholders, including, for example, teachers/caregivers, family members, administrators, specialists, assistants/paraprofessionals, and other relevant individuals. The plan is written in a manner that is clear and understood by all the stakeholders. It represents what is known as best and effective practice (for example, NAEYC, DEC, and state standards and guidelines) related to positive child guidance and positive behavior supports. Although everyone will most certainly not agree on all counts, to the maximum extent possible the plan reflects a shared vision and agreed-upon beliefs, goals, and actions. And last, the plan is available, referenced, and used on a regular basis, making it an active plan rather than one that is filed away and forgotten.

Level 1 Behavior Support Planning for School-Age Children and Youth

It is useful here to consider the distinctions that may be made among prevention, support, and intervention as they relate to schoolwide behavior support planning in elementary, middle, and secondary school educational environments. Schoolwide plans are intended to support the desired behavior of all students and to prevent acute or chronic challenging behavior of students by providing positive environments and supports, thus avoiding the necessity of interventions at Level 2 or Level 3. The assumption is that the development and implementation of a sound schoolwide plan will decrease the numbers of students who will require intervention. Schoolwide behavior support is proactive and preventive as opposed to a reactive response to the occurrence of challenging behaviors. Intervention is, after all, an intrusion, and the more intensive the intervention, the more it draws attention to differences and potential exclusion rather than similarities and inclusion. This is not to say, of course, that interventions do not have or cannot achieve the objective of facilitating a student's learning of more acceptable behaviors and therefore more inclusion with their peers and in the classroom. Keep in mind that the mission of PBIS is to improve quality of life, including independence and inclusion.

Successful SWPBIS are characterized by defining behavioral expectations, teaching students about these expectations and reinforcing students for their efforts aimed at engaging in these behaviors throughout the school year. All students have opportunities to learn self-control and social skills. There is a creative and individualized system for rewarding desired behaviors, and immediate feedback is provided for undesirable behavior. Problematic behavior has clear consequences, but much more emphasis is given to rewarding desired behavior. Settings that prove to be problematic are changed. All school employees are involved. The plan includes a clear means of monitoring and evaluating whether the schoolwide system (plan) is achieving the desired intents. Last, there is the recognition that approximately 5% of students have chronic challenging behavior and will benefit from Level 2 or 3 PBIS.

PBIS may be thought of as a continuum of support for children and youth in educational environments, from systemic, schoolwide supports to highly individualized and intensive interventions. The approaches, formats, and purposes of planning may also be understood as occurring on this continuum. Planning for schoolwide systems of PBIS are distinct from Level 2 and Level 3 planning, but they too include the idea of focusing on inputs, process, and outputs as part of planning. Input is the assessment and collection of information needed to develop the plan. It might include the school mission and beliefs, quantifiable data regarding retention rate, referrals related to behavior, staff turnover, information on classroom behavior incidences, and suspensions. It might also include the points of view of families, teachers, administrators, and students. These are examples of the input needed to develop a plan. Process is the implementation of the plan and on-going efforts to monitor how it is going. Continued reference to and use of the plan during the process of implementation is important. It might be necessary to make adjustments and refinements as experience dictates during implementation. Outputs are the outcomes of implementation of the schoolwide behavior support plan. Outcomes (outputs) may be used to sum up (summative) what and how much has been accomplished by the plan or may be used to formulate new and revised plans (formative). Sugai, Lewis-Palmer, Todd, and Horner (2001) provided an instrument useful in evaluating and assessing the critical features of a schoolwide behavior support plan. The Systems-Wide Evaluation Tool: School-Wide (SET-SW) applies multiple steps to gather information from multiple sources, including review of permanent products (such as school improvement plan goals or discipline handbooks), observations, staff and student interviews, and surveys. Many planning and evaluation tools focusing on schoolwide PBIS have been developed and researched over the past decade. A number of them are listed online at http://www.pbis.org/evaluation/evaluation-tools, the website of the OSEP Technical Assistance Center on Positive Behavioral Interventions and Supports—Effective Schoolwide Interventions.

Weber (2002) provided an outline for efforts to develop a SWPBIS plan. Although procedures will vary according to variables such as student age, school setting, and characteristics of the population and community, eight procedures are typically needed in the planning and preparation stages. It is recommended that the SWPBIS plan developed by a committee that include both a lead group and a secondary group that participates periodically to provide feedback. A statement of purpose and an associated set of values or beliefs and principles should be developed. Next, a list of clearly defined behavior expectations for all students in the school should be developed. Development of a program that helps students understand and display the desired behaviors should be articulated as a part of the plan. A sequence or continuum of consequences should be devised to apply when students violate the behavior expectations. Fostering of a total staff commitment and a sense of common purpose is necessary. Last, there should be an awareness and teaching effort designed to help the students understand and also feel ownership of the behavior support plan and system.

Vignette 7.1

Schoolwide PBIS in an Inner-City Elementary School

Scott (2001) initially described the effects of SWPBIS in an inner-city elementary school. He found that a SWPBIS resulted in both a decrease in the number of problem behaviors of students, specifically decreasing those excluded from classrooms for problem behaviors, and a clearer focus for intervention on the students with needs for intense support and intervention. Specifically with regard to the planning process, this study applied the principles of effective SWPBIS introduced earlier. The commitment of school personnel was gained through a process of three meetings; resulting in a unanimous vote to adopt a schoolwide PBIS plan for the upcoming year.

School personnel then participated in a process that generated a list of predictable problem behaviors in the school and the places, times, and conditions under which they would occur. Next, groups of school personnel worked to brainstorm prevention strategies and develop a consensus regarding strategies to be applied. Finally, the school personnel determined schoolwide expectations predictive of student success and agreed to consistently reinforce compliance with behavior expectations and to enforce and reteach for students who were not complying. From the school personnel participating in the planning process, a schoolwide team was created to meet monthly, look at data, report to others on progress, and facilitate changes as needed.

PLANNING FOR LEVEL 2 PBIS

Remember that although Level 1 PBIS is comprehensive, schoolwide, and limited in intensity, Level 2 PBIS is of moderate intensity, is for some students in school settings, and is often paired with response-to-intervention (RtI) strategies as targeted intervention strategies aimed at remediation of both academic and behavioral difficulties in need of skill enhancement. In general it is reasonable to assume that a successful schoolwide system of PBIS might reduce the number of students needing Level 2 or Level 3 support from 20% to between 10% and 15%. For that 10% to 15%, perhaps half of them might benefit from Level 2 PBIS. There will consistently be about 5% of the population in a given school that will require Level 3 or tertiary PBIS. We therefore may estimate that the population of students that will benefit from Level 2 PBIS will be 5% to 10%. Of course, this percentage varies as a result of the success of the schoolwide plan, the nature of the population, the skill of the teachers, and other factors.

A primary distinction between Levels 1 and Level 2 PBIS is that Level 2 supports are individualized and are primarily interventions rather than focused on groups and on prevention usually at the classroom level. There are many circumstances in which young children or school-age children and youth need individual support of moderate intensity but have not been classified as having a disability. One example might possibly be the preadolescent and adolescent youth who has been removed from school and placed in an alternative school environment, who have not been classified as having serious emotional disturbance or any other disability but nonetheless are in need of Level 2 (and frequently Level 3) PBIS. For students who require Level 2 PBIS, but who have not been identified as having a disability, the behavior support plan may be the single document and guide for addressing the student's challenging behavior(s). One obvious difference is that the law does not mandate the development and implementation of a plan.

Consider This

Children and youth in a sense might fall between the cracks because Level 1 support isn't sufficient, but they do not have a disability, and their challenging behavior(s) may not be chronic and intense to the extent that Level 3 intervention and support is required.

- How might you, as an educator, provide the support and reinforcement that children in this category need to replace their present behavior with more acceptable behavior(s) in your setting?

In a comprehensive review of the effects of Level 2 PBIS for individuals with disabilities, Carr and others (1999) looked at outcomes. Their synthesis of the research yielded some important findings and conclusions. Beyond the finding that Level 2 supports made a significant difference in reducing the impeding behaviors of most of the instances, other findings are useful in guiding planning. Functional behavior assessment (FBA) was important to planning, adults significant in a child's life must also change their behavior, environments should frequently be reorganized, and people who have central and meaningful relationships with the person targeted for behavior change are most important. One might think of these factors as they relate to successful IEP planning. The plan is based on multiple sources of assessment data including data from an FBA and it is undertaken and monitored by a team of people who care about the child, and it includes a focus on how others (for example, teachers, family members, or classmates) might change and how the environments might also change. We now turn our attention to some of the considerations associated with Level 2 PBIS planning in either preschool or school-age educational environments.

Level 2 Behavior Support Planning for Young Children

The myriad of effective positive child guidance techniques that are typically applied by parents, caregivers, and preschool teachers are not always sufficient to address the challenging behaviors of young children. When these usually effective strategies, specified as a part of schoolwide (preschool) PBIS planning are not sufficient, it is necessary to respond by developing plans that are more individualized and that apply different strategies or more intense versions of existing strategies. In the development of behavior support plans, it is important to keep in mind that intervention is by nature intrusive and that it focuses on differences rather than likenesses between children. Therefore, it is desirable to plan Level 2 PBIS only at the level of intensity needed to affect desired behavior change. Vignette 7.2 illustrates how Level 2 planning might be applied in a preschool classroom environment.

Vignette 7.2

Alyshea

Alyshea is a 3½-year-old girl who is enrolled in Noah's Ark, a community-based and church-affiliated private preschool. Her classroom has 15 children ages 3 to 5, reflecting the movement in early childhood education and the benefits associated with multi-age grouping. Alyshea is chronologically the youngest child in her room. She is also developmentally the youngest because she functions in general more like a child of 3 years of age. Alyshea has been described by her pediatrician as immature and may be showing some indications of ADHD. There is a lead teacher and teaching assistant in the room, which is organized into activity centers. Emphasis is placed on child-initiated and -directed activities. Noah's Ark is accredited by the NAEYC, and the beliefs and principles of developmentally appropriate practice are followed.

In this child- and family-friendly environment, Alyshea functions quite well, with one notable exception. Each morning there is a circle time during which the teacher reads a book to the group for 15 minutes. The children are seated on a rug in a semicircle and listen to the teacher as she reads. The teacher engages the children by asking them questions and having them name and describe characters in the book. The teacher's plan (Level 1) for all the children to achieve the desired behaviors or outcomes of listening to the story, interacting, increasing attention span, increasing vocabulary, appreciating books, and fostering preliteracy skills include the following: she selects books that are of high interest and developmentally appropriate, she introduces the children to the book the day prior to reading it, she provides frequent opportunities for the children to interact as she reads, and she has her teaching assistant circulate and verbally prompt and redirect children as needed. This approach works reasonably well for all of the children—except Alyshea. She has difficulty sitting for more than a few minutes, so she stands up and runs around the room. She also has verbal outbursts that interrupt the teacher and the other children. With the support and technical assistance available from the local school behavior specialist for young children and with the support and acceptance of the parents, the teacher, teaching assistant, and director, a team is established to develop a plan for Alyshea.

Reflective Moment

Note that Alyshea does not have a formal disability diagnosis, so she is not eligible for an IEP as a part of special education services. What implications might this fact have, either positive or negative, for the planning and delivering of PBIS for Alyshea? What might be some of the alternative strategies chosen by the team to include in a plan to improve Alyshea's circle time behavior?

Level 2 Behavior Support Planning for School-Age Children and Youth

Consider the forms that the challenging behavior of school-age children from kindergarten through high school might take. It might be anything from noncompliance, refusal to follow instruction or do assignments, aggressive behavior or bullying toward peers, verbal outbursts, cursing, other forms of class disruption, or withdrawn, overly shy behavior. Also, think about the children and youth who exhibit those behaviors. They might be students who have been classified as having a disability, emotional/behavior disorders, another type of disability, or a combination of all three. Or they might be students who are not classified as having special needs but who do have an acute challenging behavior that is not responsive to the broader structure and approach (Level 1) to preventing misbehavior and fostering desired behavior in school settings.

As noted previously, when students exhibit challenging behavior that is not successfully addressed by schoolwide behavior support, they frequently require and benefit from a more individualized and systematic intervention based on data gathered from a functional behavior assessment. Keep in mind the distinction (although it is frequently difficult or even unnecessary in practice to do so) between Levels 2 and 3 PBIS planning. Level 2 targets challenging behavior that is singular, is more situation-specific, and necessitates interventions of moderate intensity. Level 3 targets challenging behavior of fewer students, require more intensive interventions, and are comprehensive in nature. That is, it occurs across various environments and suggests the need for persons representing all those environments as participants in the planning (as well as implementation and evaluation) process. One might argue that although children and youth experiencing challenging behavior at either level will have a diminished quality of life, those for whom Level 3 PBIS and interventions are needed will predictably experience a more substantial and comprehensive negative impact on their quality of life and that of their families, teachers, classmates, and others.

Carr and colleagues (1999) with regard to Level 2 PBIS reached several conclusions that have direct relevance for the planning process. Interventions and supports are more successful when functional behavior assessments are the basis for the plan when significant individuals, in addition to the student targeted, change their behavior when the environment is reorganized and when intervention is carried out by persons with whom the student has on-going and meaningful relationships. All these dimensions of successful Level 2 PBIS should be evident in the planning process and documents. Most certainly the school team will have conducted a functional behavior assessment and developed a behavior support plan (BSP) using these data with multiple inputs from team members including the student's parents and family.

There are a number of behavior support plan formats and processes from which to choose as have been described in the literature (Anderson, Russo, Dunlap, & Albin, 1996; Jackson & Veeneman-Panyan, 2002; Janney & Snell, 2000; O'Neill et al., 2014; Scott, Liaupsin, & Nelson, 2001). These forms and processes vary somewhat and must be individualized to address the unique circumstance of a particular student, family, and school environment. They do, however, have the following components and emphases largely in common in varying amounts.

Such processes are frequently entitled "behavior support plan," "positive behavior support plan," "plan for positive behavior support," or "behavior intervention plan." Jackson and Veeneman-Panyan (2002) used the term *solution-focused behavior intervention planning form* to guide what they describe as a "different planning and implementation format that is inspired by solution-focused concepts, grounded in theories of discourse and collaborative processes for the construction of shared knowledge, and structured as an on-going guided inquiry activity" (p. 215). Most planning forms and formats include either the complete results of the functional behavior assessment or a summary of that assessment. Most forms and formats include a description of the challenging behavior(s), and some differentiate in the description between the form and function of the behavior(s). Stated another way, what does the behavior look like (form), and what purpose does it serve for the child in meeting his or her needs (function)? Essentially, all plans and formats require the inclusion of an operational definition of the behavior(s). The definition must be operationally defined and easily understood by everyone. Some plans include a section in which previous strategies are described or summarized. Most plans and formats include a hypothesis regarding the function of the behavior, which might be a brief description of what individuals believe is the function of the behavior. The hypothesis might be specific, global, or both. It might be argued that in practice and with a number of team members involved, the global hypothesis is more useful. It is generated from data attained through the functional behavior assessment and might be described as an "educated guess" about how the challenging behavior is associated with the needs of the child being met.

Most approaches apply some version of what O'Neill and others (2014) referred to as the **competing behaviors model**. In the competing behaviors model, the following elements are used to identify desirable and replacement behaviors to compete with the impeding, challenging behaviors. Setting events associated with the challenging behavior are described when possible. Antecedents associated with the challenging behavior, the desired behavior, and/or replacement behavior is stated. The desired behavior is stated in the plan. The consequences assumed to be reinforcing the challenging behavior and those to be associated with the desired or replacement behaviors are stated. You'll frequently find in plans summaries or descriptions of antecedents, including changing environmental arrangements and teaching strategies.

Also, plans may include detail about the reinforcing consequences of desired behavior. Some plans include a section on written behavior objectives, but most treat them as part of the implementation and do not include them in the plan. Other components that are occasionally included in planning formats and forms are descriptions of long-term prevention strategies or crisis plans (what to do if the student experiences a crisis that has an acute potential for endangering him- or herself, others, or property). Although most plans provide a place where names and roles of team members might be stated and signatures provided, fewer provide information about action planning (who will do what, when, and where) and what supports will be given to particular team members. And some forms and formats include a section for formative and summative evaluation of the plan's implementation. They are largely focused on outcomes of the intervention and answering the question about whether desired behaviors increased or undesired behaviors decreased.

In summary, there are numerous planning forms and formats for PBIS. Some are simple and straightforward. Others are more complex and comprehensive. Some include content that addresses the team and collaborative nature of PBIS assumed, especially in Level 3 interventions and supports. Figure 7–2 illustrates one example of behavior support plan forms for Level 2 or Level 3 positive behavior intervention and support planning.

PLANNING FOR LEVEL 3 PBIS

Remember that children and youth who require Level 3 PBIS are those for whom the planning and implementation of Levels 1 and 2 are insufficient to address their challenging behavior. That is, Level 3 PBIS is used only when there is a need for an intensive

FIGURE 7–2

Behavior Support Plan Forms

Child's Name Daniel E   **Date** 03/16/12

Age: 6   **Review/Revision Date(s)** 09/01/12

E/BD w/communication delays

Team Members Classroom Teacher   Miss Hasenfuss

S/L Therapist   Laura Logan

Parents   Bill and Pam Eshler

Functional Assessment Summary (attach complete assessment):

Structured interview completed by classroom teacher, speech language therapist, and parents.

Motivation Assessment Scale—Completed by teacher and S/L Therapist; Scatter-plot—Completed by teacher.

Behavior Description:

Verbal and physical aggression, destructive behavior, tantrums, and noncompliance.

Behavior Definition:

Incidents of challenging behavior are defined as any acts of verbal or physical aggression (yelling at teacher, hitting, kicking), tantrums as evidenced by crying and shouting at the teacher, and noncompliance.

Summary of Previous Strategies:

Daniel appears to be a "visual learner" and performs well when working one-on-one with the teacher or in small groups of fewer than three children. Daniel can also display appropriate behavior when working on preferred tasks.

Hypothesis—Function of Behavior:

Global

Primary Function—Attention;
Secondary Function—
Escape/Avoidance

Specific

When presented with nonpreferred tasks, Daniel will display one or more
forms of challenging behavior.

ABC:

Antecedents	Behavior (desired)	Consequences
Setting Events: Large group or classwide setting event	To consult his schedule as a means of promoting task engagement and to communicate his need for teacher assistance by raising his hand.	Use of differential reinforcement in the form of praise for approximations at "task engagement," appropriate use of schedule, and for raising his hand to seek teacher assistance. Present Daniel with increased opportunities for choices in tasks during the day.
Antecedents: Unpreferred tasks presented by teacher		
Strategies: Develop a picture schedule to serve as a cue to help Daniel in understanding task sequences.	**Strategies:** Actively teach Daniel in using his schedule and raising hand.	

Implementation Notes (including behavior objectives):

Antecedent Management Strategies—Use of picture/word schedules, advanced prompts, and verbal reinforcement for approximating compliance and task engagement.

Replacement Behaviors—Actively teach and reinforce how to seek teacher assistance appropriately. Use a system of least-to-most prompts and modeling.

Consequences—Using differential reinforcement, verbally praise Daniel for attempts at desired behavior in the absence of challenging behavior.

Team Action Plans: Who	What	When	Where	Support
Classroom Teacher	Picture/Word Schedule +	Daily	Classroom Setting	Daniel's team will provide support if needed.
Speech/Language Therapist	Use of Differential Reinforcement +			
	Opportunities for Choice			

Long-Term Prevention Strategies:

Use of creative scheduling and interspersed requesting by building in opportunities for choice and performance of preferred activities.

Crisis Plan:

If Daniel's aggression is perceived as invasive or as a threat to the well-being of his classmates, he will be escorted to the principal's office.

Tentative Evaluation Plans: Inputs (looking at the plan)	Processes (looking at the implementation)	Outcomes (looking at the results)
Are the behavior expectations stated in the plan developmentally appropriate for Daniel? Plan reviewed and commented on by teacher's first-grade colleagues and by parents.	Team meeting, including parents, after 2–3 weeks of implementation to discuss progress to date and consider any needed adjustments to plan.	At 6 weeks, observation and frequency count of increase in raising hand and consulting schedule and decrease in aggressive behaviors. Also, meeting with parents to determine satisfaction with plan and possible impacts at home.

and comprehensive plan that is not provided by less-intrusive approaches. Planning for Level 3 PBIS is complicated by the fact that the challenging behavior(s) occur across multiple settings (home, school, and community), requiring a high level of coordination and collaboration from individuals who are especially concerned about the well-being of the child.

We intentionally avoid use of the term *stakeholders* because that term seems to suggest that the child is an object or a commodity. Also, the family should certainly be seen and understood as more than just one of several stakeholders. The teaming and shared beliefs necessary to successfully plan Level 3 support suggest the need for intraschool (between and among personnel, and possibly students, in the school or preschool) connections as well as between school personnel and others, such as family members and other persons who are significant in the child's life (for example, minister or coach). The difficulties here are obvious. It is challenging in many schools to find time, opportunity, and willingness for teachers to meet and plan together. Also, it has been noted (Turnbull & Turnbull, 2001) that most schools do not have comprehensive services, so the important connections between a student (who needs a Level 3 PBIS plan) and his or her life at home and in the community are possibly not understood or addressed by teachers and other school personnel.

Finally, with regard to Level 3 PBIS, planning always is based on the results of a functional behavior assessment. Refer to Chapter 5 for specific procedures, processes, and instruments useful in conducting functional behavior assessments for children in need of comprehensive and intensive plans. The next two sections address considerations associated with Level 3 planning for either preschool-age children or school-age children and youth.

Level 3 Behavior Support Planning for Young Children

The preschool period refers to children whose ages range from birth through kindergarten. NAEYC takes the position that kindergarteners are preschoolers. Therefore, very young children may be understood as including newborns, infants, toddlers, preschoolers ages 3 to 5, and kindergarteners. What are the considerations associated with planning Level 3 PBIS for very young children?

The fundamental components of successful planning (see five factors described earlier in the chapter) apply, and the need for a systematic functional assessment, in which the form and function of challenging behavior are identified and operationalized, also applies. Collaborative teamwork aimed at producing a comprehensive, individualized plan with measurable outcomes applies. However, some considerations are largely unique when planning Level 3 PBIS for young children. Beyond considerations such as the developmental status of young children related to, for example, the ability to communicate and their level of dependence on adults, here are three such considerations. First, many but certainly not all of these children (see, for example, Alyshea in Vignette 7.2), will have been formally identified and certified as having special needs. As a result, they will have an early intervention (IFSP) or a special education (IEP) plan.

The IFSP or IEP can have anything from a great deal of focus on behavior support planning to none. If the primary disability is specific to behavior, one would certainly expect the IEP or IFSP to be the basis for behavior support planning. So one consideration associated with very young children is the nature of and formats for the legally mandated planning in early intervention and preschool special education. Stated another way, the IFSP is different from an IEP and is focused on children from birth to 3 years and their families, and the IEP for a preschool-age child is different from an IEP for a school-age child.

A second consideration has to do with living, learning, and developmentally appropriate environments. You have learned that Level 3 interventions and supports are comprehensive—that is, they apply across all the settings relevant to an individual child. Obviously, the typical environments in the life of an infant, toddler, or preschooler are different from a school-age child. For a very young child, it might be more focused on home, child care center, grandparents or extended family, and neighborhood settings such as the grocery market. For school-age children, school, afterschool programs, and group environments (for example, the soccer team) are more typical. These varied environments are inhabited by different individuals requiring different approaches to their participation in Level 3 planning. As you're probably aware, there is a significant emphasis on natural environments and early inclusion practices for very young children with special needs, including challenging behaviors. Therefore, planning might require more attention to the fit between the interventions and supports planned, the realities of the natural and inclusive environments, and the willingness of the persons in those environments to participate in planning and delivering Level 3 PBIS.

Suppose in the example in Vignette 7.2 that Alyshea's challenging behavior is somewhat more extreme and is not responsive to Level 2 supports. She runs around the room throughout much of the day and also hits other children, and these behaviors occur across other environments (home, Sunday school, etc.). Alyshea needs comprehensive, intensive Level 3 intervention and support. Historically, the caregiver or preschool teacher might have felt that Alyshea is now beyond his or her responsibility and expertise and should be referred for evaluation, special education, and a placement outside the preschool classroom. The challenge is clearly how to plan Level 3 support in a manner that is individualized, intensive, and measurable; works across environments; and fits with the natural and inclusive setting.

A third consideration is the role of parents and families in planning Level 3 supports for very young children. Most of the professional literature addressing interventions for children and youth experiencing challenging behavior includes a discussion of the importance of parents as part of a multidisciplinary team or as partners in a collaborative team effort. However, distinctions might be made between the focus on parents versus families and on family-centeredness versus parent involvement. For school-age children and youth (with special needs related to challenging behavior), the focus is clearly on parent involvement as a part of the team planning and delivering intervention and support to achieve education-specific objectives—that is, to change behavior that impedes educational progress.

On the other hand, for very young children and especially for early intervention, the emphasis will likely be on families rather than just parents, on family-centered practices, and on challenging behavior as it affects all aspects of a young child's quality of life, not just his or her academic performance. Neilsen and McEvoy (2004) recommended that when linking the results of functional behavior assessment to intervention for young children with challenging behavior, interventions selected must be acceptable to families and consistent with their values, skills, and resources. Understanding the role of families and knowing how to facilitate their empowerment and accepting their increased influence related to Level 3 planning proves challenging for many of us as educators.

Level 3 Behavior Support Planning for School-Age Children and Youth

The PBIS planning forms and formats appropriate for Level 3 school-age planning are essentially the same as those described earlier as appropriate for Level 2 school-age PBIS. However, there are some unique considerations associated with Level 3 school-age planning. Remember that Level 3 interventions and supports are intended for students who have a need for intensive and comprehensive interventions that are delivered by multiple individuals (team members) across a variety of settings. Turnbull and Turnbull (2001) suggested that a distinguishing characteristic of Level 3 support planning and implementation is the necessary link among home, school, and community and the pervasive collaboration among them. Peck Peterson, Derby, Harding, Weddle, and Barretto (2002) point out that "facilitating parental input in behavior support plans is especially valuable when children reach school age because of the variety of settings in which they must participate (e.g., home, classroom, bus, child care)" (p. 303). Consider how this concept complicates the planning process, given what was introduced at the beginning of the chapter as factors associated with successful planning. One such factor is the extent to which the plan is comprehensive and includes all the elements of planning (rationale or mission, goals, objectives, strategies, constraints and resources, implementation, and evaluation). An example of a model that meets these criteria for comprehensive planning is the Prevent-Teach-Reinforce (PTR) model (Dunlap, Iovannone, Wilson, Kincaid, & Strain, 2010; Dunlap et al., 2010), intended as a schoolwide process to individualize PBIS for students with serious behavior challenges in a range of school settings. The PTR model has five steps: (1) teaming, (2) goal setting, (3) functional behavioral assessment, (4) intervention, and (5) evaluation.

Development of a comprehensive plan that results from the meaningful contributions of team members representing home, school, and community takes substantial coordination, time, and effort, and it is dependent on a process of team building, establishment of trust, and problem solving over time. A second factor associated with successful planning is the extent to which it represents a partnership and a shared vision among the team members. Level 3 planning (and implementation) will be unsuccessful or minimally successful if all members of the team do not consider themselves to be a part of the plan.

The extent to which the plan is real, practical, and doable (third factor associated with success) certainly will affect success in Level 3 planning. Intervention plans have long failed because they did not have these attributes for parents, family members, and other persons in the child's life. Too often, educators and behavior interventionists have expected parents and others to plan and implement interventions that were not a good fit for them. Rao and Kalyanpur (2002) described correction of this issue as developing plans with a good conceptual fit. That is, all aspects of the intervention, including the means of reinforcing the desired behavior and the individual styles of the persons and unique aspects of the environment, should be individualized. They pointed out that "interventions that do not consider parental values or resolve the differences between parents and professionals may not address the problem behavior at all" (2002, p. 232).

A fourth factor associated with successful planning is the role of the person who is targeted for behavior change. A worthwhile goal in the development, implementation, and ongoing assessment of Level 3 planning is to work toward increased participation of the student. Remember that no one likes to have a plan imposed on them and that ownership of the plan increases likelihood of success. It is certainly dependent on the developmental and cognitive status of the child or youth, but in most instances he or she can be supported to feel a sense of ownership of the plan. Because the student is the only one who is to be found in all of the settings relevant to the plan, he or she can become an important part of ensuring continuity across environments. The last factor associated with successful planning is making the plan challenging but doable, as it is associated with Level 3 school-age planning.

Consider This

Plans and interventions at this level are intense and comprehensive; they are also more complicated and more difficult to manage. A teacher in the general education classroom, a parent, or a religious instruction teacher may feel like his or her role in the intervention is overwhelming and impossible. So it is important in the planning to take into account that the persons involved believe that as a part of the team and with the team's support, they can do their part and be successful.

SUMMARY

Planning is something that we all include in both our personal and professional lives. There is, of course, a great deal of variance among people with regard to how they view planning and how they use it to improve the quality of their lives. Sometimes planning is systematic, formal, and written, and at other times it is unsystematic and done with few if any behavior manifestations. Planning is applied in formal ways across a variety of human service disciplines and areas, such as social services, mental health, and child welfare. As professionals in education, it is important for us to think of planning as something that we do *with* people rather than something that is done *to* people. Many special educators, for example, might concur that all too often the IEP process is more consistent with the latter approach.

The planning process has been described as having seven components: a rationale or mission, goals, objectives, strategies, constraints and resources, implementation, and evaluation (evaluation is covered in detail in Chapter 8). Five factors may be associated with successful planning: comprehensive inclusion of all components; a teamwork/collaborative approach to planning; having a meaningful, relevant, and useful planning document; involving the person(s) who is (are) a target of the plan; and making the plan challenging while doable and sustainable. These components of the planning process and the five factors associated with success are applicable to behavior support plans across multiple settings and at three levels of intensity.

Although the literature in behavior support planning is largely focused on meeting the individual needs of children with challenging behaviors, behavior support planning has a broader application in supporting PBIS. Three levels of behavior support planning were introduced and examples provided. Level 1 is planning that is associated with comprehensive, schoolwide plans. It includes all students in a particular school environment, is limited in intensity, and does not include the use of functional assessment as a means of establishing the plan or evaluating its success. Level 2 behavior support plans are for a limited number of students who experience moderate levels of challenging behavior. It is typically confined to implementation in school settings and includes the use of functional assessment. Level 3 behavior support planning is for fewer students, is often associated with their IFSP or IEP, is more intense, typically extends beyond the school environment to home and community, and results from a functional assessment.

This chapter has not focused on providing a recipe for what a BSP should look like. There are many examples in the literature in which different planning processes, formats, and documents have been successfully applied (see the sections on Further Reading and Exploration for sources). The chapter has emphasized the importance of planning at the three levels of positive behavior support and the elements typically included for successful planning at each level. There are few examples in the literature of what a Level 1 schoolwide PBIS plan looks like. Rather, the emphasis is on the desired process and the elements that should be included. If one looked at comprehensive plans across a number of schools, undoubtedly some would be limited to one or two pages, whereas others might take up a volume or more to detail the plan. For Levels 2 and 3 positive behavior intervention and support—largely as a result of their connection to special education—it is likely that the plan will be rather standardized and will be written to include the elements described earlier. Regardless of the level of planning, it is important for professionals to know what planning is, what makes it succeed, and how it should be applied to support children and youth to learn and exhibit the behavior that will help them succeed in learning environments.

ACTIVITIES TO EXTEND YOUR LEARNING

1. This activity might be done over the period of several class sessions. Divide the class into small groups (teams) of four to eight members. Each team should develop a hypothetical school environment (including preschool, elementary, middle, and high school) and specify characteristics and uniqueness of the school (setting, diversity, emphasis, etc.). Establish roles for each member of the team (e.g., teacher, parent, administrator, student, other). Develop a SWPBIS plan using the guidance provided in the chapter. Complete this exercise by sharing with the class as a whole.

2. Generate as a class a list of agencies, disciplines, or programs in which there exists a formal and required planning process and document (see discussion in the chapter). Either individually or in small groups, select one planning approach. Review guidelines or talk with professionals who use the plan to gain an understanding of its application. Compare your planning process and document to the criteria provided in the chapter for a quality plan. Also compare your planning process and document to behavior support planning, IEP planning, and IFSP planning.

3. Review your state's guidelines for development of the IEP and the IFSP as well as the documents. Consider how behavior support planning might fit well or not so well, given its desired components, in your state's IEP and IFSP.

4. Identify a school in your community that has successfully implemented for 2 or 3 years a SWPBIS plan, and invite a member or members of the team to come and share with your class.

5. Identify a behavior specialist, special education consulting teacher, school psychologist, school counselor, or special education supervisor in a local education agency who is the most experienced professional at that organization related to understanding and developing PBIS plans. Invite this person and, if appropriate, a parent or family representative to provide a guest lecture to the class. Ask the guests to contrast their planning approach to the practices recommended in the chapter.

6. Several Level 2 or 3 behavior support planning forms and processes are referenced in this chapter. Go to the sources for these plan forms and processes and examine each to see what they have in common and how they are unique. Consider how they might work for Level 2 planning as compared to Level 3.

FURTHER READING AND EXPLORATION

1. Go to the website of the National Association of School Psychologists (www.nasponline.org) and look for projects and initiatives that NASP is undertaking related to safe and responsive schools and to prevention of violence.

2. Go to the website of the Center for Positive Behavioral Interventions and Supports (www.pbis.org) and look for information, articles, sources, and links that will provide you with models for both schoolwide planning as well as Levels 2 and 3 PBIS planning.

Evaluating Positive Behavioral Interventions & Supports

CONCEPTS TO UNDERSTAND

After reading this chapter, you should be able to:

- Describe evaluation as a general concept, including definitions of formal versus informal evaluation; summative and formative evaluation; input, process, outcome, and context evaluation; and program versus individual evaluation.
- Describe the place of evaluation as a component of positive behavioral interventions and supports (PBIS).
- Discuss the issues associated with evaluating PBIS, especially related to family and community participation, self-determination, and quality of life.
- Compare evaluation methods appropriate for SWPBIS to methods used for individual child interventions.
- Create a matrix illustrating the issues and practices associated with input, process, and outcome evaluation for both schoolwide and Levels 2 and 3 PBIS.
- List and describe five issues or future directions associated with evaluation of PBIS.

KEY TERMS

Accountability-driven evaluation	Interdisciplinary team evaluation
Assessment of needs	Multicomponent interventions
Competing behaviors model	Multiple-outcome measures
Continuum of behavior support	Performance-based outcomes
Ecological validity	School climate
Empowerment evaluation	Shared vision
Formal and informal evaluation	Single-case designs
Implementation fidelity	Summative and formative evaluation
Individual and program evaluations	Third-party and external evaluation
Inputs, processes, and outcomes	Treatment integrity

To evaluate is to determine the value or significance of something. As briefly discussed in Chapter 7, evaluation is an activity done on an ongoing basis in both our personal and professional lives. Three important points are made to begin our consideration of evaluation. One is that evaluation is not something that we should impose on someone in a professional–student relationship but is rather an ongoing part of our personal as well as professional lives. Second, evaluation may be understood as part of a process that includes assessing (e.g., functional assessment), planning (e.g., behavior support), and implementing (e.g., intervention). Third, evaluation is best done *with* someone rather than *to* someone. The purpose of this chapter is to overview evaluation, to examine the place of evaluation at all levels of positive behavior support, and to introduce some perspectives, methods, and procedures for implementing evaluation.

OVERVIEW OF EVALUATION

Before we consider evaluation specific to the delivery of PBIS in educational environments, we will provide a framework for what is meant by evaluation. According to Fitzpatrick, Sanders, and Worthen (2003), evaluation may be considered either formal or informal. **Formal evaluation** tends to be structured, systematic, thorough, and based on explicit criteria for what is being evaluated. **Informal evaluation** tends to be more subjective and not connected to the relative merits of varied alternatives. Both formal and informal evaluations are relevant in our personal and professional lives. We are more interested here in the formal applications of evaluation that will improve the lives of children and youth who are participants in approaches to PBIS. But it is important to recognize that, intended or not, informal perspectives will be present and should be recognized, valued, and included.

We have already noted that evaluation may be formal or informal. Summative and formative evaluation (Scriven, 1967) are additional terms often encountered in the literature to differentiate between two primary purposes for evaluation. **Summative evaluation** refers to the acquisition of information that allows determination at a specified end point of whether goals and objectives have been met or to sum up the impact of effectiveness of (for example) an intervention. **Formative evaluation** refers to information that is gathered for the purpose of formulating additional goals, objectives, and intervention or teaching practices and to inform future decisions and actions. In practice, the things that we evaluate typically have varying amounts of both types of evaluation. Both are important; their differences are at times blurred, and their purposes are frequently intertwined (Scriven, 1991).

Sanders (1994) stated that formative evaluation was designed and used to improve an object, especially while it is being developed, and that summative evaluation presents conclusions about the merit or worth of an object and recommends whether it should be retained, altered, or eliminated. Let us take as an example a behavioral intervention in which we want to apply a reinforcing "object" to assist a student to stay on task more with his math assignment. Having the student select a reinforcer from a menu of possible reinforcers (let's say he selects extra time at the computer/game center over other things offered) is an example of formative evaluation. We are doing this formative evaluation to formulate and develop our intervention to increase on-task behavior. After a period of time, we will look at the data on amount of on-task behavior to judge the worth and merit of our reinforcement strategy in order to decide whether to retain it. This is an example of formative evaluation.

Consider This

A teacher finds that her cooperative learning approach (providing students opportunities to work in pairs) has resulted in improved task engagement among her students.

- What kind of data might she have to demonstrate the positive impact of the strategy?
- How might she use her data summatively? Formatively?

Another way to understand the evaluation process is to differentiate among evaluation of **inputs, processes, and outcomes**. For understanding PBIS evaluation in this chapter, these three types of evaluation will be used.

The study of this textbook as well as other education sources shows that there is growing emphasis on accountability in general education and special education as expressed by measurable outcomes. The salient point here is that although outcomes are certainly important, it is also frequently important as a part of the evaluation process to examine the inputs and processes. Inputs are the elements that go into the plan before it is implemented. Development of the behavior support plan itself is an example of inputs. Processes are the events and actions that occur as a part of implementing the plan. Vignette 8.1 provides an example of how these elements of evaluation are integrally related.

Vignette 8.1

Classroom Evaluation of Reading Skills

A classroom teacher is interested in determining how much gain his students have made both as a group and individually in their reading skills. He is interested in outcomes—that is, what are the quantifiable scores in reading at the end of a specified period of instructional time? He is also interested in outcomes associated with how both the students and the parents experienced the reading program. However, the curriculum that he chose (inputs) was not very effective for teaching reading, and he is not very pleased with the way he organized and presented his reading lessons (process). The reading test scores and other outcome measures are disappointing.

Reflective Moment

It is frequently difficult to effectively evaluate outcomes without also evaluating inputs and processes. Evaluation of inputs and processes should be done substantially during the time that they are occurring, rather than as a look back at the end. Of course, it is easier to focus on outcomes because they are often specific and quantifiable. Can you think of ways that the teacher might have conducted input and process evaluation related to the reading instruction? In what ways might the children and their parents or families have been involved in input and process evaluation?

In addition to understanding evaluation as either summative or formative and as focused on inputs, processes, and outcomes, another distinction is that which is made between **individual and program evaluations**. This distinction is certainly an important one as we consider the varying needs for evaluating the three levels of PBIS. Program evaluation, as the term suggests, is aimed at determining the effectiveness of a program-wide or schoolwide plan and the implementation of that plan. This definition would certainly apply to the implantation of SWPBIS, as Individual evaluation is aimed at making judgments about the impact of (in this case) PBIS on the behavior of individual children and youth. As is the case with summative and formative evaluation, these two purposes sometimes overlap.

EVALUATION AND PBIS

It is important to keep in mind, as methods and practices for evaluation of PBS are discussed in this chapter, that no one especially likes to have his or her behavior judged and evaluated. Just as in collaboration, teamwork, and partnerships among professionals, families and others are viewed as important in the process of planning behavior supports at all levels and in carrying them out. They are equally important in determining how the inputs, processes, and outcomes will be evaluated. As discussed in previous chapters, over the past 20 years the PBIS movement has—largely as an extension of applied behavior analysis—broadened principles of behavior to include all children and youth. As a result, attention is given to preventing challenging behavior by attending more to setting events and antecedents and by emphasizing a partnership between professionals and families.

PBIS is applied at three levels. Each of these levels presents unique opportunities and considerations for evaluation. Historically, evaluation in applied behavior analysis has focused primarily on measurement of outcomes through quantifiable data resulting from **single-case designs** that affected targeted challenging behaviors. These approaches certainly continue to be important tools for evaluation, especially Levels 2 and 3 of PBIS. However, this chapter, although it includes these applied research approaches, also provides information and suggestions for additional means to evaluate PBIS. Evaluation methods and practices are multifaceted and often require a period of time for team members to think divergently about possible ways to evaluate inputs, processes, and outcomes and also the opportunity to discuss and problem solve to arrive at a shared view of how the usefulness of PBIS (at any level) may be determined.

Carr and colleagues (1999) early on pointed out that one of the distinguishing features of the PBIS approach is that it requires **multicomponent interventions** that address the many factors that might influence behavior. Multicomponent interventions require multiple means of assessment and evaluation and might focus on antecedents, setting events, intervention process, outcomes, or broader community, family, and quality-of-life variables.

Another important connection to be made related to the evaluation of PBIS is with the concept of **ecological validity**. Ecological validity refers to the meaningfulness and usefulness of behavior supports in the context of an individual's life and daily routines, experiences, and settings. Doing so will improve the addressing of impeding and challenging behaviors in relevant contexts, such as home and family. Obviously, broadening the contexts, service systems, and professionals involved will require expanding our ways of evaluating effectiveness.

One way to understand the relationship between PBIS and evaluation is to examine the different purposes of program evaluation and individual evaluation (introduced earlier) as they are applied in PBIS. Historically, applied behavior analysis has emphasized focusing on the impact of intervention on individuals' discrete challenging behaviors using quantifiable outcome measures. Systems serving groups of individuals (such as school environments), when formal evaluation was desired or mandated, have tended to use various program evaluation designs in which a broader variety of indicators of success have been applied. Often program evaluation designs include measurable outcomes, but they may also include more subjective indicators. Some focus on inputs and processes and the intent of generalizing evaluation findings beyond the group targeted. Part of the PBIS movement has been to work toward bringing together these disparate approaches and intents of evaluation to best serve its delivery at the three levels of PBIS.

In a discussion of the evolution of PBIS as an applied science, Carr and colleagues (2002) point out that one is required to change and expand one's view of assessment practices (the means by which the success of PBIS is determined). The authors suggested that in the future the who, where, how, and what of assessment–evaluation is likely to change as a function of further experience with PBIS. Because of the PBIS focus on quality of life, life span development, community, various stakeholders, and social validity, persons other than experts will be increasingly involved directly in evaluation (i.e., the who). Schoolwide PBIS, rather than focusing only on individuals in specific environments, certainly represents a change in evaluation (i.e., the where). Use of indirect and less formal and quantifiable means of evaluation will be applied (i.e., the how). And the tools of assessment and evaluation (i.e., the what) are likely to change; for example, they might include an analysis of documents and sociometric measures to determine the effects of PBIS.

An example of this concept can be demonstrated through a study designed to evaluate the effects of PBIS in a broader sense related to quality of life, social validity, and behavior and ecological outcomes. Kincaid, Knoster, Harrower, Shannon, and Bustamante (2002) applied both survey and interview methods to ascertain the views of 397 individuals on 78 child-centered behavior support teams across three states. The researchers found that the behavior support plans demonstrated social validity and were believed to positively affect quality of life (interpersonal relationships, self-determination, social inclusion, personal well-being, and emotional well-being). We suggest the need for future expansion of collaboration among policy makers, practitioners, and stakeholders and the use of varied research and evaluation methods (such as interviews, rating scales, and checklists that are family and practitioner friendly). The point is that the advancement of PBIS at all levels requires rethinking the manner in which professionals design and carry out evaluation.

Not only is it important to think about the relationship between individual evaluation and program evaluation as elements of PBIS when conducting it at the different levels, but it is also important to understand that Level 3 or Tertiary PBIS requires that the context of evaluation be broadened to demonstrate social validity and to include other stakeholders, family, and community. We will next examine issues and practices in PBIS evaluation, using the three levels of PBIS and the distinction among input, process, and outcome evaluation as the structure on which to base understanding (see Figure 8–1).

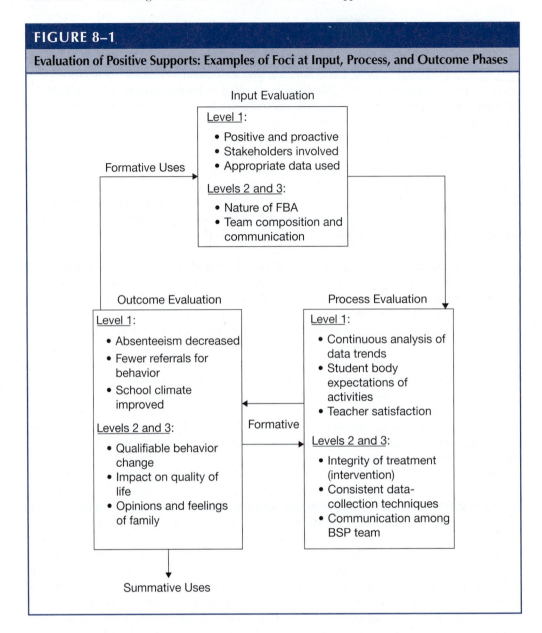

FIGURE 8–1

Evaluation of Positive Supports: Examples of Foci at Input, Process, and Outcome Phases

EVALUATING SCHOOLWIDE PBIS (SWPBIS)

The evaluation of Level 1 (primary prevention) PBIS requires the use of a program evaluation design rather than an individual evaluation approach. That is, we are interested in the quality of the plan (inputs), the ways in which it is implemented (processes), and the extent to which it affects/impacts the behavior of a group of students in a school environment (outcomes). As was stated in Chapter 7, an effective and successful schoolwide (Level 1 primary prevention) behavior support plan (BSP) is assumed to be comprehensive, developed by a team, and relevant; involve meaningful participation by the persons targeted by the plan; and be possible and sustainable. It is reasonable to assume that you, as an educator currently teaching or as a student preparing for a career in preK–12 education, have been or will be at some point a member of a team charged with responsibility for planning, implementing, and evaluating a schoolwide positive behavior support program.

In some of the early work done to lay the foundation for PBIS, the federal Office of Special Education Programs Technical Assistance Center on Positive Behavioral Interventions and Supports (OSEP, n.d. [a]) suggested that schools that are successful in developing proactive approaches to schoolwide discipline (schoolwide PBIS approaches) are those that develop procedures to accomplish seven actions: (1) behavior expectations are defined, (2) behavior expectations are taught, (3) appropriate behaviors are acknowledged, (4) behavior errors are corrected proactively, (5) program evaluations and adaptations are made by a team, (6) administrative support and involvement are active, and (7) individual student support systems are integrated with schoolwide discipline systems. For our purpose here, it is especially important to note action 5: *program evaluation and adaptations are made by a team*. A great deal of work has been done over the past decade on developing, testing, and refining a number of instruments and procedures for evaluating PBIS, in particular schoolwide programs. Information about these tools, how they have been developed, and how to access and apply them may be found at the website of the Center on Positive Behavior Interventions and Supports (OSEP, n.d. [b]). In particular, you may want to become familiar with a tool developed by Todd, Lewis-Palmer, Horner, Sugai, Sampson, and Phillips (2012) called the School-wide Evaluation Tool (SET) Implementation Manual: Version 2.0. Its purpose is "to assess and evaluate the critical features of schoolwide behavior support across each academic school year."

What is important here is the focus on the role of a schoolwide behavior support team in evaluation and on an ongoing process (formative evaluation) of monitoring based on data (formal evaluation). In describing the consistent themes of schoolwide behavior support efforts, Horner and Sugai (2000) mentioned that "information on student performance was collected continuously and summarized for decision making by local teams" (p. 231). These considerations all lend themselves to program evaluation, along with judgments made about the desired outcomes (for example, a reduction in the number of students referred to the office for disciplinary action or the percentage of student absenteeism).

Empirical Evidence for SWPBIS

Research and the associated methods used to evaluate those plans, especially for elementary and middle school-age students, have become increasingly more prevalent in the literature. In an early longitudinal study of the effects of SWPBIS in a middle school setting, Luiselli, Putnam, and Sunderland (2002) found substantial benefits over a 4-year period. Student detentions issued for disruptive–antisocial behavior, vandalism, and substance abuse decreased, and student attendance increased each year, as did the portion of students earning positive reinforcement. A unique feature of this study was the fact that it was a long-term, 4-year effort. The exclusive means of evaluation of effectiveness in this study were quantitative outcome measures; that is, the frequency (increase or decrease) of behaviors measured at the end of each of the three years. Because a team approach was applied (students, teachers, administrators, parents, and community members), this program met the criteria stated previously for an effective schoolwide plan. However, the evaluation criteria did not include any methods other than student-specific outcomes.

Scott (2001) in an early study examined the effects of SWPBIS plan in an inner-city K–5 school characterized as a school in crisis with students at risk. A process of obtaining unanimous school personnel commitment, identifying predictable problem behavior contexts, brainstorming prevention strategies, developing consensus, and determining schoolwide expectations and teaching was used. Following that process, a behavior support team—representing all job responsibility groups, the principal, and a school-based student services coordinator—was established. The plan focused on decreasing the number of SAFE referrals and on decreasing suspensions. SAFE is an acronym for "suspension and failure eliminated," and in this school was a room used much like an in-school suspension site. Many proactive prevention strategies targeting the environments of most concern—cafeteria, halls, stairs, and gymnasium—were agreed on and implemented. Results of the program after 1 year indicated that both SAFE referrals and suspensions were substantially reduced in number. As with the study summarized previously (Luiselli et al., 2002), the evaluation of effectiveness was limited to quantitative outcome measures. The team did not include family, community, or student representatives, and it is not clear how the team was involved in making judgments about the program's effectiveness.

LaBrot and colleagues (2016) in a recent investigation examined the efficacy of a Check-In Check-Out program, an approach typically used as a Tier 2 intervention within SWPBIS model within an Early Head Start program serving young children. They evaluated this Tier 2 intervention for its portability within early childhood settings, its social validity as rated by the Head Start teachers, and lastly on its effects toward improving behavior of Early Head Start students at-risk for emotional and behavioral disorders. Findings revealed that it was deemed feasible for an Early Head Start setting, socially valid, and with positive effects on student behavior as evaluated by teachers.

Numerous reports in the literature describe the merits of SWPBIS. Some describe programs and methods, whereas others provide empirical data from formal research or evaluation efforts. Teams, sometimes including parents or families and other stakeholders, are frequently cited as responsible for development and overseeing implementation, but it is often unclear how their role might be related to evaluation. Reports of SWPBIS focus largely on measurable outcomes such as decreases in office referrals, absenteeism, and suspensions as examples.

Input Evaluation for SWPBIS

Remember that input evaluation is evaluation of the contexts, actions, events, documents, attitudes, and beliefs that precede the implementation plan as well as evaluation of the development of the plan itself. Input evaluation, the precursor to implementation (and process evaluation) of SWPBIS, is the assessment of needs and contributions to the plan. It is evident that insufficient and bad information will limit the ability to develop an effective plan. The questions become the following: *Who* are the participants in the input phase and its evaluation? *What* inputs should be evaluated? *Why* are they important? *How* might they be evaluated (criteria, methods of evaluation)? Figure 8–2 provides a summary of how these questions might be answered.

A concern central to determining the quality of input evaluation in SWPBIS planning is to what extent and in what ways the primary stakeholders are participatory. *Who* might those individuals be? They should be the persons most directly affected by the benefits of having a workable schoolwide behavior support plan (or negatively affected by the absence of a plan). Schoolwide personnel might be those persons who would be helpful resources and have expertise and experience with behavior support planning. Parent or family representation and participation may be solicited in a variety of ways, including individual contacts, parent–teacher organizations, newsletters, phone surveys, email distribution, class parent meetings, and parent-to-parent networks.

Keep in mind the distinction between input prior to the plan and input as a part of development of the plan. The individuals noted previously are appropriate for the broader context—that is, the **assessment of needs** for the schoolwide plan and the formulation of a **shared vision** regarding the overall mission, goals, and objectives of the plan. Shared vision refers to the efforts of a group (for example, the stakeholders noted earlier) to come to a reasonable level of agreement about what the major mission, principles, and goals of

---

FIGURE 8–2

Elements of SWPBIS Input Evaluation

Who are the individuals (input evaluators) on the team?

The stakeholders will most likely include school personnel (teachers, administrators, supervisors, specialists, teacher assistants, cafeteria workers, custodians, and other volunteer and support staff), students, parent/family representatives, and potentially schoolwide personnel and community representatives.

What are the inputs to be evaluated?

Inputs include the needs assessment document and results, evidence of a shared mission and consensus, frequency of team meetings, and a complete planning document signed by team members.

Why are the inputs important for evaluation?

Success of the schoolwide plan begins with a systematic and thorough effort to involve all stakeholders, build consensus, assess needs, and write a plan directed to the needs.

How might the inputs be evaluated?

Use both quantitative and qualitative methods (e.g., questionnaires, interviews, document analysis, focus groups) to examine opportunities for participation, documents, satisfaction, and fit of plan with recommended practice.

---

a program (SWPBIS)—and the schoolwide behavior expectations—should be. That is, they have a shared view of why this is being done, generally how it is being done, and what goals will be achieved. It is, of course, unrealistic to assume that a large group of diverse stakeholders will arrive at full consensus, but the extent to which this is accomplished will affect the success of the development of the plan and its subsequent implementation.

Consider This

A team develops a SWPBIS plan for their high school, and the team arrives at a shared vision and agrees on content. The plan is reviewed by outside experts, including local university faculty and other school districts in which plans have succeeded. Everyone concurs that it is a sound plan. However, no students or parents are involved in plan development.

- What might the students and parents say about the plan (input evaluation)?
- Will they feel ownership of the plan?

As has been stated, the success of SWPBIS planning is partially dependent on the establishment and continuous functioning of a team. Who should be on the team that develops the plan? The membership should include representatives from all the stakeholders noted. How many members should it have? Although there is much variance in team size, it is reasonable to assume that at least 6 to 8 members would be needed, and as many as 12 to 15 are possible. The challenges associated with too few or too many team members are obvious. Too few will limit the perspectives and possibly not represent all the stakeholders. Too many will make the team unwieldy and possibly disrupt the team's ability to reach consensus and make decisions. So the input evaluation question related to *who* is broadly stated as follows: Are the appropriate persons included in the wider context, and are the stakeholders represented on a behavior support team?

What are the inputs that should be included in the evaluation effort? Prior to establishing the team and development of the plan, several inputs are especially important and should be the focus of formative evaluation. The ethical standards and codes and guidelines for best and effective professional practice (see Chapter 3) related to discipline and behavior in schools would certainly constitute one possibility for inclusion. The points of view of students of what will contribute toward positive behavior and learning and minimal conflict in their school is important. The beliefs, values, and preferences of parents and family members should, of course, be included. And the beliefs, values, and experiences of school personnel related to behavior expectations in school and effective methods of fostering desired behavior and preventing challenging behavior are important.

Finally, data from a needs assessment process in which all stakeholders are given an opportunity to provide input on plan content should be included. Once the schoolwide behavior support team is established, what should one look for in the plan? Is the plan a written, public document, widely available to all, produced from contributions of all team members? Does the plan have a clear statement of the school's PBS mission, goals, and objectives? Do the mission, goals, and objectives reflect content from the broader stakeholder group? Is the plan based substantially on quantifiable data related to goals and objectives and measurable benchmarks to judge success?

Why are the inputs noted of importance as targets for evaluation? If there is to be a partnership among various stakeholders in whom collaboration and teamwork are demonstrated toward the development of a sound schoolwide behavior support plan, then everyone with an interest must have a genuine opportunity for input. Primarily, the input evaluation is to examine the extent to which relevant persons (who) had opportunity to contribute (what) to the preliminary steps and development of the plan.

How might these inputs be evaluated? As with all forms of evaluation, one can apply both quantitative and qualitative methods. With regard to the quantitative dimension and input evaluation, these might primarily be yes or no questions. Did the specified stakeholders have an opportunity to contribute to the preliminary planning? Did these stakeholders arrive at a specified level of consensus? Was a preliminary set of school behavior expectations developed? Was one representative from each stakeholder group elected or appointed to serve on the schoolwide behavior support team? Did the team meet multiple times? Was a schoolwide plan written? Are the objectives in the plan measurable?

How to evaluate input qualitatively is somewhat more complicated and time-consuming but still very useful in getting off to a good start. Qualitative methods might include using interviews, focus groups, or questionnaires to get at the beliefs, values,

Vignette 8.2

Ms. Thornton Participates on the SWPBIS Development Team at Central High

Alycia Thornton received her bachelor's degree, along with dual teacher licensure in special education–emotional disturbance and secondary English. Alycia was able to get a teaching position in the small, rural community in which she grew up and at the high school she attended: Central High. As part of her undergraduate program, Alycia took two classes in PBIS, one on theory and principles and one on applications. Despite her professors' insistence that she could very likely be employed in a school or school system that believed in and promoted PBIS, Alycia was skeptical. Upon beginning her new job, she was pleasantly surprised to find that Central High would be the first to plan a comprehensive PBIS system and would serve as a pilot, with other schools in the system to follow suit over a period of several years. She found out that the school superintendent, Mr. Griffith, along with the system's principals and other administrative staff, had received some PBIS training from the state department and determined from that along with support from the school board, that their system would "buy in." The state also had in place a program to provide additional training, technical assistance, and support. Ms. Sorensen (the school principal) established a 12-member team to do the planning for SWPBIS at Central High. Membership included the vice principal, the special education behavior specialist, a bus driver, a cafeteria worker, the school guidance counselor, a community agency representative (YMCA director), a state department PBIS consultant, two parent/family representatives, a current student at Central, and two subject area teachers, including a math teacher and a grade 11 English teacher—Alycia Thornton! The vice principal served as the committee chair, and the committee was given a charge to develop over a 17-month period (August 2014–December 2016) the SWPBS plan for Central. They would meet weekly and/or as needed to produce a plan for implementation in January 2017. The team determined that the first order of business was to develop a vision/mission statement and to establish the broad goals for SWPBIS. They understood that these elements would be the foundation and that everything else in the plan should flow from the mission and goals.

After a month, the team had hammered out a statement and six broad goals. Now they needed to pause and determine whether they were on the right track (input evaluation). The team decided to use primarily qualitative methods to judge where they stood, including focus groups and interviews conducted by all team members. Group discussions and interviews included student groups, parents, building faculty, support staff, community representatives, and others. The team also wanted to compare what they had done to some established models for high school PBIS programs, so they asked the state PBIS consultant to collect samples. Alycia's participation in this part of evaluation was to co-lead with the student representative meetings with Central High student groups. After collecting this input, the committee went back to work to incorporate changes and develop the next version of mission and goals.

and preferences of various stakeholders; asking teachers, parents, and students if they are satisfied with their opportunity to provide input; comparing the plan to other plans (considered model plans) for inclusion of the desired elements; and comparing the plans, goals, and objectives to established professional ethical codes, standards, and guidelines for behavior and school discipline.

Process Evaluation for SWPBIS

Frequently, schoolwide behavior support plans are implemented on an academic year calendar. That is, they are carried out as planned for one school year, and judgments are made about the extent to which goals and objectives were met (outcomes). The successes or failures of the implementation (summative evaluation) are used to inform decisions about the future (formative evaluation). The process, or implementation, lends itself to numerous opportunities for evaluating how the methods and strategies applied are working to address the mission, goals, and objectives of the plan. Evaluation of the process allows for any midcourse adjustments and fine-tuning as needed to keep the plan on track. Evaluation of the process of implementing schoolwide behavior support plans can also be understood by examining the who, what, why, and how questions. Figure 8–3 provides a summary of how these questions might be answered.

FIGURE 8–3

Elements of SWPBIS Process Evaluation

Who are the evaluators of the process?

The same group as in the input phase, including the schoolwide team, students, parents and family representatives, and community members.

What are the processes to be evaluated?

The processes include the written plan, data trends relating to behavior change, school social climate, and evidence that the plan has been communicated consistently and continuously to school personnel and students.

Why are these processes important for evaluation?

Ongoing evaluation (formative) will allow for changes and improvements along the way. Data on trends (e.g., how absenteeism is being affected) will be helpful.

How might the processes be evaluated?

The means of evaluation should be consistent with the who, what, and why answers introduced previously. Some of the likely means of doing process evaluation are ongoing quantifiable measures such as frequency and percentage of behavior; structured, semistructured, or unstructured interviews of students, teachers, family members, or other stakeholders; focus groups; analysis of documents; and questionnaires related to knowledge, attitudes, and beliefs.

Who are the key persons related to the evaluation of the process of implementing a schoolwide behavior support plan? For the most part, they are the same individuals and groups that participated during the input phase. The schoolwide behavior support team must certainly play a central role in the ongoing evaluation of the effectiveness of the plan. Feedback from the students about how the implementation of the plan is working for them is necessary. Provide a mechanism for the larger stakeholder group to continue to influence implementation. Finally, parents or families of the students should not only be kept informed of the plan's progress, but should also have the opportunity to provide formal or informal evaluation information along the way. These four groups—the team, the students, the stakeholders, and the parents or family members—are the key to ongoing evaluation of the process.

What are the processes, products, actions, documents, and behaviors that should be part of the process evaluation? What should be evaluated during implementation of the schoolwide plan? The written plan itself should be periodically reviewed, discussed, and modified as needed so that it becomes, as intended, a working and useful document rather than a perfunctory exercise. The data reflecting trends related to the goals and objectives of the plan should be analyzed by the team and by others. This analysis might occur monthly or even quarterly and will be useful in making adjustments and changes in strategies. For example, given the goal of reducing suspensions, are the data showing a trend toward a decrease in the number of students suspended? Changing attitudes and beliefs of the various stakeholders should be assessed as a part of the process, as well as attitudes and beliefs of the students about the schoolwide plan. Although the notion of **school climate** may be somewhat abstract and difficult to measure, it is nonetheless important, and it is useful to ask the teaching staff and support staff of the school to evaluate how they and the school have been affected by the behavior support plan.

Why are the process evaluation activities important and desirable? As stated earlier, process evaluation will allow for fine-tuning and making adjustments as the plan is implemented. It also provides for strengthening and advancing the shared vision that was fostered as a part of the initial development and planning effort. Documenting the experiences of implementing the plan in a qualitative and descriptive fashion will potentially be useful as formative information when plans are made for a subsequent year's plan. Stated in a straightforward manner, it is not only necessary to judge what we intended to do (input) and what we did (outcome) but also to consider carefully how we got there (process).

How might these processes be evaluated? Numerous methods, strategies, and instruments might be developed or applied to evaluate the process of implementing SWPBIS. They are, of course, situation specific and dependent on the needs and goals of the school, team, and other stakeholders.

Outcome Evaluation for SWPBIS

Outcome evaluation is the judgment made about the results of a schoolwide behavior support plan, usually after a period of 1 year. In a study reported by Scott (2001), the results of an inner-city elementary SWPBIS plan were provided after 1 year of implementation, and two dependent variables were addressed. These variables (referral to an in-school suspension room and suspension from school) were seen to be dependent on the success of the behavior support plan. Desired outcomes were for both variables to decrease in frequency over the period of the year. The outcome evaluation in this instance consisted of monthly and end-point quantifiable measures of frequency. This example likely represents the most frequently applied and traditional means of outcome evaluation. Others might serve to complement and expand this strategy. Outcome evaluation, like input and process evaluation, may be understood by considering who, what, why, and how (see Figure 8–4).

Who might be the participants in the evaluation of the outcomes of a schoolwide behavior support plan? Three approaches to this question are presented. It is logical and appropriate for the SWPBIS team to be primarily responsible for the formative and summative evaluation of the outcomes of the effort. A second approach is a **third-party or external evaluation**. Third-party or external evaluation includes the use of a presumably unbiased evaluator or team from outside the school and school system.

FIGURE 8–4

Elements of SWPBIS Outcome Evaluation

Who are the evaluators of the outcomes?

The evaluators are the schoolwide team, an outside evaluator(s), or a combination of both.

What are the outcomes to be evaluated?

Measurable intended outcomes to be evaluated include absences, suspensions, discipline referrals, and student, teacher, and family attitudes about the school, based on goals and objectives in the plan. Unintended outcomes, such as promoting interest of some teachers to learn more about PBIS, should also be evaluated.

Why are these outcomes important for evaluation?

Outcome evaluation serves the dual purposes of providing end-of-the-year evidence of the impact of the schoolwide effort (summative) and information useful for formulating a new plan for the next year (formative).

How are outcomes evaluated?

Evaluation tools include group trend data analysis, behavior observations, interviews, focus groups, and questionnaires.

There are advantages to both external and internal evaluation approaches. Internal evaluators (for example, the PBIS team) presumably have more contextual information and are familiar with the implementation. Having an outside evaluation does not necessarily ensure objectivity and credibility (Scriven, 1993). A third approach regarding evaluation outcomes of a schoolwide plan is to use a combination of the behavior support team and representatives from other schools experienced in PBIS and possibly university professors experienced in program evaluation and PBIS.

What are the elements that might be evaluated at the outcome stage? The extent to which the mission or vision of the plan, its overriding goals, and its specific objectives are accomplished should be evaluated at the end of an established period (often one school year). Although the mission and goals tend to be less measurable and lend themselves to more qualitative analysis, the objectives should be written in a manner that makes them quantifiable and measurable. For example, the objectives might have been to reduce (perhaps by an established percentage or frequency) measurable behaviors such as in-school suspensions, suspensions, discipline referrals, disruptive behavior incidents, or absences.

Why is outcome evaluation important? Keep in mind that SWPBIS requires a program evaluation approach rather than a focus on individuals. Program evaluation targets program (school) processes and outcomes, aggregate data, judgments about achieving goals, and producing data for decision makers. Patton (2015) points out that outcomes evaluation has become a central focus of **accountability-driven evaluation**. The accountability movement is not so much about achieving quality as it is about demonstrating responsible use of public funds to achieve politically desired results. The trend toward accountability and **performance-based outcomes**, although it certainly has advantages, also has the potential weakness of minimizing or excluding important outcomes that do not fit well with the objectives or do not lend themselves to quantitative methods.

How might one evaluate outcomes of a schoolwide behavior support plan? Suppose that the stated objectives of the plan are to reduce in-school suspension referrals, school suspensions, discipline referrals to the office, and absences, and to increase student/faculty/staff/parent satisfaction with the school climate related to behavior and discipline. All these variables may be evaluated quantitatively as outcomes using data counts taken on a monthly basis and questionnaires using a Likert-type scale to measure attitudes and beliefs related to the changing school climate. Interviews and focus groups may be used to add qualitative data, targeting any or all stakeholders. Kim, McIntosh, and Hoselton (2014) reported on the extent that schools having adequate Tier I supports have stronger implementation at Tiers II and III using the Schoolwide Evaluation Tool (SET). The results were significant that in over 1400 schools sampled those having adequate Tier I supports had substantially more effective implementation at Tiers II and III on the BAT. Their research points to the reliability, validity, and efficiency of the *Benchmarks of Quality (BoQ)* as a tool for measuring the fidelity of implementation of PBIS. The BoQ provides a format for members of the PBIS team to complete a checklist indicating where the school currently stands (in place, needs improvement, or not in place) on 10 critical elements of a schoolwide plan.

EVALUATING LEVEL 2 AND LEVEL 3 POSITIVE BEHAVIOR SUPPORTS

Crone and Horner (2003) pointed out that evaluation is essential to successful PBIS and that it should be a part of its initial design. They suggested that evaluation procedures should be simple and efficient and should include three elements: the assessment of changes in behavior, the feasibility and acceptability of the plan, and the satisfaction with the plan and implementation of students, parents, and teachers. Also, evaluation of PBIS should conclude with plans for maintenance of behavior improvement. This point of view is consistent with the position taken in this chapter that PBIS should be evaluated at all points, including inputs, processes, and outcomes. Further evaluation must go beyond merely assessing behavior change.

Because Levels 2 and 3 PBIS both focus on individuals (and pairs or small groups for Level 2) and their challenging or impeding behavior, they both require individual evaluation (as opposed to program evaluation) approaches. Also the input, process, and outcome elements are very similar, with the distinctions mainly related to the intensity and comprehensiveness of the interventions. The methods of evaluation at all phases are comparable. For example, antecedents, setting events, and functional behavior assessment and analysis are likely to be important to both. The process of delivering Levels 2 and 3 PBIS will require evaluation of progress by collection of ongoing measurable effects. Observation of discrete behaviors, multiple baselines, and collaboration among persons responsible for implementation will help. The evaluation of outcomes for Levels 2 and 3 will both include quantifiable data and issues of self-determination and social or ecological validity. Following are some issues and ideas related to evaluation at the three points in the process.

Input Evaluation for Level 2 and Level 3 PBIS

What are the input variables associated with individual positive behavior supports, and how might they be evaluated? Keep in mind that the objective is to evaluate them prior to the process and outcome stages to establish the best start possible, as opposed to waiting until the implementation is in process or is completed, then looking back to consider whether the inputs were appropriate and useful.

Most often the inputs for Level 2 and Level 3 PBIS planning are identifying goals, gathering information, developing a hypothesis or best guess statement, and designing the behavior support plan. Each of these four steps involves specific actions. *Identifying goals* includes establishing a team, establishing rules and guidelines for the team's functioning, formulating a picture (profile) of the child or youth, consideration of the broader goals or enhancement of quality of life for the child or youth, and defining the target behavior(s). *Gathering information* is conducting a functional behavior assessment. O'Neill and colleagues (2015) posited five primary outcomes for functional behavior assessment: (1) describing the problem behaviors; (2) identifying events, times, and situations that may predict problem behavior across daily routines; (3) identifying consequences that maintain problem behavior; (4) developing summary statement(s) that describe behaviors, situations in which they occur, and the consequences maintaining them; and (5) collecting data from direct observations (for example, scatter plots) that support summary statements. Interviewing, reviewing records, and other forms of assessment may also be useful as a part of the functional behavior assessment process.

Developing a *hypothesis* is the third step. The information gathered by the team is analyzed to identify patterns of behavior that may help clarify the contexts of challenging behavior (antecedents) and the functions of behavior (consequences). Patterns of behavior allow for the development of a hypothesis (summary statement) related to the challenging behavior. Setting events may also be relevant in developing the hypothesis. Testing the hypothesis (for example, functional analysis) may be desirable.

The fourth and last step in the input phase is *developing and designing* the plan (see Chapter 7 for planning formats). One prominent and recommended strategy is the **competing behaviors model** (O'Neill et al., 2015). "This model uses summary statement information (setting events, antecedents, behaviors, and maintaining consequences) to identify specific replacement skills and other desired behaviors" (Florida Department of Education, 1999, p. 53). Intervention strategies that are positive, educational, and functional are specified in the plan specific to the desired behavior.

One important means of evaluating the inputs described is to have a checklist to record whether these actions have been taken, on what date, and by whom (individual, team as a whole, other). Another method is to determine whether specific documents exist, such as the list of team members and the team functions and guidelines. These are quantifiable measures.

Consider This

There are also important qualitative questions in evaluating inputs:

- Is the team representative of the "stakeholders"?
- Do all of the team members feel like they had an opportunity to provide input, and were their ideas taken seriously and considered?
- Are the team members (and other relevant persons) satisfied with the portrait of the child or youth?
- Is it clear how the planning is connected to broader goals of the family and the child's quality of life?
- Is the conduct of the functional behavior assessment consistent with the literature's description of recommended practices?
- Are setting events adequately represented in development of the hypothesis?
- Is the plan itself written in a way that communicates clearly and effectively with all members of the team, other members of the family, and the child or youth who is targeted?
- Do the interventions selected to facilitate the replacement behavior meet the criteria of being positive, educational (or developmental), and functional?
- Are the planned interventions socially valid?

Qualitative questions are frequently more difficult to answer and may require methods with which behavior planners have limited experience and expertise. For example, semistructured and unstructured interviews, questionnaires, document analysis techniques, focus groups, and third-party judgments might be applied.

Process Evaluation for Level 2 and Level 3 PBIS

When the PBIS plan has been implemented and is ongoing, how might progress be evaluated? Crone and Horner (2003) suggest that numerous methods can be used and that frequency counts, individualized behavior rating scales, and observations are the more common methods. Evaluation of the ongoing intervention procedures (also referred to as "treatment," particularly in applied behavior analysis single-subject and multiple-baseline research designs) may be thought of as efforts at ensuring **treatment integrity** and **implementation fidelity** (Crone & Horner, 2003).

Treatment integrity refers to the ethics and functionality as well as the honesty of the intervention directly related to the child or youth. Implementation fidelity has been used to describe a broader perspective on how positive behavior support implementation is progressing, as it affects the child but also the team, the family, and other partners and collaborators. Just as with input evaluation, both quantitative methods (such as the ones listed) and qualitative methods are important in ongoing assessment and evaluation of the implementation of PBIS. These evaluations are formative, in that they are used to make adjustments and formulate new directions as needed in the intervention strategies to better address the goals and objectives of the plan.

Although it is efficient and appropriate for one member of the behavior support team to take primary responsibility for keeping track of the process evaluation and informing the remainder of the team, it is very important that all members of the team have meaningful input into determining the process evaluation components and how they will be continuously evaluated. It is also important that all members of the team take part in the collection of process evaluation data. For example, team members might keep a journal describing their roles and how they view their contributions.

Vignette 8.3

Ms. Thompson's Kindergarten Class

Janie Thompson has been a kindergarten teacher for 10 years, and she is widely considered to be an excellent teacher. She is especially successful with children who are determined to be at risk for challenging behavior and/or academic failure. To Ms. Thompson, ongoing professional development is important, and she is working on her master's degree in early childhood special education. Ms. Thompson is striving to apply principles and practices of both RtI and PBS in her classroom. For this school year, Ms. Thompson has 20 students in her class. Three of her students have been deemed (from a combination of preschool experiences, talking with family members, and Ms. Thompson's initial informal observations) to be at risk for challenging behavior based on their difficulties associated with being able to share with other children. For the most part, these three children are doing okay, but Ms. Thompson doesn't want to take a "wait and see" approach and assume that they will improve in their ability to share with maturation and experience. After a simple functional assessment, completed by Ms. Thompson with the assistance of the special education teacher consultant, and in partnership with the children's parents, Ms. Thompson gains a better understanding of the functions of the student's behaviors, and she plans PBIS intervention strategies for them to be done in the context of the typical classroom routines and activities. Ms. Thompson focuses on three settings: the playground, art activity time, and snack time. Her intervention strategies are not complicated. Ms. Thompson uses a combination of arranging the environments to foster sharing, teaching them specifically about how to share, demonstrating, prompting, redirecting, and descriptive verbal praise for sharing. After about four weeks of intervening, Ms. Thompson's sense is that sharing is increasing for all three of the children. She has data from the functional assessment about frequency of sharing but has not since then had time or resources to maintain a formal record and frequency count. Ms. Thompson wishes to pause and evaluate her process—to see more exactly what impact her interventions seem to be having on the student's ability to share. The special education consulting teacher is available to come to class and observe the children in the three activities and to do a sampling of frequencies of the incidences of sharing. This information, compared to the data that Ms. Thompson has from the functional assessment, tells Ms. Thompson that at least for the time being, she appears to be making progress. Ms. Thompson also meets with the parents of the three children to share with them and to solicit their thoughts/feelings about how the intervention process is going.

Outcome Evaluation for Level 2 and Level 3 PBIS

To evaluate outcomes is to make judgments at the end of a specified period of time about whether behavior change has occurred related to the objectives stated in the plan. Attention has been given (Clarke, Worcester, Dunlap, Murray, & Bradley-Klug, 2002) to the importance of using **multiple-outcome measures** in the evaluation of PBIS. In a single-case study of the use of PBIS with a 12-year-old female student having challenging behaviors and diagnosed with autism and other medical/developmental conditions, Clarke and colleagues (2002) found that in addition to direct measures of change in challenging behaviors, indirect measures such as pre- and post-quality-of-life surveys completed by teachers, parents, and peers, as well as PBIS satisfaction ratings completed by various stakeholders, were very important in evaluation. These also serve as measures of social validity and inform us as to the impact of these interventions as perceived by parents and family as well as teachers. They can also be effectively used with students themselves allowing for us to get direct feedback as to how they are perceived by the students themselves.

Questions to be answered in outcome evaluation are the following: Were the goals and objectives met? Was the intervention carried out as designed? In what ways might the intervention(s) be changed if it is to be continued? Outcome evaluation has the dual purpose of summing up the effects of the intervention (summative) and contributing to the formulation of new, revised plans (formative). The use of objective measures, such as frequency counts, duration of behaviors, or intensity of behaviors have long been useful outcome measures for applications of applied behavior analysis and PBIS. Criticisms of the PBIS movement have not been focused so much on the relevance of including dimensions such as social validity, quality of life, self-determination, person-centered planning, and effects on family but rather on the difficulties associated with quantifying those dimensions. A reasonable assumption would be that a combination of subjective, qualitative methods and objective, quantitative methods of outcome evaluation are necessary to establish a useful picture of how the intervention affected these variables.

Vignette 8.4

Calvin's Classroom, His Special Needs, and His Quality of Life

Calvin James (CJ) Owens is a 9-year-old boy who is in grade 4 at Sycamore Elementary. CJ was diagnosed at age 5 with autism spectrum disorder (ASD). For his entire school career, CJ has been included in general education classrooms, and he, his teachers, and his family have been provided with support from a special educator who has expertise in challenging behavior and ASD. CJ has had each school year an IEP and a related PBS plan. CJ's academic skills have pretty much always been at or above grade level, but his social skills and relationships, especially with other children, continue to be problematic. CJ has needed and benefited from highly specialized and individualized direct instruction and interventions, focused on supporting him and teaching him social skills. One of CJ's objectives for this school year has been to increase the amount of time in class that he spends in interactions with classmates. This objective was one of several for CJ that were included to improve his social skills and communication. A variety of intervention strategies were applied and refined throughout the year, including using a schedule and self-monitoring system, a buddy/peer model approach, verbal praise, and others. At the beginning of the year and based on the functional analysis and baseline assessments, CJ's interaction with other students averaged 10 minutes per day, or about 2.5% of the classroom day. The objective was 20 minutes per day, or 5% of the classroom day. In order to determine whether the objective was met, 2 weeks before the end of the school year, the school's behavior specialist observed and completed a record of frequency, duration, and settings. This data suggested that CJ's social interactions had increased to slightly above 5%, so the outcome was that the objective was met. Finally, CJ's teacher used a simple semistructured interview with both CJ and his parents to try and get at how this particular objective might have impacted his quality of life.

ISSUES AND FUTURE DIRECTIONS IN PBIS EVALUATION

In this section, we discuss five selected issues that are related to the future of evaluation of PBIS: (1) the behavior continuum, (2) empowerment evaluation, (3) partnerships with families, (4) measurable outcomes, and (5) unifying disciplines and fostering professional collaboration. Others could have been included here. These issues were selected because they are consistent with the content presented in this chapter and other chapters of the text.

The Behavior Continuum

Sailor and colleagues (2002) reported that "typical" and inner-city schools look quite different related to the percentage of students on the continuum of behavior. Typical schools might have 9% of students with chronic or serious behavior problems, 15% who are at risk for behavior problems, and 76% with mild or no behavior problems. Inner-city schools might have an additional category of extreme behavior problems (11%), 21% with chronic or serious behavior problems, 30% at risk for behavior problems, and only 38% with mild or no behavior problems. Consider how this affects the way we establish and evaluate behavior support plans. A growing trend treats PBIS in a given educational environment (such as a school) as a **continuum of behavior support** for all students, from those who have no challenging behavior to those who might have extreme challenging behavior. It is expected that for schools in which there is a high percentage of students with specific challenging behaviors or at-risk factors, there will be a much greater emphasis on individual, measurable outcome evaluation and possibly a school-wide focus on intervention.

Fox, Dunlap, Hemmeter, Joseph, and Strain (2003) described a model for supporting social competence and preventing challenging behavior in young children. They presented a teaching pyramid in which a continuum progresses from the least to the most intensive approaches. Positive relationships with children, families, and colleagues are at the base, followed by classroom prevention strategies, then social and emotional teaching strategies, and, at the top of the pyramid, intensive individualized interventions. This pyramid is one way of describing the connection in a learning environment among the three levels of PBIS. Given that implementing these practices depends to a large extent on the positive attitudes and abilities of teachers, the question is: in what ways should evaluation focus on the teachers' behavior and attitude changes (input and process evaluation) in addition to the evaluation of outcomes for groups of children or individual children?

Empowerment Evaluation

McCart and Sailor (2003) described the advantages of a method referred to as **empowerment evaluation** to establish and sustain schoolwide PBIS: empowerment evaluation "enables the partnerships of school personnel, families, and community members to come to perceive ownership of the process, to take an active role in structuring goals and objectives for implementation of PBIS and, over time, to become skilled in methods of data collection and evaluation" (p. 27). Helping all stakeholders make decisions based on evidence and feel ownership and helping schools become more self-evaluating and self-reliant are goals of empowerment evaluation. Given the increased emphasis on SWPBIS, often including various stakeholders and goals associated not only with academic achievement but also with discipline and school behavior climate, are encouraging indicators that empowerment evaluation could translate from theory to practice.

Partnerships with Families

The future with regard to how professionals will and should partner with families in the development, implementation, and evaluation of positive behavior intervention and support is rather complicated and unclear. This discussion is limited to considerations of parent or family roles related to evaluation of PBIS. Lucyshyn, Horner, Dunlap, Albin, and Ben (2002) advocated that a basic tenet of PBIS is for families to be seen in a positive light and from a strength (rather than deficit) perspective and that the evaluation of PBIS should be a continuous process in which parents or families are participants. They suggested that:

> evaluation of child and family outcomes is made family friendly by including parents in the selection of evaluation procedures, by choosing or designing measures that are relatively easy to use, and by ensuring that instruments not only measure problems but also child progress and family success. (p. 28)

Some of the factors that contribute to the complexity of partnerships are: (a) the ages and developmental status of the children and youth targeted, (b) the developmental status of the parents and other family members, (c) the preferences of families for participation, (d) the difference associated with various levels of PBIS evaluation (for example, individual versus program evaluation), (e) the attitudes and skills of professionals, and (f) the perceptions and policies of schools and school systems regarding partnerships with parents or families. Following is a brief consideration of each of these six factors.

The age of the child affects the partnership with parents or families in evaluating PBIS. Consider the differences among toddler, preschool, elementary, middle school, and high school environments and potential parent or family roles. Peck Peterson, Derby, Harding, Weddle, and Barretto (2002) pointed out that because of the variety of settings and related communication issues, the input of parents is especially valuable when children reach school age. What about the developmental status of parents related to participation in evaluation? Parents and family members are at different places developmentally regarding their ability to contribute to the evaluation process. How are decisions made in this regard, and how is parent or family change and growth taken into account in the process? And what about the preferences of parents or families for participation? How might professionals accurately and continuously assess parent or family preferences for levels and types of participation in schoolwide and individual behavior support planning? One size for all does not work for children, and of course the same is also true for parents.

Turnbull and Turnbull (2011) note that families are important participants in all aspects (including evaluation) of Level 1 PBIS but also that their involvement should be pervasive at Level 3 and more significant than at Level 1 or Level 2. Pervasiveness suggests that parents or families should be integral team members in evaluating PBIS at the input, process, and outcome phases of evaluation. Yet it is still common for parents or families to be viewed as recipients of a schoolwide plan, rather than as team members, and as simply one of many stakeholders responsible mostly for the consistency and generalization of intervention plans made and implemented by professionals for Level 2 and Level 3 PBIS.

Consider This

Think about the difference between parents as evaluators when the PBIS plan is for all the students in school as opposed to when the evaluation is focused on their child (and his or her challenging behavior):

- What about the attitudes and skills of professionals?
- As an educator or educator-to-be, how do you feel about the roles of parents or families in PBIS, especially as part of assessment, evaluation, and making judgments?
- Are you being prepared to value parents as team members, and are you gaining skills and practices to make that possible?

Regarding the final issue of school and school system policy and procedure related to parent or family representation on behavior support teams, it is useful to look at a school's improvement plan. Increasingly, public schools are being expected to engage in a process of continuous improvement through a formalized plan. This plan typically includes means of measuring progress toward goals. Does the school (or system) value the role of parents or families by supporting their meaningful participation in all aspects of evaluating school improvement (input, process, and outcomes)? Specifically, are there formalized position statements and guidelines promoting the roles of parents as members on schoolwide or individual PBIS teams? Professional literature is replete with arguments, empirically based and otherwise, in favor of parent or family partnerships, but it can be assumed that these practices are not yet realized.

Measurable Outcomes

A central consideration in the evolution of PBIS from its origins (Carr et al., 2002) in applied behavior analysis, the normalization–inclusion movement, and person-centered values has been how to address the need for measurable, quantifiable outcomes, given the emphasis in PBIS on quality of life, life span development, ecological and social validity, and family participation. For professionals in applied behavior analysis, this issue has been especially troublesome given the tradition in applied behavior analysis of strict adherence to scientific methods that ensure systematic and measurable examination of child-focused outcomes.

To evaluate outcomes such as quality of life, school climate, effects on the family, and social validity, it is often necessary to pair qualitative methods and instruments—for example, interviews, questionnaires, scales, focus groups, and document analysis—with quantitative methods. Certainly these social validity and quality-of-life outcomes are sometimes amenable to observation and measurement. Kincaid and colleagues (2002) recommended that future research include "longitudinal and empirically robust evaluations of assessment instruments that are sensitive to quality of life and social validity issues" but pointed out that the field of PBIS should also be "evaluating the impact of PBIS through less labor-intensive methods, including rating scales and interviews" (p. 116). A guiding principle is that the evaluation of outcomes should be done in a logical, clear, and straightforward manner that is understood and agreed upon by team members and that includes measurable child outcomes as well as the broader contexts of the plan. For all members of the team, the evaluation of outcomes should come as a natural progression from their roles in input and process evaluation activities.

Unifying Disciplines and Fostering Collaboration

Over the past 20 years or so, there has been a great deal of discussion about the need for various disciplines to be more collaborative in the planning and delivery of educational programs, in particular as they relate to children with special needs. One example is the **interdisciplinary team evaluation** approach. The basis of interdisciplinary team evaluation is that a group of professionals conducts evaluations together, transcending their individual disciplines. From the family and child perspective, this approach has potential for saving time and effort, fostering communication with professionals, and eliminating the volume of professional jargon that they must interpret. The team approach advocated in behavior support planning can be a mechanism for interdisciplinary evaluation at the input (planning), process (implementation), and outcomes stages of PBIS. However, it will require that professionals in different disciplines (for example, school psychology, general education, and special education) find ways to speak the same language and merge their evaluation instruments and methods. If the behavior support team is inter-disciplinary for the development of the plan based on evaluation of needs for behavior change, then it should continue to function in that manner as process and outcomes are evaluated.

Another future consideration related to evaluation of PBIS is the question of differences among professional organizations (see Chapter 3) in terms of the way they view discipline and challenging behavior in various learning environments. Consider, for example, the different points of view on the acceptability of punitive approaches for children and youth reflected in the ethical codes, standards, and guidelines of the NEA, the LFA, the CEC, the NAEYC, the APA, and BCBA. As has been noted repeatedly, an effective behavior support plan requires consensus building not only between professionals and family but also among professionals representing varied disciplinary perspectives. To function as a behavior support team and to monitor and evaluate interventions on a continuous basis, professionals are required to resolve differences and reach consensus about target behaviors, intervention methods, and desired outcomes.

SUMMARY

To evaluate is to determine the value or significance of something. It is important that we develop and apply effective ways of evaluating positive behavior interventions and supports. Just as planning (Chapter 7) is a process applicable in both our personal and professional lives, so too is evaluation. It is also important to keep in mind that evaluation is not exclusively a professional tool—something that we might use *on* someone—but rather that it is a process that is best done collaboratively *with* others, including the person who is the subject of the evaluation.

Evaluation may be characterized as either *formal* or *informal*. Formal evaluation tends to be structured, systematic, thorough, and based on explicit criteria for what is being evaluated. Informal evaluation tends to be more subjective and less planned. Evaluation may also be understood as a part of a *system* that includes planning, implementing, and evaluating.

The two purposes of evaluation are *formative* and *summative*. Formative evaluation refers to information that is gathered for the purpose of formulating additional goals, objectives, and intervention or teaching practices and to inform future decisions and actions. Summative evaluation refers to the acquisition of information that allows one at a specified end point to determine whether goals and objectives have been met or to sum up the impact of effectiveness of an (for example) intervention. In practice, often the same evaluation data are used for both purposes.

Evaluation may be further understood as one of two types, *program evaluation* or *individual evaluation*. Program evaluation is aimed at determining the impact and effectiveness of a program (school) for a group. Individual evaluation is aimed at making judgments about the impact of (in the case of this textbook) PBIS on the behavior of individual children with challenging, impeding behavior.

Finally, to understand broadly what evaluation is, it is necessary to think of it occurring as a part of a process that includes *inputs* (for example, contexts, setting events, environmental arrangements, and antecedents), *processes* (for example, intervention strategies or teaching methods), and *outcomes* (the results of intervention and teaching). These basic elements of evaluation are important to the understanding of evaluation as it is applied to all levels of PBIS.

Evaluation of PBIS at all levels is a topic of increasing interest in the literature. A number of issues are still unresolved with regard to how to apply evaluation methods and instruments in PBIS. One issue concerns the difference between SWPBSI and PBSI for children and youth with impeding or challenging behavior. The former requires a program evaluation approach, whereas the latter necessitates an individual evaluation approach. The two are distinct and require different methods and instrumentation.

Another issue is specific to the relative focus on inputs, processes, and outcomes as part of an overall evaluation plan for each of the three levels of PBSI. Although each is important and relevant, current emphasis in public policy is focused almost exclusively on outcomes. Finally, in examining the evolution of PBSI from its roots in applied behavior analysis, questions arise about broadening evaluation beyond quantifying child behavior outcomes to using a variety of both qualitative and quantitative approaches to answer questions of, for example, social validity, meaningfulness for parents or families, and relationships to self-determination and other aspects of quality of life.

This chapter introduced some of the fundamental issues and practices associated with evaluation of both SWPBSI programs and PBSI targeting individual children and youth (both those classified as having special needs and those not classified) who have impeding, challenging behavior and require a more intensive and systematic approach. Evaluation is an important and necessary component of any educational endeavor. Evaluation is more than merely determining what has occurred at the end point. It is best connected to inputs, processes, and outcomes. Finally, evaluation is most effective when it reflects both quantitative and qualitative information from a variety of sources.

ACTIVITIES TO EXTEND YOUR LEARNING

1. Invite the school district behavior specialist or behavior support team chair(s) to come to class and share how they evaluate the effectiveness of their plans.
2. Invite family representatives to class to serve on a panel to share their perspectives on how they evaluate the behavior support plan in which they are participants (team members or partners for Levels 1, 2, and 3). Discuss at a follow-up class meeting the connections among their perspectives and the points made in this chapter.

3. Divide the class into four research groups and assign each group one of the following topics: social or ecological validity, person-centered planning, quality of life, or self-determination. Research professional literature on these topics specific to what is being said about how each topic should be evaluated or measured. Share findings across groups and have discussions related to input, process, or outcome evaluation and methods for quantifying.

4. Use a role-playing exercise in class to learn more about the development, implementation, and evaluation of a schoolwide behavior support plan. Divide the class into stakeholder groups (students, parent or families, teachers, other school staff, and administrators). Using a hypothetical (or real) school, have the groups engage in the preliminary process of discussion and consensus building related to the desired behaviors in the school. After this step is completed, have each group select one or two members to serve on a behavior support team. The team can develop an outline of a plan and present it to the class, with particular attention to the means of evaluation (use the chapter content for assistance in choosing the who, what, why, and how of the evaluation).

5. Identify faculty members at your university who teach and perform research and who are experts on school and program evaluation, applied behavior analysis and single-case design, and qualitative research. Establish interview teams in class and conduct interviews with each of these individuals, focusing on their views about comparing program and individual evaluation and evaluation of PBSI. Report your interview findings in class or invite these professors to serve on a panel for a class presentation.

6. In small groups, review and discuss the *School-wide Evaluation Tool (SET) Implementation Manual*: Version 2.0 (Todd, Lewis-Palmer, Horner, Sugai, Sampson, & Phillips, 2012) with consideration for how the guidance that it provides relates to what you have studied in the chapter. Given that the manual is lengthy, consider having each small group address a section. Report your findings to the class as a whole.

FURTHER READING AND EXPLORATION

1. Go to the website of the Center for Positive Behavioral Interventions and Supports (www.pbis.org) and look for references and descriptions of methods of evaluation of PBSI at all three levels.

2. Survey schools in your community, city, county, or area and find out how many have established SWPBSI. Collect as many plans as possible and compare them using the evaluation criteria introduced in the chapter.

3. Look in professional journals on education and educational leadership or administration to find articles describing examples of SWPBSI. Study and compare the evaluation methods provided in each article. To what extent do these evaluation methods meet the standards for practice detailed in this chapter?

Using Reinforcement to Increase Appropriate Behavior

CONCEPTS TO UNDERSTAND

After reading this chapter, you should be able to:

- Define and discuss reinforcement.
- Describe positive and negative reinforcement.
- Identify and describe classes of positive reinforcement.
- Discuss the principles of effective reinforcement.
- List and describe methods for using positive reinforcement within learning environments, including naturally occurring reinforcers and how the use of reinforcement relates to PBIS.
- Describe the applications of reinforcement programs within the classroom, such as group contingencies.

KEY TERMS

Chaining

Classes of reinforcers

Establishing operations

Fading

Interval schedules

Naturally occurring reinforcers

Negative reinforcement

Positive reinforcement

Ratio schedules

Reinforcement

Shaping

Stimulus control

One of the major goals of PBIS is to foster learning environments that promote positive behavior in all learners. Teachers can facilitate the development of appropriate behaviors in learners through the use of positive reinforcement. Positive reinforcement is a critical piece of any instructional package in the development of new behaviors. Previously learned skills can also be maintained through the application of reinforcement procedures. Reinforcement is a vital component of all effective instructional or behavioral intervention programs. It is important that teachers be fluent in their understanding of these principles to accomplish desired instructional and learning outcomes aimed at promoting positive behavior change.

So how does positive reinforcement fit into the PBIS model? As discussed previously, a comprehensive PBIS intervention applied to an individual learner seeks to: (a) identify setting events and antecedents most frequently associated with challenging behaviors, (b) actively teach replacement behaviors that serve the same function for the learner, and (c) use differential reinforcement in the form of desired consequences to reinforce these skills. You have also learned that when teaching learners replacement behaviors, you must make their attempts at acquiring these skills efficient and use positive reinforcement to reinforce their approximations at performance until they acquire the skill and build fluency. We also see the use of reinforcement in the delivery of classwide and school-wide models of PBIS through the administration of tickets for performance to students that can be redeemed for tangibles or privileges. These are designed to acknowledge student behavior for schoolwide, classwide, and/or individual student performance at school assemblies, which serve as celebration days for schools who are engaging in SWPBIS. All of these serve as examples of positive reinforcement.

Reinforcement is defined as the contingent delivery of a consequence following a behavior that increases the future probability of the behavior (Cooper, Heron, & Heward, 2007). Reinforcement strengthens behavior and can occur naturally within one's environment or can be part of an intervention plan aimed at teaching new behaviors (Sulzer-Azaroff & Mayer, 1991). In this chapter, we examine how positive reinforcement can be used to promote the development of new behaviors and skills in learners.

WHAT IS REINFORCEMENT?

Reinforcement is a consequence that follows a behavior and that strengthens the behavior. What this means is that the contingent delivery of the reinforcing consequence must maintain or increase the behavior in terms of its rate, frequency, duration, and/or intensity. If it does not do so, then the consequence is not considered to be reinforcement.

Reinforcement is a part of everyday life. The term *reward* comes to mind for many when speaking of positive reinforcement. We all seek reinforcing outcomes in life, such as in our work, social network of friends, and/or leisure-time pursuits. The work of B. F. Skinner (1953) enlightened us on the topic of operant conditioning and the role of reinforcement in promoting behavior change. Operant behaviors are those behaviors that operate on the environment and generate consequences and as a result are influenced by these consequences (Martin & Pear, 2015). Behaviors that are reinforced over time are strengthened. Reinforcement can occur naturally as part of everyday life or can be planned, as in an educational or learning setting, or within the home, as when parents provide incentives to their children for picking up their rooms or assisting with household chores. Unplanned or naturally occurring reinforcement could include a child who works diligently on a class assignment because his teacher has recently commented about how she appreciates his efforts in her class. Planned reinforcement used by a teacher could include developing a point scheme for homework assignments turned in early or on time or the use of verbal praise by a parent for a child's attempt at performing a specific household chore.

An individual's behavior is influenced by the interactions between that individual and his or her environment. These interactions over time result in the development of an individual's reinforcement history (Cooper et al., 2007). A reinforcement history is developed through the culmination of these life and learning experiences that mold and shape what we as individuals define as reinforcing. To be effective, reinforcement should be individualized and should take into consideration the preferences of individual learners to the greatest extent possible. Another important point to remember as a teacher when working with students is that we should not underestimate the power of reinforcing consequences to change and or maintain desired behavior in learners. However, it is equally as important to understand how reinforcement can be used to enrich the quality of the learning environment, subsequently enhancing the quality of life for the learner, as illustrated in Vignette 9.1.

Vignette 9.1 reminds us of just how important positive reinforcement can be in a learning environment. To begin and end each school day with a statement of positive regard or a kind gesture toward students from their teacher is invaluable. To receive acknowledgement for one's effort can enhance a child's or adolescent's self-esteem and desired behavior to learn. In contrast, consider Vignette 9.2.

Vignette 9.1

Quality-of-Life Reinforcement at School

An adolescent girl who had just entered her first year of high school came home from school one day and proclaimed to her parents how much she enjoyed school and what supportive teachers she had. A few days passed, and the young girl again came home ecstatic about her day at school. When asked by her father as to what made her day so special, she replied, "My teachers are simply great! My English teacher told us how special we were and how she looked forward to our class every day because we worked so hard, and that we were wonderful students. And my history teacher always says how much he appreciates our giving it our best in his class, and my computer science teacher told me how impressed she was with my knowledge of computing." The father smiled and said to his daughter, "Positive praise goes a long way, doesn't it? Do you think this is why you are enjoying school so much this year?" The girl replied, "Absolutely, Dad. This is the first time I have ever felt this level of encouragement from my teachers. I actually look forward to going to school each day and finding out what I am going to learn from each of my teachers."

Reflective Moment

How can a teacher influence the performance of his or her students? What can you as a teacher do to help learners engage in learning and at the same time contribute to their self-esteem?

Vignette 9.2

A Failure to Provide Reinforcement

A 6-year-old child named Ethan, who has mild cerebral palsy, was given an assign-ment to color a picture from his workbook that accompanied a story he and his class were asked to read. He worked very hard at selecting the right colors and care-fully traced the picture with his crayons, being cautious to color the picture just right. Upon completing his masterpiece, he proudly went up to the teacher's desk and said, "Would you like to see my picture?" The teacher looked up and said, "Oh, you are finished? Well, you colored outside the lines, didn't you?" Tearfully, Ethan went back to his chair and muttered quietly to himself under his breath. Unfortunately, his teacher reprimanded him, and this later escalated in more externalized behaviors, thus result-ing in a less-than-positive day at school for him. A caring teacher could have avoided the entire situation and that sad unnecessary moment in Ethan's life.

Reflective Moment

Describe how you feel the teacher should have responded to Ethan concerning his work. How would you have given feedback to Ethan?

After reflecting on the material covered to this point, decide how you as a teacher could respond to the situation in Vignette 9.2 in a more reinforcing manner. Another important point to consider from the previous example is that the child in this case, Ethan, is attempting to recruit reinforcement from his teacher (i.e., he is attempting to get affir-mation or validation from the teacher regarding his work). For the teacher in this instance, it is important to respond favorably to Ethan's attempts at performance, being mindful to recall that he was engaged in completing the task, that he genuinely put forth his very best effort in completion of the task, and that he sought affirmation for his work. It is important to remember how a teacher's response can make or break the spirit of a child.

POSITIVE REINFORCEMENT

Positive reinforcement is perhaps the most well-known form of reinforcement pro-cedure practiced among educators. Positive reinforcement is defined as the contingent presentation of a stimulus that increases the probability of the occurrence of the behavior in the future. Translated to practice, what does this mean? If a teacher provides a learner with a choice of preferred activities consisting of library time, computer time, or time with the teacher following the completion of an assigned task and this procedure results in strengthening the behavior (task completion), then positive reinforcement has been demonstrated. Positive reinforcement is widely used within classroom settings and other learning environments. Examples of positive reinforcement can include verbal praise, smiles, teacher proximity, access to preferred activities, and choice. The key points to remember are that reinforcers should be individualized and must be valued by the indi-vidual to be effective. Also, regardless of the type of reinforcers that are selected (e.g., praise or activities), to qualify as a positive reinforcer they must increase the occurrence of the target behavior. Positive reinforcement is an effective tool when used by a skillful and caring teacher within any teaching and learning context.

Consider This

An example of positive reinforcement is the use of the Premack Principle (Premack, 1959). This has also been referred to as "Grandma's Law" (Cooper et al., 2007). The Premack Principle states that the opportunity to engage in a high-probability behavior can be used to reinforce a low probability of behavior. An example of the Premack Principle is: "When you complete your dinner, you may have a piece of chocolate pie." The high-probability behavior (eating a slice of chocolate pie) will have a greater value, especially if an unpreferred dish happens to be the entrée for dinner that evening.

Another example is something like this: "When you complete the assignment, you may play your favorite game on the computer." Each example clearly specifies that if the learner performs the desired behavior (a low-probability behavior) that they will be reinforced by a desired consequence (a higher-probability behavior). This technique can be very effective for classroom teachers when attempting to promote task engagement and task completion with learners.

NEGATIVE REINFORCEMENT

Negative reinforcement occurs when an occurrence of the target behavior is followed by the removal of an aversive stimulus, ultimately resulting in an increase in the target behavior (Miltenberger, 2015). This procedure is often misunderstood and considered to be a punishment procedure. However, it does not reduce behavior, as would be the case with punishment; rather, it strengthens the probability of a target behavior. One of the most frequently witnessed examples within classroom settings is contained in Vignette 9.3.

In examining Vignette 9.3, it is apparent that Aaron has difficulty completing the task. In response to his frustration, he is unable to communicate his need for assistance in an effective manner, resulting in behaviors that are inappropriate and not helpful to Aaron. The teacher's response in this case is to send Aaron to the principal's office, allowing him to escape the task demand and ultimately serving to negatively reinforce and strengthen this behavior. Often, escape behaviors—those behaviors that are directed at escaping from an aversive situation—as demonstrated in Vignette 9.3 are strengthened by negative reinforcement. With regard to positive behavior supports, individual and specific classroom supports—once identified and implemented—can be used to successfully eliminate such problems from occurring.

Avoidance behavior is also associated with negative reinforcement, with the intent being aimed at avoiding an aversive stimulus rather than terminating it (Cooper et al., 2007). Some more prominent examples of avoidance behavior include pretending to be ill hoping to stay home from school to avoid a threat from a school bully or having to sit for an exam, failing to verbally express their feelings to avoid conflict with a parent or sibling, and losing homework assignments to avoid receiving a poor grade. In each of these examples, the aversive consequence was avoided. When these behaviors are negatively reinforced over time, the individual fails to develop a repertoire of alternative social and communication skills that would address such conflicts in his or her life in a more direct and deliberate manner. Many behaviors such as task disengagement and disruptive

Vignette 9.3

Strengthening Challenging Behavior Through Negative Reinforcement

Aaron is a 14-year-old learner with an identified learning disability. School has served as a constant source of frustration for him over the past several years, and after his recent transition to high school, he feels more out-of-sorts about it than ever—especially in math. He is in a pre-algebra class and receives some tutoring and assistance from the resource teacher but is struggling in the regular classroom. Upon receiving math problems to complete during class, he attempts a few and then becomes increasingly frustrated, shouting expletives about how he thinks the work is useless, resulting in a heated verbal exchange between him and his teacher and then in Aaron being sent to the principal's office.

Reflective Moment

As a teacher, how would you respond to a learner like Aaron who is obviously "turned off" to school? How can we promote Aaron's success through our instructional efforts and in turn lessen his ill feelings toward school?

behavior are aimed at escape or avoidance from instructional tasks (Cipani, 1995). Cipani recommended the following approaches for determining whether negative reinforcement is maintaining a problem behavior:

1. Does the behavior result in the termination of instructional demands or activities?
2. Does the learner experience difficulties with regard to the instructional tasks or demands in question?
3. Do the behaviors occur most frequently in those academic subject areas that the learner has difficulty with versus those tasks that the learner has greater degrees of ability in? (pp. 36–39)

There are some potential solutions for addressing behaviors that are linked to negative reinforcement. One of the most obvious is to alter task demands that would result in promoting participation on the part of the learner. A second strategy is to teach alternative skills or learning strategies to the learner to address the areas of deficiency. Last, one could use positive reinforcement to acknowledge attempts at performance and for the absence of the problem behavior.

SELECTION OF REINFORCERS

Reinforcement is an important element of quality of life for everyone, yet the types of reinforcers preferred by individuals are numerous and varied. Basic human needs such as food, clothing, and shelter are consistent for most people, and certainly toys are meaningful to all children. Yet it is very important to consider the individual preferences of each learner when developing a program using positive reinforcement. It should also be noted that reinforcers often work best when they are paired. The right combination of

FIGURE 9–1

Pairing Reinforcers

- "I like the way you did such a good job of expressing yourself on your essay, and I am going to give you an additional 5 bonus points for your hard work."
- "Excellent job cleaning your room, son. How about an ice-cream cone for such good work?"
- "Thank you for the beautiful picture that you made," said the mother, giving her child a hug and smiling.
- "I like how hard you are working on your assignment. If there is time remaining when you complete it, choose a free time activity that you would like to do."
- "Great job! Here is a bonus for your excellent work."

These examples emphasize how reinforcers can be paired. Usually this type of reinforcing means pairing a social reinforcer with an activity, edible, or tangible reinforcer.

edibles, activity, tangibles, and social reinforcers paired with one another can have a significant and lasting impact on promoting positive behavior in each of us. Figure 9–1 contains examples of how reinforcers can be paired to promote and affirm positive behavior.

CLASSES OF REINFORCERS

Reinforcement can be classified using the following labels: edibles, activity, tangibles, social, and tokens. Examples from various **classes of reinforcers** include the following:

- *Edibles—food and drink preferences:* Juice, water, milk, fruit, cereal, pudding, peanut butter, crackers, raisins, cookies, popcorn
- *Activity—preferred activities enjoyed by the individual within work, play, and leisure-time contexts:* Computer games, reading a book, playing with puzzles, playing basketball, listening to music, playing a game, completing an art project, assisting the teacher, free time, swimming, jobs in the classroom, no homework days
- *Tangibles—preferred items such as toys, personal possessions, and clothing:* Books, backpack, notebooks, pencils, logo apparel such as a jacket or hat, makeup, magazines, miniature cars, action figures
- *Social—social praise, conversation, hugs, smiles, social attention, and eye contact, which can be applied to individual learners or used within an entire class:* Smiles from the teacher or parent, nodding in affirmation, recognition for attempts at performance, "Good work," "Nice improvement," "Thanks for your efforts," "That's great," "Thank you for being so patient," "I like the way you have gotten your materials out and are ready for work"
- *Tokens—can be exchanged for a specific reinforcer that is valued by the learner:* Candy, free time, computer access, bonus points, homework free pass, library time, tickets to a movie, free meal coupons, gift certificate, money
- *Naturally occurring reinforcers—although not formally defined as a reinforcer class that is facilitated by a classroom teacher,* **naturally occurring reinforcers** *represent a very rich array of reinforcers available to a teacher and students found within the day-to-day classroom and home environments of children.* Baer (1999) advocated

that when selecting target behaviors, one should select only those that will result in positive reinforcement within the natural environment. Thus, naturally occurring reinforcers should be considered first as teachers attempt to teach and promote the acquisition and fluency of new behaviors.

When constructing an intervention plan, it is important to list reinforcers that have been effective in the past as part of the learner's reinforcement history. Several methods can be used to identify reinforcers for a specific learner that he or she prefers, including the following:

1. Asking the parents and family what the learner enjoys most, such as a favorite toy, activity, social amenity, or other.
2. Asking the learner what he or she enjoys most. Assessing personal preference is important, and everyone likes to be considered. Ask the learner to complete a reinforcer survey in which he or she circles or lists most preferred reinforcers in the following areas: edibles, tangibles, activities, and social.
3. Providing the learner with choice and allowing the individual to select his or her preferred reinforcers from a reinforcer menu or by choosing preferred reinforcers as they are presented. This is known as reinforcer sampling.
4. Performing a review of past educational records to identify reinforcers that were successfully used in the past.

An important consideration to remember is that for learners who have well-developed communication skills and who are of school age, the direct approach is often best when trying to identify reinforcer preferences. Asking the learner is the best and most timely method for ensuring what the learner likes most and least prefers. Another method that is often effective is presenting students with a reinforcer menu and asking them to circle their preference. However, for learners who are young, or for students with significant challenges in communication associated with comprehensive disabilities, the use of parent interviews, record review, and presenting the student with choice-making opportunities is recommended.

Reinforcer assessment can be accomplished through allowing a choice-making opportunity for a child, such as presenting the student with a choice of two objects (e.g., toys or activities) or using picture symbols or photos of actual activities. Provide a verbal cue paired with a gesture if necessary, such as a pointing motion while asking the student to "pick the toy you want to play with" or "choose the activity you want." It is important to recognize how to accommodate individual needs when presenting them with a choice-making opportunity to assess reinforcers. For example, if severe cognitive disabilities and subsequent communication difficulties are present, often allowing the child to point or approximate by pointing to the desired object is sufficient. Bambara and Koger (1996) described a procedure for teaching how to make choices. Their recommendations were formulated from a review of pertinent literature in this area and included the following steps:

1. Provide the learner with an opportunity to sample the options that are available to him or her. These options should be based on personal preferences.
2. Present the options before a student and allow the student to visually or tactilely scan each option.
3. Verbally prompt the learner to choose by asking, "Which one do you want?"
4. Wait approximately 5 to 10 seconds to allow the learner to respond.
5. Reinforce immediately if an independent choice occurs by giving the preferred choice to the student with verbal praise.

6. Provide prompting if the independent choice response does not occur immediately.
7. Repair the situation if a student refuses an option, take it away, and never force choice.
8. Repeat steps 2–7 for another choice opportunity, continue as long as the student is receptive, and vary options from left or right on each trial.

PRINCIPLES OF EFFECTIVE REINFORCEMENT

To ensure effective reinforcement, here are some basic rules for delivery of reinforcers:

1. *Reinforcement must be contingent.* It is important that teachers establish the contingencies or rules related to the administration of reinforcement. Clear guidelines concerning classroom behavior must be established, and contingencies must be clearly explained to all learners. Guidelines for administering reinforcement must also be clear and concise so that learners understand the expectations and consequences associated with desired behavior.
2. *Reinforcement needs to be immediate.* For reinforcement to be effective, it must be delivered immediately following the desired behavior. When a teacher asks a child to complete a task, the teacher must administer the appropriate reinforcer immediately following performance of the behavior on the part of the learner.
3. *Establishing operations will increase the value of the reinforcer.* This item refers to the factors that affect the reinforcing value of a particular stimulus (Michael, 1993). Deprivation and satiation are most frequently cited as examples of **establishing operations** (Martin & Pear, 2015). A reinforcer is more effective when an individual has been deprived of it for a substantial period of time. An example of this principle is when you have not eaten a favorite food or dessert for a long period of time. You will experience a heightened sense of fulfillment from this favorite food upon eating it. On the other hand, satiation occurs when a previously reinforcing consequence loses its value and is therefore no longer reinforcing. For example, if you eat your favorite Thanksgiving dessert (pumpkin pie), and then repeatedly snack on it two or three more times before nightfall, it will eventually lose its value, despite how much you like it as a dessert. And when you have viewed the same movie more than two or three times, it eventually loses its value and is at that point no longer of interest to you.
4. *Intensity of the reinforcer will result in more effective outcomes.* Reinforcement is generally more effective if the intensity or magnitude of the reinforcer is greater (Miltenberger, 2015). Individuals are more likely to expend greater amounts of effort if the yield in terms of reinforcement is greater. Consider student athletes who are willing to work extra hours to perfect their skill and earn a starting berth on the team (something that they value as a goal). The intensity associated with the consequence could be the enjoyment they derive from playing their chosen sport, the increased social attention that they receive, and generalized emotional and social fulfillment. Another example is the academic dean at a major state university who uses her personal leave time so that she can be compensated financially for teaching a class that she enjoys.
5. *The quality of a reinforcer will also be a determinant in the effectiveness of a reinforcer.* Kazdin (2008) made the distinction that quality of the reinforcer differs from the intensity or magnitude of a reinforcer in that the quality of a reinforcer is

determined by the learner and is linked to the preferences of individual learners. As we have previously mentioned, it is important to ask the learner what his or her preferences are, as the quality of a reinforcing consequence as determined and valued by the learner will influence the effectiveness of a reinforcer.

USING POSITIVE REINFORCEMENT WITHIN LEARNING ENVIRONMENTS

This section will provide examples of how teachers and others can better use positive reinforcement within learning environments. Concepts will be introduced that examine the various facets associated with positive reinforcement programs, such as schedules of reinforcement, shaping behavior, chaining, stimulus control, fading reinforcement, and enlistment of naturally occurring reinforcers.

Schedules of Reinforcement

Reinforcement schedules have been widely written about within the behavior literature. There are two major terms related to reinforcement that one should be familiar with: continuous reinforcement and intermittent reinforcement. Continuous reinforcement occurs when a target response is repeatedly reinforced following its occurrence. Consider the following examples that illustrate the concept of continuous reinforcement:

- Each time Alli, a young student driver, gets into the car and puts her safety belt on, her teacher verbally praises her.
- When Duncan picks up each individual toy and places it in his toy chest, his mother says, "Good job picking your toys up."
- The teacher praises Curt each time he attempts and completes a math problem.
- Ben's father verbally reinforces him for each step that Ben approximates or successfully attempts in his pursuit to learn to ride his bicycle independently.

Continuous reinforcement is most frequently used during the skill acquisition stage of learning when someone is attempting to learn a new skill. Parents and teachers alike can best use this approach to reinforce children when learning a new skill or routine within the home. The more frequently a teacher reinforces desired behaviors, the better, as these patterns of responding will be more likely to occur. Sulzer-Azaroff and Mayer (1991) recommend that a dense or continuous schedule of reinforcement (CRF) should be used when the goal of the instructional program is to increase or stabilize a behavior. Teachers and parents should rely on high rates of reinforcement during this initial stage of learning. By doing so, they will increase the likelihood that the learner will approach and attempt the task or behavior and ultimately result in the acquisition of the skill. As skill acquisition occurs and the behavior is established, reinforcement can be thinned and applied intermittently. Instead of each response being reinforced, every second or third response is reinforced, until ultimately natural consequences or naturally occurring reinforcement associated with successful completion of the task will ultimately become reinforcing enough and aid in maintaining the behavior. Once again, this is a prime example of how reinforcement applies to the PBIS model at the tertiary or individual student level.

An intermittent reinforcement schedule is used during the fluency- and maintenance-building stages of learning. As students become more fluent in performing a new task, intermittent reinforcement is provided at key points during the performance of the task or following the completion of the task. Fluency is the ability of an individual to perform a skill or behavior with minimal or no assistance at a reasonably fast rate with few or no errors. Intermittent reinforcement is typically used during this phase of learning to promote ongoing refinement and performance maintenance of the skill or behavior over time. Intermittent schedules of reinforcement consist of four different types of schedules. These include fixed interval, variable interval, fixed ratio, and variable ratio schedules of reinforcement (Ferster & Skinner, 1957). **Interval schedules** are connected to periods of time, whereas **ratio schedules** are associated with an average number of responses.

When using fixed and variable interval schedules of reinforcement, a behavior is reinforced after a designated time interval has passed. Fixed interval (FI) schedules use the same time period—for instance, FI 30 would mean that the first occurrence of the behavior on or following when 30 seconds have elapsed would be reinforced. Conversely, when using a variable interval schedule, the amount of time is based on an average. An example of this is a variable interval (VI) schedule of VI 30; the behavior would on average be reinforced at approximately 30 seconds. The obvious difficulty for a teacher in a busy general or special education classroom is the degree to which they could consistently adhere to such a strict reinforcement schedule.

Ratio schedules of reinforcement are based on the number of responses that must occur before reinforcement is given. An example of a fixed ratio (FR) schedule follows:

> Curtis receives a stamp on his paper after he completes every third problem. His teacher is using an FR 3 schedule of reinforcement.

Fixed-ratio schedules of reinforcement are very effective within classroom settings. Teachers can effectively use this approach when teaching certain academic tasks such as completing math problems. It is also an effective approach for use within job settings in which parts assembly is a required task. An example of this applied to a job setting follows:

> Roger, an adolescent with Asperger's syndrome, is employed at a grocery store. His primary job is stocking shelves. His supervisor has worked out a fixed ratio schedule (FR 9) of reinforcement in which Roger is given a token after he has completed stocking the ninth shelf unit in the aisle. He can redeem the tokens for food and beverage items in the store during his break and lunch periods.

Variable ratio (VR) schedules also deliver reinforcement based on the number of responses that occur but are based on the average number of responses. Variable ratio schedules can also be used within school settings related to the performance of academic tasks. Classroom teachers would therefore administer reinforcement based on a range of responses. In the case of Lawrence, a student in grade 4 who receives a good-job stamp for successive problems completed in math, he may receive a stamp every 3 problems, every 6 problems, every 8 problems, or every 10 problems. The average number of these constitutes the variable ratio schedule being used. One important point to consider when using a variable ratio schedule is that the learner is not "tipped off" as to when the reinforcement will be administered and thus is more likely to continue to be engaged in the task, hoping at some point for the reinforcer to be administered.

Shaping

When teaching a new behavior or skill, reinforcement is necessary to initiate skill acquisition. One effective teaching method that employs reinforcement in the development of new skills is **shaping**: the reinforcement of successive approximations of a target behavior. Successive approximations are attempts at performing a desired behavior that gradually resembles the desired response over time and with practice (Cooper et al., 2007). The idea is that reinforcement is applied incrementally as the behavior more closely resembles the terminal behavior that you are trying to teach:

> A father teaching his son to hit a ball begins by first using an oversized softball, perhaps a plastic ball in order to minimize injury. He continues by reinforcing his son's crude approximations at holding the bat and continues to reinforce his son's efforts at refining his stance and holding the bat. The father then initiates pitching to his son, maintaining a close proximity and slowly pitching the ball underhand so that his son will have a greater chance of striking the ball with his bat. As these steps take place, the father continues to reinforce his son's attempts at approximating a swing and continues the process until his son does indeed hit the ball. As his son's abilities increase, he will "raise the bar" and gradually move farther away and pitch the ball slightly harder until his son has refined his skill to a more advanced level. Once he has acquired the skill, the father will gradually move to a regulation-sized ball to aid his son in generalizing the skill to more natural contingencies.

To use shaping, the teacher must identify a target behavior. The next step is to identify a starting point or an initial approximation. The teacher then reinforces the learner for engaging in the approximation. As the learner refines the ability to perform the initial step with ease and proceeds to the next step, the teacher gets excited at the learner's progress and begins to provide reinforcement for each of those subsequent steps. By doing so, the teacher's use of differential reinforcement is enhancing the learner's desire to proceed to the next step and move closer toward performance of the target behavior. Consider the example in Vignette 9.4 of shaping as applied to teaching a young boy with Down syndrome how to ride his bicycle.

Vignette 9.4

Learning to Ride a Bike

Jared, a 7-year-old boy with Down syndrome, wanted desperately to ride a bike but was somewhat fearful and apprehensive when his parents tried to teach him. His parents contacted the motor development clinic at the local university, and they invited Jared to attend the clinic to assess how they might help in teaching him the skill.

They began the session by assessing Jared's ability to perform the desired motor sequence needed for riding a bike. They placed him at first on an exercise cycle to reduce his anxiety and to reinforce his approximation at sitting on a bike. They also wanted to determine whether Jared could independently pedal in sequence; the exercise bike was a perfect answer, given that it was stationary and lessened Jared's fear of falling from the bike. Jared had some obvious difficulty with pedaling independently that became noticeable almost immediately. The clinic's instructional staff began by verbally praising Jared for his attempt at keeping his feet on the pedals. As each assistant moved Jared's left and then right foot in sequence, repeating the pedaling motion over and over again, they verbally praised Jared's performance.

As Jared assumed greater levels of independence in performing the pedaling sequence at the close of the first session, the staff then began to use a timer on the bike to encourage Jared to maintain his pedaling for extended periods of time. At the end of each time period, Jared was given a break and allowed to play basketball. The team began by setting the timer on the bike for 1 minute, in which they praised Jared for pedaling independently during this time period, then gradually increased the timer to 5 and then 10 minutes. At that point, the instructors mounted Jared's bike on an adapted bike rack used by competition cyclists to train indoors during inclement weather. The team continued with the timer and reinforced Jared for his independent pedaling. As Jared began to display less fear on the bike and continued to improve in his ability to pedal independently without physical prompts, the team then proceeded to mount training wheels to Jared's bike. They then used the same shaping method, in which they reinforced Jared for his attempt at each successive approximation of the target behavior, such as his ability to sit and independently pedal and steer his bicycle. This process went on weekly for nearly three months, ultimately resulting in Jared learning to ride his real bike independent of assistance and training wheels, which led to a very happy outcome for Jared and his family.

Reflective Moment

What recommendations would you have in teaching Jared to ride his bike? Was this a socially valid skill to teach, and why?

As a rule, shaping can be used to teach and increase new behaviors and also to systematically reduce excessive or problematic behavior over time. The benefits of shaping as a teaching procedure are many. It is a positive procedure that is learner centered, individualized, and promotes the delivery of reinforcement for successive approximations, thus placing other behaviors on extinction (Cooper et al., 2007). Shaping is a long-term and systematic goal-setting process that can often serve to enlist greater degrees of learner participation. The obvious challenge when using shaping procedures within any learning setting is that it is a time-consuming method that does require a great deal of attention and monitoring on the part of the teacher and other instructional staff. However, the instructional progress that is made possible to a learner through this practice and the ultimate learning outcomes that are likely to ensue provide a great return on the time investment that is required.

Chaining

When teaching a new skill or behavior to a student, it is important to focus on the entire skill or behavior. This method is referred to as **chaining**. Chaining involves a sequence of related steps or behaviors or discriminative stimuli (SDs) and responses (Rs) that are linked together like links in a chain. For example, when children arrive home from school, their parents might have a routine comprising a sequence of behaviors that must be accomplished: having a light snack, completing their homework, washing their hands, and having supper together as a family. Each of these activities can be taught individually or can be linked and taught as a sequence or behavior chain.

How does this concept apply to a school setting? Consider the behavior chain associated with arriving at school and attending the first-period class. Upon arriving at school, Kaitlin will go to her locker, retrieve her books and notebooks needed for her first- and second-period classes, go to her first-period class, take her assigned seat, place her instructional materials on her desk, stand for the Pledge of Allegiance, remain standing for the moment of silence, and then sit down and wait for instructions from her teacher. For Kaitlin, each of these behaviors serves as a discriminative stimulus for the next response. A discriminative stimulus (SD) is defined as an antecedent stimulus associated with the availability of reinforcement for a particular response class (Cooper et al., 2007). Think of each step in performing a behavior or skill as an individual link in the chain (Martin & Pear, 2015). Chaining is an important method in the development of behavior, in that it will frequently result in the delivery of reinforcement.

Three methods of chaining have been traditionally used in teaching: total task presentation, backward chaining, and forward chaining. However, before a chain can be taught, it is important to develop a task analysis, which is a method designed to break down a complex behavior into small components or steps. Task analysis has been instrumental as a teaching method almost since the inception of special education. It is conceivable that any instructional task can be task analyzed. This can include academic skills, social skills, and functional self-help skills, to name a few of the possible categories. To task analyze a skill, one should observe others performing the skill and write down the essential steps of the task, being mindful of the entire process. Next, perform the skill yourself, noting the chain of SD and responses that constitute the task. As noted by Cooper and colleagues (2007), there are three methods that can be used to validate the sequencing in a task analysis. The authors recommend the following:

1. The behaviors required in the sequence are developed after observation of others performing the task.
2. Request consultations with experts or persons who are recognized for their abilities in performing the task.
3. Perform the task yourself to aid in refining the movements and sequence that are required for optimal performance of the entire task.

Whatever the method that you select for validating the task analysis, be sure that attention is given to identifying the most efficient sequence of steps and note the SD for each response to ascertain whether the learner will be able to discriminate the individual stimulus–response chains. Figure 9–2 provides an example of a task analysis for going through the lunch line in the school cafeteria.

The various stimulus–response units are easily identified when one examines this task analysis. If any one of these steps fails to be performed, the entire behavior chain is disrupted and ultimately the reinforcing outcome may not be realized. Task analysis is important in teaching; it allows a task to be broken down into smaller steps. Skills are more efficiently taught in smaller steps. Another benefit is that it allows the teacher to

---

FIGURE 9–2

Going Through the School Lunch Line

1. Enter the cafeteria.
2. Pick up tray and wait in line.
3. Proceed through the line as it slowly progresses forward.
4. Select food items and place on tray.
5. Select desired drink (milk, chocolate milk, or juice).
6. Give student identification number to the cashier.
7. Pick up utensils and napkins.
8. Pick up condiments (mayonnaise, ketchup, mustard).
9. Locate a seat and begin eating.

assess a student's performance on each component of the skill sequence, thus enabling individualized instruction at different skill levels. We will examine that you can use chaining with a task analysis for teaching new behaviors.

Total Task Presentation

The total task presentation method of chaining basically involves allowing the student to attempt each step in the task analysis from beginning to end. In this method, the teacher provides the necessary instructional assistance in the form of instructional cues (verbal, gestural, and physical prompts) as needed to assist the learner in completing the sequence of behaviors. Miltenberger (2015) indicated that graduated physical guidance has been widely used with this type of chaining procedure. Graduated physical guidance is a term used to describe a form of physical prompting that uses a hand-over-hand procedure provided by the teacher to assist the student in completion of the task (Sulzer-Azaroff & Mayer, 1991).

We often witness examples of this form of chaining being used to teach new and complex motor skill behaviors, such as feeding oneself, using utensils, and drinking from a cup, and also with adult learners, such as learning to swing a golf club or a tennis racket. As the student becomes proficient in performing each step in the task analysis, the teacher can begin to back off or fade the use of physical prompts or graduated guidance as a means of promoting independence on the part of the student.

Backward Chaining

Backward chaining involves teaching a task beginning with the last step and then moving in a descending order: the next-to-last step, the third-from-last step, and so on. Backward chaining has been a successful teaching method for teaching a variety of skills, including dressing, grooming, and feeding. This method was widely used in the early days of applied behavior analysis when teaching functional skills to persons with developmental disabilities living within institutional settings. One advantage to backward chaining is that the student receives reinforcement for completion of the last step, thus reducing the wait time and making the reinforcing consequence more effective.

When using backward chaining, the teacher must first establish the performance criteria that must be attained before introducing subsequent steps. The teacher begins by assisting the student with all of the early steps in the task analysis and continues until the very last step. The student is then instructed by the teacher on how to complete the last step, which may require use of a verbal, gestural, or physical prompt on the part of the teacher to assist the student. If, for example, the teacher has established as a performance criterion that the student must perform the last step of the task analysis for three consecutive trials without assistance, then upon meeting that performance criterion, the teacher will initiate teaching the next-to-last step in the skill sequence. This pattern continues until each step in the task analysis has been mastered. For example, if we examine the task analysis in Figure 9–2, we would assist the student in completion of steps 1–8 and then teach step 9 until mastery. The process would then be repeated. We would assist the learner through steps 1–7 and then teach step 8 until mastery, and the learner would complete step 9 independently.

Forward Chaining

Forward chaining takes the opposite approach from backward chaining. With forward chaining, the first step in the task analysis is taught first. Typically, the first step is taught to the student until a predetermined performance criterion is attained before introducing the second step of the task analysis. However, there are variations to this approach, as identified by Zirpoli (2015). This approach includes teaching more than one step of the task analysis concurrently. This method is referred to as concurrent task training (Zirpoli, 2015). Using this method allows for the presentation of multiple steps of the task analysis and affords learners a better instructional context for learning more complex behavior chains.

Stimulus Control

Stimulus control is a process by which a stimulus assumes control of a behavior that has been previously reinforced in the presence of that stimulus: the ability of a student to successfully discriminate the antecedent stimulus and voluntarily respond to it in an appropriate manner within the natural environment. When a response receives reinforcement repeatedly over time, it is strengthened and learning occurs. This is a process that occurs over time through repeated practice and through trial and error on the part of the student. Consider some examples of stimulus control from everyday life: When driving a car, most people are prompted to stop at the presence of a red light or to pull over to the edge of the road when seeing a flashing red light and hearing the sound of a siren from a police car, fire truck, or ambulance. Other examples could be purchasing your favorite soft drink from a vending machine; when you see that your choice's button on the machine is lit up, upon depositing the correct change and pushing the button, the can tumbles out of the bottom of the machine. Other examples include answering the telephone when it rings or answering the door on hearing the sound of the doorbell. These responses are likely to be reinforced by a voice on the other line or a visitor at your door.

From a teaching and learning perspective, it is important to understand how discrimination training is essential to the learning process. Discrimination training refers to assisting a learner in discriminating the presence or absence of an SD. The discriminative stimulus basically serves as a cue that the behavior, once emitted, will be reinforced. For example, when the teacher prompts a child to take out his or her book, and he or she complies, the teacher verbally reinforces the student with a statement such as, "Good listening." The chaining techniques previously described in this chapter serve as examples of teaching methodologies that support the development of discrimination in learners as response chains are taught and reinforced within task analyses. If the behavior is emitted in the presence of an antecedent stimulus and is not reinforced, it is termed an S-Delta. These moments also assist the student with discrimination by identifying those antecedent stimuli that are not associated with reinforcement, thus strengthening the student's ability to discern the correct cues. When attempting to promote stimulus control, Martin and Pear (2015) recommend the following guidelines:

1. Select distinct cues and make them apparent to the learner so that he or she can readily identify the discriminative stimulus. Doing so will minimize errors and frustration and lead to reinforcing outcomes. One example is being precise about directions for completing an assignment or operationally defining what constitutes a "clean room." Another could be defining for learners which assignments must be completed before they are "finished."

2. Use errorless learning procedures to control for errors. When possible, teachers should use errorless learning approaches to teaching as a method for promoting the stimulus–response patterns and avoiding mistakes. As students are first learning to recognize the distinct instructional cues (SDs), attempts should be made to make these as obvious as possible to reinforce correct responding, thus leading to stimulus control.

3. Provide frequent opportunities for practice. When teaching new skills, learners must be afforded numerous opportunities to practice the desired behaviors and to receive reinforcement for appropriate responses before learning can occur. Frequent

repetitions or trials are needed during the acquisition and fluency stages of learning to reinforce both the recognition of SDs and the refinement of responses. But, as the old adage goes, "Practice makes perfect."

4. Use rules and contingencies. When teachers or parents state their performance expectations and are clear and consistent in their reinforcement of these rules or contingencies, children and youth will most likely demonstrate the desired behavior. Recognition of desired behavior through the administration of reinforcement and the withholding of reinforcement for undesired or incorrect responses will assist the learner in making the necessary discriminations, provided that these rules are maintained and are consistent.

This section has attempted to familiarize you with methods for promoting stimulus control. It is the ultimate goal of every teacher to facilitate learning. As we have discussed in this section of the text, the importance of reinforcement used in conjunction with systematic teaching techniques and repeated trials can result in the attainment of desired instructional and learning outcomes.

Fading

Fading is a procedure designed to systematically remove instructional prompts so that a behavior occurs under natural conditions. Fading is a process that teachers frequently use over time to reduce the amount of instructional prompts provided to the learner to allow for independent performance on the part of the learner.

Prompting is a teaching method designed to provide instructional support to the learner in completing a task. Prompt hierarchies, as you have learned, can involve a system of least-to-most prompts or, conversely, a series of most-to-least prompts, depending on the nature of the skill, the skill abilities of the learner, and general complexities associated with teaching the task. When using a system of prompts, a time-delay element is also typically incorporated, which allows for a 3- to 5-second time delay between the presentation of a prompt and a learner's response before initiating the next level of prompt. Time delay can be classified as an errorless learning approach. It involves systematically fading teacher-delivered prompts so that behavior is controlled by naturally occurring contingencies.

There are generally two types of time-delay procedures that can be used. The first is a constant time-delay procedure that basically uses no time delay between a teacher-delivered prompt and learner performance. The constant time-delay procedure does not allow for independent performance on the part of the learner, the instructional cue is given by the teacher, and subsequently the teacher assists the learner in the performance of the task, relying on prompts to assist the learner in task completion. The second type of time-delay procedure is a progressive procedure. The goal of the progressive time-delay procedure is to slowly lengthen the time delay following the instructional cue, thus allowing for independent performance on the part of the learner. As the learner's proficiency increases, the time delay is slowly lengthened to a maximum of approximately 5 seconds before assistance in the form of a prompt is provided by the teacher to the learner. The ultimate goal, of course, is the transfer of stimulus control from teacher-delivered prompts to the naturally occurring contingencies found within the task and environment. Examples of prompting approaches are displayed in Figure 9–3.

Fading procedures allow the teacher to systematically withdraw the level of teacher assistance in the form of prompts over time as students become fluent in their performance and maintain high levels of performance. Fading can take on many forms, such as the reduction of stimulus prompts in terms of their frequency and intensity. One example

---

FIGURE 9–3

Prompt Hierarchies

A least-to-most prompt hierarchy is as follows:
Independent—Allow for independent performance on the part of the learner.
Verbal—Following a 3- to 5-second time delay, initiate a verbal prompt (e.g., "Pick up the cup.")
Gesture—Allow for a 3- to 5-second time delay for a response to occur. If no response occurs, initiate a gestural cue paired with a verbal cue such as "Pick up the cup" while pointing to the cup.
Physical—Following a 3- to 5-second time delay, initiate a physical prompt (light touch on the hand or graduated physical guidance) paired with a verbal prompt: "Pick up the cup."

In contrast to this approach, a system of most-to-least prompts is as follows:
Physical—Using a graduated physical guidance procedure, the instructor provides hand-over-hand guidance to the learner in performing the task in conjunction with a verbal cue.
Gesture—As the learner acquires the ability to perform the task, the teacher gradually fades physical assistance and relies on a gestural prompt to initiate the learner's performance, also paired with a verbal cue.
Verbal—As the learner exhibits fluency in his or her ability to perform the desired task, the teacher fades to the use of verbal prompts to assist the learner in task performance.

---

of this was a widely cited study conducted by Massey and Wheeler (2000). The study demonstrated a systematic reduction of both the frequency and intensity of prompts delivered to a young child with autism. Massey and Wheeler (2000) in their study used a system of most-to-least prompts to teach the child how to successfully use a picture activity schedule as a method for promoting increased task engagement and reducing problematic behavior. The authors determined that prompts would be systematically faded if the child reached a performance criterion of 80% for task engagement across six consecutive sessions. It is important to gradually and systematically change these antecedent stimuli over time in a stepwise fashion based on the performance indicators of the student. A rapid or premature reduction of these important instructional prompts could result in disaster and likely in having to reteach the skill.

It is important to know when to reduce prompts and subsequently fade them in an effort to transfer stimulus control, thus promoting learner independence. There are some effective strategies that can assist in this process, including reinforcing correct responses and reinforcing independent performance on the part of the student. Other strategies include errorless learning approaches, such as building embedded cues within the task as much as is possible.

APPLICATIONS OF CLASSROOM-WIDE REINFORCEMENT PROGRAMS

We have examined the principles and guidelines for using reinforcement within instructional programs for individual learners. The following section provides examples of reinforcement programs that are classroomwide. Classroomwide program of reinforcement generally are reinforcement programs that are administered to the class as a whole based on their performance. One of the most commonly found system is the token economy program.

Token Economy Programs

Token economy programs have been widespread in a variety of educational and habilitation settings for a number of years. Originally developed within state institutions for use with adults who are mentally retarded, this method was designed as an incentive system to promote behavior change within these settings (Ayllon & Azrin, 1968). The token economy has also been extensively used within classroom and school settings, largely within educational programs serving children and youth with special needs. Within these settings, token economies seem to be most prevalent in serving learners identified with emotional and behavior disorders as a means of promoting positive behavior change.

The basic design of a token economy is that point values are attached to desired behaviors. The tokens or points earned by students can be redeemed later for various backup reinforcers (e.g., food, tangible, social, and activities). There are numerous examples of backup reinforcers that can be included within such a program. These could include stickers, pencils, fruit snacks, free time, library time, free time to choose an activity, and so on. A token economy can be applied classwide with individuals and in collaborative learning situations. In establishing a token economy, the teacher must take into consideration several key elements, including the following:

1. Defining desired behaviors within the classroom. The behaviors that are operationally defined should be those that are expected within the classroom, such as:

   - Coming to class on time
   - Sitting in assigned seat
   - Being prepared for class with the appropriate materials
   - Raising a hand for teacher assistance

2. Determining the tokens or other currency used within the classroom. These could include chips, hole punches on a card, stickers, point cards, ribbons, and play money, to name a few.

3. Determine which backup reinforcers will be used in conjunction with the tokens. Identify and list those backup reinforcers that are available to you within the classroom or that could be easily developed. Keep in mind that if these backup reinforcers are linked to more naturally occurring consequences, it's even better, as they will be much easier to implement within the classroom setting. Also, aside from ease of administration, affordability must be taken into consideration. Too often, teachers develop token systems out of pocket with limited resources, thus bearing the cost of purchasing backup reinforcers by themselves.

4. Define how the system will be implemented, such as the frequency by which tokens will be given and exchanged, the token or point value of backup reinforcers, and how to maintain records of individual learner performance.

5. Train staff and inform families of the system as a means to ensure consistency and support in terms of implementation.

6. Develop methods for fading the procedure, maintaining behavior change, and transferring to naturally occurring contingencies.

Team-Based Models of Reinforcement

Team-based contingencies (Kazdin, 2008) represent another alternative within classrooms and schools and are consistent with the values of PBIS. These can be used in the classroom to encourage a positive peer culture. Team-based contingencies assign students to teams, which then compete for points relative to assigned academic tasks or in adherence of classroom or school rules and policies. Kazdin (2008) recommended team-based contingencies as highly effective, largely because both teams accrue reinforcers and the winning team earns an additional positive consequence.

The benefits of classroomwide contingencies are many. They generally provide the teacher with comfort and ease in their administration, and they promote positive peer cultures within the classroom and school. Of course, the obvious issue is the potential limitations it places on individual learners who are well behaved, are compliant, and exceed the minimum standards. Such oversight of individual student performances can serve as a disincentive for performance; thus care must be taken in the design of these systems.

Consider This

When using token economies, make sure that the token reinforcers used are valued by the learner(s) and that they are efficiently administered, contingent on performance of the desired behavior.

USING POSITIVE REINFORCEMENT WITHIN THE PBIS MODEL

As mentioned at the beginning of the chapter, positive reinforcement is an element within the PBIS model at all levels. Consider how schoolwide positive behavior support (SWPBIS) uses PBIS across an entire school and with all students across all environments. SWPBIS is built around the notion of transforming the school culture to develop a more positive and affirming environment for students to learn and grow. When using a SWPBIS approach, schools begin by identifying a set of performance expectations with regard to student behavior that is embraced by all within the school. As a part of this process, schools then identify positive reinforcers that can be used to acknowledge the performance of these behaviors. Schools typically have celebration days that bring attention to the student body on how well "they" as a school are doing in terms of their SWPBIS implementation. Awards may be presented to individual students who exemplify these behaviors, or a class may be recognized for its efforts, and perhaps all students in the school will receive some small affirmation that will serve as a reinforcer for their attempts.

Within the classroom, positive reinforcement can be applied in much the same way. A set of performance expectations in terms of student and class behavior is defined, and positive reinforcers are identified for acknowledging the class in their efforts to honor these behavioral expectations. Often such reinforcers take the form of tokens or tickets that will earn the class a groupwide privilege.

Finally, when using PBIS with individual learners, the use of positive reinforcement procedures is perhaps most obviously useful. When teaching new behaviors (replacement behaviors), we must find reinforcing consequences to promote the acquisition of these skills; often, teacher praise will be effective as learners' approximate steps in the performance of these behaviors. The more enriching we can design our learning environments to be, the greater the likelihood that we can fade to more naturally occurring forms of reinforcement to enhance the maintenance and generalization of these replacement skills. It is, however, very important to remember the value of feedback in the form of praise for all learners and the importance of positive reinforcement in helping all learners develop their repertoire of skills.

SUMMARY

This chapter has provided you with an introduction and overview of reinforcement and the application of positive reinforcement procedures within instructional programs. Specifically, the use of positive reinforcement procedures within intervention programs designed to increase appropriate behavior in learners were described. The terms *positive reinforcement* and *negative reinforcement* were also defined, and the point was made that reinforcement strengthens behavior. Negative reinforcement is not to be confused with punishment, as is often the case. Selection of reinforcers was described, along with various methods for determining individual preference. These methods included reinforcer sampling, providing opportunities for choice, asking parents and family members (if not the learner directly), and reviewing past educational records to obtain insights as to previously effective reinforcers.

Classes of positive reinforcement were also described. These included the following: edibles, activity, tangibles, and social reinforcers. Principles of effective reinforcement were discussed, along with guidelines for administering reinforcement. These principles included making reinforcement contingent on behavior, administering reinforcement immediately, and establishing operations, including deprivation and satiation. Deprivation is important for reinforcer effectiveness, in that when an individual has been deprived of a reinforcer for a period of time, the reinforcer will have greater effectiveness. Satiation, on the other hand, is when the reinforcer has lost its value because the individual has received too much of it.

Schedules of reinforcement were also introduced within the chapter. Continuous reinforcement means that each occurrence of a behavior is reinforced, and intermittent reinforcement means that a behavior is reinforced on an intermittent basis with either a ratio or interval schedule of reinforcement. Ratio schedules of reinforcement involve reinforcing the average number of behaviors with either a fixed ratio (a fixed number) or a variable ratio (an average number of responses intermittently reinforced). Interval schedules of reinforcement involve administering reinforcement for a fixed time interval (e.g., 2 minutes) or for a variable interval schedule, which would involve intermittently reinforcing a behavior an average of every 2 minutes.

The chapter also introduced the principles of shaping (reinforcing successive approximations of a terminal behavior) and fading (systematic withdrawal of instructional prompts and reinforcement). Prompt hierarchies and time-delay procedures were introduced with applied examples of how these instructional procedures are used to teach new behaviors and how they coincide with fading. The importance of systematically fading external prompts and reinforcers was described as related to transfer of stimulus control to natural contingencies. Last, the application of token economies within schools and classrooms was described. The efficacy of such programs and considerations for the implementation of token systems within the classroom were identified.

In conclusion, this chapter introduced important concepts related to reinforcement and tied these to their use within instructional situations. These principles will be elaborated on in later chapters as we explore how to teach positive alternative behaviors and reduce problematic behavior.

ACTIVITIES TO EXTEND YOUR LEARNING

1. Identify and list within the various classes of reinforcement (edibles, tangibles, activity, and social) your preferred reinforcers. Note the frequency of occurrence of each of these respective reinforcers in your life and identify which activities (e.g., work, leisure, and or school) they are most frequently associated with.

2. Conduct an observation within a classroom and note the presence of reinforcement. Identify the types of reinforcers used by the teacher and whether they are individualized for each child.

3. Create an assessment tool for use within home, community, and school environments that you live and work in, and identify the level of reinforcement found within these settings. Are these environments dense or lean in terms of reinforcement? How might these settings be enhanced to provide a more reinforcing environment that could enhance your own quality of life?

FURTHER READING AND EXPLORATION

1. Develop a database of teaching-related articles on reinforcement from such journals as *Teaching Exceptional Children*. Develop these strategies into a file that you can later refer to when you have your own classroom.

2. Visit the website of OSEP (www.pbis.org) and note articles and resources related to using positive reinforcement in the development of behavior intervention plans for learners with challenging behavior.

CHAPTER
10

Teaching Positive Replacement Behaviors

CONCEPTS TO UNDERSTAND

After reading this chapter, you should be able to:

- List and describe the factors that contribute to skill deficits.
- Describe and discuss the methods for selecting positive replacement behaviors.
- List and describe the considerations for design of a behavioral support plan (BSP).
- Describe methods for formulating goals and objectives.
- Identify and describe how to design a plan to teach replacement behaviors.

KEY TERMS

Differential reinforcement of alternative behavior (DRA)	Positive replacement behaviors
	Self-management
Functional communication training (FCT)	Skill deficits

A major goal of PBIS is to identify and teach replacement behaviors that will result in enhanced educational and lifestyle outcomes for students. These lifestyle outcomes might include increased satisfaction with school, improved academic skills, increased social opportunities, and success on the job or in the community. Regardless of the outcome, the major focus of PBIS is facilitating greater degrees of personal and lifestyle freedoms for the individual. There are several factors to consider in the selection of replacement behaviors and in the creation of an intervention plan aimed at teaching these new behaviors. In this chapter, we examine these factors and describe how PBIS can facilitate such behavior change. We also identify how these outcomes can be realized through the use of systematic instruction to foster meaningful behavior change on the part of all students. Finally, we explore the topics related to the development of positive alternative behaviors in learners with challenging behavior.

UNDERSTANDING SKILL DEFICITS EXPERIENCED BY STUDENTS

Students who engage in challenging behavior may often experience skill deficits in one or more areas as a result of a disability or a lack of previous learning experience pertaining to a specific skill or skill set. **Skill deficits** often result when students have not been taught the targeted skill or when they have failed to develop mastery of the skill before instruction on that skill was terminated. A simple illustration of this concept is when a student fails to master the requisite skills in a content area such as math, yet the work proceeds at a faster and more complex level over time. Because the student has failed to learn the necessary requisite steps, he or she falls increasingly behind as the skill demands continue to accelerate. This problem often occurs because the student did not fully master a specific skill set before instruction on that skill was terminated and the new material introduced.

Failure to learn a skill can occur because the student did not develop fluency (i.e., high rate of performance with minimal or no errors) or because a lack of time was designated for promoting generalization and maintenance of the skill before terminating instruction. Another plausible explanation is that there was a failure to employ naturally occurring reinforcement from within the learning environment during instruction that would help maintain the rate of behavior and result in durability of the skill for an extended period of time.

Reasons for Skill Acquisition Failures

- The student was never fluent in the skill before skill instruction was terminated.
- The activity was too challenging for the developmental level of the student.
- There was a lack of emphasis placed on promoting maintenance and generalization during instruction.
- The instructor failed to employ naturally occurring reinforcement during instruction.
- The skill was not functional or relevant in the life of the student.
- Inconsistent use of cues and teaching techniques were employed during instruction, resulting in a failure to develop fluency on the part of the learner.

When students experience skill deficits, other forms of behavioral fallout occur. One common side effect for many children and youth is frustration. Chronic frustration resulting from a failure to achieve desired learning outcomes often leads to problematic behavior such as noncompliance, interpersonal problems with teachers and peers, and school refusal behavior. These behaviors develop over time and are often directly related to performance problems in school stemming from specific skill deficits.

Communication skill deficits are also a common cause of challenging behavior among children and youth with disabilities (Durand & Moskowitz, 2015). These deficits are more common with students who experience moderate and severe disabilities and who may also have limited communication abilities, such as in the case of some children and youth with autism and intellectual disabilities (Durand & Moskowitz, 2015; Lanovaz & Sladeczek, 2012). Communication skill deficits often result in behaviors that are neither socially acceptable nor functional in the long run to obtain needs. Yet these behaviors may have been efficient for the individual, given an absence of socially appropriate responses in their behavior repertoire from which to select. These problematic behaviors persist for several reasons, which may include one or more of the following:

- A failure by educational or related professionals to understand and modify the triggers or antecedents associated with the problem behavior
- An inability on the part of the student to select alternative responses due to a limited skill repertoire
- Behaviors continue to be reinforced unknowingly by persons in their environments and therefore persist and are frequently used by the learner

Consider This

Remember as a teacher that when learners fail to perform a desired behavior, it is your responsibility to first examine whether you are using teaching strategies that are appropriate and individualized for the needs of the specific student.

- What are some instructional and behavioral support methods that you as a teacher can use to minimize failure on the part of your students?

In light of these factors, it is important in such cases to identify **positive replacement behaviors** that can serve as alternative responses for many reasons, including the following:

- Positive replacement behaviors promote the best overall interests of the student.
- The presence of these skills affords the student increased lifestyle options.
- Replacement behaviors reduce the likelihood that challenging behaviors will occur.
- The development of functional replacement behaviors can lead to a greater sense of independence and self-determination on the part of the student.

Bambara and Knoster (1998) recommended that skill instruction aimed at replacing challenging forms of behavior be grouped into the following categories: (a) teaching replacement skills and behaviors, (b) teaching general skills, and (c) teaching coping strategies. Replacement skills refer to socially acceptable behaviors that serve the same function as the target behavior of concern, but in a positive form. Therefore, emphasis is given to teaching alternative forms of the behavior that are also socially acceptable. When teaching replacement skills, the focus of an intervention is directed toward changing the form of the behavior to that of a more socially acceptable behavior and maintaining the function, thus allowing the students to obtain their needs but in a socially acceptable manner. Effort is placed on changing the form (what the behavior looks like, in other words) rather than the function (purpose of the behavior).

An example of this is anger associated with frustration. Everyone experiences anger related to frustration when they fail to perform a particular task in a desirable manner. If you were to consider anger placed on a continuum from basic to refined forms of responding, then you can see how replacement behaviors can serve the same function but look different.

Examine Figure 10–1 and reflect on how many ways anger associated with frustration can be expressed. At the basic end of the continuum, a person could choose some form of aggression; at the refined end of the continuum, anger can be expressed in a calm and rational manner by communicating feelings through self-talk ("That really makes me angry") or through talking to someone else ("You know, I got so frustrated by that problem, and it made me so incredibly angry that I just could not come up with the answer"). The function of the behavior is the same across the range of options—only the form varies.

One aspect to consider when examining Figure 10–1 is the range of behavior options available; however, the presence of skill deficits in the areas of social coping skills may not exist in a student's behavior repertoire. As evident from this example, teaching replacement behaviors to broaden the behavior options for the individual learner is most important.

FIGURE 10–1

Behavior Continuum for Expressing Anger

1. Aggression toward self, others, or property destruction and use of profanity, screaming, crying, and withdrawal
2. Attempts at communicating one's feelings and resolution
3. Calm and rational communication concerning one's anger with self or others

---

The emphasis in intervention is devoted to developing new skills, thus providing the student with expanded behavioral options to select from and ideally resulting in the reduction of problem behavior. Consider the previous example highlighted in Figure 10–1. Later in the chapter, we will discuss the use of self-management skills as one form of intervention for behavioral self-regulation.

When determining your course of action as a teacher, it is important to examine evidence-based practices that have been documented in the literature to be effective in the development of acceptable replacement behaviors. The choice of *how* to intervene would obviously be determined by evaluating the specific needs of the student. To aid in understanding some of the intervention options that are available and that are recognized as best and effective practice, consider the following methods identified from the literature as options to select from in this area.

Carr and colleagues (1999) identified two major categories of PBIS interventions from the literature: (1) stimulus-based interventions, such as antecedent-management and environmental modifications, and (2) reinforcement-based interventions that were directed toward replacing behavior skill deficits.

Antecedent-based strategies (i.e., stimulus-based interventions) were described at length in Chapter 4. For the purposes of this chapter, reinforcement-based interventions designed to teach replacement behaviors will be highlighted.

METHODS FOR SELECTING REPLACEMENT BEHAVIORS

Carr and colleagues (1999) described three prominent methods to select from when teaching replacement behaviors to learners with challenging behaviors:

- Functional communication training (FCT) approaches
- Self-management
- Differential reinforcement of alternative behavior (DRA)

Functional communication training (FCT) was first described by Carr and Durand (1985) and involves teaching a functionally equivalent communication behavior to a student with challenging behavior. The efficacy of this procedure has been well established across classroom settings (Mancil & Boman, 2010) and also across learners with a variety of challenging behaviors in community settings (Tiger, Hanley, & Bruzek, 2008). After 30-years of research on this method, the results from these studies reinforces the efficacy of FCT as a viable method for teaching replacement behaviors (Durand & Moskowitz, 2015). As indicated by Durand (1990), FCT consists of two primary components: (1) teaching learners an alternative communicative response that serves the same function as the problem behavior and (2) making the problem behavior nonfunctional for the individual. The first component of FCT is directed toward the development of new skills, and the second component is directed toward teaching the student that the problem behavior no longer controls the environment and is no longer efficient in obtaining their needs. An example of how to use FCT in teaching a replacement skill would include teaching a child to communicate the need for a break not by having a tantrum but by using a sign or by raising their hand and asking the teacher for a short break, depending on the communicative abilities of the learner. The use of FCT to communicate these needs eventually reduces problem behavior (aggression) as a means of obtaining teacher attention. The child's needs are now met in an efficient and socially acceptable manner using functional communication. Vignette 10.1 provides another example of how FCT can be used to teach replacement behaviors.

Vignette 10.1

Eliminating Challenging Forms of Behavior

Samantha, an 8-year-old child who has autism, frequently engages in extended periods of screaming as a way of escaping the demands associated with instruction. Essentially, over the course of time, this has become her way of regulating the environment around her, given that she has limited communication abilities. She becomes increasingly agitated as her teacher attempts to provide her with instructions for completing a task. She screams very loudly and continues to persist. Her teacher continues to offer instructions as a means of redirecting Samantha and not reinforcing her screaming by allowing her to use it as a means to escape instruction. When these efforts continued to be unfruitful, her teacher initiated FCT to teach Samantha how to communicate when she needs assistance and or when she is in need of a break from instruction. The program consists of teaching Samantha to approximate simple verbalizations paired with picture symbols, such as "I need help," or "I need a break, please." The object of FCT in this example is to teach Samantha that when she attempts to use positive replacement behaviors to meet her needs, persons in her immediate environments will respond accordingly and she will obtain her needs and be reinforced for engaging in the replacement behavior.

Another functional communication strategy that has been widely employed among students with autism spectrum disorders has been the Picture Exchange Communication System (PECS). PECS was developed by Bondy and Frost (1994) and was initially used with young children diagnosed with autism who had limited verbal communication skills. It involves the use of pictures as a means to communicate. Tien (2008), in a synthesis of research on PECS, pointed out that PECS differs from any other form of communication system in that it does not require the learner to have any prerequisite skills, it facilitates the opportunity for social reinforcement (something that often has little consequence to learners with autism), and it promotes initiation on the part of the learner. A more recent meta-analysis conducted on the use of PECS with learners with ASD reported PECS to be a very promising intervention method, stating that preschool-age children with autism generally showed the greatest training effects and that the more phases a child progressed through, the greater the outcomes (Ganz, Davis, Lund, Goodwyn, & Simpson, 2012).

There are six phases in PECS training (Frost & Bondy, 2002). These phases have been synthesized in a review by Tien (2008): (1) *How to Communicate*, which involves

continued

the child selecting the appropriate picture that represents a desired object and presenting it to the partner with whom they are communicating; (2) *Distance and Persistence*, in which the child selects the desired picture from his or her communication book and presents it to a teacher or parent; (3) *Picture Discrimination*, in which the child learns to discriminate from an array of items and selects a preferred item when prompted with a question such as "What do you want?" at which point he or she selects the corresponding picture from the communication book and presents it to a teacher or parent; (4) *Sentence Structure*, in which the desired outcome is for the child to request items using pictures from the communication book and placing them in sequential order incorporating the statement "I want" followed by a picture of the desired object or activity and then placing them on a sentence strip; (5) *Responding*, during which the child is taught how to appropriately respond using his or her pictures to the question, "What do you want?" so that receptive language and responding skills are taught; and (6) *Commenting*, which is designed to foster more spontaneous responding on the part of the child to various queries such as "What do you see?" "What do you want?" "What do you have?" thereby promoting expressive communication or commenting on the part of the child through the use of his or her pictures accordingly.

The successes of PECS as documented in the literature have been that acquisition rates were faster than sign language, an increase in overall communication and language has been reported, and children appear to prefer PECS as a preferred mode of communication over sign language (Tien, 2008). Another important benefit of teaching young children with autism the PECS method is that it serves to prevent and reduce challenging behavior (Charlop-Christy, Carpenter, Le, LeBlanc, & Kellet, 2002; Machalicek, Ganz et al., 2012; Machalicek, O'Reilly, Beretvas, Sigafoos, & Lancioni, 2007). Charlop-Christy and colleagues (2002) investigated the use of PECS with three boys of varying ages—12 years old; 3 years, 8 months; and 5 years, 9 months—all having been given the diagnosis of autism and displaying limited communication skills, with two of the three children displaying various forms of challenging behavior, including aggression, tantrums, and throwing and grabbing objects. Results from this study indicated that after 23 sessions, all three children met a performance criterion of 80% for each PECS phase of training with an accompanying increase in spontaneous speech and a systematic decrease in challenging behavior across all participants from baseline to post-training phases (Charlop-Christy et al., 2002).

Reflective Moment

What are some examples of how you could use functional communication training methods for learners who engage in challenging forms of behavior? Do you think that such training and skill development would assist in the prevention of challenging behavior?

A second type of reinforcement-based intervention strategy for teaching replacement behaviors advocated by Carr and colleagues (1999) is **self-management**, a cognitive–behavior intervention method originally designed for teaching learners to self-direct their behavior (Kanfer, 1975; Meichenbaum, 1974). Self-management has been around for a very long time and is composed of three major types of interventions: self-monitoring, self-instruction, and self-reinforcement. Self-management became very popular in the 1970s–1980s and has been widely documented in the literature in terms of its efficacy and widespread applications with children and youth with emotional and behavior disorders (DiGangi & Maag, 1992; Dunlap et al., 1995; Miller, Miller, Wheeler, & Selinger, 1989), learning disabilities (Webber, Scheuermann, McCall, & Coleman, 1993), and also with persons with intellectual disabilities (Agran, 1997; Wheeler, Bates, Marshall, & Miller, 1988). Self-management promotes the central involvement of the individual in the selection of goals, monitoring of behavior, and implementation of the intervention procedures (Sulzer-Azaroff & Mayer, 1991). More recently, it has also been used as part of a classroom intervention package with success (Chafouleas, Sanetti, Jaffrey, & Fallon, 2012).

One of the most popular forms of self-management intervention that has been used extensively within school settings is self-monitoring. Self-monitoring is directed toward teaching students to monitor their behavior, noting the occurrence or nonoccurrence of the behavior through self-recording. This process is often done using some form of cue, as provided by an iPad set at varying intervals and designed to deliver an auditory prompt, such as a beeping sound or bell. Upon hearing the auditory cue, the student self-records the occurrence or nonoccurrence of a specific target behavior with a plus (+) or minus (−) on a data sheet. Another example of self-monitoring could include monitoring the completion of class assignments as reflected on a to-do list (Figure 10–2) and recording the occurrence or nonoccurrence of the behavior on a checklist. In this example, the checklist becomes the cue, and completion of a task marks the point at which the learner would then self-record, thus placing a check next to the completed task listed on the checklist.

Dunlap and colleagues (1991) outlined the essential steps in developing and using a self-monitoring program in the classroom:

1. Operationally define the target behavior. This step requires the teacher to operationally define the target behavior in specific terms that the child can understand, such as "having class materials out and ready," "remaining seated while in class," or "raising hand for teacher assistance."

2. Identify functional reinforcers. The teacher identifies reinforcers that are functionally relevant to the child and setting. These can be activities or other tangibles that are appropriate within the setting. Identifying preferred reinforcers can be accomplished through observation of the child, by asking the parents, and even by allowing the child choice-making opportunities. Reinforcers could include free time, access to the library or computer, fruit snacks, or assisting the teacher.

3. Design the self-monitoring method or device to be used. As the authors recommend, these devices should be nonintrusive and portable. There are plenty of downloadable apps for an iPad that will emit a sound such as a chime to serve as a prompt. Attention should be given to what is functional (whether it gets the job done) and what is developmentally appropriate, given the child's age and abilities (e.g., using picture symbols and single functional vocabulary words for a child with moderate intellectual disabilities who has difficulty reading).

4. Teach the child how the procedure works. The teacher should provide the learner with direct instruction in how to use the self-monitoring device. The teacher should

---

FIGURE 10–2

To-Do List of Assignments

Name: Trevor Date: 10/4/12

1. Math Problems—Nos. 10–25, pages 45–47   ☑
2. Language Arts—2-page essay on your favorite food   ☑
3. Social Studies—Color and label the map of Europe   ☑
4. Science—Complete short-answer questions at the end of Chapter 3   ☐
5. Chorus—Bring $10.00 for the chorus T-shirt tomorrow (Friday, 10/5/17)   ☐

model how to use the device for the child and then provide opportunities to rehearse or practice the skill, with the teacher providing instructional feedback.

5. Fade the use of the self-monitoring device. It is important to fade the self-monitoring device as a method for increasing independence. The authors recommend that this be accomplished in two ways. First, thin the schedule of reinforcement, thus gradually increasing the number of responses required before the child obtains the preferred reinforcer. The second method is to reduce or fade the use of cues provided by the self-monitoring device. Examples of this method are fading the number of embedded instructions on the checklist or reducing access to the self-monitoring device.

Holifield, Goodman, Hazelkorn, and Heflin (2010) investigated the use of a self-monitoring procedure on task engagement and academic accuracy in two elementary students with autism within a self-contained classroom. Results from this study demonstrated that self-monitoring was effective in promoting task engagement, though the results were variable concerning the accuracy of responding. Perhaps one of the most impressive aspects of self-monitoring is that this form of cognitive-behavioral intervention has been around for quite awhile and continues to demonstrate its utility by remaining an effective approach.

Self-instruction (Meichenbaum & Goodwin, 1971) represents another form of self-management and involves teaching a learner a set of instructional steps related to social, academic, vocational, or community living tasks. An early reference to self-instruction and behavior regulation was offered by Luria (1961) in *The Role of Speech in the Regulation of Normal and Abnormal Behaviour*, whereby he explained how in typical child development, a child is first exposed to verbal cues by adults as a means of regulating their behavior. As children age, they then begin to use self-generated overt verbalizations as a way to self-regulate their behavior. As they continue to grow and develop, these processes become internalized and result in covert verbalizations as a means for self-directing their behavior. Imagine how could you apply this process in your own life related to such behaviors as studying. As a child develops, parents provide support to encourage studying behavior, such as organizing assignments, following a schedule, and allotting time for this important activity through verbal cues paired with some modeling. As children begin to learn these processes, they practice them by using overt self-verbalizations to serve as cues and reinforcement until these patterns become learned and more internalized, eventually eliminating the need for external verbal directives from their parents.

With self-instruction, students are taught a set of statements related to the task that they recite to themselves when in certain situations (Zirpoli, 2015). This process is initiated first through models provided by the teacher; the learner then practices the self-instruction sequence through overt verbalization. As acquisition occurs, the learner gradually replaces the overt verbalization with "quiet speech," followed by "whispers," until eventually these become covert speech.

The final form of self-management intervention is self-reinforcement. Self-reinforcement emerges as a method for teaching students to self-administer their preferred reinforcement on performance of a desired behavior. Many examples of how this process works can be found in our daily lives, such as treating ourselves to a cold drink after mowing the yard, playing a game after finishing work, or choosing a favorite television show after completing homework. Within educational settings, self-reinforcement could involve any number of things, including self-administering a token reinforcer for completion of a task or using a system of self-checks for each step of the task that has been completed. This procedure can be most effective within educational settings with children and youth when trying to develop a student's ability to sustain and tolerate performance of a task that he or she may not be fond of.

Goal-setting strategies, skills instruction, and the opportunity for a student to select a preferred reinforcer are powerful tools for teaching alternative behaviors and warrant the use of self-reinforcement in certain instances. Some key points to consider when using self-reinforcement in the classroom are:

- Involve the student in goal-setting activities related to performance of the target behavior and selection of preferred reinforcers.
- Ensure that the student is fluent in performing the procedure (i.e., self-monitoring and self-reinforcement).
- Evaluate progress and fade the intervention over time as the student meets the pre-established goals.

In summary, self-management interventions are designed to promote the acquisition of replacement behaviors through engaging the student in the behavior-change process and by teaching a learning process that can promote self-sufficiency and consistency. Through the successful use of self-management procedures, individual students can be taught a method that will result in increased task engagement and personal independence and less reliance on teacher-delivered instructional cues and reinforcers.

Consider This

Self-management interventions can be effective in promoting academic task engagement and greater degrees of independence in students, including the development of self-determination skills. List and describe some applications of these procedures with various academic tasks.

The final consequence-based intervention identified by Carr and colleagues (1999) was **differential reinforcement of alternative behavior (DRA)**. DRA is a procedure designed to increase the frequency of a desirable behavior and to reduce challenging behavior through the delivery of reinforcement for positive alternative behavior (Miltenberger, 2015). The problem behavior is thereby placed on extinction and is no longer reinforced when using a DRA procedure, resulting in a decrease of the future probability of the problem behavior. Differential reinforcement is discussed in greater detail in Chapter 11.

Guidelines for Selecting Positive Replacement Behaviors

When selecting positive replacement behaviors, it is important to take into consideration the function of the challenging behavior that you are seeking to replace. As discussed in an earlier chapter, challenging behavior occurs for a reason and is linked to skill deficits. Once the function of these behaviors has been determined, a replacement behavior can be better identified for instruction. Replacement behaviors serve as functional equivalent responses, in that the replacement behavior should serve the same function (be functionally equivalent) as that of the target behavior. Our intervention goal in positive behavior supports centers around teaching the student an alternative form of the behavior (what it looks like and the outcomes it results in), rather than changing the function for the learner.

Consider when a child pulls his or her hair as a means of obtaining attention from the teacher. Teaching that same child to raise a hand for teacher assistance or to communicate a need for teacher assistance in some other alternative form of communication would better meet the child's needs and in turn be more socially acceptable. One key point about teaching functionally equivalent responses is that the replacement behavior must be efficient in meeting the learner's needs. That is, it needs to be as effective and efficient to use for the child as was the challenging form of the behavior. Failure to meet the learner's needs in an efficient manner results in the learner being less likely to rely on the replacement behavior and more apt to revert to the challenging behavior. This situation occurs when the challenging behavior has been more efficient over time for the child in obtaining his or her needs.

A central component to this phase of the intervention process is teaching the new skill or behavior to the student. This may be a timely process, and direct instruction should be used to encourage acquisition of the new skill. Scott and Nelson (1999) provided three recommendations for facilitating the development of positive replacement behaviors:

1. Select a functionally equivalent replacement behavior (a behavior that serves the same function).
2. Use direct instruction in teaching the behavior to the student.
3. Facilitate access to the same functional outcome for the student, thus making the replacement behavior efficient for meeting the learner's needs.

In summary, it is important to remember that when positive replacement behaviors should do the following:

- Ideally, serve the same function as the target behavior.
- Facilitate the desired outcome for the learner within a positive context.
- Be efficient in meeting the needs of the student, as this is essential for promoting acquisition of the replacement skills.
- Be systematically taught to the learner using direct instruction methods.

Some examples of positive replacement behaviors are shown in Figure 10–3.

FIGURE 10–3

Examples of Positive Replacement Behaviors

Target Behavior: Getting out of seat and avoiding work

Function: Escape

Replacement Behavior: Raising hand for teacher assistance and allowing a short break on completion of the task

Target Behavior: Verbally refuses to complete the task, thus resulting in being sent out of class

Function: Escape from completing the task

Replacement Behavior: Direct instruction on the requisite skills per content area and teaching self-management skills aimed at increasing task engagement; access to free time on completion of assigned work

Target Behavior: Taking toys or materials away from peers

Function: Social attention from peers

Replacement Behavior: Teaching appropriate requesting behavior and contingent access to preferred toys when playing with peers

Target Behavior: Stereotypical rocking while at seat and task disengagement

Function: Sensory feedback

Replacement Behavior: Contingent access to music on completion of short tasks, gradually increasing task engagement time

Consider This

When selecting replacement behaviors, remember that they should serve the same function as the problem behavior. Yet they should be in a socially acceptable form, and consideration should be given to the efficiency of replacement behaviors in addressing the needs of the individual.

DESIGNING AN INTERVENTION PLAN

The next step in the process is designing an instructional plan that will systematically address all relevant factors related to promoting the successful acquisition of positive replacement behaviors on the part of the student. Within the intervention plan are several components that must be taken into consideration.

Albin, Lucyshyn, Horner, and Flannery (1996) introduced the concept of "contextual fit" when developing behavior support plans. Their model consists of three major classes of variables that should be considered by professionals while in the formative stages of developing a behavior support plan: (1) characteristics of the individual for whom the plan is being designed, (2) variables related to the people responsible for implementing the plan, and (3) features of the environments in which the plan will be implemented. These same considerations also apply when considering the development of an intervention plan to teach positive replacement behaviors. Specific items to consider when constructing such a plan aimed at teaching replacement behaviors are:

1. *What are the desired learning outcomes that you hope to achieve?*

   Identify the goals that you hope to achieve with the intervention. First identifying the outcome measures that you seek to attain as a result of the intervention can provide a social validity check of whether the goals are relevant and significant to the student. It also provides clarity as you formulate the components of an intervention plan.

2. *What specific skills does the student currently have that can be expanded in teaching the new behavior?*

   Identify the student's strengths and current skills and abilities that could assist in acquiring the new behavior. Also, the individual's learning style and primary input mode (how he or she processes information during instruction) are relevant to the design and ultimate success of the program.

3. *Are the replacement behaviors socially valid and functional for the student's needs? Do they serve the same function?*

   Be sure to consider whether your selected behaviors are socially valid, given the student's needs, and whether they serve to provide the student with an expanded repertoire of behavior options.

4. *How do parents and family members feel about the intervention? What type of input have they had in the planning process? Will there be a home and school component for teaching replacement behaviors across both environments?*

   Seek family partnerships in the development of the intervention so that family and school environments are in harmony in terms of intervention goals and in carrying out the procedures. Also, be conscious of the degree of family involvement in carrying out procedures based on where individual families are developmentally.

The interests and ability levels of family members in carrying out procedures should be considered.

5. *Who are the professionals who will be implementing the intervention, and what level of expertise do they have?*

Identify who will be delivering the intervention (i.e., teachers or teaching assistants or other educational and related services professionals). Have they had experience in the area of PBIS? Will they need training and support in the implementation and delivery of the intervention? Is there support among professionals for implementing the procedure?

6. *Is additional training needed to equip the staff with skills to implement the instructional program?*

Determine the extent of training required and how training will be provided. Will a skilled professional need to model how to implement the intervention with the learner? Design feedback loops so that professionals carrying out the intervention will have opportunities to share feedback and address any concerns.

7. *What are the specific contexts in which instruction on replacement behaviors will occur?*

Will the intervention be carried out exclusively at school or across multiple environments such as school, home, and the community? Who will be responsible within each of these respective settings for overseeing that the intervention plan is carried out as planned? (This is called "treatment fidelity.")

8. *Identify the environmental strengths and barriers that will facilitate and/or impede instruction.*

Are there any environmental variables that serve to support the delivery of the intervention, and consequently, what are the environmental limitations that could hinder the intervention from being successfully carried out? Is the student-to-teacher ratio manageable, or will teaching assistants be required to assist in the delivery of instruction? Is the classroom organized environmentally to facilitate ease in the delivery of the intervention?

9. *What are the specific formal and informal supports available to the learner within home, school, classroom, and community environments that will facilitate successful acquisition and generalization of the replacement behaviors?*

Identify existing supports (both formal and informal) that are currently available to the learner in home, school, classroom, and community environments that will assist the learner in the acquisition and generalization replacement behaviors. Also, identify the significant others in the life of the individual who will play an instrumental role in the development of replacement skills.

10. *Identify the student's typical daily classroom routine and plan how instruction can be best included within natural contexts.*

Identify whether the learner has a current schedule within the classroom. If so, what form does the schedule take (object, picture, written)? Is the schedule individualized to the needs of the learner, or is the schedule for general classroom use? Identify the time periods that coincide with activities that are conducive for teaching the replacement behavior.

11. *Will the intervention plan receive support from all team members and the administration?*

Does the intervention plan have the unanimous support of all parties who are directly or indirectly involved? These parties include teacher, family, related school personnel, and administrators. If not, what level of communication needs to occur to facilitate this level of commitment?

FORMULATING GOALS AND OBJECTIVES

After selecting a replacement behavior or new skill to be taught, the teacher must develop a set of goals and objectives before proceeding with instruction. Goal statements are broad encompassing statements that identify the skill area or behavior and whether the goal is to increase, decrease, or maintain the identified skill or behavior. Aside from serving as statements of directionality, they also define the level of performance to be attained. Frequently, goals are confused with instructional objectives: objectives are substeps or subgoals that contribute to the broader goal. One important component of developing goals is to use goal-setting strategies. Goal setting is an important step when developing an instructional program because goals define the instructional outcome we are trying to obtain.

Martin and Pear (2015) identified some basic elements of goal-setting strategies to consider in promoting the attainment of goals. Among their suggestions were: (a) set realistic and attainable goals; (b) establish clear consequences for meeting or not meeting the goal; (c) develop goals that are of short-, intermediate-, and long-term duration; (d) establish performance deadlines for meeting the desired goal; (e) provide team-based support to facilitate attainment of goals on the part of the student; (f) evaluate progress toward goals through a system of monitoring; and (g) provide encouragement and positive reinforcement to the student throughout the process.

If at all possible, it is advisable to encourage student participation in establishing goals, which enables the student to be engaged in the behavior change process; thus the student is more likely to attain the goal. Some guidelines to consider when formulating instructional goals are:

- Consider why the behavior should be taught. Provide a clear and concise rationale as to the importance of the goal in terms of the overall development of the student.
- Is the skill a logical replacement behavior? Will the skill serve as an efficient means by which the student can meet his or her needs?
- Will the replacement behavior provide the student with needed skills that are consistent with demands found in his or her current and future environments?
- Must prerequisite skills first be taught to ensure overall success?
- Can the goal be accomplished, given the competencies of the teaching staff, or will additional training be required of the teachers?
- Is the goal socially valid, given the needs of the student, and will such a goal positively affect the quality of life of the child?

These considerations are meant to serve as guideposts to enable teachers to carefully plan and consider the instructional goals they develop for students. These considerations stress the importance of goals related to the learning and behavior needs of the individual child, the capacity of educational environments to nurture and foster acquisition of these goals, and the impact of the instructional goals that teachers develop in the lives of children and their families.

Consider This

Goals are broad and encompassing statements of desired learning outcomes. How do objectives relate to goal statements?

Goals are dependent on the development of objectives or substeps that approximate components of a goal. Figure 10–4 provides an illustration of how objectives formulate a

FIGURE 10–4

Elements of Effective Instruction

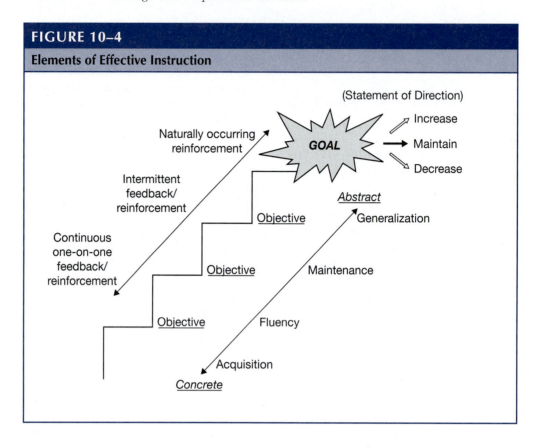

stepwise development of these subskills, which are directly linked to the broader goal. Also relevant to understanding the relationship of goals to instructional objectives are the four stages of learning: (1) skill acquisition, (2) fluency, (3) maintenance, and (4) generalization. Each of these stages serve as a building block for subsequent stages in the learning process.

Acquisition is the introductory phase associated with the initial learning process. It is concerned with the development of new skills, and accuracy of performance generally improves during this phase because students are presented with multiple opportunities for performing the desired skill or behavior. The goal of acquisition is to embed the basic steps of performing a new skill in the repertoire of the student and to subsequently move to a more refined performance of the skill over time. Reinforcement is generally carried out on a one-to-one ratio during this phase and is directed at reinforcing successive approximations of correct performance of the target skill.

The second stage of learning, fluency, is directed toward increasing the learner's accuracy of skill performance as well as speed or rate of performance. It is at this stage of the learning process that reinforcement becomes intermittent, with the intention that performance associated with the task and performance outcomes will replace externally administered reinforcement. However, verbal praise and corrective feedback are important to ensure performance accuracy and the rate associated with performing the target skill.

The maintenance stage that follows is devoted to facilitating use of the newly learned skill over time in relevant learning contexts. This phase of the process is aimed at promoting durable and lasting behavior change or learning that will stand the test of time and ultimately be retained in the student's repertoire.

The final stage of learning is generalization. This stage is concerned with promoting the transfer of skills to untrained settings and situations, such as various classrooms or learning environments with different teachers and materials. Generalization is a critical and often-overlooked portion of the teaching and learning process. If students are taught a particular skill or behavior that cannot transfer beyond the specific setting or conditions that were used to teach that skill, it serves no lasting purpose in the life of the students. This problem can often occur when teachers teach the skill from a tight and narrow focus. It is important to introduce students to sufficient exemplars, such as the range of stimulus-and-response variations, when learning a new skill. As an example, consider the stimulus-and-response variations that exist in terms of teaching a child to put on shoes. There are shoes that lace up and tie, shoes with zippers, and shoes that use Velcro straps. The subtleties of these stimulus-and-response variations should be taught to the child to promote generalization in learning how to independently put on shoes.

Mager (1997) asserted that objectives are useful for providing both measurable instructional results and also a means by which to realize instructional efficiency. When developing objectives, we typically begin with the most concrete skills and move to the more complex or abstract as acquisition and fluency in the skills occur. In Figure 10–4, notice that the first objective in the sequence is also the most concrete step in the sequence of skills that constitute the goal. As students proceed through all the objectives, they reach a point in the learning process at which they have the ability to generalize across variations of the task. A simple example is teaching a child to use scissors to cut paper.

Goal: To increase fine motor skills

> (Several activities could be used with a young child; however, for this example, we will use cutting paper with scissors.)
>
>> We will list objectives in descending order to be consistent with the information in Figure 10–4.

Objective: Cutting out shapes (abstract) (square, circle, triangle)

Objective: Cutting curved lines

Objective: Cutting angled lines

Objective: Cutting straight lines

Objective: Holding the paper and using the scissors to cut (concrete)

If you examine the list of objectives relative to the goal statement, it is evident that the targeted skill (using scissors to cut lines) moves from the very basic, or concrete (holding scissors and paper, cutting straight lines), to the abstract (cutting curved lines and shapes) as the objectives ascend. We also can see that as children learn and acquire the basic elements of the task and begin to generalize and refine their skills, they are then able to move to more complex levels of performance, thus mastering the task and its variations.

When developing instructional objectives, note that objectives should contain three important criteria: specify the *conditions* that surround the performance, state the *performance* or behavior in measurable and observable terms, and indicate the performance *criteria*. When writing behavior objectives, it is important that the objective be clearly stated, be succinct, and reflect observable and measurable behaviors. Some examples of behavior objectives follow.

Objective

Jennifer, when confused by math problems that she does not understand, will stop, raise her hand, wait, and ask for teacher assistance 100% of the time.

Objective

Sam, when given a toothbrush, toothpaste, and the instructional cue to brush his teeth, will initiate and complete each step of the task analysis 90% of the time for five consecutive trials.

Objective

Louis, when needing teacher attention during vocational/technical education class, will say, "Please excuse me, I need your help," rather than interrupting, for 10 consecutive trials.

Objective

Jacob, when asked by his teacher or peer during cooperative play, "Please share your toy with me," will share his toy without prompts from his teacher for five consecutive sessions.

Objective

When given a written assignment by the teacher, Susan will outline the lesson using the previously learned skill strategy designed for outlining 100% of the time, with performance feedback and praise being provided by the teacher.

Examine each of these objectives and review them to determine whether the three components (conditions, performance, and criteria) are reflected. Identify these elements within each of the example objectives. Critique these examples and offer your input on how they might be modified or improved.

Key Points to Consider When Developing Objectives

When developing behavioral objectives, be sure to include the following:

- *Conditions:* What are the conditions (equipment, materials, aids) that the student will be allowed to use during the performance of the behavior?
- *Performance:* What is the measurable and observable behavior that the learner will be asked to perform?
- *Criterion:* The criterion measure should communicate to the student how well he or she has performed the skill against a performance standard. An example is scoring 92 points on an exam with a maximum score of 100 points. When constructing the performance criterion related to an objective, the teacher should consider the practical importance (Baer, Wolf, & Risley, 1968) to determine whether behavior change has occurred.

When developing your objectives, pay particular attention to the following issues:

- Consider whether the objective clearly communicates to the student what, when, how, and where the behavior is to be performed and specifies the performance expectation for the student.
- Ensure that the objective is written in terms that are measurable and observable and that each objective contains the three elements (conditions, performance, and criteria).
- Consider the social relevance of the objective to the learner's needs (known as social validity).
- Assess how the objectives relate to one another and to the attainment of the overall goal.

Careful consideration of the relationship of goals and objectives in the design of the instructional plan can ensure a greater probability of success when teaching replacement behaviors. The following section addresses how to design an instructional plan for teaching replacement behaviors.

DEVELOPING A PLAN FOR TEACHING REPLACEMENT BEHAVIORS

A systemic instructional plan for teaching replacement behaviors should be comprehensive, with careful consideration given to all aspects of ensuring acquisition and ultimately to generalization of the new behavior. There are numerous varieties of instructional program formats from which to choose, and often school districts have their own for teachers to use. Some basic elements should be inclusive of any instructional plan, regardless of format. Overall, the instructional plan should give consideration to the following basic elements:

Elements of an Instructional Program

A. *Rationale:* The instructional program should provide a brief rationale of why the skill should be taught, its overall importance to the well-being of the student, and implications of the skill in terms of longitudinal learning outcomes. Parental input should be sought concerning the development of any instructional plan. When selecting replacement behaviors, consideration should be given to individual, family, and cultural values that should be honored in the planning process. The selection of any replacement behavior should also consider the long-term implications of the behavior in terms of future planning for the individual.

B. *Identify the learner:* The program should be designed and individualized to the needs of a specific child or adolescent. List and describe any of the individual's learning strengths and relevant educational or behavior challenges that should be considered. Also, individual student likes and dislikes should be factored into the development of the plan. Record review should be used to ascertain this information, as well as parental input. Asking for student input into the process is a means of promoting self-determination.

C. *Materials:* List and describe any instructional materials that will be needed as part of the instructional program.

D. *Describe instructional antecedent arrangement:* Provide a description of instructional antecedents, such as how materials will be presented to the learner, seating arrangements, and other variables relevant to the instructional setting and delivery.

E. *Instructional procedures:* List and describe how the skill will be taught to the student. Include instructional goals and objectives, a task analysis of the targeted skill, teaching strategies that will be employed, prompt hierarchy, and error correction procedures.

F. *Evaluation procedures:* Describe how baseline assessment of student performance on the behavior will be conducted and evaluated. Include any data collection forms that will be used, define how learner progress will be assessed and measured throughout the instructional phase, and determine whether performance data will be graphed.

G. *Generalization:* Indicate how generalization will be addressed within the instructional phase and assessed following instruction, which could include any number of generalization strategies, such as introducing natural contingencies (cues and consequences) found within the natural environment. This strategy is usually an effective approach for promoting generalization, in that it seeks to use contextual variables specific to the environments where we hope the behavior will occur. These variables could consist of the typical daily schedule found within the classroom and building in cues and consequences designed to prompt and maintain the replacement behavior.

In summary, to use a program of systematic instruction within the classroom or other learning environment as a means for teaching replacement behavior, Browder (2001) recommended the following four steps:

1. Define the skills to be taught, and develop a data sheet to assess the skill and determine an instructional objective related to mastery.
2. Define the specific methods used to teach the skill, such as systems for instructional prompts and instructional feedback, and develop a systematic instructional plan.
3. Implement the instructional plan by determining when, where, how, and why the skill will be taught until performance criterion is reached.
4. Evaluate and review student performance on a daily, weekly, or biweekly basis; chart progress; and modify the program based on the performance data.

In conclusion, it is important to remember the considerations that should be taken into account when developing a plan for teaching replacement behaviors. The goal of an intervention plan should be to reduce the rate of challenging behavior and increase the replacement behavior. The steps in this process include understanding the function of the target behavior, selecting an appropriate replacement behavior, addressing the efficiency of the replacement behavior in terms of effort required from the student, considering the social validity or acceptability of the replacement behavior, and ensuring the long-term implications of the intervention.

SUMMARY

This chapter provided a conceptual and applied overview in developing an instructional plan designed to teach replacement behaviors. It was organized around three major themes. The first theme addressed the issue of understanding skill deficits. As you learned, often children and youth within classroom environments who experience challenging behaviors exhibit skill deficits in major areas, such as academic and social skills. The presence of challenging behaviors in these children can often be attributed to the absence of socially appropriate alternative skills coupled with academic and other learning and lifestyle challenges that they may be confronting. The combination of these life events and the frustration encountered from academic failure can result in challenging behavior.

In an effort to address these skill deficits, it is important to understand the role that replacement behaviors have in reducing problem behavior. As described, the second theme addressed the importance of selecting and teaching replacement behaviors. Replacement behaviors are socially acceptable and designed to serve the same function as the challenging behavior (i.e., escape, attention, tangibles, or sensory). By selecting behaviors that serve the same function, it is hoped that these skills can be developed to meet the needs of the learner efficiently in academic and social contexts. Important to this concept is the development of an intervention plan, the third major theme in this chapter.

When developing an intervention plan, care must be given to design and engineer learning environments that promote the success of our intervention efforts with youngsters. Central to this is the use of schoolwide PBIS plans that are designed to improve school climate and buy-in on the part of all stakeholders, thus creating an optimal backdrop for the prevention of challenging behavior and the success of individual interventions.

Of course, any intervention plan must be accompanied by goals and objectives, and the chapter discussed the relationship between these two important instructional components. Last, the chapter examined how to assemble an instructional plan for teaching replacement behaviors, with attention given to the rationale of selecting behaviors to teach and the various elements of instruction and evaluation needed in the design of a systemic instruction plan.

ACTIVITIES TO EXTEND YOUR LEARNING

1. Select and review samples of instructional plans designed for teaching replacement behaviors from web-based and text sources. Examine their characteristics, and compare and contrast each of these sources for continuity in the components recommended for instructional plans.
2. Develop a resource file for later use on the design of instructional plans.
3. Evaluate the format and contents of instructional plans for teaching replacement behaviors within the context of practicum placements to ensure your knowledge and understanding of the process.
4. Use a case study approach to develop an instructional plan for teaching replacement behaviors.
5. Within your practicum settings, identify replacement behaviors for some of your students who may be experiencing challenging forms of behavior in need of intervention.
6. Develop a sample instructional program for teaching a replacement behavior from an applied example within your practicum, and discuss it with your instructor.

FURTHER READING AND EXPLORATION

1. Compile a list of articles from journals such as *Teaching Exceptional Children, Young Exceptional Children*, and *Intervention in School and Clinic* on the use of various instructional methods for teaching academic and social behaviors. Contrast how these resources illustrate instructional goals and objectives and teaching methodologies.
2. Conduct a systematic review from behavioral journals such as the *Journal of Applied Behavior Analysis, Journal of Positive Behavior Interventions, Education and Training in Autism and Developmental Disabilities, Research in Developmental Disabilities*, and *Focus on Autism and Other Developmental Disorders* to name a few and compile resources on teaching replacement behaviors.
3. S. L. Carter's (2009) book on social validity, *The Social Validity Manual: A Guide to Subjective Evaluation of Behavior Interventions*, provides a more in-depth examination of the importance of social validity when constructing interventions.

Minimizing Challenging Behavior

CONCEPTS TO UNDERSTAND

After reading this chapter, you should be able to:

- List and describe the factors that influence challenging behavior.
- Discuss alternatives for the prevention of challenging behaviors, such as the concept of capacity building through SWPBIS and environmental engineering within both classroom and school settings and the development of alternative replacement behaviors that provide students with increased academic and social success.
- Identify and describe how SWPBIS can be used in minimizing challenging behavior and the potential cost/benefits associated with this philosophy and practice.
- List and describe the methods that have been historically used to reduce challenging behavior, such as differential reinforcement, extinction, response cost, and time-out.

KEY TERMS

Non-invasive treatment

Differential reinforcement

Continuum of intervention alternatives

Preventing and minimizing the occurrence of challenging behavior within the classroom is one of the most frequently cited concerns expressed by teachers and school administrators. Challenging behaviors can serve to disrupt the classroom for all parties concerned, including the child affected, students within the class, and teachers. Not surprisingly, the lifestyle outcomes for students who experience chronic behavioral challenges are often bleak and plagued with problems that frequently include academic and social difficulties in school, school failure, suspensions, expulsions, increased difficulty in social and interpersonal relationships, and brushes with the criminal justice system.

Traditionally, many public schools have in the past responded to these forms of behavior through the use of *rapid-suppression* approaches (Durand, 1990) aimed at quickly reducing and ultimately eliminating these behaviors. These methods have historically included a variety of punitive consequences, such as loss of privileges, time-outs, in-school suspension, corporal punishment, and expulsion. These approaches have also failed repeatedly over time to promote lasting behavior change, are reactive in their response to the problem, and they also fail to teach positive replacement behaviors that may have a more positive and enduring effect for the student. Changing how problem behavior is viewed and responded to within a school is the greatest challenge to any teacher. These issues are the focus of this chapter, along with how we can design not only individual interventions but also systems (i.e., schools) to better respond to the challenging behaviors that interfere with learning and the educational success for children and youth.

HOW CHALLENGING BEHAVIOR IS PERCEIVED

One of the most important insights gleaned from the research findings in the area of PBIS has been that challenging behaviors need not always be considered for behavior reduction, but rather for behavior *replacement*. This evidence-based practice has indeed prompted a new way of thinking about challenging behavior as well as about how teachers and school systems respond. Early work by Sulzer-Azaroff and Mayer (1991) recommended a three-step intervention model for promoting positive replacement behaviors as a constructive approach to reducing challenging behavior. This includes the following elements:

1. Assess the function of the problem behavior, and, if feasible, alter conditions to allow the individual access to the same or added reinforcing contingencies by means of a more acceptable action.
2. If that solution proves unworkable, before proceeding, consult laws and policies within the respective school or program.
3. Select the least-restrictive method supported by research to promote optimal results.

This approach addresses excessive behaviors from a *constructive approach* aimed at supporting the learner through skills building and the engineering of relevant environments, including classrooms, school, home, and community. These approaches have been expanded through the refinement of PBIS and have served to enlighten professionals on the many alternatives for addressing challenging behaviors. PBIS places a great deal of emphasis on prevention and minimizing challenging behaviors rather than responding to them in a reactive manner. Challenging behavior infringes on the potential of students to fully participate and achieve success within school and other settings. PBIS as a philosophy of practice served to bridge the gap in facilitating an acceptance of behavioral procedures in schools among teachers and school personnel. PBIS has also reinforced the basic premise that challenging behavior serves a function for an individual—it does not occur in isolation but rather it is often associated with environmental events and circumstances that serve to trigger and reinforce it—and finally, that challenging behavior most often stems from skill deficits on the part of the student.

Sadly, the case can be made that educators and parents alike often look only at the challenging behavior displayed by children as a problem rather than how to promote the development of appropriate skills, and too often these perceptions result in the deployment of punitive consequences and an absence of any skills training. In short, it often becomes a habit to address challenging behavior from a reactive, after-the-fact response that is directed toward its rapid elimination rather than to consider other options aimed at teaching meaningful replacement skills.

Consider This

It is important to remember that when selecting replacement behaviors that they should be efficient. In other words, that the learner should be able to learn and use them efficiently. This concept also applies when training teachers and other professionals to rely on PBIS rather than reactive methods. These methods need to have portability for teachers and provide an ease and efficiency in their use in the classroom.

Constructional approaches such as PBIS advocate that behavioral repertoires not be eliminated but built upon through the development of enriched environments that are designed to promote the development of new and appropriate behaviors. PBIS builds interventions that are designed to enable children to obtain reinforcing consequences within their environments through expanded skill repertoires; these skill repertoires should be inclusive of those skills that are desired within their environment and that also serve a functional purpose for the student. PBIS demonstrates this concept rather well across all three tiers: primary, secondary, and tertiary. Primary is aimed at universally applying these principles across all students through schoolwide implementation directed towards promoting positive behaviors and the prevention of at-risk and or challenging behaviors. At the secondary levels we see these principles applied within the classroom most notably paired with other notable practices such as response to intervention (RtI). Finally, for those students with more significant support needs, the use of PBIS at the tertiary or individual level allows for more concentrated efforts to build effective and positive replacement behaviors for students.

Jackson and Panyan (2002) provided some interesting historical perspectives on the response from public education toward challenging behavior in the past. They indicated that the focus on behavior change was largely focused on a fix-it mentality among professionals, thus lending itself to the use of rapid-suppression approaches as a means of fixing the problem behavior by squelching its occurrence. Second, as a result of children being labeled with problem behavior, specialists trained exclusively to address such problems were given the charge of fixing the problem, rather than seeing the broader context that contributes to these responses. In addition, the authors also reported that many children identified with behavior support needs may be experiencing these behaviors as a response to the practices of some schools that are insensitive to the individual needs of the child and to their diverse familial and cultural factors.

PBIS has informed us that (a) human behavior is functional, people behave the way they do for a reason, and even challenging behavior serves a function for the individual; (b) human behavior is predictable and directly related to the environments that children and youth are a part of; and (c) human behavior is changeable, and through the practices associated with PBIS, such as functional behavior assessment, challenging behavior can be reduced or eliminated (Crone & Horner, 2003).

Since the most recent Reauthorization of IDEA in 2004, schools have begun to address challenging behavior more proactively; thus, meaningful strides have been realized as a result of these promising practices. One of the biggest remaining challenges confronting the SWPBIS agenda is ensuring that all teachers are trained in these skills from both a philosophical and applied perspective and that schools are reinforced for their attempts at systemic change in reference to schoolwide behavior support initiatives. It is also critical that the schools embrace SWPBIS as a systems change initiative in order to be successful. This means allocating resources, administrative support and buy-in at all levels to ensure success.

A consistent challenge that confronts administrators and teachers alike in working toward these goals is that such an initiative competes with numerous other mandates, thus making it difficult to be accountable, given the constant shifting of energy and degree of effort required to accommodate these competing demands (Coyne, Simonsen, & Faggella-Luby, 2008). In response to this challenge, Coyne and colleagues recommended that schools develop a comprehensive framework that encompasses all areas of school improvement and encourages the use of evidence-based practices and capacity building to initiate and sustain these practices over time. The implementation of a schoolwide behavior support initiative requires high commitment and leadership at all levels to carry it out in practice. Such systemic efforts are needed in promoting a climate within schools that encourages and supports children and promotes appropriate prosocial behavior among all persons within the learning community. This climate should be the standard against which schools measure themselves with regard to student behavior.

ALTERNATIVES FOR THE PREVENTION OF CHALLENGING BEHAVIOR

In understanding how to provide alternatives that are directed toward the prevention of challenging behaviors, it is necessary to view PBIS from a systems perspective. Within schools, multiple behavior support systems (Horner, Sugai, Todd, & Lewis-Palmer, 1999–2000) are present. These include classroom systems, nonclassroom systems, and individual student support systems (Horner et al., 1999–2000).

At the base of the continuum of behavior supports model (OSEP Center on PBIS, 2000) are universal interventions, which consist of a schoolwide system that encompasses individual classrooms and is also directed at the primary prevention of problem behaviors among the majority of students within a school (80% to 90%). This population of students is composed of those who do not exhibit serious behavior problems and who require no specialized interventions targeted for behavior concerns. Secondary prevention is the next level on the continuum and targets students who are identified as at risk and who represent approximately 5% to 15% of the student population. The focus at this level is to prevent further problems for these students and to provide a model of support that is aimed at skills building and prevention. The final level on the continuum is tertiary prevention. This level is designed for students with chronic and ongoing behavior challenges that require specialized interventions developed for individual students. It has been estimated by Sugai and colleagues (OSEP Center on PBIS, 2000) that students who display intense and chronic behavior challenges account for 1% to 7% of students within schools.

PBIS consists of a systemic and proactive approach to promoting optimal behavior across multiple contexts, including community, families, schools, classrooms, playgrounds, and nonclassroom settings such as cafeterias, hallways, and playgrounds. The focal point of a systemwide PBIS model such as those presented is prevention. It represents a proactive model aimed at understanding the problem and responding to the problems in a systematic manner. Features of a systems-based model of behavior support are built on a philosophy that is carried out effectively within the daily operations of a school.

In summary, the most important point to remember about developing comprehensive systems of support within school settings is that a school must first commit to change. Such a commitment is the first step in acknowledging that the current methods used to address challenging behaviors are suboptimal and that improvement is needed to promote enhanced learning outcomes for all students. At the core of this philosophical change is the need for capacity building in the area of PBIS. With this in mind, Wheeler and Hoover (1997) identified some of the most relevant competencies required of school-based behavioral support teams as they prepare for schoolwide implementation:

Philosophy of Practice

- Ensure a common understanding of the principles of PBIS.
- Develop teaming and collaboration strategies aimed at solutions.
- Focus on joint problem-solving methods aimed at improved outcomes.

Behavior Support Strategies

- Use Functional Behavior Assessment (FBA) as a tool for understanding challenging behavior.
- Analyze functional assessment data to make informed, data-based decisions.
- Develop function-based hypotheses development based on the FBA data.
- Develop Behavior Support Plan (BSP) aimed at:
  a. Antecedent management approaches focusing on prevention
  b. Development of replacement skills designed to make these more efficient for the learner
  c. Reinforcement strategies to assist the learner in maintaining these replacement skills

Program Evaluation

- Evaluate performance data across all three tiers on a daily, weekly, and monthly basis.
- Collect social validity measures as to satisfaction among students, family members, and teachers relative to the intervention outcome.
- Track student outcomes in terms of academic, social, and behavioral improvements realized.
- Evaluate team outcomes and how the team functioned and performed.
- Evaluate school outcomes and how individual student success positively affects the school at large.

The next step in the process is the stepwise systematic implementation of a systemswide model of behavior support. Research findings have indicated that some unique performance indicators are associated with SWPBIS approaches. Sugai and Horner (2001) identified the following characteristics found within schools that are actively engaged in SWPBIS:

1. An agenda aimed at primary prevention is visible schoolwide.
2. Students and staff members within the school have been taught the expectations and have had regular intervals to practice and rehearse them and to be positively acknowledged by peers and supervisors alike for engaging in the practice of these skills.
3. A majority of students, staff, and families (in excess of 80%) can state the schoolwide positive behavior expectations and provide examples for each.
4. The majority of contacts between faculty, staff, and students are positive.
5. A full continuum of behavior supports exists at the school and district levels.
6. Personnel are well trained and competent in the use of PBIS procedures.
7. A function-based approach serves as the foundation for addressing challenging behaviors.
8. All faculty, staff, and administrators participate in the delivery of SWPBIS practices.
9. A schoolwide behavior support team serves in the role as a designated leadership team committed to the use of research-based practices in behavior support.
10. Schoolwide data are reviewed at regular intervals and are instrumental in decision making and planning.

The final step in the process involves the evaluation of these procedures and their impact on schoolwide behavior outcomes. Sugai and Horner (2001) concluded that the implementation of SWPBIS is feasible within a 1- to 2-year period; that office referrals typically decrease between 40% to 60%, with increases in academic performance measures occurring as more time is devoted to academic instruction when behavior improves; and that lasting impact can endure over a 5- to 7-year period when implementation includes systems change and the use of validated practices.

Finally, Sugai and Horner (2001) recommended the following suggestions for the successful implementation of SWPBIS:

- Concentrate on doing what is possible within your given resource structure, but be persistent over time in capacity building within the school.
- Invest in practices that work.
- Invest in outcomes that the school hopes to achieve.
- Be mindful of individual and cultural differences in the delivery of supports.
- Make data-based decisions as a means of promoting informed decision making.
- Work collaboratively as teams to attain desired outcomes.
- Work hard to develop the professional knowledge and skills among on-site personnel as a method for promoting buy-in and lasting change.

The merits of SWPBIS are numerous and beneficial as a *prevention tool* for challenging behavior. Individual schools have the license to adapt SWPBIS to fit their individual needs as Horner and Sugai (2015) have emphasized. Through the implementation of these practices systemwide, schools are transformed as the cultures within these environments become more proactive in understanding the behavior support needs of the learners they serve. The outcomes for teachers, administrators, and staff members are also apparent as schools transform into a collective team-based unit committed to maintaining an environment of behavior support for all children. To date, over 21,000 schools in the U.S. have adopted SWPBIS nationwide. There have been four key points learned to this point according to Horner and Sugai (2015). These include: (a) identifying the core features needed in a respective school with sensitivity given to the specific culture, resources, and demands found within a school. In other words, adapting to the unique circumstances specific to the setting as each school will be different: (b) implement systems that support and sustain effective practices, meaning the provision of resources and support to school-based teams to deliver high quality evidence-based practices consistently over time and the evaluation of these practices to ensure their efficacy specific to local school needs; (c) the use of data in evaluating the implementation fidelity (are core practices implemented consistently?) and the continuous measurement and evaluation of student behavior through measures such as numbers of office referrals for disciplinary action as one example; and (d) how individual schools implement SWPBIS in their respective locales and the evaluation of these implementation practices such as the adoption of core practices, the development of schoolwide implementation teams and data systems needed to monitor and evaluate progress.

MINIMIZING CHALLENGING BEHAVIOR

As we have learned earlier in the chapter and previously from the text, PBIS is aimed at developing meaningful behaviors that are socially valid for the individuals concerned (Carter, 2007). As noted, PBIS when implemented across all three tiers is focused on prevention at the primary level through the practice and reinforcement of the core elements within a SWPBIS model. At the secondary level, more deliberate interventions ensue directed toward remediation, and at the tertiary level more intense and individualized behavioral supports are designed and implemented. It is at this level where some more persistent and severe behaviors may need to be addressed. When this occurs, questions concerning the nature and severity of the behavior need to be examined. For example, does the behavior in question really pose such a significant challenge that it needs to be reduced? Are we being objective when looking at the behavior of an individual, or is it a subjective bias based on a conflict between personalities? Does the behavior of concern limit the options and personal freedoms of the learner? Additional considerations should include whether there is consensus among staff or other team members that a student's behavior is in need of reduction.

There are, however, instances in which behaviors are of such a magnitude that minimizing and reducing challenging behavior is important for the well-being of the individual such as those that cause a risk to the individual or others or cause damage to property and impede the quality of life for the individual or others (Sulzer-Azaroff & Mayer, 1991). Some examples of these are David, who has autism and is so fascinated by the rotation of the wheels of a car that he runs from his classroom and out onto the edge of the street to watch the cars so he can fixate on the spinning motion of the tires as they pass by; Julie, whose teeth grinding has become so chronic and persistent that she has caused permanent damage to her teeth; Jacob, who has been persistently pinching his classmates to the point that they choose to avoid him and are fearful of him; and Beth, whose chronic self-injury has nearly cost her the use of one eye from her repeated hitting in and about the tissues surrounding her eye. These are examples of behaviors where we must try to minimize their occurrences and hopefully implant replacement behaviors that ultimately serve to eliminate them. They are of concern because they interfere with learning, they pose a threat to the learner or others, and they greatly inhibit the learner's quality of life by limiting his or her personal freedoms.

In times like these it is important that care and consideration be given to conducting a thorough functional behavior assessment (FBA) to ascertain the function of the behavior. In conducting the FBA Sulzer-Azaroff and Meyer (1991) stress that we are attempting to determine the specific antecedent and consequence events that are correlated with the occurrence of the behavior as well as interpersonal and physical or health issues that may be influencing high rates of the behavior. If the functional assessment reveals antecedents that can be altered to prevent the occurrence of the behavior or indicates that alternative behaviors are needed to remediate the problem, then attention should be given to these areas.

PBIS stresses the importance of teaching replacement behaviors that serve the same function as the challenging behavior as we have discussed previously in the text. After identifying the replacement behavior, we actively teach that skill to the student and reinforce his/her approximations in performing the replacement behavior. When addressing severe and challenging forms of behavior, it is important that we are fluent in our understanding of school policies and remain in compliance with these as well as state and federal laws to ensure the rights of the individual and compliance with all laws and policies.

The right to **non-invasive treatment** continues to be an area of justified concern among professionals and advocates of persons in the areas of special education and services to persons with disabilities. The injustices suffered by persons with disabilities in the past led to the formation of human rights committees within state institutions serving persons with developmental disabilities and mental illness and led to the development of nonaversive behavior interventions and the development of PBIS. Substantial progress has been made over time in this area through a greater awareness among professionals, families, self-advocates, and policies that reinforce these beliefs and practices.

The PBIS movement has also contributed to understanding of the limitations of restrictive procedures and their overall impact on the student. Within school settings, for example, a common debate in some geographic areas is whether to permit the use of corporal punishment in schools. Corporal punishment has been defined as the intentional application of physical pain as a method of changing behavior (National Association of School Psychologists [NASP], 2003; Society for Adolescent Medicine, 2003). Corporal punishment does not include physical restraint by school officials to protect students from physically harming themselves or others (American Academy of Pediatrics, 2000). Currently, 19 states in the United States still authorize the use of corporal punishment in schools. It has been estimated that 160,000 students in these states will be subjected to corporal punishment each year. Data indicates that physical punishment is more prevalent in grades K–8, in rural schools versus urban, in boys versus girls, and in disadvantaged children and children of color versus middle-class and upper-class Caucasians (Gershoff & Font, 2016).

There are many problems associated with the use of corporal punishment. Among these are the lack of punishment procedures to produce lasting changes in behavior, not to mention the modeling of physical aggression against children to control their behavior; the reinforcement of escape and avoidance behaviors in children to avoid punishment in the first place; and the reinforcement gained by the user as a means of exerting control. In spite of decades of research and advocacy denouncing corporal punishment, it still remains a viable discipline alternative within almost half the states in the United States. The American Academy of Pediatrics (2000) and the Society for Adolescent Medicine (2003) recommended that corporal punishment be abolished in all states by law and that alternative forms of behavior management be used. The evidence against corporal punishment serves to reinforce the lack of effectiveness of this method for promoting behavior change. The Society for Adolescent Medicine (2003) also concurred within their position paper on corporal punishment in the schools that these methods were also not being used as methods of last resort. Their findings reported that corporal punishment is an ineffective method of disciplining children and that it has serious and damaging effects on the physical and emotional health of those children who have it inflicted on them. Sadly, these outcries still continue, and despite these data as to the harmful effects of corporal punishment, 19 states continue the practice.

Furthermore, the use of corporal punishment does not contribute to the moral development of children, nor does it increase their respect for their teachers or authority figures, as many proponents of this practice believe. On the contrary, the use of corporal punishment promotes fear and distrust of authority figures and models aggression as a means of control. Serious psychological side effects can also result, such as school refusal behavior and other stress-induced behaviors, which are collateral effects of corporal punishment in some children. Such evidence has led many organizations affiliated with medical and related professions to reject corporal punishment as a practice of addressing excessive behavior in the schools. Given the acceptable alternatives for treating behaviors through the use of applied behavior analysis and PBIS, the practice of corporal punishment is unnecessary and unacceptable in our nation's schools.

A related issue that must be discussed is crisis intervention. What is a teacher to do in such a situation? The need for crisis intervention is a growing concern among school professionals and involves something completely different from suppressing behavior through the administration of corporal punishment. However, in the event of escalating behaviors that constitute a crisis, procedures need to be developed to address these circumstances. Crisis intervention procedures are essential as a component of a systemswide positive behavior support model in the event that behaviors escalate to the point that they endanger the safety of the learner or others. These plans should identify the procedures to be used in addressing serious problem behaviors, the roles and responsibilities of personnel involved, and the plan of operation in a crisis and should also ensure that personnel are trained and certified in techniques designed to de-escalate the situation.

CONTINUUM OF INTERVENTION ALTERNATIVES

The **continuum of intervention alternatives** that we will examine includes: (a) differential reinforcement procedures, (b) extinction, (c) response cost, and (d) time-out procedures. With the exception of differential reinforcement, the remainder of these methods are not regularly found within school settings ascribing to a PBIS model, however it is important to briefly understand them as you will encounter them in the literature of the field.

Differential Reinforcement

Differential reinforcement is a method that uses reinforcement to increase desired behavior in the absence of challenging behavior. This form of intervention is called a *positive reduction procedure* (Cooper, Heron, & Heward, 2007).

There are four distinct types of differential reinforcement procedures that can be selected: (1) differential reinforcement of alternative behavior (DRA), (2) differential reinforcement of incompatible behavior (DRI), (3) differential reinforcement of other behavior (DRO), and (4) differential reinforcement of lower rates of behavior (DRL).

The first method, DRA, reinforces a behavior that is a designated alternative behavior for the behavior targeted for reduction (Cooper et al., 2007). For example, if Josh continues working on his assignment rather than putting his head down on the desk and complaining, he is given praise and a token from his teacher; thus he is reinforced for his continued task engagement in the absence of the target behavior. Subsequently, attempts or approximations that Josh makes towards assignment completion are recognized and given praise by the teacher.

DRI is very similar to DRA; however, with DRI the incompatible behavior is topographically incompatible with the target behavior. This is not the case with DRA. For example, in the case of an adolescent boy who engages in hitting classmates in his vocational class, keeping his hands busy with meaningful activity related to his metals class is the desired behavior; thus, when he is not hitting but working on class projects, his teachers reinforce him verbally. A groupwide illustration of this might be the formation of evening recreation programs or sports leagues designed to attract adolescents toward appropriate use of time within a structured setting as a means of curbing youth violence or less than healthy behavioral choices.

When using DRA or DRI procedures, the following guidelines are recommended (Cooper et al., 2007):

1. Select behaviors that are in the student's repertoire of responses that he or she regularly uses.
2. Select behaviors that are reasonable expectations, given the student's current skill level, to ensure rapid acquisition of the new skills.
3. Select behaviors that will be supported within the student's natural environment upon completion of training.

DRO occurs when a behavior is not reinforced for a specific period of time. In other words, a child is reinforced for zero occurrences of a behavior for a specified period; if

Jacob remains in his seat for the 20-minute period, he will earn points. If he leaves his seat only one time during that period, he will fail to earn his reinforcer. This method is very widely applicable within classroom settings and has been reported to reduce a broad range of behaviors, including aggression, spitting, hyperactivity, stereotypy, disruption, and so forth (Sulzer-Azaroff & Mayer, 1991). The benefits of DRO are numerous and include the following:

- It is applicable across learning environments.
- Behavior reduction is possible in a short time frame.
- DRO procedures have been demonstrated to maintain and generalize.

However, there are some negative attributes associated with this strategy, one of which is that DRO does not teach a replacement behavior. It also attends to the undesired behavior, and it can strengthen other undesired forms of behavior because only the targeted behavior cannot receive reinforcement when using a DRO procedure. Teachers must be careful not to reinforce other problematic behaviors when using a DRO procedure.

The last form of differential reinforcement procedure is DRL, which is an effective procedure to use when a behavior can be systematically reduced over time. Reinforcement would be provided for a gradual reduction of the target behavior over time, such as reducing caloric intake and then administering the desired reinforcer on meeting that goal.

To implement DRL procedures, it is recommended that reinforcement be provided in small incremental steps to facilitate sustained behavior change. If expectations for appropriate behavior exceed student capabilities and the time intervals reflect too significant a change, a regression in behavior change is apt to occur.

Extinction

Extinction occurs when a previously reinforced behavior is no longer reinforced. As an example of extinction, Louis continually interrupts his teacher during his interactions with other students. His teacher, Mr. Wilson, being new and concerned about the well-being of all his students, continually stopped what he was doing and gave his immediate attention to Louis. After reading about behavior redirection and extinction, Mr. Wilson no longer stopped what he was doing for Louis's interruptions, and they reduced. Coupled with direct instruction on how to obtain Mr. Wilson's attention, Louis developed appropriate skills for obtaining teacher attention as well.

If a behavior receives continuous or intermittent reinforcement, it will continue to occur (Miltenberger, 2015). One thing to consider when using extinction is that the phenomenon known as extinction burst can occur when a previously reinforced behavior is no longer reinforced. An extinction burst occurs when the intensity or frequency of a behavior increases or escalates in an effort to obtain reinforcement. This increase may also result in the manifestation of novel behaviors that occur with the extinction burst, such as swearing or crying as emotional outbursts due to frustration (Miltenberger, 2015). An example of this occurred when Mac inserted the coins into his favorite vending machine and pushed the accompanying numbers for his favorite snack. As his favorite snack began to drop off its hook, it was snared and did not release. Mac pushed the button for a refund and nothing happened. As he became more frustrated, he kicked the machine as he feverishly pushed the coin return button. Finally, in his efforts to obtain his snack, he began rocking the machine back and forth, but to no avail. His snack stayed hooked, and he walked away exhausted and frustrated by his efforts.

Extinction can result in the reduction of the behavior and has been shown to be lasting in terms of its effects on challenging behaviors. As noted, however, the disadvantages associated with this procedure are as follows:

- Increased rates of behavior or behavioral escalation will most often ensue.
- Development of novel behaviors may also develop as part of the escalation process.
- Aggression may result from frustration.
- Time required to produce the desired effects could be lengthy.

So when assessing the feasibility of extinction procedures in the behavior change process, carefully consider whether you have the willingness and patience to accommodate the slow and gradual reduction in behavior.

Response Cost Procedures

Response cost programs have been used within school settings for a number of years as part of a classroom management system and have been largely prevalent within programs serving students with behavior disorders. Response cost is a behavior reduction procedure that attempts to reduce behavior through the removal or withdrawal of a quantity of reinforcement contingent on a response (Sulzer-Azaroff & Mayer, 1991). In other words, a loss of something of worth or value to the individual is a consequence for inappropriate behavior. You can think of this loss as a penalty or fine.

Perhaps one of the best examples comes from the game of ice hockey. When a player commits a rule violation against another player, this is called a *penalty*; the player who has violated the rules of the game then receives a penalty of two minutes or more, depending on the seriousness of the violation—that is, he or she must sit out the assigned penalty minutes in a penalty box. This is an example of a response cost procedure.

Response cost programs have also been frequently used by parents in managing children's behavior through the loss of privileges such as driving the family car, being grounded (i.e., unable to go out), or through loss of allowance following the occurrence of a problem behavior (i.e., a rules violation). Response cost has been a widely used procedure for students with behavior disorders. With this population of students, response cost has been used in conjunction with level systems that are tied to points students may earn and then be redeemed for various forms of reinforcers that are made available to them within their classroom or school environments. These programs also remove points from students for problem behaviors through the deduction of points, tokens, or privileges as a penalty or fine. One of the major concerns with response cost programs is that teachers frequently err in their design and implementation of these programs: for instance, they remove points from students and provide no mechanism that allows them to earn points back. Therefore, students with chronic behavior challenges are continually in debt or in a position of loss (see Vignette 11.1). This deficit creates an emotional burden for learners and results in a "what do I have to lose" mentality as a result of point deficits that have ensued. The creation of such a climate within a classroom increases problem behavior. It is therefore a better option to use reinforcement with response cost programs as a method for developing desired responses.

Is the loss of the reinforcer ethical, and does it infringe on the child's rights? Consider the following example:

The teaching assistant verbally reprimanded Jim for not engaging in his work and not completing his assignment. Jim, who was diagnosed with autism, sat expressionless in his seat. The teaching assistant elevated her voice and said, "I told you to start working, and because you did not, I am going to have your snack today." After that she proceeded to eat Jim's snack from his lunchbox.

Vignette 11.1

The Limitations of Response-Cost Procedures

The teacher informed Alex that he should stop bothering his classmates and complete his work or lose 5 points for this infraction. Alex persisted and was warned a second time by his teacher, who also told him that she was subtracting 10 points from his total for not following her instructions. On receiving this reprimand, Alex, who was already more than 50 points in debt in terms of total point value, screamed at the teacher and threatened to do "a lot worse." At this point, the teacher deducted another 25 points as a consequence for issuing a verbal threat. Now that Alex has surpassed 75 points in the hole, he feels he has nothing to lose and has escalated his behavior by shouting profanities at the teacher, thus earning him a detention and the loss of another 25 points.

We see from this illustration the perpetual cycle that can result from administering a procedure such as response cost in an inappropriate manner.

Reflective Moment

What recommendations might you have in altering how this response cost procedure was implemented? Identify how this situation could have been prevented.

This example illustrates a very unethical response on the part of the teaching assistant that does indeed violate the rights of the child in this case. Frankly, one of the criticisms associated with the use of punishment procedures is that these procedures become reinforcing to the user. Too often, these programs belittle children and adolescents, as they are most often not implemented carefully nor monitored in terms of their treatment integrity.

Time-Out

Time-out is a procedure commonly used to remove a child from access to reinforcement for a period of time following the occurrence of problem behavior. There are two forms of time-out. Exclusionary time-out refers to the student being taken out of the room or area where the behavior occurred and placed in another area. The second form of time-out procedure is called nonexclusionary time-out and involves the student remaining in the room or area where the behavior occurred but being denied access to positive reinforcement (Miltenberger, 2015).

Time-out has been noted to be an effective procedure to use with behaviors that are maintained by social or tangible reinforcers because time-out denies access to these reinforcers by removing the individual from the environment in which the reinforcers are available (Miltenberger, 2015). Time-out procedures are relatively easy to use within classroom settings and have been deemed to be generally acceptable by professionals, and the use of time-out procedures suppresses behavior rapidly and generalizes across time and settings (Cooper et al., 2007). Time-out procedures require strict adherence to policies within the school and the permission of families. As with any behavior reduction procedure, it should not be the first intervention of choice, and care should be taken in the development of guidelines to be adhered to in administering time-out procedures. The limitations of time-out are many, as pointed out by Sulzer-Azaroff and Mayer (1991). These include the following:

- Time is lost from instruction. When in time-out, the learner loses valuable time from instruction.
- Time-out is not universally effective among all learners, yet is often deemed as such and is overly relied on for that reason.
- Time-out represents a negative contingency, in that it removes the learner from reinforcing environments.
- The lack of procedural safeguards and legal liabilities associated with time-out are cause for concern in terms of its implementation with school-age children and youth.
- The potential for abuse exists because time-out is easy to use and can be overused.
- The generalized suppression of other behaviors can occur, especially when the cues associated with the administration of the time-out procedure are not clear and consistent.

One point to consider when assessing the feasibility of using time-out procedures within your setting is to also assess how to make time in class more reinforcing (Sulzer-Azaroff & Mayer, 1991). Enriching learning environments through the design and delivery of exciting, stimulating, learner-centered activities represents a positive option when considering how to reduce or eliminate challenging behaviors of concern. After all attempts have been exhausted in terms of positive practices, consideration can be given to procedures such as time-out.

If time-out is selected as a behavior-reduction procedure, all personnel must adhere to consistent implementation guidelines involved in the administration of the time-out procedures. Sulzer-Azaroff and Mayer (1991) recommend that staff clearly communicate the conditions for time-out. The procedures must be consistent, staff must be trained and supervised in implementing the procedures, and the transition back to the classroom from the time-out must be planned to ensure that the student reenters the learning environment with appropriate behavior. It is important to reinforce behaviors that are appropriate and desired within the learning environment before the student re-enters the setting.

SUMMARY

The purpose of this chapter has been to explore how PBIS can be used to prevent and minimize challenging behavior. The chapter began with a discussion of how challenging behavior is perceived by professionals and caregivers and how these perceptions can result in our responses to behaviors that we often find annoying or overly problematic.

The importance of how behaviors are viewed by professionals and staff result in the responses that are selected to address these behavior challenges. Excessive behavior often occurs as a result of skill deficits paired with environments that are neither supportive nor instructive of skill deficiencies. This combination of personal and environmental skill deficits often results in high rates of problem behaviors that interfere with learning and the overall ease and functioning of the learning environment. The chapter also presented how, within certain environments, skill deficits that result in excessive behavior in students become the major focal point with no attention given to understanding the skills needed by the learner to eliminate the need for these responses. The need for a constructive approach (Sulzer-Azaroff & Mayer, 1991) in how we respond to challenging behavior was also presented. This viewpoint looked at adding skills to the behavior repertoires of individuals through the selection and teaching of positive replacement behaviors.

One element that has emerged from the field of PBIS has been the schoolwide application of these principles within school systems as a means of preventing problem behaviors from occurring, which has been accomplished through the deployment of a continuum of supports within the school's behavioral support philosophy. The continuum of support (OSEP Center on PBIS, 2000) identified three distinct levels within this continuum. At the base of the continuum is the primary prevention level. This level accounts for approximately 80% to 90% of the students within the school population. Interventions at this level are schoolwide and preventive in nature. The second level within the continuum is that of secondary prevention. This level on the continuum comprises approximately 5% to 15% of the school population, and interventions here focus on the unique needs of students who have been identified as at risk. The final level, tertiary prevention, is directed toward individualized behavior support interventions for approximately 1% to 7% of the population.

The final portion of the chapter introduced and discussed traditional methods for minimizing and reducing challenging behaviors. These included the use of differential reinforcement as a method designed to promote the development of replacement behaviors. Extinction was discussed, along with the application of this procedure in the classroom as well as its limitations. More invasive procedures such as response cost and time-out were described to help students in gaining a clearer understanding of what they are and their limitations.

We hope that the material provided in this chapter offers a clearer picture of the methods that have been traditionally used to address excessive behavior and the merits of the alternatives provided through PBIS. The reality is that children and youth will challenge the abilities of teachers and educational systems to proactively address their behavior and educational needs. It is imperative that educational personnel and systems be trained in the development of effective schoolwide systems designed to meet these challenges at every level for every student. The far-reaching benefit of PBIS is that the quality of life of these students will be considered as part of our response as educators in addressing their behavioral challenges. We hope that through prevention and the development of personal competencies and skills within caring and supportive environments that children and youth will learn positive alternatives to the behaviors that infringe on their potential.

ACTIVITIES TO EXTEND YOUR LEARNING

1. Conduct a review of existing sources from the literature concerning the selection of replacement behaviors.
2. Interview the parent of a child with a disability and have him or her offer perspectives on addressing challenging behavior.
3. Visit a school and interview a principal, a general education teacher, a special education teacher, perhaps a counselor, and a group of students to determine whether a schoolwide behavior support model exists. Assess the availability of such models within area schools and determine whether these models provide a continuum of support, as described in the model by Sugai and colleagues (2001).
4. Contact your local school system and ask for information pertaining to existing policies governing the use of behavior intervention approaches for responding to challenging behaviors.

FURTHER READING AND EXPLORATION

1. Consult the websites www.pbis.org, www.nasponline.org, www.nasdse.org, and www.cec.sped.org for information pertaining to the use of positive interventions designed to address challenging behavior.

2. Assess the content of selected textbooks in the areas of PBIS and ABA and compare the content from these sources as it pertains to the use of preventing and minimizing challenging behavior. How are these texts similar in their presentation of the topics, and do they promote PBIS as the method of choice in addressing challenging behavior? If not, what are the recommended practices in these resources?

3. Contact your local school system and ask for information pertaining to their policies governing the use of behavior intervention approaches for the reduction of challenging behaviors.

PBIS and Self-Determination

CONCEPTS TO UNDERSTAND

After reading this chapter, you should be able to:

- Define and describe quality of life.
- Define and describe self-determination.
- Describe and discuss the relationship between PBIS and self-determination.
- Discuss the relationships among quality of life, social validity, and self-determination of persons with disabilities.
- Describe and discuss Bronfenbrenner's bioecological systems theory and its relationship to self-determination.
- List and describe the four subsystems of the systems theory perspective, and provide examples of quality of life and self-determination in each.
- List and describe the 12 teaching components of self-determination.
- Discuss how quality of life improvement and self-determination are included in PBIS for children and youth with challenging behavior at different ages, including infants and toddlers, early childhood, middle school years, and high school years.

KEY TERMS

Autonomy	Microsystem
Bioecological model	Outcomes
Chronosystem	Outputs
Exosystem	Personal appraisal
Feedback	Person-centered planning (PCP)
Functional behavior assessments	Processes
Inputs	Psychological empowerment
Macrosystem	Quality of life
Mesosystem	Self-determination

Self-management   Social validity

Self-realization   Systems theory perspective

Self-regulation

The concepts of quality of life and self-determination for children and youth with challenging behavior and families were mentioned briefly in previous chapters. It is most appropriate for them to be discussed in detail at the end of the text because the overriding mission of PBIS is to improve quality of life: "A hallmark of PBIS planning is its emphasis on improving overall lifestyle quality (relationships, activities, health) as an integral part of behavior support. PBIS focuses not only on reducing behavior problems, but on enhancing a person's overall quality of life" (Association for Positive Behavior Support [APBS], n.d.). Stated another way, everything that has been introduced up to this point is intended to make it possible for persons with or at risk for challenging behavior to have an improved quality of life and to be more self-determined—that is, to be more independent and in charge of their own lives.

Before getting into the specifics of self-determination as an outcome that educators seek in their work with all children and youth, in particular with those who have special needs, it is useful to consider self-determination more broadly. Most people seek opportunities for and the ability to self-determine. Self-determination can be thought of as a lifelong pursuit for human beings. Individuals want to be "financially independent," to "do our own thing," to "not be under someone else's thumb," to "be our own person," to have opportunities and options, and to decide for ourselves what we will do to meet our needs and wants and how our behavior will be rewarded. Yet people are constantly faced with the reality that they are interdependent on others and that others have substantial influence on their behavior. The quality of our lives is not, of course, solely determined by the extent to which we are independent.

In his classic work *Beyond Freedom and Dignity*, noted psychologist, Harvard professor, and father of modern behaviorism (leading to the experimental analysis of behavior, applied behavior analysis, and now, many suggest, positive behavior support) Skinner (1971) concludes his treatise on the necessity of a scientific view of human behavior by pointing out that each human being ("man") is controlled by the environment but that environments are largely of his or her own making. Skinner writes, "The evolution of a culture is a gigantic exercise in self-control" (1971, p. 215). So rather than being a victim or passive observer of what happens to them, individuals can influence the environments, demands, expectations, and conditions that influence their behavior. Skinner further points out that the experimental analysis of behavior (now largely evolved to applied behavior analysis and PBIS) changes the focus of human behavior as being grounded in their environments rather than being autonomous.

Viewed in this manner and related to self-determination, it may be logical to think of self-determination as being facilitated by the nature of the ecology—the environments in which we spend our time. For example, if one's work environment is monotonous, repetitive, highly controlled, constantly monitored, and requires no independent decision making, one might conclude that it is inconsistent with an individual's self-determination. One might conclude that a classroom teacher who must strictly adhere to the state-prescribed curriculum has no say in which students are assigned to his or her class, has little planning time, and has hardly enough time to go to the restroom during the school day is not self-determined in his or her work environment. Both of the preceding examples are overly simplistic with regard to whether an individual is self-determining, as you will learn on further exploration of what is meant by self-determination.

In this chapter, the importance of self-determination as a component of quality of life is explored, as is what educators might do to foster the acquisition and use of self-determination skills in the children and youth for whom they have responsibility is discussed. In particular, the emphasis is on individuals (with disabilities and/or challenging behavior) who have historically been deprived of sufficient opportunities for achieving self-determination.

THE RELATIONSHIP BETWEEN PBIS AND SELF-DETERMINATION

In Chapter 1, we introduced the various philosophical and theoretical perspectives that have been used to explain and to intervene with children and youth who demonstrate challenging behavior. Behaviorism and its application as represented by ABA are described as the approach that has produced the best outcomes in programs and services for children and youth with emotional and behavior disabilities. PBIS is understood as having evolved from ABA as an extension thereof. PBIS relies on the use of person-centered interventions and employs meaningful consequences to enhance the quality of life of individuals with behavior issues.

Anderson and Freeman (2000) described PBIS as having three prominent features: (a) person-centered values (attention to individual needs, preferences, and socially valid goals); (b) recognition of individual needs and flexibility to accommodate them; and (c) meaningful outcomes that enhance the quality of life of individuals, including participation in inclusive educational and community settings. Although some argue that there is little if any difference between ABA and PBIS, most experts in the discipline believe that PBIS has brought greater focus to interventions that are socially valid, emphasize prevention and antecedent and environmental management, have wider relevance than exclusively special education populations, are positive and proactive, and are evaluated by the extent to which they improve the quality of life of individuals with challenging behavior. The quality of life for everyone, including those with challenging behavior, is in no small measure connected to the extent to which they are self-determined. Self-determination is inseparable from the planning, delivery, and evaluation of PBIS. In the Standards of Practice (see Chapter 3) developed by the APBS (2008), there is significant emphasis on the importance of addressing self-determination as an integral part of behavior support planning and implementation by practitioners.

It is useful to understand how self-determination, as it is represented and advanced as a part of PBIS, is connected to more traditional and established behavior interventions and ABA. The goal as educators is to teach students how to direct their behavior in optimal ways as to promote increased quality if life options for them. One method by which to do this is through instruction in self-management skills. **Self-management** may be thought of as self-control or self-discipline and the ability to function to some extent independent of others in both determining aspects of the environment and in determining what the reinforcers are and how they are applied. Although this is only one way in which we might connect self-determination to prior descriptions of behavior interventions and ABA, it is very significant. For a number of years, the guidance provided to educators through professional literature (textbooks and journal articles) on classroom management, ABA, and behavior interventions has emphasized the necessity of helping children and youth become more self-reliant and less dependent on external sources for antecedents (for example, environments, expectations, and consequences both rewarding and punitive).

Typically, the goal of helping students become more self-managed has been associated with their ability to apply the desired behaviors that they have learned to settings and circumstances in which there may be no adult supervision. It might be argued that although self-management and self-control have been much discussed in the special education discipline, they have all too often received insufficient attention compared to external controls. One area of criticism of special education is that it tends to make students with disabilities passive learners and overly dependent on adults for both direction and reinforcement. Although this criticism may be in part fair, it is certainly important to note that the nature and severity of particular disabilities affects the extent to which individuals may be expected to become self-managed, self-reliant, and self-controlled.

QUALITY OF LIFE AND PERSONS WITH DISABILITIES

In recent years, increased attention has been given in special education to enhancing the quality of life of persons with disabilities. Frequently included in the consideration of quality of life are issues and practices associated with socially valid outcomes, person-centered planning, and development of the individual across the life span, roles and functions of the family, joy and happiness, personal well-being, and self-determination. In his review of how the concept of quality of life has developed, Schalock (2000) pointed out that in the field of intellectual disabilities quality of life was embraced in the 1980s and clarified in the 1990s. He suggested that in the decade of the 2000s, quality of life would be understood and applied more intensely by advocates, service providers, and those persons who evaluate quality outcomes. Most would agree that this in fact has become the reality, and professionals in regular education, special education, and related disciplines, have increased their roles in planning, delivering, and evaluating educational services to children and youth with disabilities specific to the goal of quality of life and self-determination as one of its components.

Schalock (2000) defined **quality of life** as "a concept that reflects a person's desired conditions of living related to eight core dimensions of one's life: emotional well-being, interpersonal relationships, material well-being, personal development, physical well-being, self-determination, social inclusion, and rights" (p. 121). In the 1990s, substantial changes were made with regard to moving the concept of quality of life more toward an outcome that may be assessed and measured (Schalock, 2000) through the use of both personal appraisal and functional assessment. Personal appraisal is largely qualitative in nature and refers to asking an individual how satisfied he or she is with aspects of his or her life. Functional assessment (see Chapter 6) refers to the application of various methods and instruments to observe and quantify (though some include qualitative methods, such as interviews in functional assessments) how an individual functions in various environments. The combination of these two measures allows for a useful assessment of a person's quality of life, including on the dimension of self-determination.

Self-determination, as a dimension of quality of life for persons with disabilities, has been explored in professional literature. For example, Wehmeyer and Schwartz (1998), in a study of adults with intellectual disabilities, found that people who were more self-determined reported a higher quality of life. This is certainly true for all of us as when we are making the choices that affect our lives we have a greater sense of satisfaction and are more apt to have a more meaningful quality of life. Self-determination was advanced as an important goal in continued efforts to improve the quality of life for individuals with mental retardation and developmental disabilities. Wehmeyer and Schalock (2001) offered a perspective on the future roles of quality of life and self-determination in the planning and delivery of special education supports and services. They concluded that the emphasis on quality of life and self-determination could have the effect of fostering the further integration of special education and general education (see the discussion of unified systems reform in Chapter 2). That is, the emphasis on quality of life and self-determination is likely to become more important in the future in educational environments for all children and youth, and the systems of accountability will reflect more than just quantifiable, testing outcomes, such as personally valued outcomes. In a position paper on the future of PBIS and its growth, expansion, and (our term) maturity, Carr (2007) described the importance of systems change and collaboration among disciplines in order to support quality of life for individuals. As for the future view of PBIS, Carr stated that it should be "a vision that impels us to create meaningful lives and not simply to eliminate psychopathology, a vision that spurs us to change systems and not just people, a vision that motivates us to seek collaborative possibilities with our colleagues in many different sciences" (Carr, 2007, p. 12). As you think about the ways that as an educator, you might go about improving quality of life for students and the broader implications that your efforts might have, it is important to include family. Applying common sense, we might argue that the quality of life of a child affects the quality of life of that child's family. Smith-Bird and Turnbull (2005) underscored this point and suggested that plans and actions to improve the family quality of life are necessary outcomes. And it is interesting to think of the focus of educators on the quality of life and self-determination of their students and their families as a means of advancing the cause of integration and inclusion and full participation of children and youth with disabilities.

SOCIAL VALIDITY

Social validity refers to the extent to which the objectives and outcomes of intervention are meaningful (valid) for the lives of the individuals for which they are intended. That is, does the education—and special education—intervention result in behaviors, skills, and attitudes that are usable and functional in the context of a person's everyday life? The connection between social validity, quality of life, and self-determination is certainly clear. Quality of life is enhanced when a person's repertoire of skills has utility and meaning in his or her life. Carpenter, Bloom, and Boat (1999) suggested that four criteria related to social validity and quality of life be kept in mind when providing special education services: a focus on increasing self-esteem of students, producing high levels of self-determination, increasing empowerment, and promoting joy in the lives of students. As noted earlier in the discussion of quality of life, the focus on socially valid outcomes has as much relevance for general education as for special education. Scott (2007) addressed the relationship between personal dignity and social validity in schoolwide systems of PBIS. He emphasizes that as we further develop and refine PBIS, we should continue to enlist the participation of varied stakeholders in researching and better understanding how personal dignity (an individual's perception of his or her standing) and social validity (meaningfulness of objectives and outcomes) are connected.

An important concern that arises when the matter of socially valid outcomes are examined more closely is determining whose point of view is represented in the judgments about the outcomes. To what extent are the outcomes agreed upon and determined by the person who is targeted for education and behavior change versus, for example, teachers, parents, or other family members? Social validity has relevance for not only outcomes but also goals and procedures, and that social validity may be seen as the extent to which programs and procedures are acceptable to its consumers (Carter, 2009).

There are many consumers, or stakeholders, and it is reasonable to assume that there will be times of disagreement between an individual's wishes (for self-determination) and the wishes of others. For example, in a study (Fox & Emerson, 2001) in which the researchers examined what different stakeholders viewed as socially valid outcomes for people with mental retardation and challenging behavior, clinicians and academics viewed direct efforts to reduce the challenging behaviors as more important and valid as outcomes than did the persons with developmental delays, their parents, or direct service providers. The point is that professionals must exercise caution in the conclusions they draw about what constitutes social validity in intervention goals and outcomes.

DEFINING AND DESCRIBING SELF-DETERMINATION

There are many ways to define the term **self-determination**. For purposes of this chapter, several definitions are useful. Turnbull and Turnbull (2001) define self-determination as "living one's life consistent with one's own values, preferences, strengths, and needs" (p. 13). Turnbull and Turnbull equate the terms *self-determination* and *empowerment* but pointed out that self-determination is more often associated with an individual who has a disability, whereas empowerment is more often associated with a family. Other definitions have been provided as the concept of self-determination has taken form over the past decade. For example, several early studies, including Wehmeyer (1992; 1996) and Wehmeyer, Kelchner, and Richards (1996) suggested that self-determination referred to "acting as the primary causal agent in one's life and making choices and decisions regarding one's quality of life free from undue external influence or interference" (Wehmeyer, 1996, p. 22). Taken together, these definitions of self-determination address: the ability to make one's own decisions free from undue interference; the consistency of options with one's own values, preferences, and needs; and the application of self-determination across various environments (home, school, work, leisure). An organization of adults with disabilities, Self-Advocates Becoming Empowered (1996), defines self-determination as follows:

> speaking up for our rights and responsibilities and empowering ourselves to stand up for what we believe in. This means being able to choose where we work, live, and our friends; to educate ourselves and others; to work as a team to obtain common goals; and to develop the skills that enable us to fight for our beliefs, to advocate for our needs, and to obtain the level of independence that we desire. (p. 3)

Finally, with regard to defining self-determination, a consensus definition was provided (Field, Martin, Miller, Ward, & Wehmeyer, 1998) that appeared to take into account all the elements and emphases of the others:

> Self-determination is a combination of skills, knowledge, and beliefs that enable a person to engage in goal-directed, self-regulated, autonomous behavior. An understanding of one's strengths and limitations together with a belief in oneself as capable and effective are essential to self-determination. When acting on the basis of these skills and attitudes, individuals have greater ability to take control of their lives and assume the role of successful adults. (p. 3)

Something to keep in mind in the understanding and application of definitions of self-determination is the effect that chronological and developmental ages have on the development of self-determination. Obviously, the younger a child is (with or without a disability), the less ability (and opportunity) he or she will have for self-determination, independence, and autonomy. However, there is a growing emphasis (Erwin et al., 2009) on the importance of and methods for fostering self-determination of young children with disabilities and their families.

The elements and characteristics of self-determination have been described in various ways. As a part of the previous definition (Wehmeyer, 1996), four characteristics for determining the extent to which behaviors are self-determined are provided. They are **autonomy** (acting according to one's preferences), **self-regulation** (engaging in self-management, goal setting, and problem solving), **psychological empowerment** (having and exercising skills to exert control and reach desired outcomes), and **self-realization** (acting on an accurate knowledge of one's strengths and limitations) (Wehmeyer, 1999). These characteristics may be seen as developing as outcomes of particular skills and attributes that may be acquired and reinforced as part of a student's educational program and experience. Wehmeyer (1996) identified eleven components (skills and attributes) that accompany the four characteristics of self-determination: (1) choice-making skills, (2) decision-making skills, (3) problem-solving skills, (4) goal-setting and attainment skills, (5) self-management skills, (6) self-advocacy skills, (7) leadership skills, (8) internal locus of control, (9) positive attributions of efficacy and outcome expectancy, (10) self-awareness, and (11) self-knowledge.

Self-determination has been defined and described largely as it is associated with the skills and attributes of an individual who manifests the ability to self-determine. Various environments support or interfere with one's ability to self-determine, and those environments certainly include much more than educational settings. In their foundational book on self-determination, *Self-Determination Across the Life Span*, Sands and Wehmeyer (1996) provided perspectives on how this ability is important throughout one's entire life and in various settings, such as school, home, community, and place of work, and they suggest that the self-determination movement is a necessary part of other current social and educational movements, including school reform (unified systems) and inclusion. As noted earlier in the chapter, although self-determination might be a goal for which to strive, it is not synonymous with independence. Sands and Wehmeyer (1996) cautioned that misrepresenting self-determination as being the same as absolute individual control (independence) will interfere with educators' ability to address self-determination as an instructional goal, process, or outcome.

It is helpful in understanding self-determination to examine its relationship to the human ecology of children and youth. Self-determination—like other behaviors of children and youth, regardless of whether they have a disability—is built and maintained as a result of interactions across the various environments having relevance at various points in their lives. For example, with regard to choice-making skills, if a child has the opportunity to learn and maintain this skill in school, but the skill is ignored or even countered in other significant environments (for example, home, religious classes, T-ball, scouting), then it may be only partially or unsuccessfully acquired as an element of the child's repertoire for self-determination.

SELF-DETERMINATION AS AN ECOLOGICAL PERSPECTIVE

One prominent perspective on understanding the development of children and youth in the context of their environments is provided by Urie Bronfenbrenner as a part of his bio-ecological systems theory. The ecological model, introduced in Chapter 1, "views the child as developing within a complex system of relationships affected by multiple levels of the surrounding environment" (Berk, 2002, p. 27). Bronfenbrenner (1998) extended his perspective and characterized it as a **bioecological model**, taking into greater account the interaction between heredity and environment in influencing development and behavior.

Bronfenbrenner's bioecological systems theory is represented as nested circles, with the individual in the center surrounded by five concentric circles detailing the various contexts and systems within which the individual develops. The first is the **microsystem**, which is the bidirectional relationship and influence of the child and her immediate environment, such as family and school. If interactions in the microsystem occur often and over time, they tend to have a more significant and lasting effect (Collins, Maccoby, Steinberg, Hetherington, & Bornstein, 2000).

Adding to this ecological and developmental perspective the emphasis in Albert Bandura's social learning theory (1977) (see Chapter 1) on the importance of imitation of models for learning and the behavior principles specific to environmental arrangements and positive consequences, it is clear how experiences in the microsystem influence development and, in particular, the acquisition of specific skills associated with self-determination. One of the characteristics of self-determination is self-regulation. For example, children learn to self-regulate (self-manage) from the opportunities provided them by parents and teachers as they are modeled by important persons in a child's immediate environment and because the behaviors associated with self-regulation are valued and rewarding (either intrinsically or extrinsically).

The second level of Bronfenbrenner's bioecological systems theory is the **mesosystem**. Whereas the microsystem focuses on the relationship of the child to various near environments and influences (such as home and family members or school and teachers), the mesosystem is defined as the connections between microsystems (for example, the connection between home and school). Brotherson, Cook, Cunconan-Lahr, and Wehmeyer (1995) provided an earlier model for how three components (home, school, and community) might collaborate to build self-determination skills for children. Among a number of practical suggestions provided in the model, examples include expanding daily activities to encourage independence and choice (home), teaching choice, decision making, and self-advocacy (school) and providing accessible stores, theatres, offices, and programs (community). The actions associated with home, school, and community, taken together, contribute substantially to a child's opportunities for gaining self-determination skills.

The third level of the bioecological model is the **exosystem**, which refers to settings such as the parent's workplace that do not directly include children but that are likely to have a significant impact on their development and skill acquisition. Other examples of the exosystem are extended family, friends, and neighbors. Brotherson and colleagues (1995) pointed out that current federal policy associated with laws (such as the Americans with Disabilities Act and IDEA) support and expect the use of PBIS for persons with disabilities across collaborative environments.

The fourth level of the Bronfenbrenner model is the **macrosystem**, which is made up of laws, customs, cultural values, and resources. There are connections between a child's acquisition of self-determination skills and the macrosystem. As stated earlier, current federal (as well as state and local) laws and associated policies support the need to prepare children and youth with disabilities to be more self-determined. At the same time, self-determination is not always a cultural value; the extent to which it is valued varies considerably within and between cultures. For that matter, it also varies considerably depending on other factors, such as parenting styles, socioeconomic levels, and spiritual beliefs. These issues should be carefully considered and understood in the context of the family when assisting persons who are gaining self-determination skills.

The last element of the Bronfenbrenner model is the **chronosystem**, which is not a context for the development of children but rather a subsystem reflecting change over time. That is, life events change over time, and children experience developmental changes that affect their development in areas such as self-determination. It would be expected that as children get older and become more autonomous and (hopefully) more self-managed, they would more likely exhibit choice and influence their environments.

SELF-DETERMINATION AS A SYSTEMS PERSPECTIVE

A system is "an integrated set of parts that function together for some end purpose or result" (Goldsmith, 2000, p. 32). Systems are made up of subsystems. Urie Bronfenbrenner's ecological systems theory and bioecological model is intended to explain child development in the context of the five subsystems described. Many models and frameworks related to children and families have been used in education and other human service disciplines. Turnbull, Summers, and Brotherson (1984) provided a family systems framework to understand in particular what happens in families in which there is a member with a disability. Using their systems perspective, the first subsystem is input, which refers to the characteristics of families. The second subsystem is process, which refers to the family's interactions. The third subsystem is output, which refers to how the family functions—what it does. One might use other terms to describe these three subsystems. Process in systems theory terms is sometimes referred to as *throughput*. These are the three basic elements of systems theory. Further systems theory assumes that when output is returned in some fashion to input, feedback has occurred.

Applying a **systems theory perspective** to educational environments and especially to the intent of helping children and youth gain skills in self-determination, one might use the following structure. Inputs may be considered the actions taken and information provided in relation to determining how an individual might be supported in gaining self-determination skills. Therefore, activities such as IFSPs, IEPs, PCP, functional assessment and other forms of assessment, and other means of establishing an individual's needs, strengths, and wishes related to self-determination are inputs. Processes (throughputs) might be thought of as the teaching, intervention, environmental arranging, and uses of particular methods, procedures, strategies, and curricula associated with self-determination. Outputs are the results of the processes. In educational terminology, outputs are most often referred to as *outcomes*. In fact, much of the literature on self-determination has focused on desired outcomes. However, the extent to which persons with disabilities at all developmental levels and ages have gained in self-determination as a result of special education intervention is somewhat undetermined empirically.

This systems approach of four subsystems—**inputs** (assessment and planning), **processes** (teaching and intervening), **outputs** (outcomes and results), and **feedback**—has long been used in special education as a means of understanding how special education is designed to function most effectively. To illustrate, it might be determined in the context of the evaluation and assessment process that a student needs to be more autonomous and self-managed, that is, to have better self-determination skills (see Vignette 12.1). The student's IEP and PCP, with the student's contribution, includes goals and activities specifically aimed at increasing self-determination. These are parts of the input subsystem.

Vignette 12.1

Self-Determination Process and Outcomes for Rhonda

Rhonda is a 17-year-old high school student who receives special education. She wishes to be more independent, to make some money on her own, and to spend less time around parents and teachers. She is placed in a part-time job in the community and then provided with support and training under the life coaching approach in which emphasis is placed on learning on the job rather than in a prevocational setting. These are parts of the throughput (process) subsystem. Formative and summative judgments are made about how Rhonda is doing in her development of autonomy and self-management and the degree to which she is experiencing success and satisfaction in her job. These are parts of the output, or outcomes subsystem.

Reflective Moment

Rhonda's placement is with a veterinary clinic where she works 3 hours each weekday afternoon doing a variety of jobs around the clinic, including routine care, feeding, and watering of the animals; clean-up and maintenance of the cages as well as the floors and exam and surgery rooms; some assistance in the office with clerical tasks; and occasionally serving as assistant to the veterinarian during routine exams or surgery. Given this placement and these responsibilities, can you think of some methods or strategies that Rhonda and others might employ to make judgments about her job satisfaction and her development of self-management and self-determination skills? What about ways to measure quality of life related to her job placement?

For the remainder of this chapter, a systems perspective will be used to examine the acquisition and maintenance of self-determination skills and improving quality of life in children with and without disabilities across the lifespan. Several fundamental assumptions are made. One is that improving quality of life and becoming self-determined is a lifelong process for all people, regardless of whether they have disabilities. Other assumptions are that self-determination is an important teaching and intervention goal and that it can be planned for and assessed; it can be systematically taught through methods, procedures, and curricula; and it is an outcome that can and should be measured and evaluated.

Assessing and Planning for Self-Determination (Input)

Numerous approaches have been used to assess children and youth to gain information useful in making plans for their education. There is an obvious close link between assessment and success in teaching. Generally, it has been held that the more program-relevant the assessment procedures and instruments are (the extent to which they produce information that is directly applicable to intervention and teaching), the more useful and appropriate they are. **Functional behavior assessment** (FBA) is the most prominent means of assessment of PBIS. Functional assessment of challenging behavior makes four primary assumptions (Chandler & Dahlquist, 2002): Behaviors are supported by the current environment, behavior serves a function, positive interventions will change challenging behavior, and FBA should be a team process.

Earlier in the chapter, self-determination was introduced as one important dimension of quality of life. The indicators of self-determination might include a person's level of autonomy, the extent to which the individual makes his or her own choices and decisions, personal control, the individual's role in determining personal goals and values, and the extent to which he or she is self-directed. How do we assess these indicators? One way, of course, is through functional assessment, or looking at the degree to which they are present in real-life environments. Another way is through the use of **personal appraisal** (Wehmeyer & Schalock, 2001), or asking the person about how satisfied he or she is with various facets of his or her life. Although this approach may be somewhat oversimplified, it is useful to think of functional assessment as more of a quantifiable, measurable approach and personal appraisal as more of a qualitative and subjective approach.

As with other assessments, the primary purpose of assessment of self-determination is for instructional planning. The assessment of self-determination should be a team process, and the student should most certainly participate and be central to the process, along with professionals and the family. Measurement procedures might include interviews, behavior observations (for example, as a major component of functional assessment), psychometric tests, and curriculum-based assessment techniques, including portfolio assessment.

Largely through the support of the U.S. Department of Education, Office of Special Education and Rehabilitative Services (OSERS), several assessment instruments on self-determination were developed. Five of the more frequently used instruments have included *The AIR Self-Determination Scale and User Guide* (Wolman, Campeau, DuBois, Mithaug, & Stolarski, 1994), *The ARC Self-Determination Scale* (Wehmeyer, 1995), *Choice-Maker Self-Determination Assessment* (Martin & Marshall, 1996a), the *Self-Determination Assessment Battery* (Hoffman, Field, & Sawilowsky, 1996), and *The Self-Determination Profile: An Assessment Package* (Curtis, 1996).

Various planning processes and products result from the use of assessment information. For children with disabilities, planning will be manifest in the IFSP for infants and toddlers from birth to 3 years of age and their families. For school-age children with disabilities, assessment data are found in the IEP plan. Preschoolers with disabilities (ages 3 to 5), depending on the state and LEA, will have either an IFSP or an IEP. Specific behavior support plans might also be used, in particular for children and youth with challenging behavior. **Person-centered planning (PCP)** has been defined (Turnbull & Turnbull, 2001) as "a process that was created to listen to the great expectations of individuals with disabilities and their families and to tailor lifestyle support to actualize those great expectations" (p. 296). Holburn (2001) pointed out that PCP and ABA, rather than being at odds with each other, share many features with regard to improving the lives of persons with disabilities in natural environments and through enhancing skills in autonomy and self-management.

The McGill Action Planning System (MAPS) serves as one primary example of PCP (Forest & Lusthaus, 1990). The MAPS process provides the opportunity for a student with a disability and his or her friends, teachers, parents, and siblings to get together and develop a vision as well as creating an action plan for the student to achieve the vision. All of these planning formats—the IFSP, IEP, behavior support, and PCP—are opportunities to address quality of life and skills, support, and actions needed to facilitate self-determination.

Teaching Self-Determination Skills (Process)

As noted previously, the teaching and learning of self-determination skills for children and youth of all ages, whether or not they have a disability, is a worthwhile part of the mission of the educational enterprise in various environments. In fact, self-determination may be seen as an overriding ability that students need to benefit from much of their educational experience. Field and colleagues (1998) described self-determination as being both a focal point of teaching and an umbrella for making curricular decisions. The DCDT of the CEC (Field et al., 1998) said, "Self-determination instruction during the elementary, middle, and secondary transition years prepares *all students* for a more satisfying and fulfilling adult life" (p. 118, emphasis in original). In understanding this description in the context of teaching strategies, procedures, and curricula, it is helpful to view self-determination as being defined by 12 teaching components (Browder, Wood, Test, Karvonen, & Algozzine, 2001): (1) decision making; (2) choice making; (3) problem solving; (4) independent living; (5) goal setting and attainment; (6) self-observation, evaluation, and reinforcement; (7) self-instruction; (8) self-understanding; (9) self-advocacy and leadership; (10) positive self-efficacy and outcome expectancy; (11) internal locus of control; and (12) self-awareness. More recently, Rowe, Mazotti, and Sinclair (2015) describe how teaching self-determination skills in the general curriculum can be successfully done within the common core and as part of a multi-tiered system of support (MTSS). The MTSS refers to that blend of RtI and PBIS that we previously eluded to in the text.

Consider This

- Because it is desirable and possible to teach self-determination skills in the classroom, what are some ways in which the 12 components might be included directly and indirectly in preK–12 instruction?
- How might the instruction be the same or vary, depending on whether the student has a disability and, if so, the nature and severity of the disability?

PBIS has relevance for all students; it is not used exclusively as an intervention approach for children with challenging behavior or other special needs. Further, PBIS is described as having at its center the mission of improving quality of life. One important component of quality of life (for all people) is the ability and opportunities to develop self-determination. Like most other abilities and skills, self-determination may be taught, learned, and maintained by the extent to which it is rewarding and rewarded. It is, of course, necessary to ask the question: under what circumstances and in what environments are self-determination behaviors valued and rewarded? At the risk of extreme oversimplification, educators are sometimes criticized for attending too much to compliance of students and too little to teaching in ways consistent with students' development of autonomy, independence, and personal responsibility. Further, special educators are sometimes criticized for over-addressing management and control of behavior and under-addressing self-management, self-control, self-rewards, and control of students' own lives (Martin & Marshall, 1996b).

The rationale for teaching self-determination is related to criticisms of public education in the United States and the need to prepare students to be successful in adult life.

The emphasis on self-determination as an important component of curriculum and teaching strategies in special education is relatively recent. IDEA (1997, PL 105–17), the reauthorization in 2004, and the focus therein on the importances of engagement of students in learning, active student involvement, inclusion, and family partnerships have contributed to the development of curricula and strategies. Leaders in research and practice related to self-determination (Wehmeyer, Agran, & Hughes, 2000) concluded that the rationale for teaching self-determination was well established and that it is time to focus on providing educators with methods, materials, and instructional strategies. They emphasized that this need for strategies and resources applies to all students, including those who have severe disabilities. Empirical evidence of the effects of specific strategies and curricula designed to address self-determination has begun to be published in the literature over the past 15 years. For example, in a study (Agran, Blanchard, & Wehmeyer, 2000) designed to test the effects of the Self-Determined Learning Model of Teaching (Mithaug, Wehmeyer, Agran, Martin, & Palmer, 1998)—a model intended to enable teachers to teach goal setting, related actions, and associated adjustments to students with disabilities—the researchers found that 17 of 19 high school students made dramatic gains in their self-determination abilities. Although limited in scope, this study adds to the empirical evidence of the effectiveness of teaching self-determination for students with special needs. Other recent studies have produced similar results, but additional evidence is needed on the impact of self-determination teaching strategies for students in grades K–12, both with and without disabilities, and to students with disabilities in inclusive settings.

Educators recognize that the teaching of self-determination in the classroom is important (Bohannon, Castillo, & Afton, 2015) and that it should be a high priority; educators have been often unaware of the curricular and other resources available to help them incorporate self-determination into classroom instruction (Test, Karvonen, Wood, Browder, & Algozzine, 2000). So resources for understanding self-determination and applying established procedures and curricula are available, but many teachers are unaware of their availability or of how to apply them. You might consider the extent to which self-determination and its component parts are included as a part of your preparation to be an educator, whether at the early childhood, middle school, or high school level. Along these lines, Bohanon and colleagues (2015) advocate an approach to infusing self-determination for students within the common core framework in a schoolwide context. The authors demonstrated the use of RtI (Response-to-Intervention) and SEL (Social and Emotional Learning), also a schoolwide approach to teaching social and emotional skills to students, as mechanisms for infusing the teaching of self-determination skills for students. These two platforms embedded within a schoolwide PBIS (SWPBIS) model served to provide instructional opportunities for a student with challenging behavior in an urban high school.

Often one of the challenges for teachers is understanding how to procure resources for teaching self-determination. Along these lines, Browder and colleagues (2001) suggested that teachers could use a map for locating sources on teaching self-determination. One path of the map might address the conceptual literature and helps teachers understand the concept, its specific components, and the rationale for its inclusion in instruction both as an overriding principle and as specific teaching content. The authors cautioned that there are potential pitfalls in teachers' conceptual understanding of self-determination, including: (a) failing to account for and respect a person's freedom of choice, (b) ignoring cultural values, (c) neglecting collaboration with families, (d) requiring prerequisites for self-determination, and (e) ignoring the social environment of the student (learning to be self-determined means little if the student's environments do not allow and support it). A second path suggested by Browder and colleagues (2001) was the identification of curricular and other resources for teaching. Questions teachers might ask as they pursue this path are: (a) Is the resource supported in research? (b) Can the resource be used in IEP development? (c) Are teaching strategies described? (d) How can I create an environment that promotes self-determination? and (e) Does this resource make me a more self-determined teacher?

Outcomes of Teaching Self-Determination (Outputs, Results)

The third subsystem used to understand the systems approach to self-determination is the output or outcomes subsystem. The intent is that the assessment of the self-determination status of a child, youth, or adult (using, for example, personal appraisal and functional assessment and/or the instruments available) leads to a plan (IFSP, IEP, BSP, transition plan, PCP plan) associated with operationally defined and measurable objectives. The plan leads to the selection and implementation of useful, practical, and measurable methods, procedures, teaching, intervention, and curricula. The process (teaching/intervention) leads to outcomes that lend themselves to measurement in relation to self-determination skills and, more broadly, quality of life. The **outcomes** may be used to sum up (summative evaluation) the extent to which self-determination has been acquired, used, and maintained and to formulate (formative evaluation) new plans, goals, objectives, and activities aimed at improving self-determination skills. When feedback is provided from the evaluation for the purpose of revising plans and actions, the loop of the system is closed.

QUALITY OF LIFE, SELF-DETERMINATION, PBIS, AND CHALLENGING BEHAVIORS

PBIS is used to affect behavior change for students with problematic and challenging behavior. PBIS focuses on assessment of environments and environmental modifications (Horner, 2000) so that students "with problem behaviors experience reductions in their problem behaviors and increased social, personal, and professional quality of their lives" (p. 181). Once again, the connection has been made between PBIS and quality of life. Self-determination is one fundamental component of quality of life. Therefore, supporting children and youth with challenging behavior through applications of PBIS requires attending to self-determination and to the means by which it is assessed and planned for (input), acquired and maintained (process), and evaluated (outcomes). Following are brief examples of how self-determination might be included in interventions for children at various ages and their families.

Infants and Toddlers

Early intervention services for infants and toddlers from birth to 3 years of age who meet states' definitions for eligibility are provided by federal legislation (IDEA, Part C) and through a family-centered approach. Services are based on what is specified in the IFSP, which is intended to include outcomes and associated action steps that are both family focused and child focused; however, the child is always viewed in the context of his or her family. Turnbull (2001) and Smith-Bird and Turnbull (2005) addressed how the early years of a child with disabilities can serve as the launching pad to family quality of life. In other words, the supports, accommodations, and services are provided in accordance with the families' priorities related to the quality of life of all family members. This concept certainly has implications for what is stated in the IFSP and how outcomes and action steps are addressed (see Vignette 12.2).

Vignette 12.2

Bekah

Bekah is a 2½-year-old girl with spina bifida. Bekah is enrolled in a half-day, private, church-based toddler nursery school five mornings per week. The room is a natural environment for a toddler; there are nine other toddlers who are typically developing in the program. Bekah receives early intervention in the context of this environment. Both the early interventionist and physical therapist serve Bekah and her family by consulting with the teacher and doing periodic observations and functional assessments. Bekah's IFSP includes the following outcome statement: "Bekah will share materials and toys with others and maintain her engagement during independent play." Action steps include things that could be done in the nursery school room as well as at home and in other environments. One action step is to provide Bekah with developmentally appropriate toys and materials and to encourage her choosing among them (choice-making skills and decision-making skills). This step might be done as turn taking with another child to whom she would be close to while playing. Another action is to provide toys and materials that require Bekah to find hidden objects or complete steps in a sequence (problem-solving skills). Some of this activity might be done as a shared activity with another child—for example, alternating putting shapes in a shape ball. Bekah might also have an action step that encourages her outcome to state what toys or materials she wants and have the adult confirm by saying, "This is what you asked for" (self-advocacy skills).

Reflective Moment

How are this outcome and the associated action steps for Bekah relevant for the development of self-determination skills? Consider the four characteristics (autonomous functioning, self-regulation, psychological empowerment, and self-realization) introduced earlier in the chapter.

Early Childhood

It has become increasingly recognized that self-determination is an important goal or outcome for all students across the lifespan. With regard to early childhood education we see more attention being given to self-determination and promoting the importance of it in the education of young children. Erwin and colleagues (2009) describe four basic home-based strategies: (1) engagement (supporting prolonged attention to activities and positive interactions with others), (2) choice and decision making (for example, the choice of toys in a play space), (3) control and regulation (for example, creating a personal space for the child), and (4) self-esteem support activities. We suggest that activity-based intervention, or ABI (Johnson, Rahn, & Bricker, 2015), is also an effective approach because it includes the elements of self-determination. ABI emphasizes natural environments, logically occurring antecedents and consequences, child-directedness, child-initiations, and active engagement (see Vignette 12.3).

Vignette 12.3

Theron

Theron is a 5-year-old boy who has a label of pervasive developmental disorder and has associated challenging behaviors. Theron is in an inclusive public preschool for children ages 3 through 5. He will soon be transitioning to a developmental kindergarten. Theron's IEP includes an objective to decrease instances of him hitting other children when he is frustrated or upset. Theron's PBIS plan is activity based—that is, addressing this objective will be undertaken in the context of the typical activities and routines of the classroom.

Reflective Moment

How might Theron be more self-determined related to this objective? One way would be to provide him with a concrete and simple means of keeping track of periods of time or units of activity when he has not hit another child (self-management) and associate the desired behaviors with a reward of his choosing (self-rewarding). With regard to activity-based intervention, this intervention is largely child directed, and Theron is actively engaged in a natural setting. Can you think of other ways that Theron might be self-determined?

Palmer and colleagues (2013) described the Early Childhood Foundations Model for Self-Determination. The model is built on that premise that young children need to support of caring adults in their lives and benefit from these relationships through a partnership and collaboration between classroom and home settings. Their model advocates that self-determination is fostered in young children through allowing for (a) choice-making and problem solving, (b) self-regulation, and (c) engagement. These three focal areas are consistent with the themes throughout the chapter.

Middle School Years

Students in the middle school years find themselves at a challenging point in their development. These years bring with them the desire for students to assert themselves and define their capabilities. Skill development at this stage is critical, especially in the development of social and emotional skills. These skills are vital for promoting self-determination, as illustrated in Vignette 12.4.

Vignette 12.4

Jason

Jason is a 10-year-old student attending Preston Middle School. He is a fifth-grader, and changing classes each period is new for him this year. Jason was recently diagnosed and certified to receive special education under the classification of emotionally disturbed. He is also certified as intellectually gifted. Preston Middle School has a well-established and successful schoolwide behavior support system, and Jason requires support and intervention at the most intensive level of the support system. That is, he needs an individualized, systematic, data-based, and quantifiable intervention. He is included in all classes and does fine in his academic work. Each morning, Jason starts the day by visiting the school counselor's office for a few minutes.

Jason's IEP team includes Jason; his mom, dad, and older sister; his homeroom teacher (math); the special education consulting teacher; and the school counselor. Jason's IEP includes an objective focusing on increasing his interactions with peers. He tends to isolate himself and disconnect from children his age, and he has no friends. To develop the IEP, a functional assessment was conducted along with a personal appraisal approach. The personal appraisal and IEP participation contribute to Jason's self-determination (choice-making and decision-making skills, goal-setting skills, and self-advocacy as well as leadership skills). Jason recognizes, although it is not particularly pleasant for him, that he needs to be more sociable with others his age. One of the interventions used is a systematic analysis of decisions and cost/benefit approach (Doll et al., 1996), in which Jason writes down issues (for example, he doesn't enjoy the usual chatter that goes on across the table in the lunchroom) at the top of a page and then lists possible choices and related benefits and costs of each choice. This approach contributes to the characteristics of self-determination related to internal locus of control, positive attributions of efficacy and outcome expectancy, and self-management. Jason has a student partner in each class who helps by looking at his analysis pages and making comments, with support from the consulting teacher. Jason also shares his papers with the school counselor in the mornings and sometimes at the end of the day. Input and comments from other children and adults help Jason with self-realization, self-awareness, and self-knowledge.

Reflective Moment

This approach to supporting Jason in establishing and maintaining peer relationships is especially designed to fit Jason's needs. It is rather unique and creative compared to typical intervention strategies. What are the elements that might make it work for Jason? What are the possible pitfalls?

High School Years

Students at the secondary-school age level typically are able to apply similar abilities for systematic decision making that are comparable to adults, which is important in planning and implementing self-determination for them. Doll and colleagues (1996) stated that, "because most of the precursors to self-determination are intact in the typical adolescent, the primary emphasis of adult support for students at this level is the provision of frequent and varied opportunities to practice self-determination behaviors" (p. 85). The focus of Vignette 12.5 is Annie, who has Down syndrome resulting in mild to moderate cognitive delays; this reality for typical adolescents also applies to her needs.

Vignette 12.5

Annie

Annie is 19 years old and is a student in the school-to-community transition program at her high school. She has the benefit of both a transition plan and a person-centered plan that are consistent and complementary. Watching movies and listening to music give Annie the greatest sense of joy and fulfillment. She enjoys all types of music, and she sings proudly in her church choir. Annie's plan is that she will soon have a job in the community where she will earn a salary. She wants to live in an apartment with a friend or friends. A great deal of work has been done previously with Annie in her school experience and at home, as well as in her mesosystem—the connections between environments and people important in Annie's life. She is at a point where she is prepared to acquire more advanced self-determination skills.

The plan for Annie is that she will have a supported employment placement at the local bookstore/coffee shop. She will learn on the job, but experiences at school will reinforce the skills she needs at the bookstore. The positive behavior plan for Annie is that she will be supported and provided practice and skill refinement on the job, at school, and at home.

Reflective Moment

Given this brief description of the plan for Annie, how might her experience contribute to her autonomy? Self-regulation? Empowerment? Self-realization? How is the plan for Annie potentially connected to the enhancement of her quality of life?

SUMMARY

PBIS has as a central mission the improvement of the quality of life for children and youth with special needs as well as those who do not have disabilities. Schalock (2000) defined quality of life as "a concept that reflects a person's desired conditions of living related to eight core dimensions of one's life: emotional well-being, interpersonal relationships, material well-being, personal development, physical well-being, self-determination, social inclusion, and rights" (pp. 1–2). We have focused in this chapter on one component of quality of life: self-determination. Although self-determination has been defined in various ways, a consensus definition has emerged (Field et al., 1998) stating that knowledge, skills, and beliefs combine to support persons in being goal directed, self-regulated, and autonomous. Self-determination requires that persons understand their strengths and limitations, along with a belief in their capability. Behaving in self-determined ways allows persons to take control of their lives and to be successful adults.

Various methods have been applied to assess self-determination in children, youth, and adults, including most commonly personal appraisal and functional assessment. Assessment information is used to develop plans, such as the IFSP, the IEP, BSPs, or PCP. Self-determination is frequently not included in planning for students with special needs through the IEP.

Self-determination as a skill, attitude, and belief has relevance for all children and youth, not just students who have disabilities. PBIS and its components, such as self-determination, are seen as initiatives that will facilitate the movement toward inclusion and unified systems reform in education.

With the current status of reforms in education, including unified systems reform and inclusion, self-determination is receiving increased attention as both a specific component of curricula and classroom instruction at all grade levels as well as a broader mission.

In this final chapter, we have used a number of descriptors to help define and describe self-determination as a part of quality of life and therefore an important component of positive behavior supports. Some of those descriptors are self-reliance, self-management, self-control, social validity, empowerment, primary causal agent, choice making, self-regulated, goal directed, autonomous, self-realization, self-advocacy, self-awareness, self-knowledge, and self-rewarding. All of these descriptors are part of an understanding of what composes self-determination. These behaviors, beliefs, and attitudes are acquired over the life span as a result of experiences. They may be systematically planned and assessed, taught, and evaluated.

ACTIVITIES TO EXTEND YOUR LEARNING

1. Find additional definitions of self-determination in the literature, compare them to the five definitions provided in the chapter, and develop your own composite definition.
2. In small groups of three to five participants in class, develop an outline of what you would consider a curriculum for teaching self-determination at the levels of preschool, early childhood years, middle school, and high school.
3. Invite a group of college students with disabilities on your campus to visit your class to share their perspectives on quality of life. Be sure to prepare them by letting them know about the chapter content—in particular, the definition from the Self-Advocates Becoming Empowered organization. You can make this contact through the office for students with disabilities on your campus. You will probably want to meet with them prior to their coming to class to share your goals and what they might expect, as well as how they think you might enhance the activity.
4. In the chapter (under the section on assessing and planning for self-determination), develop a rubric for understanding the features of various instruments, with your professor's assistance and as an entire class activity. In small groups, with each group taking one of the five instruments, use the rubric to gain an understanding of the assessment tool. Then report back to the class as a whole.

FURTHER READING AND EXPLORATION

1. Go to the sources provided for the assessment tools introduced in the chapter and determine to what extent each is curriculum based, what age levels are covered, and for what children and/or youth they are intended.
2. Find journal articles on current movements for school restructuring and reform and accountability; see if you find quality of life and self-determination discussed as important parts of the process. Two good places to start are the journals *Phi Delta Kappan* and *Educational Leadership*.
3. For an early childhood and early childhood special education perspective on challenging behavior, PBS, and self-determination, read the monograph *Young Exceptional Children Monograph Series No. 1*, "Practical Ideas for Addressing Challenging Behaviors," from the DEC of the CEC (Sandall & Ostrosky, 1999). In particular, look for guidance and examples of strategies that in your view reflect self-determination.

4. To better understand the connections between individual quality of life and family quality of life outcomes, take a look at the Beach Center Family Quality of Life Survey (The FQOL) at www.beachcenter.org/resource_library/beach_resource_detail_page.aspx?intResourceID=2391&Type=Tool&JScript=1.

5. To deepen and enrich your understanding of how positive behavior support over the lifespan has a profound impact on lifestyle change, quality of life and human dignity, and how PBS is the "right science," read the personal account provided by Ann Turnbull and Rudd Turnbull (2011) in the *Journal of Positive Behavior Interventions*.

References

CHAPTER 1

Anderson, C. M., & Freeman, K. A. (2000). Positive behavior support: Expanding the application of applied behavior analysis. *The Behavior Analyst, 23,* 85–94.

Anderson, C. M., & Kincaid, D. (2005). Applying behavior analysis to school violence and discipline problems: Schoolwide positive behavior support. *The Behavior Analyst, 28*(1), 49.

Anderson, G. M. (2015). Autism biomarkers: Challenges, pitfalls and possibilities. *Journal of Autism and Developmental Disorders, 45*(4), 1103–1113.

Bandura, A. (1973). *Aggression: A social learning analysis.* Upper Saddle River, NJ: Prentice Hall.

Bandura, A. (1977). *Social learning theory.* Upper Saddle River, NJ: Prentice Hall.

Bandura, A., Ross, D., & Ross, S. A. (1961). Transmission of aggression through imitation of aggressive models. *Journal of Abnormal and Social Psychology, 63,* 575–582.

Barnes, T. N., Smith, S. W., & Miller, M. D. (2014). School-based cognitive-behavioral interventions in the treatment of aggression in the United States: A meta-analysis. *Aggression and Violent Behavior, 19*(4), 311–321.

Bettelheim, B. (1967). *Empty fortress.* New York: Simon and Schuster.

Bijou, S. W. (1963). Theory and research in mental (developmental) retardation. *The Psychological Record, 13,* 95–110.

Bijou, S. W. (1970). What psychology has to offer education now. *Journal of Applied Behavior Analysis, 3,* 65–71.

Bronfenbrenner, U. (1994). Ecological models of human development. In T. Husen & T. N. Postlethwaite (Eds.), *International encyclopedia of education* (2nd ed., vol. 3, pp. 1643–1647). Oxford: Pergamon Press/Elsevier Science.

Charach, A., Yeung, E., Volpe, T., & Goodale, T. (2014). Exploring stimulant treatment in ADHD: narratives of young adolescents and their parents. *BMC Psychiatry, 14*(1), 1.

Cobb, N. J. (2001). *The child: Infants and children.* Mountain View, CA: Mayfield.

Copple, S., & Bredekamp, S. (2009). *Developmentally appropriate practice in early childhood programs serving children birth through age 8.* Washington, DC: NAEYC.

Cortese, S., Holtmann, M., Banaschewski, T., Buitelaar, J., Coghill, D., Danckaerts, M., . . . & Sergeant, J. (2013). Practitioner review: Current best practice in the management of adverse events during treatment with ADHD medications in children and adolescents. *Journal of Child Psychology and Psychiatry, 54*(3), 227–246.

Dunlap, G., Kincaid, D., Horner, R. H., Knoster, T., & Bradshaw, C. P. (2014). A comment on the term "positive behavior support." *Journal of Positive Behavior Interventions, 16*(3), 133–136.

Dunlap, G., & Fox, L. (2011). Function-based interventions for children with challenging behavior. *Journal of Early Intervention, 33,* 333–343.

Dunlap, G., Kern, L., DePerczel, M., Clarke, S., Wilson, D., Childs, K. E., White, R., & Falk, G. D. (1993). Functional analysis of classroom variables for students with emotional and behavioral disorders. *Behavioral Disorders, 18,* 275–291.

Dunlap, G., Kern-Dunlap, L., Clarke, S., & Robbins, F. R. (1991). Functional assessment, curricular revision, and severe behavior problems. *Journal of Applied Behavior Analysis, 24,* 387–397.

Dunlap, G., White, R., Vera, A., Wilson, D., & Panacek, L. (1996). The effects of multi-component, assessment-based curricular modifications on the classroom behavior of children and behavioral disorders. *Journal of Behavioral Education, 6,* 481–500.

DuPaul, G. J., Gormley, M. J., & Laracy, S. D. (2012). Comorbidity of LD and ADHD: Implications of DSM-5 for assessment and treatment. *Journal of Learning Disabilities,* 0022219412464351.

DuPaul, G. J., Weyandt, L. L., & Janusis, G. M. (2011). ADHD in the classroom: Effective intervention strategies. *Theory into Practice, 50,* 35–42.

Dwyer-Moore, K. J., & Dixon, M. R. (2007). Functional analysis and treatment of problem behavior of elderly adults in long-term care. *Journal of Applied Behavior Analysis, 40,* 679–683.

Engelman, K. K., Altus, D. E., & Mathews, R. M. (1999). Increasing engagement in daily activities by older adults with dementia. *Journal of Applied Behavior Analysis, 32,* 107–110.

Erikson, E. (1950). *Childhood and society.* New York: W. W. Norton.

Fabiano, G. A., Pelham, W. E., Coles, E. K., Gnagy, E. M., Chronis-Tuscano, A., & O'Connor, B. C. (2009). A meta-analysis of behavioral treatments for attention-deficit/hyperactivity disorder. *Clinical Psychology Review, 29*(2), 129–140.

Folstein, S., & Rutter, M. (1977). Infantile autism: A genetic study of 21 twin pairs. *Journal of Child psychology and Psychiatry, 18*(4), 297–321.

Freud, S. (1961). *Collected works* (standard ed.). London: Hogarth Press.

Friedman, L. A., & Rapoport, J. L. (2015). Brain development in ADHD. *Current Opinion in Neurobiology, 30,* 106–111.

Fries, D., Carney, K. J., Blackman-Urteaga, L., & Savas, S. A. (2012). Wraparound services infusion into secondary schools as a dropout prevention strategy. *NASSP Bulletin, 96*(2), 119–136.

Gliga, T., Jones, E. J., Bedford, R., Charman, T., & Johnson, M. H. (2014). From early markers to neuro-developmental mechanisms of autism. *Developmental Review, 34*(3), 189–207.

Gold, M. (1980). *"Did I say that?"* Champaign, IL: Research Press.

Greydanus, D. E. (2015). Stimulant misuse: Strategies to manage a growing problem. (*PDF*). *American College Health Association (Review Article). ACHA Professional Development Program, 20.*

Heard, K., & Watson, T. S. (1999). Reducing wandering by persons with dementia using differential reinforcement. *Journal of Applied Behavior Analysis, 32,* 381–384.

Hobbs, N. (1974). A natural history of an idea: Project Re-ED. In J. M. Kauffman & C. D. Lewis (Eds.), *Teaching children with behavior disorders: Personal perspectives* (pp. 146–163). Columbus, OH: Merrill.

Horner, R. H., & Carr, E. G. (1997). Behavioral support for students with severe disabilities: Functional assessment and comprehensive intervention. *Journal of Special Education, 31,* 84–104.

Horner, R. H., Dunlap, G., Koegal, R. I., Carr, E. G., Sailor, W., Anderson, J. . . . O'Neill, R. E. (1990). Toward a technology of "nonaversive" behavioral support. *Journal of the Association for Persons with Severe Handicaps, 15,* 125–132.

Horner, R. H., & Sugai, G. (2000). School-wide behavior support: An emerging initiative. *Journal of Positive Behavior Interventions, 2,* 231–232.

Horner, R. H., & Sugai, G. (2015). School-wide PBIS: An example of applied behavior analysis implemented at a scale of social importance. *Behavior Analysis in Practice, 8*(1), 80–85.

IDEA Amendments of 1997, Public Law 105–17. ERIC Document Reproduction Service.

Juul, K. D. (1977). Models of remediation for behavior disordered children. *Educational and Psychological Interactions* (Rep. No. 62). Malmo, Sweden: School of Education.

Kanner, L. (1943). Autistic disturbances of affective contact. *Nervous Child, 2*(3), 217–250.

Kazdin, A. E. (2012). *Behavior modification in applied settings* (7th ed.). Long Grove, IL: Waveland Press.

Kern, L., Childs, K. E., Dunlap, G., Clarke, S., & Falk, G. D. (1994). Using assessment-based curricular intervention to improve the classroom behavior of a student with emotional and behavioral challenges. *Journal of Applied Behavior Analysis, 27,* 7–19.

Koegel, L. K., Koegel, R. L., & Dunlap, G. (1996). *Positive behavioral support: Including people with difficult behavior in the community.* Baltimore: Brookes.

Lovaas, I. (1993). The development of a treatment-research project for developmentally disabled and autistic children. *Journal of Applied Behavior Analysis, 26,* 617–630.

Martin, G., & Pear, J. (2014). *Behavior modification—What it is and how to do it* (10th ed.). Upper Saddle River, NJ: Merrill/Pearson Education.

Martorell, G., Papalia, D., & Feldman, R. (2013). *A child's world: Infancy through adolescence* (13th ed.). Boston: McGraw-Hill.

McEachin, J. J., Smith, T., & Lovaas, I. (1993). Long-term outcome for children with autism who received early intensive behavioral treatment. *American Journal on Mental Retardation, 97,* 359–372.

Miller, M., Miller, S. R., Wheeler, J. J., & Selinger, J. (1989). Can a single-classroom treatment approach change academic performance and behavioral characteristics in severely behaviorally disordered adolescents: An experimental inquiry. *Behavioral Disorders, 14,* 215–225.

Odom, S. L. (2016). The role of theory in early childhood special education and early intervention. In *Handbook of early childhood special education* (pp. 21–36). Springer International Publishing.

Pavlov, I. P. (1927). *Conditioned reflexes: An investigation of the physiological activity of the cerebral cortex* (W. H. Grant, Trans.). London: Oxford University Press.

Poppen, R. (1988). *Behavioral relaxation training and assessment.* New York: Pergamon Press.

Ratajczak, H. V. (2011). Theoretical aspects of autism: biomarkers—A review. *Journal of Immunotoxicology, 8,* 80–94.

Reid, D. H., Phillips, J. F., & Green, C. W. (1991). Teaching persons with profound multiple handicaps: A review of the effects of behavioral research. *Journal of Applied Behavior Analysis, 24,* 319–336.

Richey, D. D., & Wheeler, J. J. (2000). *Inclusive early childhood education: Merging positive behavioral supports, activity-based intervention, and developmentally appropriate practice.* Albany: Delmar.

Sadler, C. (2000). Effective behavior support: Implementation at the district level. *Journal of Positive Behavior Interventions, 2,* 241–243.

Scheerenberger, R. C. (1987). *A history of mental retardation: A quarter century of promise.* Baltimore: Brookes.

Skinner, B. F. (1953). *Science and human behavior.* New York: Macmillan.

Skinner, B. F. (1968). *The technology of teaching.* New York: Appleton-Century-Crofts.

Sugai, G., Horner, R. H., Dunlap, G., Heineman, M., Lewis, T. J., Nelson, C. M., Scott, T, Liauopsin, C., Sailor, W., Turnbull, A., Turnbull, H. R., Wickham, D., Wilcox, B., & Ruef, M. (1999). *Positive behavioral interventions and supports under the Individuals with Disabilities Education Act.* Lawrence: University of Kansas, Beach Center on Families and Disability, OSEP Center on Positive Behavioral Interventions and Supports.

Sugai, G., Horner, R. H., & Sprague, J. (1999). Functional-assessment-based behavior support planning: Research to practice research. *Behavioral Disorders, 24,* 253–257.

Sulzer-Azaroff, B., Mayer, G. R., Wallace, M. (2013). *Behavior analysis for lasting change.* (3rd ed.). Cornwall-On-Hudson, NY: Sloan Educational Publishing.

Taylor-Greene, S. J., & Kartub, D. T. (2000). Durable implementation of school-wide behavior support. *Journal of Positive Behavior Interventions, 2,* 233–234.

Tharinger, D. J., & Lambert, N. M. (1990). The contributions of developmental psychology to school psychology. In T. B. Gutkin & C. R. Reynolds (Eds.), *The handbook of school psychology* (2nd ed., pp. 74–103). New York: Wiley.

Thorndike, E. L. (1911). *Animal intelligence: Experimental studies.* New York: Macmillan.

Umbreit, J. (1995). Functional assessment and intervention in a regular classroom setting for the disruptive behavior of a student with attention deficit hyperactivity disorder. *Behavioral Disorders, 20,* 267–278.

Vygotsky, L. S. (1978). *Mind and society: The development of higher psychological processes.* Cambridge, MA: Harvard University Press.

Watson, J. B. (1924). *Behaviorism.* New York: Norton.

Wheeler, J. J., Bates, P., Marshall, K. J., & Miller, S. R. (1988). Teaching appropriate social behaviors to a young man with moderate mental retardation in a supported competitive employment setting. *Education and Training in Mental Retardation, 23,* 105–116.

Wisocki, P. A., & Powers, C. B. (1997). Behavioral treatments for pain experienced by older adults. In D. I. Mostovsky & J. Lomranz (Eds.), *Handbook of pain and aging* (pp. 365–382). New York: Plenum.

Zuvekas, S. H., & Vitiello, B. (2012). Stimulant medication use in children. *American Journal of Psychiatry, 10,* 1176.

CHAPTER 2

Act, E. S. S. (2015). of 2015, Pub. L. No. 114– 95, § 1177. *Stat.*

Anderson, C. M., & Freeman, K. A. (2000). Positive behavior support: Expanding the application of applied behavior analysis. *The Behavior Analyst, 23,* 85–94.

Assistance to States for the Education of Children with Disabilities and the Early Intervention Program for Infants and Toddlers with Disabilities: Final Regulations, 64 Fed. Reg. 12, 406–12, 672 (1999). Washington, DC: Department of Education.

Barr, M. W. (1913). *Mental defectives: Their history, treatment, and training.* Philadelphia: Blakiston.

Bengtson, V. L. (2001). Beyond the nuclear family: The increasing importance of multi-generational bonds. *Journal of Marriage and Family, 63*(1), 1–16.

Blair, K. C., Lee, I., Cho, S., & Dunlap, G. (2010). Positive behavior support through family-school collaboration for young children with autism. *Topics in Early Childhood Special Education, 31*(1), 22–36.

Bricker, D., Pretti-Frontczak, K., & McComas, N. (1998). *An activity-based approach to early intervention.* Baltimore: Brookes.

Brookman-Frazee, L., & Koegel, R. L. (2004). Using parent-clinical partnerships in parent education programs for children with autism. *Journal of Positive Behavior Interventions, 6*(4), 195–213.

Brown v. Board of Education, 347 U.S. 483 (1954).

Buschbacher, P., Fox, L., & Clarke, S. (2004). Recapturing desired family routines: A parent–professional behavioral collaboration. *Research and Practice for Persons with Severe Disabilities, 29*(1), 25–39.

Cancino, A. (2016, February 16). More grandparents raising their grandchildren. *Associated Press.* Retrieved from http://www.pbs.org/newshour/rundown/more-grandparents-raising-their-grandchildren/

Education for All Handicapped Children Act of 1975, 20 U.S.C. § 1401 *et seq.*

Epstein, J. L. (2010). *School/family/community partnerships: Preparing educators and improving schools.* Boulder, CO: Westview Press.

Epstein, J. L., & Sanders, M. G. (2002). Family, school, and community partnerships. In M. H. Bornstein (Ed.), *Handbook of parenting: Vol. 5. Practical issues in parenting* (2nd ed., pp. 407–437), Mahwah, NJ: Lawrence Erlbaum Associates.

Fisher, C. (2000). Ripple or tidal wave: What can make a difference? *Journal of Positive Behavior Interventions, 2*(2), 120–122.

Fuchs, D., Fuchs, L. S., & Stecker, P. M. (2010). The "blurring" of special education in a continuum of general education placements and services. *Exceptional Children, 76*(3), 301–323.

Harry, B. (2008). Collaboration with culturally and linguistically diverse families: Ideal versus reality. *Exceptional Children, 74*(3), 372–388.

Henderson, A. T. (1987). *The evidence continues to grow.* Columbia, MD: National Committee for Citizens in Education.

Henderson, A. T., & Berla, N. (1995). *A new generation of evidence: The family is critical to student achievement.* Washington, DC: Center for Law and Education.

Hunt, J. (Ed.). (1972). *Human intelligence.* New Brunswick, NJ: Transaction Books.

Individuals with Disabilities Education Act (IDEA), 20 U.S.C. § 1400 *et seq.*

Kleinhammer-Tramill, J., & Gallagher, K. (2002). The implications of Goals 2000 for Inclusive Education. In W. Sailor (Ed.), *Whole-school success and inclusive education* (pp. 26–41). New York: Teachers College Press.

Lucyshyn, J. M., Albin, R. W., Horner, R. H., Mann, J. C., Mann, J. A., & Wadsworth, G. (2007). Family implementation of positive behavior support for a child with autism: Longitudinal, single-case, experimental and descriptive replication and extension. *Journal of Positive Behavior Interventions, 9*(3), 131–150.

Lucyshyn, J. M., Blumberg, E. R., & Kayser, A. T. (2000). Improving the quality of support to families of children with severe behavior problems in the first decade of the new millennium. *Journal of Positive Behavior Interventions, 2*(2), 113–115.

Martin, G., & Pear, J. J. (2015). *Behavior modification: What it is and how to do it* (10th ed.). Psychology Press.

McLaughlin, M. L. (1998). *Special education in an era of school reform: An overview.* Washington, DC: Federal Resource Center, Academy for Educational Development.

McWayne, C. M., Melzi, G., Schick, A. R., Kennedy, J. L., & Mundt, K. (2013). Defining family engagement among Latino Head Start parents: A mixed-methods measurement development study. *Early Childhood Research Quarterly, 28*(3), 593–607.

McWilliam, R. A. (2009). *Family-centered intervention planning: A routines-based approach.* Chattanooga, TN: Siskin Children's Institute.

Meadan, H., Halle, J. W., & Ebata, A. T. (2010). Families with children who have autism spectrum disorders: Stress and support. *Exceptional Children, 77*(1), 7–36.

Mills v. Board of Education of the District of Columbia, 348 F. Supp. 866 (D.D.C. 1972).

National PTA. (December, 2016). *National standards for parent/family involvement programs*. Retrieved from: http://www.pta.org/nationalstandards

No Child Left Behind Act of 2001, Pub. L. No. 107–110, 115 Stat. 1425 (2002).

Pennsylvania Association for Retarded Citizens (PARC) v. Commonwealth of Pennsylvania, 343 F. Supp. 279 (E.D. Pa. 1972).

Richey, D. D., & Wheeler, J. J. (2000). *Inclusive early childhood education: Merging positive behavioral supports, activity-based intervention and developmentally appropriate practice*. Albany: Delmar/Thomson Learning.

Safer, N. D., & Hamilton, J. L. (1993). Legislative context for early intervention services. In W. Brown, S. K. Thurman, & L. F. Pearl (Eds.), *Family-centered early intervention with infants and toddlers: Innovative cross-disciplinary approaches* (pp. 1–17). Baltimore: Brookes.

Silverstein, R. (1989). A window of opportunity: P.L. 99–457. In *The intent and spirit of P.L. 99–457: A sourcebook* (pp. A1–A7). Washington, DC: National Center for Clinical Infant Programs.

Steiner, A. M. (2011). A strength-based approach to parent education for children with autism. *Journal of Positive Behavior Interventions, 13*(3), 178–190.

Stichter, J. P., & Caldicott, J. M. (1999). Families, school collaboration, and shared vision in the context of IDEA. *Journal of Positive Behavior Interventions, 1,* 252–255.

Sugai, G., Horner, R. H., Dunlap, G., Hieneman, M., Lewis, T. J., Nelson, C. M., . . . Wilcox, B. (2000). Applying positive behavior support and functional behavioral assessment in schools. *Journal of Positive Behavior Interventions, 2*(3), 131–143.

Summers, J. A., Hoffman, L., Marquis, J., Turnbull, A., Poston, D., & Nelson, L. L. (2005). Measuring the quality of family–professional partnerships in special education services. *Exceptional Children, 72*(1), 65–81.

Turnbull, A. P., Turnbull, H. R., Erwin, E. J., Soodak, L. C., & Shogren, K. A. (2015). *Families, professionals, and exceptionality: Positive outcomes through partnerships and trust* (7th ed.). Upper Saddle River, NJ: Pearson Education.

U.S. Census Bureau. (2016). 2016 Current Population Survey Annual Social and Economic Supplement. Release Number: 16–192. Washington, DC.

U.S. Department of Education. (n.d.). *Choices for parents*. Retrieved March 3, 2012, from http://www2ed.gov/nclb/choice

Vaughn, B. J., White, R. Johnston, S., & Dunlap, G. (2005). Positive behavior support as a family-centered endeavor. *Journal of Positive Behavior Interventions, 7*(1), 55–58.

Wang, M., McCart, A. & Turnbull, A. P. (2007). Implementing positive behavior support with Chinese American families: Enhancing cultural competence. *Journal of Positive Behavior Interventions, 9*(1), 38–51.

Wehmeyer, M. L., Martin, J. E., & Sands, D. J. (1998). Self-determination for children and youth with developmental disabilities. In A. Hilton & R. Ringlaben (Eds.), *Best and promising practices in developmental disabilities* (pp. 191–204). Austin, TX: PRO-ED.

Yell, M. L. (2015). *The law and special education* (4th ed.). Columbus, OH: Pearson.

CHAPTER 3

Association for Positive Behavior Support. (2008). *APBS standards of practice*. Retrieved May 17, 2017, from http://www.apbs.org/standards_of_practice.html

Behavior Analysis Certification Board. (2017). *Professional and ethical compliance code for behavior analysts*. Retrieved May 17, 2017.

Council for Exceptional Children. (n.d.). *Ethical Principles and Practice Standards*. Retrieved April 15, 2017, from http://www.cec.sped.org/Standards/Ethical-Principles-and-Practice-Standards

Division for Early Childhood. (2007, August). *DEC concept paper on the identification of and intervention with challenging behavior*. Retrieved May 17, 2017, from http://www.dec-sped.org/position-statements

Garfinkel, I., Hochschild, J. L., & McLanahan, S. S. (Eds.). (2001). *Social policies for children*. Brookings Institution Press.

Houten, R., Axelrod, S., Bailey, J. S., Favell, J. E., Foxx, R. M., Iwata, B. A., & Lovaas, O. I. (1988). The right to effective behavioral treatment. *Journal of Applied Behavior Analysis, 21*(4), 381–384.

Learning First Alliance. *Every child learning: Safe and supportive schools*. Retrieved April 11, 2017, from https://learningfirst.org/issues/safeschools

Lewis, R. B., Wheeler, J. J., & Carter, S. L. (2017). *Teaching students with special needs in general education classrooms*. Columbus, OH: Pearson.

National Association of the Education of Young Children. (2011). NAEYC Code of Ethical Conduct. Washington, DC: Author.

National Association for the Education of Young Children. (2017). *Code of ethical conduct and statement of commitment*. Retrieved April 11, 2017, from http://www.naeyc.org/files/naeyc/image/public_policy/Ethics%20Position%20Statement2011_09202013update.pdf

National Association for the Education of Young Children. (2017). National standards for early childhood preparation. Retrieved April 11, 2017, from http://www.naeyc.org/caep/standards

National Education Association. (2017). *Code of ethics of the education profession*. Retrieved April 11, 2017, from http://www.nea.org

Schalock, R. L. (2000). Three decades of quality of life. In M. I. Wehmeyer & J. R. Patton (Eds.), *Mental retardation in the 21st century* (pp. 116–127). Austin, TX: PRO-ED.

Sugai, G., Horner, R. H., Dunlap, G., Hieneman, M., Lewis, T. J., Nelson, C. M., . . . Ruef, M. (2000). Applying positive behavior support and functional behavioral assessment in schools. *Journal of Positive Behavior Interventions, 2*(3), 131–143.

Sulzer-Azaroff, B., & Mayer, G. R. (1991). *Behavior analysis for lasting change*. Orlando: Harcourt Brace Jovanovich.

Turnbull, A. P., Turnbull, H. R., Erwin, E. J., Soodak, L. C., & Shogren, K. A. (2015). *Families, professionals, and exceptionality: Positive outcomes through partnerships and trust* (7th ed.). Upper Saddle River, NJ: Pearson Education.

CHAPTER 4

Berkeley, S., Bender, W. N., Peaster, L. G., & Saunders, L. (2009). Implementation of response to intervention. *Journal of Learning Disabilities, 42,* 85–95.

Bijou, S. W. (1970). What psychology has to offer education—now. *Journal of Applied Behavior Analysis, 3,* 65–71.

Carr, E. G. (1994). Emerging themes in the functional analysis of problem behavior. *Journal of Applied Behavior Analysis, 27,* 393–399.

Childs, K. E., Kincaid, D., George, H. P., & Gage, N. A. (2016). The relationship between school-wide implementation of positive behavior intervention and supports and student discipline outcomes. *Journal of Positive Behavior Interventions, 18*(2), 89–99.

Conroy, M. A., & Stichter, J. P. (2003). The application of antecedents in the functional assessment process. *The Journal of Special Education, 37,* 15–25.

Crosland, K., & Dunlap, G. (2012). Effective strategies for the inclusion of children with autism in general education classrooms. *Behavior Modification, 36,* 251–269.

Cummings, K. D., Atkins, T., Allison, R., & Cole, C. (2008). Response to Intervention: Investigating the new role of special educators. *Teaching Exceptional Children, 40,* 24–31.

Dunlap, G., & Kern, L. (1996). Modifying instructional activities to promote desirable behavior: A conceptual and practical framework. *School Psychology Quarterly, 11*(4), 297.

Dunlap, G., Kern-Dunlap, L., Clarke, S., & Robbins, F. R. (1991). Functional assessment, curricular revision, and severe behavior problems. *Journal of Applied Behavior Analysis, 24,* 387–397.

Durand, V. M. (1990). *Severe behavior problems.* New York: Guilford.

Durand, V. M., & Crimmins, D. B. (1988). Identifying the variables maintaining self-injurious behavior. *Journal of Autism and Developmental Disabilities, 18,* 99–117.

Horner, R. H., & Carr, E. G. (1997). Behavioral support for students with severe disabilities: Functional assessment and comprehensive intervention. *Journal of Special Education, 31,* 84–104.

Individuals with Disabilities Education Improvement Act of 2004, P.L. 108–466.

Jolivette, K., Scott, T. M., & Nelson, C. M. (2000). *The link between functional behavioral assessments and behavioral intervention plans.* Arlington, VA: ERIC Clearinghouse on Disabilities and Gifted Education (ERIC Document Reproduction Service No. E592).

Kern, L., & Dunlap, G. (1998). Curricular modifications to promote desirable classroom behavior. In J. K. Luiselli & M. J. Cameron (Eds.), *Antecedent control: Innovative approaches to behavioral support* (pp. 289–307). Baltimore: Brookes.

Lewis, R. B., Wheeler, J. J., & Carter, S. L. (2017). *Teaching students with special needs in general education classrooms* (9th ed.). Columbus: OH, Pearson.

Lord, C., & Schopler, E. (1994). TEACCH services for preschool children. In S. L. Harris & J. S. Handleman (Eds.), *Preschool education programs for children with autism* (pp. 87–106). Austin, TX: PRO-ED.

Mager, R. F., & Pipe, P. (1997). *Analyzing performance problems* (3rd ed.). Atlanta: Center for Effective Performance.

Massey, N. G., & Wheeler, J. J. (2000). Acquisition and generalization of activity schedules and their effects on task engagement in a young child with autism in an inclusive preschool classroom. *Education and Training in Mental Retardation and Developmental Disabilities, 35,* 326–335.

Mesibov, G. B., Browder, D. M., & Kirkland, C. (2002). Using individualized schedules as a component of positive behavioral support for students with developmental disabilities. *Journal of Positive Behavior Interventions, 4,* 73–79.

Mesibov, G. B., & Shea, V. (2010). The TEACCH program in the area of evidence-based practice. *Journal of Autism and Developmental Disorders, 40,* 570–579.

Miltenberger, R. G. (2015). *Behavior modification: Principles and procedures* (6th ed.). Belmont, CA: Wadsworth.

Miltenberger, R. G., Rapp, J. T., & Long, E. S. (1999). A low-tech method for conducting real-time recording. *Journal of Applied Behavior Analysis, 52,* 119–120.

No Child Left Behind Act of 2001, P.L. 107–110.

O'Neill, R. E., Horner, R. H., Albin, R. W., Sprague, J. R., Storey, K., & Newton, J. S. (1997). *Functional assessment and program development for problem behavior: A practical handbook.* Pacific Grove, CA: Brooks/Cole.

Schalock, R. L. (2000). Three decades of quality of life. In M. I. Wehmeyer & J. R. Patton (Eds.), *Mental retardation in the 21st century* (pp. 116–127). Austin, TX: PRO-ED.

Stichter, J. P., Lewis, T. J., Johnson, N., & Trossell, R. (2004). Toward a structural assessment: Analyzing the merits of an assessment tool for a student with E/BD. *Assessment for Effective Intervention, 30,* 25–40.

Stichter, J. P., Sasso, G. M., & Jolivette, K. (2004). Structural analysis and intervention in a school setting. *Journal of Positive Behavior Interventions, 6,* 166–177.

Sugai, G., Horner, R. H., Dunlap, G., Hieneman, M., Leis, T. J., Nelson, C. M., Scott, T., Liauopsin, C., Sailor, W., Turnbull, A., Turnbull, H. R., Wickham, D., Wilcox, B., & Ruef, M. (2000). Applying positive behavioral support and functional behavioral assessment in schools. *Journal of Positive Behavior Interventions, 2,* 131–143.

Touchette, P. E., MacDonald, R. F., & Langer, S. M. (1985). A scatter-plot for identifying stimulus control of problem behaviors. *Journal of Applied Behavior Analysis, 18,* 343–351.

Wacker, D. P., Cooper, L. J., Peck, S. M., Derby, M. K., & Berg, W. K. (1999). Community-based functional assessment. In A. C. Repp & R. H. Horner (Eds.), *Functional analysis of problematic behavior* (pp. 32–56). Belmont, CA: Wadsworth.

Wehby, H. H., & Hollahan, M. S. (2000). Effects of high probability requesting on the latency to initiate academic requests. *Journal of Applied Behavior Analysis, 77,* 259–262.

Wheeler, J. J., Carter, S. L., Mayton, M. R., & Thomas, R. A. (2002). Structural analysis of instructional variables and their effects on task engagement and self-aggression. *Education and Training in Mental Retardation, 37,* 391–398.

CHAPTER 5

Algozzine, B., Horner, R. H., Sugai, G., Barrett, S., Dickey, S. R., Eber, L., Kincaid, D., Lewis, Y., & Tobin, T. (2010). *Evaluation blueprint for school-wide positive behavior support.* Eugene, OR: National Technical Assistance Center on Positive Behavior Interventions and Support. Retrieved from http://www.pbis.org

Asmus, J. M., Vollmer, T. R., & Borrero, J. C. (2002). Functional behavioral assessment: A school based model. *Education and Treatment of Children, 25,* 67–90.

Bailey, J. S., & Burch, M. R. (2002). *Research methods in applied behavior analysis.* Thousand Oaks, CA: Sage.

Bambara, L. M., & Knoster, T. (1998). Designing positive behavior support plans. In *Innovations* (Vol. 13). Washington, DC: American Association on Mental Retardation.

Beavers, G. A., Iwata, B. A., & Lerman, D. C. (2013). Thirty years of research on the functional analysis of problem behavior. *Journal of Applied Behavior Analysis, 46*(1), 1–21.

Bruni, T. P., Drevon, D., Hixson, M., Wyse, R., Corcoran, S., & Fursa, S. (2017). The effect of functional behavior assessment on school-based interventions: A meta-analysis of single case research. *Psychology in the Schools, 54*(4), 351–369.

Carr, E. G. (1977). The motivation of self-injurious behavior: A review of some hypotheses. *Psychological Bulletin, 84,* 800–816.

Carr, E. G., & Durand, V. M. (1985). Reducing behavior problems through functional communication training. *Journal of Applied Behavior Analysis, 18,* 11–126.

Carr, E. G., Langdon, N. A., & Yarbrough, S. C. (1999). Hypothesis-based intervention for severe problem behavior. In A. C. Repp & R. H. Horner (Eds.), *Functional analysis of problem behavior* (pp. 9–31). Belmont, CA: Wadsworth.

Carr, E. G., & Newsom, C. D. (1985). Demand-related tantrums: Conceptualization and treatment. *Behavior Modification, 9,* 403–426.

Chandler, L. K., & Dahlquist, C. M. (2002). *Functional assessment: Strategies to prevent and remediate challenging behavior in school settings.* Upper Saddle River, NJ: Merrill/Pearson Education.

Conroy, M., Fox, J., Crain, J., Jenkins, A., & Belcher, K. (1996). Evaluating the social and ecological validity of analog assessment procedures for challenging behaviors in young children. *Education and Treatment of Children, 19*(3), 233–256.

Demchak, M. A., & Bossert, K. W. (1996). Assessing problem behaviors. In *Innovations* (Vol. 4). Washington, DC: American Association on Mental Retardation.

Dunlap, G., & Fox, L. (2011). Function-based interventions for children with challenging behavior. *Journal of Early Intervention, 33,* 333–343.

Dunlap, G., Kern, L., dePercezel, M., Clark, S., Wilson, D., Childes, K. E., White, R., & Falk, G. D. (1993). Functional analysis of classroom variables for students with emotional and behavioral disorders. *Behavioral Disorders, 18,* 275–291.

Dunlap, G., & Kinkaid, D. (2001). The widening world of functional assessment comments on four manuals and beyond. *Journal of Applied Behavior Analysis, 34,* 365–377.

Durand, V. M. (1990). *Severe behavior problems: A functional communication training approach.* New York: Guilford.

Horner, R. H. (1999). Positive behavior supports. In M. Wehmeyer & J. Patton (Eds.), *Mental retardation in the 21st century* (pp. 181–196). Austin, TX: PRO-ED.

Horner, R. H. (2007, February 6). *School-wide positive behavior support.* Retrieved May 9, 2008, from http://www.pbis.org/pastconferencepresentations.htm

Horner, R. F., & Sugai, G. (2015). School-wide PBIS: An example of applied behavior analysis. Implemented at a scale of social importance. *Behavior Analysis in Practice, 8,* 80–85. doi: 10.1007/s40617-015-0045-4

Individuals with Disabilities Education Act. 20 U.S.C. § 1401 *et seq.* National Association of State Directors of Special Education. (1997). IDEA information: A reauthorized IDEA is enacted: Comparison of previous law and Pub. L. No. 105–17 (1997 Amendments). Unpublished document.

Iwata, B. A. (1994). Functional analysis methodology: Some closing comments. *Journal of Applied Behavior Analysis, 27,* 413–418.

Iwata, B., Dorsey, M., Slifer, K., Bauman, K., & Richman, G. (1982). Toward a functional analysis of self-injury. *Analysis and Intervention in Developmental Disabilities, 6,* 1–4.

Kern, L., Dunlap, G., Clarke, S., & Childs, K. E. (1994). Student assisted functional assessment interview. *Diagnostique, 19,* 29–39.

Kincaid, D., Childs, K., Blasé, K. A., & Wallace, F. (2007). Identifying barriers and facilitators in implementing school-wide positive behavior support. *Journal of Positive Behavior Interventions, 9,* 174–184.

O'Neill, R. E., Albin, R. W., Storey, K., Horner, R. H., Sprague, J. R., & Storey, K. (2015). *Functional assessment and program development for problem behavior: A practical handbook* (3rd ed.) Stamford, CT: Cengage Learning.

O'Reilly, M. F. (1997). Functional analysis of episodic self-injury correlated with recurrent otitis media. *Journal of Applied Behavior Analysis, 30,* 165–168.

Peck Peterson, S. M., Derby, M. K., Berg, W. K., & Horner, R. H. (2002). Collaboration with families in the functional behavior assessment of an intervention for severe behavior problems. *Education and Treatment of Children, 25*(1), 5–25.

Sidman, M. (1960). *Tactics of scientific research.* New York: Basic Books.

Skinner, B. F. (1974). *About behaviorism.* New York: Knopf.

Strickland-Cohen, M. K., Kennedy, P. C., Berg, T. A., Bateman, L. J., & Horner, R. H. (2016). Building school district capacity to conduct functional behavioral assessment. *Journal of Emotional and Behavioral Disorders*, *24*(4), 235–246.

Sugai, G., Horner, R. H., Dunlap, G., Hieneman, M., Lewis, T. J., Nelson, C. M., Scott, T., Liaupsin, C., Sailor, W., Turnbull, A. P., Turnbull, H. R., Wickham, D., Ruef, D., & Wilcox, B. (2000). Applying positive behavior support and functional behavior assessment in schools. *Journal of Positive Behavior Interventions*, *2,* 131–143.

Touchette, P. E., MacDonald, R. F., & Langer, S. M. (1985). A scatter plot for identifying stimulus control of problem behaviors. *Journal of Applied Behavior Analysis*, *18,* 343–351.

Ulman, J. D., & Sulzer-Azaroff, B. (1975). Multi-element baseline design in educational research. In E. Ramp & G. Semb (Eds.), *Behavior analysis areas of research and application* (pp. 377–391). Upper Saddle River, NJ: Prentice Hall.

U.S. Department of Education Office of Special Education and Rehabilitative Services. (1999). *Applying positive behavioral support and functional behavior assessment in schools* (OSEP Center on Positive Behavioral Interventions and Supports Publication Technical Assistance Guide #1). Washington, DC: Author.

Wacker, D. P., Cooper, L. J., Peck, S. M., Derby, K. M., & Berg, W. (1999). Community-based functional assessment. In A. C. Repp & R. H. Horner (Eds.), *Functional analysis of problem behavior* (pp. 32–56). Belmont, CA: Wadsworth.

Weber, K. P., Killu, K., Derby, K. M., & Barretto, A. (2005). The status of functional behavioral assessment (FBA): Adherence to standard practice in FBA methodology. *Psychology in the Schools*, *42*(7), 737–744.

Yell, M. L., Shriner, J. G., & Katsiyannis, A. (2006). Individuals with Disabilities Education Improvement Act of 2004 and IDEA regulations of 2006: Implications for educators, administrators, and teacher trainers. *Focus on Exceptional Children*, *39,* 1–24.

CHAPTER 6

Alberto, P. A., & Troutman, A. C. (2012). *Applied behavior analysis for teachers* (9th ed.). Upper Saddle River, NJ: Pearson Education.

Ayllon, T., & Azrin, N. H. (1968). Reinforcer sampling: A technique for increasing the behavior of mental patients. *Journal of Applied Behavior Analysis*, *1,* 13–20.

Baer, D. M., Wolf, M. M., & Risely, T. R. (1968). Some current dimensions of applied behavior analysis. *Journal of Applied Behavior Analysis*, *1,* 91–97.

Bailey, J. S., & Burch, M. R. (2002). *Research methods in applied behavior analysis*. Thousand Oaks, CA: Sage.

Barlow, D. H., & Hersen, M. (1984). *Single case experimental designs: Strategies for studying behavior change* (2nd ed.). New York: Pergamon Press.

Bijou, S. W. (1970). What psychology has to offer education now. *Journal of Applied Behavior Analysis*, *3,* 65–71.

Bolt, D. M., Ysseldyke, J., & Patterson, M. J. (2010). Students, teachers, and schools as sources of variability, integrity, and sustainability in implementing progress monitoring. *School Psychology Review*, *39,* 612–630.

Brooks, A., Todd, A. W., Tofflemeyer, S., & Horner, R. H. (2003). Use of functional assessment and a self-management system to increase academic engagement and work completion. *Journal of Positive Behavior Interventions*, *5,* 144–152.

Carnine, D. (1997). Bridging the research-to-practice gap. *Exceptional Children*, *63,* 513–521.

Carnine, D. (1999). Perspective: Campaigns for moving research into practice. *Remedial and Special Education, 20,* 2–6.

Carr, E. G., & Durand, V. M. (1985). Reducing behavior problems through functional communication training. *Journal of Applied Behavior Analysis, 18,* 111–126.

Carter, S. L. (2009). *The social validity manual: A guide to subjective evaluation of behavior interventions.* London: Elsevier.

Cooper, J. O., Heron, T. E., & Heward, W. L. (2007). *Applied behavior analysis* (2nd ed.). Upper Saddle River, NJ: Merrill/Pearson Education.

Gersten, R., Fuchs, L. S., Compton, D., Coyne, M., Greenwood, C., & Innocenti, M. S. (2005). Quality indicators for group experimental and quasi-experimental research in special education. *Exceptional Children, 71,* 149–164.

Gersten, R., & Smith-Jones, J. (2001). Reflections on the research to practice gap. *Teacher Education and Special Education, 24,* 356–361.

Gettinger, M. (1993). Effects of invented spelling and direct instruction on spelling performance of second-grade boys. *Journal of Applied Behavior Analysis, 26,* 281–291.

Grad, R., Macaulay, A. C., & Warner, M. (2001). Teaching evidence-based medical care: Description and evaluation. *Family Medicine, 33,* 602–606.

Green, M. L. (2001). Evidence-based medicine training in graduate medical education: Past, present, and future. *Journal of Evaluation in Clinical Practice, 6,* 121–138.

Guyatt, G. H., O'Meade, M., Jaeschke, R. Z., Cook, D. J., & Haynes, R. B. (2000). Practitioners of evidence-based care. *British Medical Journal, 320,* 954–955.

Hall, R. V., Panyan, M., Rabon, D., & Broden, M. (1968). Instructing beginning teachers in reinforcement procedures which improve classroom control. *Journal of Applied Behavior Analysis, 1,* 315–322.

Horner, R. H., Carr, E. G., Halle, J., McGee, G., Odom, S., & Wolery, M. (2005). The use of single-subject research to identify evidence-based practice in special education. *Exceptional Children, 71,* 165–179.

Johnston, J. M., & Pennypacker, H. S. (1993). *Strategies and tactics of behavioral research* (2nd ed.). Hillsdale, NJ: Lawrence Erlbaum.

Kazdin, A. E. (1982). *Single-case research designs: Methods for clinical and applied settings.* New York: Oxford University Press.

Kortekaas, M. F., Bartelink, M. E. L., Zuithoff, N. P. A., Van der Heijden, G. J. M. G., De Wit, N. J., & Hoes, A. W. (2016). Does integrated training in evidence-based medicine (EBM) in the general practice (GP) specialty training improve EBM behaviour in daily clinical practice? A cluster ran domised controlled trial. *BMJ Open, 6*(9), e010537.

Lewis, R. B., Wheeler, J. J., & Carter, S. L. (2017). *Teaching students with special needs in general education classrooms.* Boston: Pearson.

Lowe, M. L., & Cuvo, A. J. (1976). Teaching coin summation to the mentally retarded. *Journal of Applied Behavior Analysis, 9,* 483–489.

Massey, N. G., & Wheeler, J. J. (2000). Acquisition and generalization of activity schedules and their effects on task engagement in a young child with autism in an inclusive preschool classroom. *Education and Training in Mental Retardation and Developmental Disabilities, 35,* 326–335.

Odom, S. L., Brantlinger, E., Gersten, R., Horner, R. H., Thompson, B., & Harris, K. R. (2005). Research in special education: Scientific methods and evidence-based practices. *Exceptional Children, 71,* 137–148.

Poche, C., McCubbrey, H., & Munn, T. (1982). The development of correct toothbrushing technique in preschool children. *Journal of Applied Behavior Analysis, 15,* 315–320.

Richards, S. B., Taylor, R. L., Ramasamy, R., & Richards, R. (1999). *Single subject research: Applications in educational and clinical settings.* San Diego: Singular.

Sansoti, F. J., & Powell-Smith, K. A. (2008). Using computer-presented social stories and video models to increase the social communication skills children with high-functioning autism spectrum disorders. *Journal of Positive Behavior Interventions, 10,* 162–178.

Schepis, M. M., Reid, D. H., Behrmann, M. M., & Sutton, K. A. (1998). Increasing communicative interactions of young children with autism using a voice output communication aid and naturalistic teaching. *Journal of Applied Behavior Analysis, 31,* 561–578.

Schreibman, L., Whalen, C., & Stahmer, A. C. (2000). The use of video priming to reduce disruptive transition behavior in children with autism. *Journal of Positive Behavior Interventions, 2,* 3–11.

Sidman, M. (1960). *Tactics of scientific research.* New York: Basic Books.

Simonsen, B., Shaw, S. F., Luby, M. F., Sugai, G., Coyne, M. D., Rhein, B., . . . Alfana, M. (2010). A schoolwide model for service delivery: Redefining special educators as interventionists. *Remedial and Special Education, 31,* 17–23.

Sulzer-Azaroff, B., & Mayer, R.G. (1991). *Behavior analysis for lasting change.* Fort Worth, TX: Harcourt Brace.

Ulman, J. D., & Sulzer-Azaroff, B. (1975). Multielement baseline design in educational research. In E. Ramp & G. Semb (Eds.), *Behavior analysis: Areas of research and application* (pp. 377–391). Upper Saddle River, NJ: Prentice Hall.

Zirpoli, T. J. (2015). *Behavior management: Positive applications for teachers* (7th ed.). Upper Saddle River, NJ: Merrill/Pearson Education.

CHAPTER 7

Anderson, J. L., Russo, A., Dunlap, G., & Albin, R. W. (1996). A team training model for building the capacity to provide positive behavioral supports in inclusive settings. In L. K. Koegel, R. L. Koegel, & G. Dunlap (Eds.), *Positive behavioral support: Including people with difficult behavior in the community* (pp. 467–490). Baltimore: Brookes.

Carr, E. G., Horner, R. H., Turnbull, A. P., Marquis, J. G., Magito-McLaughlin, D., McAtee, M. L., . . . Doolabh, A. (1999). *Positive behavior support as an approach for dealing with problem behavior in people with developmental disabilities: A research synthesis.* Washington, DC: American Association on Mental Retardation Monograph Series.

Dunlap, G., Iovannone, R., Kincaid, D., Wilson, K., Christiansen, K., Strain, P., & English, C. (2010). *Prevent-teach-reinforce: The school-based model of individualized positive behavior support.* Baltimore: Brookes Publishing Company.

Dunlap, G., Iovannone, R., Wilson, K. J., Kincaid, D. K., & Strain, P. (2010). Prevent-teach-reinforce: A standardized model of school-based behavioral intervention. *Journal of Positive Behavior Interventions, 12*(1), 9–22.

Forest, M., & Lusthaus, E. (1990). Everyone belongs with the MAPS action planning system. *Teaching Exceptional Children, 2*(22), 32–35.

Fox, L., & Little, N. (2001). Starting early: Developing school-wide behavior support in a community preschool. *Journal of Positive Behavior Interventions, 3,* 251–254.

Horner, R. H., & Sugai, G. (2000). School-wide behavior support: An emerging initiative. *Journal of Positive Behavior Interventions, 2,* 231–232.

Individuals with Disabilities Education Act, PL 94–142, 20 U.S.C. § 1400 *et. seq.* (1975).

Individuals with Disabilities Education Act (IDEA) Amendments of 1997, PL 105–17, 20 U.S.C. § 1400 *et. seq.*

Jackson, L., & Veeneman-Panyan, M. (2002). *Positive behavioral support in the classroom: Principles and practices*. Baltimore: Brookes.

Janney, R., & Snell, M. E. (2000). *Behavioral support: Teachers' guide to inclusive practices*. Baltimore: Brookes.

National Center on Education, Disability and Juvenile Justice. (n.d.). *Levels of prevention*. Retrieved January 11, 2012, from http://www.edjj.org/prevention/LevelsPrevention.html

Neilsen, S. L., & McEvoy, M. A. (2004). Functional behavioral assessment in early childhood settings. *Journal of Early Intervention, 26*(2), 115–131.

O'Neill, R. E., Albin, R. W., Storey, K., Horner, R. H., & Sprague, J. R. (2014). *Functional assessment and program development for problem behavior: A practical handbook* (3rd ed.). Stamford, CT: Cengage Learning.

Peck Peterson, S. M., Derby, K. M., Harding, J. W., Weddle, T., & Barretto, A. (2002). Behavioral support for school-aged children with developmental disability and problem behavior. In J. M. Lucyshyn, G. Dunlap, & R. W. Albin (Eds.), *Families and positive behavior support: Addressing problem behavior in family contexts* (pp. 287–308). Baltimore: Brookes.

Rao, S., & Kalyanpur, M. (2002). Promoting home-school collaboration in positive behavior support. In J. M. Lucyshyn, G. Dunlap, & R. W. Albin (Eds.), *Families and positive behavior support: Addressing problem behavior in family contexts* (pp. 219–239). Baltimore: Brookes.

Scott, T. M. (2001). A school-wide example of positive behavioral support. *Journal of Positive Behavior Interventions, 3,* 88–94.

Scott, T. M., Liaupsin, C. J., & Nelson, C. M. (2001). *Behavior intervention planning: Using the functional behavioral assessment data: Users guide*. Longmont, CO: Sopris West.

Steed, E. A., Pomerleau, T., Muscott, H., & Rohde, L. (2013). Program-wide positive behavioral interventions and supports in rural preschools. *Rural Special Education Quarterly, 32*(1), 38–46.

Sugai, G., Horner, R. H., Dunlap, G., Hieneman, M., Lewis, T. J., Nelson, C. M., . . . Wilcox, B. (1999). *Applying positive behavioral support and functional behavioral assessment in schools* (Technical Assistance Guide). OSEP Technical Assistance Center on Positive Behavioral Interventions and Supports. Retrieved September 22, 2012, from http://pbis.org/english/default.htm

Sugai, G., Lewis-Palmer, T., Todd, A., & Horner, R. (2001, November). *Systems-wide evaluation tool: Educational and community supports*. Eugene: University of Oregon.

Turnbull, A. P., & Turnbull H. R. (1996). Group action planning as a strategy for providing comprehensive family support. In L. K. Koegel, R. L. Koegel, & G. Dunlap (Eds.), *Positive behavior support: Including people with difficult behavior in the community* (pp. 99–114). Baltimore: Brookes.

Turnbull, A. P., & Turnbull, R. (2001). *Families, professionals, and exceptionality: Collaborating for empowerment* (4th ed.). Upper Saddle River, NJ: Merrill/Pearson.

Turnbull, A. P., Turnbull, R., Erwin, E. J., Soodak, L. C., & Shogren, K. A. (2015). *Families, professionals, and exceptionality: Positive outcomes through partnerships and trust* (7th ed.). Columbus, OH: Pearson Education.

Turnbull, H. R., Wilcox, B. L., Turnbull, A. P., Sailor, W., & Wickham, D. (2001). IDEA, positive behavioral supports, and school safety. *Journal of Law and Education, 30*(3), 445–504.

Weber, M. (2002). *Developing a school-wide behavior management system*. Retrieved October 3, 2002, from http://maxweber.hunter.cuny.edu/pub/eres/EDSPC715_MACINTYRE/school-wideSystem.html

CHAPTER 8

Carr, E. G., Dunlap, G., Horner, R. H., Koegel, R. L., Turnbull, A. P., Sailor, W., . . . Fox, L. (2002). Positive behavior support: Evolution of an applied science. *Journal of Positive Behavior Interventions*, *4*(1), 4–16.

Carr, E. G., Levin, L., McConnachie, G., Carlson, J. I., Kemp, D. C., Smith, C. G., . . . McLaughlin, D. (1999). Comprehensive multisituational intervention for problem behavior in the community: Long-term maintenance and social validation. *Journal of Positive Behavior Interventions*, *1,* 5–25.

Clarke, S., Worcester, J., Dunlap, G., Murray, M., & Bradley-Klug, K. (2002). Using multiple measures to evaluate positive behavior support: A case example. *Journal of Positive Behavior Interventions*, *4*(3), 131–145.

Crone, D. A., & Horner, R. H. (2003). *Building positive behavior support systems in schools: Functional behavioral assessment.* New York: Guilford.

Fitzpatrick, J. L., Sanders, J. R., & Worthen, B. R. (2003). *Program evaluation: Alternative approaches and practical guidelines* (3rd ed.). Boston: Allyn & Bacon.

Florida Department of Education. (1999, November). *Facilitator's guide: Positive behavioral support.* Tampa: Rehabilitation Research & Training Center on Positive Behavioral Support, University of South Florida.

Fox, L., Dunlap, G., Hemmeter, M. L., Joseph, G. E., & Strain, P. S. (2003). The teaching pyramid: A model for supporting social competence and preventing challenging behavior in young children. *Young Children*, *58*(4), 48–52.

Horner, R. H., & Sugai, G. (2000). School-wide behavior support: An emerging initiative. *Journal of Positive Behavior Interventions*, *2*(4), 231–232.

Kim, J., McIntosh, K., & Hoselton, R. (2014). Do schools with adequate tier I SWPBIS implementation have stronger implementation at tiers II and III? *Technical Assistance Center on Positive Behavioral Interventions and Supports.*

Kincaid, D., Knoster, T., Harrower, J. K., Shannon, P., & Bustamante, S. (2002). Measuring the impact of positive behavior support. *Journal of Positive Behavior Interventions*, *4*(2), 109–117.

LaBrot, Z., Dufrene, B., Radley, K., & Pasqua, J. (2016). Evaluation of a modified check-in/check-out intervention for young children. *Perspectives*, *1*(1).

Lucyshyn, J. M., Horner, R. H., Dunlap, G., Albin, R. W., & Ben, K. R. (2002). Positive behavior support with families. In J. M. Lucyshyn, G. Dunlap, & R. Albin (Eds.), *Families and positive behavior support: Addressing problem behavior in family contexts* (pp. 3–432). Baltimore: Brookes.

Luiselli, J. K., Putnam, R. F., & Sunderland, M. (2002). Longitudinal evaluation of behavior support intervention in a public middle school. *Journal of Positive Behavior Interventions*, *4*(3), 182–188.

McCart, A., & Sailor, W. (2003, January/February). Using empowerment evaluation to establish and sustain school-wide positive behavior support. *TASH Connections*, *29,* 25–27.

O'Neill, R. E., Albin, R. W., Storey, K., Horner, R. H., & Sprague, J. R., (2015). *Functional assessment and program development for problem behavior: A practical handbook* (3rd ed.). Stanford, CT: Cengage.

OSEP Technical Assistance Center on Positive Behavioral Interventions and Supports. (n.d. [a]). *School-wide PBIS*. Retrieved January 16, 2003, from http://www.pbis.org/school/default.aspx

OSEP Technical Assistance Center on Positive Behavioral Interventions and Supports. (n.d. [b]). *Evaluation/evaluation tools.* Retrieved March 29, 2012, from http://www.pbis.org/evaluation/evaluation_tools.aspx

Patton, M. Q. (2015). *Qualitative research and evaluation methods* (4th ed.). Thousand Oaks, CA: Sage.

Peck Peterson, S. M., Derby, K. M., Harding, J. W., Weddle, T., & Barretto, A. (2002). Behavioral support for school-age children with developmental disabilities and problem behavior. In J. M. Lucyshyn, G. Dunlap, & R. W. Albin (Eds.), *Families and positive behavior support: Addressing problem behavior in family contexts* (pp. 287–304). Baltimore: Brookes.

Sailor, W., Edmondson, H., & Fenning, P. (2002, October). *Implementing school-wide positive behavior support in urban settings including high schools.* Paper presented at the meeting of the Implementers' Forum on Systems Change, Naperville, IL.

Sanders, J. R. (1994). *The program evaluation standards: How to assess evaluations of educational programs* (2nd ed.). The Joint Committee on Standards for Educational Evaluation. Thousand Oaks, CA: Sage.

Scott, T. M. (2001). A school-wide example of positive behavioral support. *Journal of Positive Behavior Interventions, 3*(2), 88–94.

Scriven, M. (1967). The methodology of evaluation. In R. E. Stake (Ed.), *Curriculum evaluation* (American Educational Research Association Monograph Series on Evaluation, No. 1, pp. 39–83). Chicago: Rand McNally.

Scriven, M. (1991). Beyond formative and summative evaluation. In M. W. McLaughlin & D. C. Phillips (Eds.), *Evaluation and education: At quarter century* (pp. 19–64). Ninetieth Yearbook of the National Society for the Study of Education. Chicago: National Society for the Study of Education.

Scriven, M. (1993). Hard-won lessons in program evaluation. *New directions for program evaluation*, No. 58, 1–107. San Francisco: Jossey-Bass.

Todd, A.W., Lewis-Palmer, T., Horner, R. H., Sugai, G., Sampson, N. K., & Phillips, D. (2012). *School-wide evaluation tool (SET) implementation manual: Version 2.0.* Retrieved March 29, 2012, from http://www.pbis.org/common/pbisresources/tools/SET_Manual_02282012.pdf

Turnbull, A., & Turnbull R. (2011). *Families, professionals, and exceptionality: Positive outcomes through partnerships and trust.* (6th ed.). Upper Saddle River, NJ: Pearson.

CHAPTER 9

Ayllon, T., & Azrin, N. H. (1968). *The token economy: A motivational system for therapy and rehabilitation.* New York: Applegate-Century Crofts.

Baer, D. M. (1999). *How to plan for generalization* (2nd ed.). Austin, TX: PRO-ED.

Bambara, L. M., & Koger, F. (1996). Opportunities for daily choice making. *Innovations* (no. 8). Monograph. Washington, DC: American Association on Mental Retardation.

Cipani, E. (1995). Be aware of negative reinforcement. *Teaching Exceptional Children, 27,* 36–39.

Cooper, J. O., Herron, T. E., & Heward, W. L. (2007). *Applied behavior analysis* (2nd ed.). Upper Saddle River, NJ: Merrill/Pearson.

Ferster, C. B., & Skinner, B. F. (1957). *Schedules of reinforcement.* Upper Saddle River, NJ: Prentice Hall.

Kazdin, A. E. (2008). *Behavior modification in applied settings* (6th ed.). Long Grove, IL: Waveland Press.

Martin, G., & Pear, J. (2015). *Behavior modification: What it is and how to do it* (10th ed.). New York, NY: Routledge.

Massey, N. G., & Wheeler, J. J. (2000). Acquisition and generalization of activity schedules and their effects on task engagement in a young child with autism in an inclusive preschool classroom. *Education and Training in Mental Retardation and Developmental Disabilities, 35,* 326–335.

Michael, J. (1993). Establishing operations. *Behavior Analyst, 16,* 191–206.

Miltenberger, R. G. (2015). *Behavior modification: Principles and procedures* (6th ed.), Boston: Cengage.

Premack, D. (1959). Toward empirical behavior laws. I: Positive reinforcement. *Psychological Review, 66,* 219–233.

Skinner, B. F. (1953). *Science and human behavior.* New York: Macmillan.

Sulzer-Azaroff, B., & Mayer, R. G. (1991). *Behavior analysis for lasting change.* Fort Worth, TX: Harcourt Brace.

Zirpoli, T. J. (2015). *Behavior management: Positive applications for teachers* (7th ed.). Upper Saddle River, NJ: Merrill/Pearson Education.

CHAPTER 10

Agran, M. (1997). *Student directed learning: Teaching self-determination skills.* Pacific Grove, CA: Brooks/Cole.

Albin, R. W., Lucyshyn, J. M., Horner, R. H., & Flannery, K. B. (1996). Contextual fit for behavior support plans: A model for "goodness of fit." In L. K. Koegel, R. L. Koegel, & G. Dunlap (Eds.), *Positive behavioral support: Including people with difficult behavior in the community* (pp. 81–98). Baltimore: Brookes.

Baer, D. M., Wolf, M. M., & Risley, T. R. (1968). Some current dimensions of applied behavior analysis. *Journal of Applied Behavior Analysis, 1,* 91–97.

Bambara, L. M., & Knoster, T. (1998). Designing positive behavior support plans. In *Innovations* (Vol. 13). Monograph. Washington, DC: American Association on Mental Retardation.

Bondy, A., & Frost, L. (1994). The picture exchange communication system. *Focus on Autistic Behavior, 9,* 1–19.

Browder, D. M. (2001). *Curriculum and assessment for students with moderate and severe disabilities.* New York: Guilford.

Carr, E. G., & Durand, V. M. (1985). Reducing behavior problems through functional communication training. *Journal of Applied Behavior Analysis, 18,* 111–126.

Carr, E. G., Horner, R. H., Turnbull, A. P., Marquis, J. G., McLaughlin, D. M., McAtee, M. L., Smith, C. E., Anderson-Ryan, K., Ruef, M. B., & Doolabh, A. (1999). *Positive behavior support for people with developmental disabilities: A research synthesis.* Washington, DC: American Association on Mental Retardation.

Chafouleas, S. M., Sanetti, L., Jaffrey, R., & Fallon, L. N. (2012). An evaluation of a classwide intervention package involving self-management and a group contingency on classroom behavior of middle school students. *Journal of Behavioral Education, 21,* 34–57.

Charlop-Christy, M. H., Carpenter, M., Le, L., LeBlanc, L. A., & Kellet, K. (2002). Using the Picture Exchange Communication System (PECS) with children with autism: Assessment of PECS, acquisition, speech, social–communicative behavior and problem behavior. *Journal of Applied Behavior Analysis, 35,* 213–231.

DiGangi, S. A., & Maag, J. W. (1992). A component of self-management training with behaviorally disordered youth. *Behavioral Disorders, 17,* 281–290.

Dunlap, G., Clarke, S., Jackson, M., Wright, S., Ramos, E., & Brinson, S. (1995). Self-monitoring of classroom behaviors with students exhibiting emotional and behavioral challenges. *School Psychology Quarterly, 10,* 165–177.

Dunlap, L. K., Dunlap, G., Koegal, L. K., & Koegal, R. (1991). Using self-monitoring to increase independence. *Teaching Exceptional Children, 23,* 17–22.

Durand, V. M. (1990). *Severe behavior problems: A functional communication training approach.* New York: Guilford.

Durand, V. M., & Moskowitz, L. (2015). Functional communication training: Thirty years of treating challenging behavior. *Topics in Early Childhood Special Education, 35*(2), 116–126.

Frost, L., & Bondy, A. (2002). *PECS: The Picture Exchange Communication System training manual.* Newark, DE: Pyramid Educational Products.

Ganz, J. B., Davis, J. L., Lund, E. M., Goodwyn, F. D., & Simpson, R. L. (2012). Meta-analysis of PECS with individuals with ASD: Investigation of targeted versus non-targeted outcomes, participant characteristics, and implementation phase. *Research in Developmental Disabilities, 333,* 406–418.

Holifield, C., Goodman, J., Hazelkorn, M., & Heflin, L. J. (2010). Using self-monitoring to increase attending to task and academic accuracy in children with autism. *Focus on Autism and Other Developmental Disabilities, 20,* 1–9.

Kanfer, F. H. (1975). Self-management methods. In F. H. Kanfer & A. P. Goldstein (Eds.), *Helping people change: A textbook method* (pp. 309–355). New York: Pergamon.

Lanovaz, M. J., & Sladeczek, I. E. (2012). Vocal stereotypy in individuals with Autism Spectrum Disorders: A review of behavioral interventions. *Behavior Modification, 36,* 146–164.

Luria, A. (1961). *The role of speech in the regulation of normal and abnormal behaviour.* Oxford, UK: Pergamon.

Machalicek, W., O'Reilly, M. F., Beretvas, N., Sigafoos, J., & Lancioni, G. E. (2007). A review of interventions to reduce challenging behavior in school settings for students with autism spectrum disorders. *Research in Autism Spectrum Disorders, 1,* 229–246.

Mager, R. E. (1997). *Preparing instructional objectives* (3rd ed.). Atlanta: Center for Effective Performance.

Mancil, G. R., & Boman, M. (2010). Functional communication training in the classroom: A guide for success. *Preventing School Failure, 54,* 238–246.

Martin, G., & Pear, J. (2015). *Behavior modification: What it is and how to do it* (10th ed.). New York: Routledge.

Meichenbaum, D. H. (1974). *Cognitive behavior modification.* Morristown, NJ: General Learning.

Meichenbaum, D., & Goodman, J. (1971). Training impulsive children to talk to themselves: A means of developing self-control. *Journal of Abnormal Psychology, 77,* 115–126.

Miller, M., Miller, S. R., Wheeler, J. J., & Selinger, J. (1989). Can a single-classroom treatment approach change academic performance and behavioral characteristics in severely behaviorally disordered adolescents? An experimental inquiry. *Behavior Disorders, 14,* 215–225.

Miltenberger, R. G. (2015). *Behavior modification: Principles and procedures* (6th ed.) Boston: Cengage.

Scott, T. M., & Nelson, C. M. (1999). Using functional behavioral assessment to develop effective intervention plans: Practical classroom applications. *Journal of Positive Behavioral Interventions, 1,* 242–251.

Sulzer-Azaroff, B., & Mayer, G. R. (1991). *Behavior analysis for lasting change*. Fort Worth, TX: Harcourt Brace College Publishers.

Tien, K. C. (2008). Effectiveness of the Picture Exchange Communication System as a functional communication intervention for individuals with autism spectrum disorders: A practice-based research synthesis. *Education and Training in Developmental Disabilities, 43,* 61–76.

Tiger, J. H., Hanley, G. P., & Bruzek, J. (2008). Functional communication training: A review and practical guide. *Behavior Analysis in Practice, 1,* 16–23.

Webber, J., Scheuermann, B., McCall, C., & Coleman, M. (1993). Research on self-monitoring as a behavior management technique in special education classrooms: A descriptive review. *Remedial and Special Education, 14(2),* 38–56.

Wheeler, J. J., Bates, P., Marshall, K. J., & Miller, S. R. (1988). Teaching appropriate behavior to a young man with moderate mental retardation in a supported competitive employment setting. *Education and Training in Mental Retardation and Developmental Disabilities, 23,* 105–116.

Zirpoli, T. J. (2015). *Behavior management: Positive applications for teachers* (7th ed.). Columbus, OH: Pearson Education.

CHAPTER 11

American Academy of Pediatrics. (2000). Corporal punishment in schools (RE9574) [Policy statement]. *Pediatrics, 106,* 343.

Carter, S. L. (2007). Review of recent treatment acceptability research. *Education and Training in Developmental Disabilities, 42,* 301–316.

Cooper, J. O., Heron, T., & Heward, W. L. (2007). *Applied behavior analysis* (2nd ed.). Upper Saddle River, NJ: Merrill/Pearson.

Coyne, M. D., Simonsen, B., & Faggella-Luby, M. (2008). Cooperating initiatives: Supporting behavioral and academic improvement through a systems approach. *Teaching Exceptional Children, 40,* 54–59.

Crone, D. A., & Horner, R. H. (2003). *Building positive behavior support systems in schools*. New York: Guilford.

Durand, V. M. (1990). *Severe behavior problems: A functional communication training approach*. New York: Guilford.

Gershoff, E. T., & Font, S. A. (2016). Corporal punishment in US public schools: Prevalence, disparities in use, and status in state and federal policy. *Social Policy Report, 30(1).*

Horner, R. H., Sugai, G., Todd, A. W., & Lewis-Palmer, T. (1999–2000). Elements of behavior support plans: A technical brief. *Exceptionality, 8,* 205–216.

Horner, R. H., & Sugai, G. (2015). School-wide PBIS: An example of applied behavior analysis implemented at a scale of social importance. *Behavior Analysis in Practice, 8(1),* 80–85.

Jackson, L., & Panyan, M. V. (2002). *Positive behavioral support in the classroom*. Baltimore: Brookes.

Miltenberger, R. G. (2015). *Behavior modification: Principles and procedures* (6th ed.) Boston: Cengage.

National Association of School Psychologists. (2003). Position statement on corporal punishment. Retrieved from http://www.nasponline.org/about_nasp/positionpapers/CorporalPunishment.pdf

OSEP Center on PBIS. (2000). Applying positive behavior support and functional behavioral assessment in schools. *Journal of Positive Behavior Interventions, 2,* 131–143.

Society for Adolescent Medicine. (2003). Corporal punishment in schools: Position paper of the Society for Adolescent Medicine. *Journal of Adolescent Health, 32,* 385–393.

Sugai, G., & Horner, R. (2001). School climate and discipline: Going to scale. *A Framing Paper for the National Summit on the Shared Implementation of IDEA,* 1–8. Retrieved May 1, 2003, from http://www.pbis.org

Sulzer-Azaroff, B., & Mayer, G. R. (1991). *Behavior analysis for lasting change.* Fort Worth, TX: Harcourt Brace College Publishers.

Wheeler, J. J., & Hoover, J. H. (1997). A consultative model for the provision of behavioral supports to children with challenging behavior: Practical approaches for the development of school-based teams. *B. C. Journal of Special Education, 21,* 5–16.

CHAPTER 12

Agran, M., Blanchard, C., & Wehmeyer, M. L. (2000). Promoting transition goals and self-determination through student self-directed learning: The self-determined learning model of instruction. *Education and Training in Mental Retardation and Developmental Disabilities, 35,* 351–364.

Anderson, C. M., & Freeman, K. A. (2000). Positive behavior support: Expanding the application of applied behavior analysis. *Behavior Analyst, 23,* 85–94.

Association for Positive Behavior Support. (n.d.). *Introduction to PBS research.* Retrieved April 1, 2012, from http://www.apbs.org/new_apbs/researchintro.aspx

Association for Positive Behavior Support. (2008). *APBS standards of practice.* Retrieved April 1, 2012, from http://www.apbs.org/standards_of_practice.html.

Bandura, A. (1977). *Social learning theory.* Upper Saddle River, NJ: Prentice Hall.

Berk, L. E. (2002). *Infants, children and adolescents* (4th ed.). Boston: Allyn & Bacon.

Bohanon, H., Castillo, J., & Afton, M. (2015). Embedding self-determination and futures planning within a schoolwide framework. *Intervention in School and Clinic, 50*(4), 203–209.

Bronfenbrenner, U. (1998). The ecology of developmental processes. In R. M. Lerner (Ed.), *Handbook of child psychology: Vol. 1. Theoretical models of human development* (5th ed., pp. 993–1028). New York: Wiley.

Brotherson, M. J., Cook, C. C., Cunconan-Lahr, R., & Wehmeyer, M. L. (1995). Policy supporting self-determination in the environments of children with disabilities. *Education and Training in Mental Retardation and Developmental Disabilities, 30,* 3–14.

Browder, D. M., Wood, W. M., Test, D. W., Karvonen, M., & Algozzine, B. (2001). Reviewing resources on self-determination: A map for teachers. *Remedial and Special Education, 22,* 233–244.

Carpenter, C. D., Bloom, L. A., & Boat, M. B. (1999). Guidelines for special educators: Achieving socially valid outcomes. *Intervention in School and Clinic, 34,* 143–149.

Carr, E. G. (2007). The expanding vision of positive behavior support: Research perspectives on happiness, helpfulness, hopefulness. *Journal of Positive Behavior Interventions, 9*(1), 3–14.

Carter, S. L. (2009). *The social validity manual: A guide to subjective evaluation of behavior interventions.* Academic Press.

Chandler, L. K., & Dahlquist, C. M. (2002). *Functional assessment: Strategies to prevent and remediate challenging behavior in school settings.* Upper Saddle River, NJ: Merrill/Pearson.

Collins, W. A., Maccoby, E. E., Steinberg, L., Hetherington, E. M., & Bornstein, M. H. (2000). Contemporary research on parenting: The case for nature and nurture. *American Psychologist, 52,* 218–232.

Curtis, E. (1996). *Self-determination profile: An assessment package.* Salt Lake City: New Hats.

Doll, B., Sands, D. J., Wehmeyer, M. L., & Palmer, S. (1996). Promoting the development and acquisition of self-determined behavior. In D. J. Sands & M. L. Wehmeyer (Eds.), *Self-determination across the life span: Independence and choice for people with disabilities* (pp. 65–90). Baltimore: Brookes.

Erwin, E. J., Brotherson, M. J., Palmer, S. B., Cook, C. C., Weigel, C. J., & Summers, J. A. (2009). How to promote self-determination for young children with disabilities: Evidence-based strategies for early childhood practitioners and families. *Young Exceptional Children, 12*(2), 27–37.

Field, S., Martin, J. E., Miller, R., Ward, M., & Wehmeyer, M. L. (1998). *A practical guide to teaching self-determination.* Reston, VA: Council for Exceptional Children.

Forest, M., & Lusthaus, E. (1990). Everyone belongs with the MAPS action planning system. *Teaching Exceptional Children, 22*(2), 32–35.

Fox, P., & Emerson, E. (2001). Socially valid outcomes of intervention for people with MR and challenging behavior: Views of different stakeholders. *Journal of Positive Behavior Interventions, 3,* 183–189.

Goldsmith, E. B. (2000). *Resource management for individuals and families* (2nd ed.). Belmont, CA: Wadsworth/Thomson Learning.

Hoffman, A., Field, S., & Sawilowsky, S. (1996). *Self-determination assessment battery user's guide.* Detroit: Wayne State University.

Holburn, S. (2001). Compatibility of person-centered planning and applied behavior analysis. *Behavior Analyst, 24,* 271–281.

Horner, R. H. (2000). Positive behavior supports. In M. Wehmeyer & J. R. Patton (Eds.), *Mental retardation in the 21st century* (pp. 181–196). Austin, TX: PRO-ED.

Individuals with Disabilities Education Act Amendments of 1997, Pub. L. No. 105–17, 20 U.S.C. § 1400 *et seq.*

Johnson, J., Rahn, N. L., & Bricker, D. D. (2015). *An activity-based approach to early intervention.* Brookes Publishing.

Martin, J. E., & Marshall, L. (1996a). *ChoiceMaker self-determination assessment.* Colorado Springs: University of Colorado.

Martin, J. E., & Marshall, L. (1996b). Choice making: Description of a model project. In M. Agran (Ed.), *Student-directed learning: Teaching self-determination skills* (pp. 224–248). Pacific Grove, CA: Brooks/Cole.

Mithaug, D. E., Wehmeyer, M. L., Agran, M., Martin, J., & Palmer, S. (1998). The self-determined learning model of teaching: Engaging students to solve their learning problems. In M. L. Wehmeyer & D. J. Sands (Eds.), *Making it happen: Student involvement in educational planning, decision-making and instruction* (pp. 299–328). Baltimore: Brookes.

Rowe, D. A., Mazzotti, V. L., & Sinclair, J. (2015). Strategies for teaching self-determination skills in conjunction with the common core. *Intervention in School and Clinic, 50*(3), 131–141.

Sandall, S., & Ostrosky, M. (1999). Young exceptional children: Practical ideas for addressing challenging behaviors. *Young Exceptional Children Monograph Series,* (2).

Sands, D. J., & Wehmeyer, M. L. (Eds.). (1996). *Self-determination across the life span: Independence and choice for people with disabilities.* Baltimore: Brookes.

Schalock, R. I. (2000). Three decades of quality of life. *Focus on Autism and Other Developmental Disabilities, 15,* 116–127.

Scott, T. M. (2007). Issues of personal dignity and social validity in school-wide systems of positive behavior support. *Journal of Positive Behavior Interventions, 9*(2), 102–112.

Self-Advocates Becoming Empowered. (1996). *The national self-advocacy organization definition of self-determination* [Online]. Retrieved April 3, 2012, from http://cdrc.ohsu.edu/selfdetermination/leadership/alliance/documents/Self_Advocates_Becoming_Empowered.pdf

Skinner, B. F. (1971). *Beyond freedom and dignity.* New York: Alfred A. Knopf.

Smith-Bird, E., & Turnbull, A. P. (2005). Linking positive behavior support to family quality-of-life outcomes. *Journal of Positive Behavior Interventions, 7*(3), 174–180.

Test, D. W., Karvonen, M., Wood, W. M., Browder, D., & Algozzine, B. (2000). Choosing a self-determination curriculum: Plan for the future. *Teaching Exceptional Children, 33,* 48–54.

Turnbull, A. P. (2001, December). *The early years: The launching pad to family quality of life.* Paper presented at the annual meeting of the Division for Early Childhood of the Council for Exceptional Children, Boston, MA.

Turnbull, A. P., Summers, J. A., & Brotherson, M. J. (1984). *Working with families with disabled members: A family systems approach.* Lawrence: University of Kansas, Kansas University Affiliated Facility.

Turnbull, A. P., & Turnbull, R. (2001). *Families, professionals, and exceptionality: Collaborating for empowerment* (4th ed.). Upper Saddle River, NJ: Merrill/Pearson.

Turnbull, A. P., & Turnbull, R. (2011). Right science and right results: Lifestyle change, PBS and human dignity. *Journal of Positive Behavior Interventions, 13*(2), 69–77.

Wehmeyer, M. L. (1992). Self-determination and the education of students with mental retardation. *Education and Training in Mental Retardation, 27,* 302–314.

Wehmeyer, M. L. (1995). *The ARC's self-determination scale.* Arlington, TX: The ARC of the United States.

Wehmeyer, M. L. (1996). Self-determination as an educational outcome: Why is it important to children, youth and adults with disabilities? In D. J. Sands & M. L. Wehmeyer (Eds.), *Self-determination across the life span: Independence and choice for people with disabilities* (pp. 17–36). Baltimore: Brookes.

Wehmeyer, M. L. (1999). A functional model of self-determination: Describing development and implementing instruction. *Focus on Autism and Other Developmental Disabilities, 14,* 53–61.

Wehmeyer, M. L., Agran, M., & Hughes, C. A. (2000). A national survey of teachers' promotion of self-determination and student-directed learning. *Journal of Special Education, 34,* 58–68.

Wehmeyer, M. L., Kelchner, K., & Richards, S. (1996). Essential characteristics of self-determined behaviors of adults with mental retardation and developmental disabilities. *American Journal on Mental Retardation, 100,* 632–642.

Wehmeyer, M. L., & Schalock, R. L. (2001, April). Self-determination and quality of life: Implications for special education services and supports. *Focus on Exceptional Children,* 1–16.

Wehmeyer, M. L., & Schwartz M. (1998). The relationship between self-determination and quality of life for adults with mental retardation. *Education and Training in Mental Retardation and Developmental Disabilities, 33,* 3–12.

Wolman, J. M., Campeau, P. L., DuBois, P. A., Mithaug, D. E., & Stolarski, V. S. (1994). *AIR self-determination scale and user guide.* Palo Alto, CA: American Institutes for Research.

Name Index

Subject Index